THE FORD LECTURES GIVEN IN THE
UNIVERSITY OF OXFORD, 1981

Britain and the Vatican during
the Second World War

Britain and the Vatican during the Second World War

OWEN CHADWICK

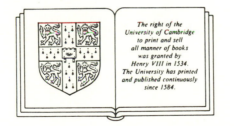

The right of the
University of Cambridge
to print and sell
all manner of books
was granted by
Henry VIII in 1534.
The University has printed
and published continuously
since 1584.

CAMBRIDGE UNIVERSITY PRESS

Cambridge
London   New York   New Rochelle
Melbourne   Sydney

Published by the Press Syndicate of the University of Cambridge
The Pitt Building, Trumpington Street, Cambridge CB2 1RP
32 East 57th Street, New York, NY 10022, USA
10 Stamford Road, Oakleigh, Melbourne 3166, Australia

First published 1986

Printed in Great Britain at
the University Press, Cambridge

British Library cataloguing in publication data
Chadwick, Owen
Britain and the Vatican during the Second World
War. – (The Ford lectures)
1. Great Britain – Foreign relations – Vatican
City 2. Vatican City – Foreign relations –
Great Britain
I. Title II. Series
327.41045'634 DA47.9.VS

Library of Congress cataloguing in publication data
Chadwick, Owen.
Britain and the Vatican during the Second World War.
(The Ford lectures/given in the University of
Oxford; 1981)
Bibliography
Includes index
1. World War, 1939–1945 – Diplomatic history.
2. Great Britain – Foreign relations – Catholic Church.
3. Catholic Church – Relations (diplomatic) – Great
Britain. 4. World War, 1939–1945 – Vatican City.
5. Vatican City – History. I. Title. II. Series:
Ford lectures; 1981.
D750.C43 1986 940.53'25'45634 86–6065

ISBN 0 521 32242 1

Contents

v

Acknowledgements

I have to acknowledge the gracious permission of Queen Elizabeth The Queen Mother to make use of material.

Documents held at the Public Record Office are crown copyright and are reproduced by permission of the Controller of H.M. Stationery Office.

In Italy I specially owe thanks to Sir Mark Heath, who at the time of writing was the first British ambassador to the Holy See; to Father Robert Graham, S.J., expert on all matters connected with the Vatican (and much else) during the Second World War; his colleague the late Father Angelo Martini, S.J.; Count Galeazzi; Professor Fabio Grassi and his colleagues at the archives of Affari Esteri in Rome; Father E. Lamalle, S.J., at the archives of the Society of Jesus; Dr Mario Serio at the Archivio Centrale dello Stato in Rome; the librarians at the Vatican Library and the Gregorian Library; Anton Call of San Vigilio; Princess Doria Pamphilj.

In France, especially to Count André d'Ormesson; and the archivists of the Quai d'Orsay.

In Belgium, to Mr and Mrs Harold Tittmann at Brussels.

In the United States, to John Taylor, at the National Archives in Washington; Mark Renovitch at Hyde Park; Larry Strawderman, Information and Privacy Coordinator of the Central Intelligence Agency; Mr and Mrs Barclay Tittmann; Father Gerald Fogarty, S.J.; Father James Hennesey, S.J.

In England, to Robin Campbell first of all; to Raleigh Trevelyan; Lady Abel Smith; Derek Hill; the Hon. Edmund Howard; the Hon. Mrs Douglas Woodruff; William Davies at the Cambridge University Press; Dr C. M. Andrew, Fellow of Corpus Christi College, Cambridge; Professor Sir Harry Hinsley; Andrzej Suchcitz at the archives of the Polish Institute at Princes Gate; D. Symington, in the Libary of the Foreign and Commonwealth Office; the archivists at the Imperial War Museum; Andrew Mussell at the Liddell Hart Centre for Military Archives at King's College, London; and of course, those who care for the books at the British Library and especially the Cambridge University Library.

The Leverhulme Foundation generously gave an Emeritus Fellowship for two years, which was indispensable for the work, particularly in Italy.

Oxford University prompted the setting of this out by its invitation to the Ford's lectureship in English history, and I am grateful to the trustees. One eminent historian doubted whether the subject is English history and whether the Reverend James Ford the Victorian endower of the lectureship would have approved. But the history of England also happens elsewhere than in England.

Abbreviations

AA	Auswärtiges Amt, Documents of the German Foreign Office
AAS	Acta Apostolicae Sedis
AC	Archivio Centrale, Rome
ADSS	Actes et Documents du Saint Siège rélatifs à la Seconde Guerre Mondiale. Vatican 1965–81
AE	Archives of Affari Esteri, Rome
AHP	Archivum Historiae Pontificiae
CAB	Cabinet Office Papers in PRO (Kew)
Civ. Catt.	La Civiltà Cattolica
DBFP	Documents of British Foreign Policy
DBI	Dizionario Biografico degli Italiani
DDI	I Documenti Diplomatici Italiani
DGFP	Documents of German Foreign Policy
FO	Foreign Office Papers, in Public Record Office (Kew)
FRUS	Foreign Relations of the United States
Huit Ans	Charles-Roux, *Huit Ans au Vatican 1932–40*, Paris 1947
NAW	National Archives, Washington
OSS	Office of Strategic Services
PREM	Prime Minister's Papers at Public Record Office (Kew)
PRO	Public Record Office (Kew)
PS	Archives of Pubblica Sicurezza, in Archivio Centrale, Rome
QO	Quai d'Orsay
WO	War Office Papers, in Public Record Office (Kew)

1

Britain and the Vatican in the last years of Pope Pius XI (1935–39)

i. The embassies at the Vatican

In the year 1936 34 nations kept ambassadors or ministers or chargés at the Holy See. But the Argentine spent a lot of time enjoying himself in other European capitals. The Belgian lived quietly to qualify for a pension. The Spaniard had been driven out by a tragi-comic siege in the Piazza di Spagna. The Peruvian was hardly ever in Rome and when he was in Rome was hardly ever seen. The Estonian was a pluralist for he was also ambassador in Paris and preferred that city. The minister of Honduras was unpaid. The Latvian had not appeared in Rome for several years and ran the Foreign Ministry in Riga. The ministers of Monaco and San Marino and of the Order of Malta hardly counted. The Nicaraguan was senile, the Panamanian disappeared in 1929 and had not been heard of since. The minister of Salvador lived at Brussels while the Liberian lived in Paris. This list shows that while it is true that 34 nations kept representatives at the Vatican, it was in part a façade.[1]

Diplomatic services need a certain number of well-paid sinecures for their members who are not good enough for important offices and not old enough to go on pension. The extraordinary case is that of the German ambassador Diego von Bergen. No one could suppose, especially after the Nazis came to power, that the post of German Ambassador could be a sinecure. And Bergen was a man of substance. He twice refused the office of Foreign Secretary in governments of the Weimar Republic, for he preferred to stay in Rome. He was the senior ambassador, the doyen of the diplomatic corps. When the Nazis came to power he disliked them and their policy. He was a professional diplomat of the old school. As the behaviour of his government grew more unpleasant, he gradually receded from affairs and did as little as possible; until by the end of his time he was almost as invisible as the ambassador of the Republic of Salvador. The Nazis were perfectly aware that he could not be said to be dedicated to their party. Nothing shows more clamorously the contempt with which they regarded the office than that they left him there undisturbed till 1943. Then they

---

[1] See the report of 5 January 1937 in FO 371/21164/6.

suddenly awoke to what chances they had missed and filled the place with the biggest man in their Foreign Service – partly because they wanted to exile him from the Foreign Office but not only for that reason.

The British had not always kept a minister at the Vatican. When the Papal State existed, they kept an unofficial official at Rome during the middle years of the nineteenth century. The remnant of the old Papal State was occupied and suppressed in 1870. Four years later someone in the House of Commons pointed out that we kept a mission attached to a non-existent State, and that there was no more reason for Britain to send an ambassador to the Pope than for the kingdom of Italy to send an ambassador to the Archbishop of Canterbury. Put like that, the British mission in Rome sounded absurd. A Conservative government withdrew its representative.

Between 1874 and 1914 certain representatives went to Rome for special and temporary missions.

When the First World War broke out, both sides competed for the alliance of Italy. Rome was the centre of intrigue to gain Italian intervention on one side or the other side. Germany had an advantage. The French were officially anticlerical, the Russians were against the Pope, the Entente had no one at the Vatican. The British decided to send back a minister to be attached to the papal Court.

When the war was over, the British government considered whether their mission in Rome was worth the expense and whether they should withdraw. They resolved that the problems of Ireland, and the problem of Malta, of Quebec, and of the Irish in Australia, warranted the maintenance of the mission. But in that maintenance prestige mattered more than political utility.

The office of British Minister started by being a quiet place for a not very distinguished diplomat, who therefore stayed several years. The first, De Salis, wrote reports which show signs of illiteracy. Odo Russell, bearer of a historic name in papal diplomacy and no doubt chosen partly for that reason, held office for five and a quarter quiet years (January 1923 to June 1928). He was succeeded by Henry Chilton, who might have had a longer tenure if a quarrel between Britain and Malta had not blown to gale force. He was moved to Chile in May 1930, and the post of Minister was left empty for almost three years because the British wished to show their disapproval of the conduct of the Vatican over the troubles of Malta. They thought it not in the least important to have a Minister in Rome. Then they began to fill the post with distinguished men, so distinguished that they used it only as a halting place on the way to higher or tenser posts: Sir Robert Clive, the most soigné and handsome of envoys, who was only there for a year and left for the anguish-ridden post of Tokyo; Sir Charles Wingfield who was only there for a year and left for the not uncomfortable and not too important post at Lisbon. At this point the Cardinal Secretary of State, Cardinal Pacelli, expressed his regret at the shortness of the tenures. D'Arcy Osborne was appointed to succeed Wingfield, but could not arrive for six months on the not very convincing plea that his present duties in Washington were too weighty.

As the relationship was partly a ritual, matters of ritual became very important, not only to the clergymen. In October 1930 the airship R 101 crashed with heavy loss of life. A telegram went out from the Pope to Cardinal Bourne, Archbishop of Westminster, asking him to convey to the King and his government condolences on the national disaster. This was awkward for it was a breach of protocol. The government was not normally willing to accept the Cardinal of Westminster as a suitable channel for communications between the Curia and the British government. However, as it was the holiday season and a slip could have occurred in the office of the Secretary of State, and as it was embarrassing to be stuffy over a kind message sent about dead men, the British government swallowed its ritual pride and was grateful.[2] But in July 1934 the government was petulant when it discovered that Cardinal Bourne's secretary delivered to Buckingham Palace a letter from the Pope to the King on official business; and Monsignor Ottaviani had to throw the blame on a minor official who failed to understand protocol. How many naval guns should be fired to salute a papal legate was another ceremonial which exercised the ministry; the Pope would receive 21 guns as a head of State, a nuncio 19 guns and an internuncio 17 guns. Such matters of protocol were important in the relationships between all States. But they were more prominent in the work of the British Legation at Rome because ceremony was a very important feature of an ancient court with many survivals, and because the Vatican State, being (whichever way you looked) a very new State or a very ancient State, was particularly sensitive that due protocol should be correctly observed in order to be certain that its status was conceded. Part of the ritual was lunches and dinners. But this was not so important as with a normal embassy. The cardinals and monsignori of the Curia thought lunches and dinners doubtful entertainments, and stayed as short a time as possible.

The British government kept two ambassadors in Rome, though one of them was not allowed the rank of ambassador. Since the Pope was the sovereign of a very small territory after 1929, which had few economic or social interests, and which had only a little ceremonial

[2] T. E. Hachey (ed.), *Anglo-Vatican Relations 1914–1939: Confidential Annual Reports of the British Ministers to the Holy See* (Boston, Mass., 1972), p. 179.

army of Swiss guards, and was thought to have small political importance, the post of envoy at the Vatican was held by men different in kind
and outlook from the men who held the post of ambassador to the
kingdom of Italy, who like their colleagues in Berlin or Paris or
Washington dealt in high politics. It was considered an easy job.

Historically, the envoy in the Vatican, whether official or unofficial,
whether resident or (as between 1874 and 1915) only visiting, had a
vital part to play in the government of the United Kingdom. Not
without reason, the British government believed that the Pope was
important to the government of Ireland. No Pope could believe in
bombs. No Pope could believe in revolution. And therefore any Pope
might help in preventing nationalist Irish priests from encouraging
their flocks to violence. This had been the historic function of the
envoys in the Vatican ever since the far off days when the Duke of
Wellington was prime minister and the country moved towards
Catholic Emancipation.

The making of the Irish Free State altered and then destroyed this
historic task. At first Ireland did not think of sending its own envoy to
Rome. But in April 1929 the Foreign Minister of the Irish Free State sent
a delegation to discuss with the Pope whether it could set up its
minister in Rome. The British government was consulted and said that
it was in favour. On 27 June 1929 the first minister of the Irish Free State
presented his letters to the Pope. Five months later the Pope
announced the appointment of a nuncio in Dublin.

This direct communication between Rome and an autonomous
government in Dublin appeared to remove the main reason for keeping a British envoy in the Vatican. However, ambassadors are not put
in places because they are useful but because they were once useful
and now cannot be withdrawn because it would offend someone.

The ritual function of any ambassador is considerable. He presents
congratulations at jubilees, receives dignitaries from kings down-
wards, stands on platforms at parades, meets personages at the
railway station, represents his people at funerals or marriages. The
Vatican was the only small State of its size where these ceremonial
functions were as arduous as those of the ambassador to one of the
great powers. If a king came to Rome he could hardly avoid visiting the
heads of both the States in Rome. Any State with a Roman Catholic
population – and that included all the Great Powers except perhaps
Stalin's Russia before 1939 – had eminent men coming on pilgrimage,
new cardinals coming to audience, groups or individuals seeking the
Pope's favour.

The Foreign Office continued to ask itself from time to time whether
the existence of the Legation in Rome was worth its expenditure of

time and people and money. In March 1935 an argument developed in the Dutch press about the absence of any Dutch representation at the Vatican, though Holland was a State containing many Roman Catholics. From Rome, Wingfield reported the argument to London, where it came to the desk of Stephen Gaselee. Gaselee's minute of 28 March 1935 ran thus:

We have some reason for our mission at the Vatican, because of Roman Catholic interests in our Empire – Ireland, Malta, French Canada – but even so we are often doubtful whether it is worth (1) its expense and (2) Protestant feeling against it. I cannot think that such a Mission would be worth anything appreciable to the Dutch.[3]

But Britain had more than a ceremonial use for its ambassador. Irish immigration, and immigration from Europe including Italy, created a far larger Roman Catholic population in Britain. The Irish Free State did not contain all the Irish. Northern Ireland was still troublesome and might become more troublesome. Canada had a problem between French and English, expressed mainly through a difference in language but partly through a difference in religion. The British colonies in Africa had questions of denominational education. Britain governed Palestine by mandate and therefore the Holy Places of Jerusalem and Bethlehem in which the Popes long had a vital interest. The British government wanted to give everyone a better or more regular Easter holiday by fixing the date of Easter and the Church of England agreed provided that the Pope would agree and the Churches act together. The Pope would not agree, and the argument fell into limbo, but it was the kind of argument which shows how a British minister in the Vatican might be needed even if Britain contained not a single Roman Catholic.

But much the largest amount of time, and much the largest amount of paper, was expended by the British minister, before the years of appeasement, on the affairs of Malta. The nationalist pressure of Mussolini's Italy generated nationalist passions among Italian speakers on the island. Since the island was very Roman Catholic, some of the most vociferous among the nationalists were clergymen. The British governor and the British government were particularly troubled by Franciscans, who being religious were under the remote control of Rome. The Vatican was particularly troubled at the growth of Anglican influence on the island, as for example when three Anglican bishops held 'propaganda lectures' in the throne room of the old Grand Master of the Order of St John of Jerusalem, and the sitting of the Maltese Parliament was suspended to do them honour.

[3] FO 371/19544/247.

Ambassadors suffer from the natural temptation to exaggerate their services to the State and their influence with the court to which they are accredited. Odo Russell in his time claimed to exercise an important influence on the appointment to bishoprics in the British Empire; and when the sees were indeed in the empire, as distinct from the British Isles, government could exercise a half-control by the threat to refuse passports to anyone of whose politics it disapproved. The custom existed of clearing the candidate with the British before the appointment was announced. In 1931 the Legation claimed, by means of its special relation with the journals *Osservatore Romano* and *Civiltà Cattolica*, to have caused Roman attacks on the Church of England to cease. Sometimes the Legation was used in ecumenical matters by the Churches. In 1931 the Pope pronounced a strenuous condemnation of Protestant propaganda in Italy and everyone grew nervous lest this condemnation apply to them. It was the secretary at the Legation and not the responsible Anglican bishop (of Gibraltar) who repudiated all connexion with the proselytism of which the Pope complained.[4]

Occasionally the Legation could help over the question of money – for example when a partly British company with a contract for building churches in Southern Italy could not get payment out of the Calabrian ecclesiastics. But this time the help was no use. They were continually in action over Malta, even when the air was cleared of friction; sometimes by trying to get more English monks or Jesuits into teaching posts there (but there were not enough Englishmen to go round). They made sure that the interest of the British government in the politics of Indians appointed to Indian bishoprics was well-known in the Vatican. As the representative of the power with the mandate in Palestine, they were concerned with the safety and welfare of the Holy Places; for though this might only concern the hanging of a tapestry in the Church of the Nativity at Bethlehem, and therefore looked as though it was essentially a ritual question, it was in fact one of the most political of all questions. Everything in Palestine was made difficult, for the Vatican even more than for the British government, because the Latin patriarch of Jerusalem, Monsignor Barlassina, was a tiresome clergyman.

The British did not know, but could guess, that the Vatican also had trouble over Malta with Mussolini's government. In 1939, for example, Italy was offended at a rumour that Maltese bishops communicated with the Vatican in the English language; and the Vatican had to contradict the report.[5]

[4] Hachey, *Anglo-Vatican Relations*, 200/142; 221/143.
[5] AE, Santa Sede, 1939, Busta 44.

ii. A Fascist Pope?

Between October 1935 and the middle of 1937 the British regarded the Pope as a man in Mussolini's pocket. This was 'a Fascist Pope'.

The causes of this belief, or the case for this belief, ran thus:

the Pope seemed rather happy than unhappy with the Italian conquest of Abyssinia;

the Pope was believed to be almost totally on Franco's side in the Spanish Civil War, since it was the other side which shot bishops, priests, monks and nuns. Mussolini's units fought on the same side;

Pope Pius XI made the Lateran treaty of 1929 by which the Vatican City State was formed and so reconciled himself to Italy. It now looked as though the status of a little neutral state inside Italy but dependent on Italy, gave him less real freedom, as well as less psychological freedom, than the old status of the prisoner in the Vatican;

the war of Abyssinia was popular in Italy, and therefore was popular among Italian churchmen.

After the Lateran treaty the Pope had a resounding quarrel with Mussolini over Catholic Action, which meant controversy about the spheres of Fascist and Catholic youth organizations. But since 1933 the relationship had been cordial. The Lateran treaty at last healed the old war between Italian nationalism and the Church. This Fascist government saw the historic Church as a main part of the international influence of Italy, both in the past and in the contemporary world.

Pope Pius XI was careful not to commit himself to Mussolini's policy. But with it he had this amount of natural sympathy: his personal experiences in Poland during the Russo-Polish war of 1920 left him with a hostility to Bolshevism and a conviction of its danger to a Christian Europe. This fear and enmity were reinforced by the terrible persecutions of innocent Catholic priests or nuns in Mexico and Spain. Many Italians believed that the only viable alternative to Mussolini's government in Italy was a Communist regime. They were not alone in this belief. The British ambassador to the King of Italy, Drummond, also believed the choice for Italy to lie between Fascism and Communism.

Early in October 1935 Mussolini invaded Abyssinia. This was abhorrent to the British government because all British foreign policy rested on the League of Nations and this invasion looked like destroying the League. They regarded it as blatant and immoral aggression.

How should you stop Mussolini from conquering Abyssinia? You could stop him by economic sanctions or deprive him of access to raw materials. Few sensible men believed that this could work. They engaged in economic sanctions more to satisfy an outraged public opinion than because they thought that they could thereby stop the Italian armies. You could stop him by an army and a navy – but that meant war, and no one was willing to go to war with Italy. Perhaps, therefore, you could stop him by moral opinion – and suddenly, in Britain, men magnified absurdly what was possible for a Pope. Most Italians are Roman Catholics – Roman Catholics are bound by their religion to do what the Pope orders – then the Pope has only to condemn this naked act of aggression and Mussolini could advance no further – such were the naive feelings in the breasts of some British democrats.

Italian bishops did not conform to this picture. Cardinal Schuster of Milan said that the Italian flag bore the Cross in triumph over the Ethiopian plains, and that the Italian army opened the gates of Abyssinia to Catholic faith and Roman civilization. The Archbishops of Brindisi, Sorrento and Amalfi attacked the League powers in violent language, accusing them of greed, egoism and hypocrisy. The Pope said nothing like this. But he said nothing to the contrary. And, therefore, among the democratic powers a lot of abuse was thrown at the Pope for not trying to stop Mussolini, or for being a secret backer of Italy, or for being an Italian instead of an international leader, or even for being a Fascist. Part of the trouble was the usual difficulty of not being able to get authentic information. The Pope said nothing. The Secretary of State Cardinal Pacelli said almost nothing. The Under Secretary of State Monsignor Pizzardo said a little but to little purpose. The British had a dubious ecclesiastic in their pay, a Monsignor Pucci. He was a free-lance journalist, with no official post in the Vatican. He had played a discreditable part in the seizure of power by the Fascists. After the death of Pope Pius XI he claimed to have been his personal friend. He made his living by selling information. The British bought it though they doubted whether it was worth buying. We shall meet Monsignor Pucci later on over questions of espionage. Pucci was in favour of the Fascist government and slanted his information to make it appear that the Vatican was more decisively on Mussolini's side than might be the case.

So if we turn to the archives of the British Foreign Office, we find a devastating series of comments on the reports out of Rome:

The Church has proved that it is purely Italian and far from 'Catholic'

or:

It is natural that anticlerical Italians should rejoice in the repeated proofs that the Church is in Mussolini's pocket or:

At present the Vatican are behaving as though Italy were the only country whose goodwill was essential to them. They seem to forget that the goodwill of Great Britain is equally important, if not to the Vatican as such, at least to the Catholic Church, the prosperity of which is the only thing that should really matter to the Holy See

or:

Vatican foreign policy seems to boil down more and more to a determination not to do anything displeasing to the present Italian government. In other words the Vatican, without perhaps being fully aware of the fact, is beginning to appear in the light of an ally of Italian imperialist and expansionist ideas.

E. H. Carr minuted on 27 November 1935:

Everyone concerned in directing Vatican policy is (so far as we can discover) 'strongly Fascist in sympathy', so that that policy is bound to be tinged by a strong Italian bias. The most that can be expected, is that they will maintain a certain semblance of decency.[6]

They watched the Pope's every move. A deputation of war-widows and mothers of the men fallen in Abyssinia came to the King to protest against sanctions, and the Pope agreed to receive them. Too late he realized that to receive them would look like taking sides against the League of Nations and its sanctions. So the Pope suffered from a diplomatic chill, suspended all public audiences, and could not receive the war-widows. The British Legation noted it down. A member of the Legation went out to a private dinner party in honour of one of the new cardinals and found Italian tricolour ribbons in front of each plate. The hostess commented on the unanimity of Italian feeling among all the guests; and then Monsignor Caccia-Dominioni, who was Master of the Pope's household, pointed at the Englishman and said 'Do not compromise me in the eyes of England'; and said of the white and red roses in the middle of the table 'Those are our colours.' The Legation noted it down.

When the *Osservatore Romano* of 7 December praised the Fascist order abolishing the fashion of Christmas trees, the Legation noted it down; and the minutes on their report show a growing obsession in the minds of good men at the desks in the Foreign Office:

There is little doubt that clerical circles in Italy tend to dance increasingly to Sig. Mussolini's tune and the Christmas tree attitude is a striking example of it (Cavendish-Bentinck)

When the Lateran treaty was concluded, the danger was foreseen that the predominantly Italian character of the Vatican might become suspect in more

[6] FO 371/19558/77, 83, 155.

than one quarter, once it and the Italian government were reconciled. It looks
as though this were now coming to pass.

(Orme Sargent)

Even E. H. Carr would not let the Christmas tree alone:

This seasonal controversy is only important as revealing the extent to which
Vatican machinery is at present at the disposal of the Italian government. It is
becoming more and more apparent that the Pope, when he ceased to be the
prisoner in the Vatican, became the prisoner of the Quirinal.
    Meanwhile I hear that the Christmas tree, banned in Italy, has been
readmitted to Soviet Russia.[7]

The British consulted the embassies round the world to find out
whether papal nuncios or apostolic delegates in the various States tried
to influence the government to which they were accredited towards
a more friendly policy to Mussolini. These reports, as they came in,
were almost universally mild or totally negative. Most of them said that
they noticed no activity by the nuncio. London was told that the
nuncio in Chile was a better ambassador on behalf of Mussolini than
was the Italian ambassador. In Buenos Aires Sir Nevile Henderson said
that he expected the anti-British Irish Passionists to be against British
policy on Italy and had been agreeably surprised. One letter is worth
quoting because it concerns a personage afterwards celebrated. The
letter came from Sir Percy Loraine, the British ambassador in Angora
(as he still called Ankara):

To judge from the practically total absence of reference to Monsignor Roncalli
in the press, it would seem that the Archbishop leads a very retiring life, and I
am informed that he is naturally of a very pious disposition and not the type of
ecclesiastic who meddles in politics.
    Briefly therefore I have hitherto been unable to detect any attempt by the
Vatican to influence opinion in this country favourably towards the Italian
thesis in the matter of the Ethiopian conflict.[8]

There is something a little obsessive about some of these minutes,
especially the vast operation of consulting embassies all round the
world to see if the Vatican secretly worked on the side of Mussolini.
    There was a feeling – not universal, but looming out again and again
in the documents – that the Pope's organization was but the international propaganda wing of Mussolini's policy. This reflected a widespread opinion among some groups in Britain. The Congregationalist
leader Dr S. M. Berry denounced the Pope for refusing to put himself at
the head of a great Christian appeal for peace. At the Whitefield
Tabernacle in London the congregation passed a resolution protesting

[7] FO 371/19558/180, 221, 292.   [8] FO 371/19227/167–9.

against the silence and the inactivity of the Pope. The Reverend F. Vince of the Wycliffe Church Mission in Sheffield accused both Mussolini and Hitler of being Jesuits, and compared Mr Eden at Geneva, defying Rome, to John Knox four centuries before.[9] The French papers of the left continued the onslaught. *Le Populaire* accused the Vatican and the Roman Catholic Church of mobilizing for war on the side of Italy, and talked of the repugnant union of the Church with Fascism.

On 24 February 1936 the *Manchester Guardian* published an article entitled 'The Vatican and Abyssinia: Pope's dilemma'. When Osborne, the British Minister at the Vatican, saw it he thought it a very good picture of the predicament. The Pope cannot act publicly because of three fears:

a. the fear of thereby provoking a kind of minor schism in the Italian Church, he and the Curia being ranged against the mass of the Italian clergy who have shown themselves ultrapatriotic
b. the fear of doing anything to weaken Fascism, to which Bolshevism or anticlericalism are regarded by the Vatican as the only possible alternatives
c. the fear that Mussolini and his Fascists might themselves, if defied by the Church, turn anticlerical and adopt Nazi methods.[10]

But the British government itself ended sanctions before long and later still recognized the conquest of Abyssinia in the desperate hope of recovering Mussolini for the cause against Hitler. By then all their comments on Vatican policy were obsolete.

Seen from a study not far from the east end of St Peter's, the Abyssinian war was to be deplored because all war was to be deplored. But this could not be said publicly except in very general terms, for several reasons: first, that it could do nothing to stop the war; second, because open support for the League would look like betraying the Italian people and in any case Pope Pius XI was no admirer of the League (where Soviet Russia was weighty); third, because amid the growing persecution of the Catholic Church in Germany the Pope had a vital interest that Catholic Austria should not go Nazi and the only person who could prevent this was Mussolini; fourth, because the alternative government to Mussolini in Italy looked to be 'anticlerical or Bolshevist' (as the Vatican described it to itself); and fifth, because Abyssinia's political arrangements, ranging from slavery to anarchy in outlying districts, were not such as to make a Pope believe that such a State must at all costs be supported. Therefore, since the conquest happened, it could be used – for it opened a large door to Roman

[9] *Tablet,* 1936/1/72 and 168.   [10] FO 371/20419/295–6.

Catholic missions in a country where hitherto they laboured under disadvantage and discouragement.

An anonymous letter to the *Tablet* at the end of July 1936, signed Sacerdos, expressed the attitude intelligently. People, said the letter, have used the Abyssinian war to beat the Pope; even Catholics are found saying 'Peter is in chains' as a way of saying that the Pope is in bondage to Italian nationalism. 'The fact is that for the first time since 1870 the Vatican finds its policy and interest closely allied with those of Italy, and this has given the impression of strong Italian influence at the Vatican.'[11]

In the Foreign Office the minutes grew still more ferocious. A press campaign mounted. What the *Osservatore Romano* described as *masonic newspapers* kept nagging at the silence of the Pope. The French Communist newspaper *L'Humanité* said that the Vatican had made a secret agreement with Italy to finance the war in Abyssinia. Someone who described himself as an officer and a gentleman went to an English tea-party and heard the ladies discussing how Mussolini could finance his war and suggesting that he used the immense wealth of the Pope and the Jesuits. It was reported that ignorant Africans heard that Rome was attacking Abyssinia and inferred that the Pope was the aggressor because among the inhabitants of Rome they had heard only of the Pope. To multiply examples of these expressions of uninformed opinion, during the winter of 1935–6, would be easy.

As late as July 1937 there was a curious incident in Oxford. A man who had links with Sir Oswald Mosley's British Fascist party wrote to the press as a Roman Catholic advocating Fascism in England because it would be as good for Catholicism here as it was in Italy, and drew attention to a pamphlet by an Irish bishop (the Bishop of Cork's *Fascism or Communism or What?*) which declared that the Church need make no apology for working with the Fascist dictatorship which pays homage to God and recognizes religion. A Dominican of Blackfriars in St Giles, Oxford wrote to the *Tablet* pouring ferocity upon this correspondent; and then came the curious thing – the highest authorities were offended, and the Dominican made a humiliating public submission in the number of the *Tablet* published on 7 August:

I am informed authoritatively that I have been mistaken in bracketing Fascism and Nazism with relation to the Church, as though both merited the same condemnation. The papal encyclicals were aimed at the excesses in both cases; but since the Concordat of 1931 [*sic*] not only have there been no cases of friction between the ecclesiastical authority and the Italian government, but for the most part the two authorities have proceeded along the lines of a fruitful

---

[11] *Tablet*, 1936/2/114.

collaboration . . . I beg to be allowed to state my unqualified acceptance of the above information.[12]

That autumn of 1937 Mussolini opened an exhibition of Roman archaeology, the *Mostra Augustea*. In the entrance hall of the exhibition was a large propagandist map of the Roman Empire at its fullest extent, from Edinburgh to the Euphrates, with the implication in the surroundings that this ought to be the extent of Mussolini's Italian Empire if justice were only to prevail in the world. But the exhibition was not only propaganda; for, on account of its imperialistic overtones, the government provided the archaeologists with lavish sums to mount whatever they wanted; and behind the entrance hall with its jarring assertions was a beautifully organized study of the history of the ancient world. But in historical hindsight, and not always realized by young students as they went daily to work in the exhibition, was the Christian cast of the exhibition. Beneath an inscription of the historic text, *Barbari discunt resonare Christum corde Romano,*[13] was a study of the civilizing and Christianizing mission of old Rome upon the barbarian peoples of Europe. In hindsight it was a swansong of the harmonies of Church and State in Italy, the civilizing mission of Fascism married to the evangelizing role of the Roman Catholic Church.

iii. Osborne

In February 1936 the new British Minister, d'Arcy Godolphin Osborne, arrived in Rome. He lived in a pleasant house with fair views at 36 Via Mercadante. He was unmarried, tall, and slim. His hair had receded, leaving a highbrow dome, and this made the face interesting and intelligent rather than handsome, indeed at times he could look comic. He had a bubbling gaiety, and was indefinably the grand seigneur in the best sense, with the simplest of manners, perfect but not too perfect courtesy and without the slightest trace of condescension. Rougher men sometimes criticized him for being formal, or overcorrect, or too tidy. He was liable to a little hypochondria. He was offended by noise, even by too loud laughter. But he was charming, and infinitely considerate. He had little money and suffered from extravagant tastes. He found it hard to resist works of art of doubtful authenticity. He liked his clothes, and wine, and whisky, and furniture, and silver, to be exactly what they ought to be. Some people thought him inclined to fuss about such outward things. He had aesthetic tastes, but was not critical in his judgments of art. He read a

---

[12] *Tablet,* 1937/2/60, 96–7, 202.
[13] 'The Barbarians learn to praise Christ's name with a Roman heart.'

lot, but not with any academic judgment. He spoke French easily, and Italian, and had a wide knowledge of French literature.

The British Minister to the Holy See must be a Protestant, lest he suffer from a conflict of loyalties. Osborne was more than a mere conformist. He was wont to lift up a prayer at bed-time. If it became his duty to go to a papal mass he could be (though he was not always) moved in soul. Once when he set out for Rome at a time when the journey was dangerous, he took the trouble to receive the sacrament in the Cornish parish church near the airfield from which he was to take off. But, at least in this stage of his life, he seldom appeared in church unless it were his duty. His mind sat loose to the orthodoxies.

He first visited Italy in 1900 but only fell in love with the country and its people during 1909–13 when he served as a junior in the diplomatic service under Lord Rennell. He looked back upon Rennell as the man who opened his eyes to the stature of Italy. When the First World War broke out he was in the embassy at Washington under Cecil Spring-Rice. He had a short spell at the Hague; was in London 1920–28; then went for a short time to be counsellor in Lisbon; was back in Rome 1929–31; and then was minister at the embassy in Washington, from which he was summoned to be the British Minister to the Holy See.

His affection for the Italian people was a merit. And unlike most Englishmen of the moment, he had an unusual aspect in his liking for the Italians. He preferred them rather than the emperor Haile Selassie to govern Abyssinia. Haile Selassie could not stop the slave-trade; the Italians could. But in that epoch of the British government's policy Osborne could not say this aloud.

His dressing-gown was of camel's hair, and he wore a George IV sovereign on his key-chain. He hated hats, especially the black hats affected by Anthony Eden and called by the name of that statesman. He hated wearing uniform and felt like a page-boy when correctly dressed as an ambassador. He refused ever to wear waistcoats. He liked pigskin, and caviare, and oysters, and Sheraton furniture, and expensive footwear. He disliked women who wore trousers. He had a touch of the introspective. People who saw him out for a solitary walk could fancy him rapt in deep thought. Certainly he was amusedly self-critical. He was amused to have his fortune told, and was interested in telepathy, and quarter-hoped that astrology might have something in it. He would have liked to believe in witches and the god Pan, though he confessed that the Vatican was not the likeliest place to see a witch sail by on a broomstick. With only a half-sceptical smile he wore a charm against cosmic rays.

He was a friend of the Duke and Duchess of York, soon to be King George VI and Queen Elizabeth. And generally he was a monarchist.

He believed that Europe was better provided with constitutional government when kings sat upon their thrones. He mildly hankered after the restoration of a sovereign in France, and Spain, and Austria. He thought democracy only to work if it continually grew an aristocracy by successive accretions. He liked Americans very much but was not sure that it was good for the North to have won the American Civil War – slavery went, that was good, but there went with it an aristocracy with its spirit of chivalry. He was talented as an artist in water-colours. Children found him an unforgettable playmate.

Osborne arrived at a time when the relations between the British government and the Vatican were at their nadir. He started with no influence and the Foreign Office expected him to exert no influence. By force of circumstances he had to spend the exceptionally long time of ten years at the Vatican and this was so long that he would never afterwards leave Rome for more than a few weeks but died there nearly thirty years later, in the last few months of his life a duke. Starting as almost a nonentity, starting as the Protestant agent of a power behaving unpleasantly to the Vatican and believed by the Vatican to be acting with unwise rigidity to Italy and tiresomely over the bishops in Malta, he took three or four years before his influence fully flowered. By the summer of 1940 we find a wholly impartial and reliable witness telling us that Osborne was *adored* in the Vatican.[14]

Not at once but little by little he began to make his way; until the time came when he was the key figure of this history, the instrument of the British government in important concerns. But in 1936–7 that was still a long way off. Osborne's first impression of Pope Pius XI ran thus: 'a very human and likeable old man, though a shade long-winded and set in his opinions'.[15] He liked the medieval clothes of the guards and functionaries. His first impression of the Secretary of State, Cardinal Pacelli, was of charm with a touch of saintliness, 'which is very refreshing'. About Fascist Rome he felt something sinister in the air, with students shouting about victories in Abyssinia, and an 'arrogant animality' which he saw on the faces of a regiment that marched up his street. The Fascist strutting lessened for him the old charm of Rome, and he confessed to uneasiness and a loss in peace of mind, and a conscious effort to keep his temper at gibes against Britain in the Italian newspapers.

The most influential ambassador at the Vatican – the only influential man outside the Italians – was the French ambassador to the Holy See, Charles-Roux. He was a very persistent man who did not mind what he said. One of the British found him 'slightly pompous' but neverthe-

[14] D'Ormesson, *Ambassade tragique*, p. 86.
[15] Osborne to the Duchess of York, 3 March 1936.

less able and ambitious and a very kind and friendly man. Osborne did not at first find him attractive. He could not speak English well. Osborne found him heavy, and always energetic for French political power, and somewhat suspicious of the motives of British policy. Two sentences of Osborne of different dates give the atmosphere. 'He . . . has no hesitation at all in telling the Vatican what he wants'; and again, much later when the worst crisis loomed, 'He is rather apt to browbeat the Vatican.' Osborne found him depressing. He told London: 'His pitilessly logical pessimism is anything but cheerful.'[16] Charles-Roux had no interests outside politics. By comparison Osborne found his wife charming, especially because she was lighthearted and spoke excellent English.

But as time went on, and Britain and France began to speak with one voice in the politics of Europe, Osborne began to like and respect Charles-Roux. He had real influence in the Vatican; partly because he was a strong personality, and partly because with the aid of Cardinal Verdier he contributed, in a much quieter way, to the détente between the Catholic Church in France and the French government. By 1938 the atmosphere between the Church and the historic anticlerical parties of French democracy was far more friendly, and this was partly due to Cardinal Verdier in Paris and Charles-Roux in Rome, before the Pope won the hearts of the French, even if they were as atheistic as possible, by his onslaughts on racialism and worship of the State.

iv. A Pope against Hitler

Hitler was the wild man of Europe. Who shall put chains on him? To someone sitting at a desk in London or Paris, it often looked as though the person with most chance was Mussolini. Twice this was seen to be effective. In the summer of 1934, London and Paris believed that Mussolini's resolution to keep Austria independent protected it from being absorbed by the Nazis. Then, in 1938, if credit were taken for the Munich settlement, that credit was given to Mussolini so far as it was not given to Chamberlain. He was the person who arranged the Conference and had the prestige of saving Europe. The idea of using Mussolini to deter Hitler from going to war was a natural wish.

In this operation the main work must be done by the Foreign Secretaries. So far as it was done in Rome it must be done by the British ambassador to the kingdom of Italy, not by that junior person, the British minister at the Vatican. But the place of that minister rose in weight nevertheless.

[16] FO 371/19544/235; 21164/6; 24959/261.

For if the question was asked, which Italian had the most chance of influencing Mussolini towards peaceful courses, only one answer was possible. The Pope, legally, was not a citizen of the kingdom of Italy. But that had in it an element of legal fiction. The Pope was an Italian by birth, by language, by education, by work. He was bishop of an Italian see. Take away in the mind's eye the high walls of the Vatican and put it back, only a few years back, only to the time before the Lateran treaty. The Pope's Curia was 90% Italian. In the Fascist dictatorship of Italy the Pope was the only Italian with independent position. He had his own newspaper, and radio, and freedom to speak to the outside world or to the Italian people. In theory he could say what he liked because he was head of a neutral State and because he had international backing as head of an international Church. This freedom was more extensive in theory than in practice. We shall see how limited was the freedom to speak. It was limited partly by treaty, and partly by helplessness if the Italian government turned rough. But it existed. And therefore, if the British Foreign Office asked itself which Italian had most chance of pushing Mussolini towards peaceful courses, it could give only one answer.

And, therefore, the British minister in the Vatican started to rise in the eyes of London. From being a ceremonial figure of prestige, or a dabbler in Maltese turmoil, he became part of that international struggle of diplomacy in which the centre was Hitler. It was a long shot. No one had much confidence that Mussolini could deter Hitler. No one had much confidence that the Pope could deter Mussolini. The Foreign Office had illusions but they were not ridiculous illusions. Nevertheless the fact was, that a powerful minister in the Vatican might help to push the Pope, who might help to push Mussolini, who might help to push Hitler, to negotiate instead of invade.

The pressure on the Pope could become important even though Mussolini had no prospect of deterring Hitler. If war had to come, better that it were war with Germany alone, and not with Germany and Italy. It might be too long a shot that the Fascist could hinder the Nazi from resort to arms. But at least, and without the slightest doubt, the Pope had influence in Italy. As the head of the Catholic Church he had weight in a largely though often nominally Catholic country. And the French and British had plenty of evidence that many sensible Italians had not the slightest desire to be taken into a war at Hitler's behest. A lot of Italian opinion wanted Mussolini not to be dragged into a Nazi war. They also looked to the Pope for help. Consequently, though the Pope could not push Hitler, he could certainly push at Mussolini. He might even be able to push Mussolini away from Hitler.

At first this was not important. But with the founding of the Axis and thereafter with the steady strengthening of the links which bound Italy to Germany and with the steady weakening of the place of Italy in the partnership which was the Axis, the desire to separate Mussolini from Hitler became more urgent. The common interest against Hitler which was shared by Mussolini, the Pope and the western democracies – the independent existence of Austria – ended when the German army occupied Austria in March 1938. Mussolini had to be tempted away from Hitler by other means – by a friendlier Foreign Secretary in London, by talk of concessions in trade or colonies, by recognizing the conquest of Abyssinia. But in this attempt to prise Mussolini from Hitler the Pope might help. And so the British minister in the Vatican became one of the instruments to stop Mussolini going to war if Hitler went to war and the Italians could not afford to lose the spoils of victory.

Whether or not the Pope had any influence on the policy of Hitler (certainly not) or of Mussolini (probably) he had another importance to the British Foreign Office as Europe rolled nearer to war. They were engaged as always in a battle for the opinion of the world. Their idea of the world usually focussed on the United States. No one was so foolish as to think that you could make the Japanese or the Russians think worse of Hitler by means of the Pope. But wherever Catholics practised their religion – and that included Austria and a third of Germany, a lot of France and nearly all Poland, Spain and Portugal and Italy, all Latin America, Belgium and Quebec Province and Ireland and a minority but a large and weighty minority in the United States – if the Pope condemned what Hitler did that must be useful to all powers that opposed him.

The Nazis played into the hands of those who saw how they could use the Pope in this way. They were unpleasant though not yet murderous to the Jews; they treated all the Churches to a form of persecution, usually mild but aspects of it were peculiarly unpleasant especially in the way Catholics were treated by the viler Nazi organs; and they flaunted an aggressive philosophy of life which shrieked a contrast with the ideals of a man of peace.

A member of the British Foreign Office had as his business to keep the peace; or, if already he thought that to be in the long run impossible, to keep the peace for months or years enough to allow Britain and France time to rearm. The Pope was another voice in international morality talking of peace. And, if in many parts of the world ears were closed to everything he might say, his voice might be heard faintly, perhaps, even in Bavaria and Austria and the Rhineland, and would be sure to be heard more loudly in the United States. This last was not to be despised, because it began to look uncertain whether

Germany could be contained unless the United States reversed its decision of 1919 to withdraw from Europe and came in its weight to stop the aggressor.

In this way also the British minister to the Vatican grew in stature in the eyes of the Foreign Office. Another reason lies in the mentality of the Foreign Office, which started to change. It began our period by thinking the Pope a broken reed, useless for any practical purpose of international morality. The scrawls made at Foreign Office desks on the reports coming in from Rome leave no room for doubt that they thought him a broken reed. The British minister to the Vatican was unimportant because he could do nothing. And he could do nothing because the power to which he was accredited either could or would do nothing. They started by thinking that the Pope was as near as makes no difference a Fascist and how shall a Fascist bring independent force to bear upon Mussolini?

Throughout the period with which this book deals, some desks in the Foreign Office thought the Pope to be a broken reed. Nevertheless the mentality of the Foreign Office changed dramatically. First, they discovered that the Pope was not after all in the pocket of the dictators as they had supposed. Second, they discovered that something could actually be achieved in Rome. Third, their own leader changed. Anthony Eden never had much use for Popes. His attitude to them was as impatient as it afterwards was to Moussadeq the Iranian in his pyjamas, or to Nasser the Egyptian. Not being even an amateur of appeasement, he could not see a professional of appeasement (which was what the Pope was) as any kind of natural ally. And Eden had a faint sensation that when he coped with ecclesiastical affairs, he dealt in things that he did not well understand. On one report from Rome he scrawled in his own hand, 'These religious ideas are apt to raise many complexities.'[17]

Part of this change of mentality had something to do with the decline in the force of Sir Robert Vansittart. Of all the scrawls on the desks at the Foreign Office, Vansittart's were the most caustic in expression. He was caustic about others besides Popes. But it was a little more than that. Sometimes Vansittart seemed to enjoy the discovery that in the game of international politics the Pope was a broken reed. The appearance of Sir Alexander Cadogan, still more the rise of Orme Sargent, made a difference.

Between the beginning of 1937 and the end of 1938, the Pope who had seemed to be in the pocket of one of the dictators came to be one of the world leaders in the fight against Nazism and Fascism. The process

[17] FO 371/37554/49, 14 December 1943.

may be taken to begin on 12 March 1937 when Osborne wrote a very private letter to Anthony Eden.[18] He warned him that the Pope had decided to send a personal message to the German people, which would be read in German pulpits on Palm Sunday or Easter Sunday. It would urge German Catholics to stand firm in the face of the persecution. Therefore it would affect Italian sentiment towards the alliance with Germany, and Austrian sentiment towards Germany. 'My Vatican source urged upon me the need for absolute secrecy.'

Eden did not file this document in the normal way but put it among the specially secret papers for confidential filing – this was not surprising for at that moment Osborne knew more than the Gestapo. The encyclical *Mit brennender Sorge* was printed in Italy, taken into Germany by couriers, distributed to the bishops and then the parish priests. Many priests only received their copies on the morning of the Palm Sunday when it was due to be read in church, and all without using the postal system. The Gestapo got hold of a number of packages before they were distributed, but the whole feat was a wonderful success in secret organization.

It denounced the various breaches of the Concordat, the encouragement of anti-Christian doctrines, the encouragement of racialism. 'Whoever gives the idea of race or people or state or form of government a value beyond that of the ordinary world and claims to make idols out of them, violates the divine order of things.' The Pope tried to protect himself from the charge of political partiality by condemning atheistic Communism almost simultaneously.

From this moment the quarrel between the Pope and the German government became very public. The Nazis said that the Pope was ungrateful and forgot how they saved Germany from Bolshevism and interfered where he had no business and passed a judgment on German affairs from a 'parliamentary and democratic outlook'. They took no notice of his various complaints and treated the Church worse rather than better. The Pope continued to stand up to Hitler. The non-effects of this encyclical were used to argue, under the next Pope, that this kind of vast public pronouncement achieves nothing and brings hurt to the work of the Churches. But the encyclical made the western democracies look with new eyes upon the man whom they had supposed to be Mussolini's Pope. The Foreign Office began to ask itself whether after all the Pope might be serviceable in the struggle for peace and justice.

They were bothered, in London – and were not the only observers to be bothered – by the personality of the Pope's nuncio in Berlin.

---

[18] FO 380/38.

Monsignor Cesare Orsenigo was very suitable as a running-mate for the new British ambassador in Berlin, Sir Nevile Henderson.

Orsenigo saw nothing but ill to come from a breach between the Church and the Nazi State. As an Italian he believed in the Fascist State. His ideas of what ought to happen in Germany were formed on the basis of what happened in Italy. Moreover he had a German secretary, Father Gehrmann. In the Russian famine of 1922 Gehrmann was sent on a commission and formed opinions of Bolshevism which made him favourably disposed to the Nazi party. He saw the results of a total breach between the Vatican and Moscow and was determined that these calamities should not be repeated in Germany. And Orsenigo had successes. He got a chaplain-general for the German army. He advised bishops to send out pastoral letters on subjects which would please the government as well as the Church, like the importance of having a lot of babies. He would wave his hands zigzag, to show that in a contrary wind tacking is the only course for a sailing ship.[19]

In Orsenigo can be found that attitude which occasionally is found later in Rome and which displeased the British. It may be called the faith of a long perspective. We are an institution which has seen a lot; we have seen a Pope in the mines of Sardinia, and a Papacy under two harlots, and a Pope kidnapped at Anagni, and Rome sacked by the mercenaries of Charles V, and two Popes kidnapped by French revolutionaries, and Italians stealing all the Pope's property – and yet here we are, still at work, still in business, still doing what we can for the human race. History is long, tyrants are short. They rise, and kill people and suppress monasteries, and close churches. But protest will change nothing; and soon tyrants come to a bad end, and the Church shakes itself after the persecution, and churches start to reopen. We bow to the storm, and put down our heads, and wait. For we have faith, and know that our day will come.

If this Pope was thought to be, after the encyclical *Mit brennender Sorge*, a stalwart standing up to Hitler, why did he keep Orsenigo in Berlin? He kept him there despite the strong protests of two or three of the German bishops. No one knows, and it is still a mystery. Perhaps the Pope remembered that they were both Lombards and had known each other from boyhood. Perhaps the Secretariat realized that Orsenigo's diplomatic bag was their securest means of communication with Germany, and what would happen to that bag if they withdrew Orsenigo? Perhaps they pondered over the difficulty that a retiring nuncio to Germany would by custom have to be made a cardinal and

[19] Walter Adolph, *Geheime Aufzeichnungen aus dem nationalsozialistischen Kirchenkampf, 1935–43* (Mainz, 1979), pp. 28, 231–2.

the prospect of promoting Orsenigo to be a cardinal looked a worse alternative. All that is guesswork. We have no evidence of the mind of the Pope on this matter.

The Foreign Office knew about Orsenigo; and were interested, and needed reassuring. During the summer of 1937 Osborne wrote to William Strang, telling him of the opinion of the French ambassador in the Vatican that 'Orsenigo does not really count for much'.[20]

If the Pope and the Nazis were at loggerheads, that was not yet true of the Pope and Italy, even while Italy and Germany forged closed links. On 12 January 1938 Osborne reported on an ecclesiastical demonstration at the Palazzo Venezia, when 60 archbishops and bishops visited Mussolini to thank him, and Archbishop Nogara of Udine made a fulsome speech, and Mussolini reaffirmed solidarity with the Church. Osborne wrote to London of Mussolini's 'nailing the Catholic flag to the Fascist flagstaff'.[21]

Between summer 1937 and April 1938, Western Europe became conscious of a conflict of world-philosophies. It looked as though two underlying sets of principles were at stake, which issued in opposed ways of thinking about society; touching the nature of justice, or the possibility of political freedom, or the rights of the individual, or even the old fraternities and equalities of the French Revolution. Men started to write books about the nature of western civilization. Writers like Arnold Toynbee or Christopher Dawson grew in influence. What are the roots of western culture? On what moral principles does Europe stand? When Nazis trampled on Jews and sniped at the Churches, what was the place of the Judaeo-Christian tradition in the European inheritance?

From the broadest viewpoint the rising interest by the Foreign Office in the Pope was nothing specially to do with that Pope. It was part of a wider and deeper and vaguer struggle within the European mind; a struggle between the traditional heritage of moral ideas in politics and society, and revolutionary doctrines of social morality which might be ascribed, not always plausibly, to Houston Stewart Chamberlain or Gobineau or Richard Wagner or Nietzsche or Charles Darwin. On 25 January 1937 Winston Churchill spoke at the annual dinner of the Leeds Chamber of Commerce. He likened Fascism and Communism to the Arctic and Antarctic zones of the world and said that he preferred a temperate zone. 'It is a strange thing that certain parts of the world should now be wishing to revive the old religious wars. There are those non-God religions Nazism and Communism. . . . I repudiate both and will have nothing to do with either. . . . They are as alike as two peas.

---

[20] FO 380/39.   [21] FO 380/40.

Tweedledum and Tweedledee were violently contrasted compared with them. You leave out God and you substitute the devil' (*Manchester Guardian*, 26 January 1937). Such a speech shows how men who were not at all ecclesiastical and not even particularly religious might see, in that war of ideologies, a conflict of men for the soul of Europe. And in such a quest for the soul of Europe the Pope could not help but be of interest.

But from another point of view the rising British interest in the Pope had much to do with the behaviour of the Pope.

They began a quest for friendliness with the Italians. In view of what had happened over Abyssinia, and of Mussolini's signed alliance with Hitler, even to threats of war, this was not a promising undertaking. How desperate at times they felt it, was shown by their behaviour when Gabriele d'Annunzio died (March 1938).

London asked the question, what notice should be taken of an Italian hero who was a repulsive man and one of the founders of Fascism? The *Osservatore Romano* wrote against his influence and declared that there was nothing in him that was 'morally useful'. The British government was much more perplexed. The idea of sending condolences on the death of d'Annunzio filled them with nausea. Some said that this unpalatable act would nevertheless be 'appropriate'. Why, it was asked, would it be appropriate? The Italian government did nothing when Rudyard Kipling died. The minutes of the Foreign Office desks are comic. Cadogan wanted a message, and wrote: 'It is true that d'Annunzio was almost the originator of international gangsterism, but we needn't praise him for that.' The minutes of Vansittart and of Lord Halifax are predictable:

Robert Vansittart: 'This seems to be going beyond the bounds of all literary proportion.

D'Annunzio was a first-class cad and a second-class writer – sometimes a rather ridiculous one. He shone in a remarkably lean period and has long been extinct outside Italy.

I hope we shall not get this right out of focus and cheapen ourselves.'

Lord Halifax: 'I think on balance of undesirables, I come down on the side of a "respectable" message.'

The letter actually sent after all this did not mention any actual merits in d'Annunzio. It expressed the condolence of the British government on the passing 'of that distinguished Italian who enjoyed so international a reputation in the world of letters'.[22]

This shows that by March 1938 the British were willing to go to further lengths in appeasing Mussolini.

[22] FO 371/22440/382.

From March 1938 onwards, after the occupation of Austria, the Pope's language became strong enough to satisfy the critics in London and Paris who wanted him to stand out for morality against aggression and racialism. When Hitler visited Rome in May 1938 the Italians decorated the streets of Rome with swastikas. Pius XI saw the swastika as a pagan symbol and regarded these banners as a pollution of the sacred city, and said what he thought. He was getting old, and knew that he had not much time, and ceased to care about discretion or the worries of his diplomatic staff. Then during the summer, Mussolini increased the anti-semitic pressure of the Italian government. These acts seemed to the Pope another pollution of Italy. Between August and December 1938 he denounced racialism and perverted nationalism in strong language. He implied that governments 'not far from here' (he was speaking at Castel Gandolfo) reminded him of Judas Iscariot in their behaviour. He went to the missionary college near Castel Gandolfo and talked loud about the evils of excessive nationalism. He got out a circular to all missionary colleges on the importance of instructing candidates in the measures to combat racialism. The Curia applied to the Ministry of Education, and received vague assurances that the new racial doctrines would not be taught formally in schools. The Inquisition condemned a German racialist book which was published in Italian translation.[23]

In one speech Pius XI went so far as to lament the mania for copying Germany; 'Catholic means universal, but not racialism, nor nationalism, nor separatism . . . One wonders therefore why Italy has felt the need, in an unfortunate spirit of imitation, to copy the example of Germany.' He lent extreme point to the utterance, saying that as a Milanese he could remember how not so long ago the men of Milan were proud to chase out the *Tedeschi*. Mussolini in a speech at Forlí, and then at Venice on 18 September, said that people who suggested that the Fascist government copied anyone over racialism were unfortunate half-wits and he did not know whether they better deserved contempt or pity. The Pope enquired privately whether this was directed at himself and was assured that it was not. But such a slanging match between the two heads of State proved that in Italy the relations between Church and State were sinking back to the stormiest years of the Risorgimento, and the cause was Italian racialism under pressure from German racialism. The Italian press reproduced an article from the German newspaper *National-Zeitung* blaming the Pope for his alliance with international Jewry.

---

[23] Raoul Heinrich Francé, *Von der Arbeit zum Erfolg* (Dresden, 1934). Francé was an Austro-Hungarian Catholic from Budapest who did serious work in plant physiology and then moved via plant psychology into a general social Darwinism which was influential among half-educated nationalistic Germans.

The Pope privately reminded the Italian government that the proposed measures against the Jews were in breach of the Concordat, which forced the government to give civil recognition to any Catholic marriage. The Pope wrote letters in his own hand both to Mussolini and to the King of Italy as this danger loomed. But the law forbidding mixed marriages was published in November 1938. The Fascists were aware that they had useful historical material if they needed. Farinacci made a speech to the Institute of Culture saying that the persecution of the Jews was in accordance with the traditions of Catholicism. He said that he could not therefore comprehend the tendency of the Church to drift into the camp of Communists, freemasons, democrats and others, 'its declared or former enemies'. Farinacci's newspaper *Regime Fascista* dug up a vehemently anti-semitic article written by a Jesuit in 1890.[24]

On Christmas Eve 1938 the Pope addressed the Consistory about the forthcoming tenth anniversary of the Lateran Treaty. He was surprisingly weak in view of all that had passed in the summer. He said that the anniversary would be a joyful occasion and one for which he could not but be grateful to the noble monarch and the 'incomparable' minister whose statesmanship had done so much to make it possible. Nevertheless, it carried bitter sorrows – the provocations of Catholic Action, the infringement of the Concordat on marriages, the swastika in the streets when Hitler came to Rome. This was so unlike the mood of the summer that the reader suspects that the drafting was beginning now to slip from the hands of the dying Pope into that of his more peaceable Secretary of State Cardinal Pacelli.

The Italian newspapers took only those parts of the speech which referred to the noble king and his incomparable minister, and the Pope's joy at the forthcoming anniversary of the Lateran treaty.

Five days later, on 29 December, Pius XI received Osborne. Because he was so ill, audiences with diplomats were now limited to five minutes. But Osborne happened to be last in the queue. The Pope kept him talking for 35 minutes; obviously very old and weak, but with mind and memory unimpaired. The Pope wanted to talk about Germany and the Germans, Hitler and the Nazis.

He started by expressing 'his admiration and affection' for Great Britain and his pleasure at the recent institution of an Apostolic Delegate in London. He was pleased at the fairness with which Britain treated the Catholics in the British Empire. 'There is no doubt', Osborne reported to Lord Halifax, 'that Nazi Germany has taken the place of Communism as the Church's most dangerous enemy.' This report made a contrast with all previous reports of that nature.

[24] 'Della questione giudaica in Europa', *Civ. Catt.* (1890), Series 14, no. 8, pp. 5ff., 385ff., 641ff.

Relations between His Majesty's Government and the Vatican at the present time are particularly satisfactory. There are various reasons for this, amongst them the Vatican's growing fear of German Nazism and, it must be added, of Italian Fascism . . . Now that conflict has been joined on the racial issue which cuts across fundamental tenets of the Roman Catholic Church, it is difficult to see how the two systems can ever again work in harmony together. In facing this threat to the work of the Church in Germany and Italy the present Pope, old in years and feeble in health, has shown great courage. He finds himself now in open conflict with the totalitarian States . . . It is natural that he should look for support to the great Democracies where Christianity is still accepted as the rule by which public and private life should be guided . . . The Pope is an old and probably a dying man; for whatever reasons he is following a policy in international affairs which on the major issues of principle corresponds very closely indeed with our own.[25]

This was the reversal of the attitude less than two years before, in the aftermath of the Abyssinian invasion and the height of the Spanish civil war.

The long interview of Christmas 1938 was unusual for Osborne. The British minister in the Vatican was not so important as he afterwards became because this was a Pope difficult to influence. Pius XI was a man without intimate friends, whose staff were afraid of him, a man autocratic and outspoken. Persuading autocrats to do something is harder than persuading people who act on other people's opinions. Under this Pope the Secretary of State had no power because the Pope listened to no one not even his Secretary of State. But ambassadors worked with the Secretary of State and his assistants; these were the people whom they saw each week and whom they got to know. It was no use trying to achieve something by persuading the Secretary of State if even the Secretary of State was not heard by his principal. For Osborne to be influential, the circumstances must change; not only the political situation of Europe, but the Pope and the Secretary of State to whom he was accredited.

Even the Italian government watched with alarm the rising Vatican hostility to the tide of racialism. On Epiphany (the feast of the Three Wise Men, 6 January) 1939 the nuncio in Turkey, Monsignor Roncalli, preached a sermon at the French Church of the Holy Spirit in Istanbul. He reminded his hearers that the bodies of the Three Wise Men lay at Cologne, in the midst of a country which proclaims 'We do not want Christ or Christianity any more'; and used the reminder to say that 'the Church does not know the division of humanity into races', and to prophesy that humanity would be reconciled on the ideas of charity and equality. About this sermon the Italian government protested to

[25] FO 371/23789/393.

the Vatican, because a Jewish journal at Istanbul (*Journal d'Orient*) took the chance to apply the condemnation to Italian racial policy.[26] The Vatican took no notice of the protest.

The dying Pope had a last triumph. In January 1939 Herriot took office again as President of the French Chamber of Deputies and made a speech. In that historically anticlerical chamber he said: 'In Rome an old man, to whom our spontaneous homage is due, armed by his spiritual gallantry, renews the grand tradition of the great Popes, as protectors of outraged weakness.' And the Chamber applauded, which some took as a sign how far and fast the French were travelling when the Pope was so anti-German.

The autocratic Pope suddenly looked like a Liberal, and Liberal Catholics started to claim him for their own. At Birmingham Town Hall (30 January) Cardinal Hinsley of Westminster said that the Catholic Church was becoming recognized as the principal bulwark of wise liberty. 'History will record that Pius XI has been the foremost and fearless champion of freedom against the enslaving forces of our time. Even at the very door of death he dauntlessly reminds democrats and dictators that man was made by God and for God . . .'

Hinsley did not forget to remind his audience that no Catholic can be a Communist: 'We condemn the errors of Communism, Fascism, or Nazism with an equal emphasis.'[27] 'I cannot understand how a Catholic in this country can adopt wisely and safely this foreign label *Fascist*, however much he may modify its underlying meaning.'

The Pope knew that he had only a few days to live. He prepared a last speech to the bishops of Italy. He said to his doctor to give him twenty-four more hours so that he could deliver the speech. The staff and the diplomats were afraid what would come, afraid of too unwise an attack upon the German or the Italian governments. But he died without delivering what he had to say.[28]

He died on 10 February 1939; once regarded by Britain and France as the Fascist Pope; at the end of his life seen as one of the saviours of Europe from racialist heresy; an autocrat who accepted that the Church could live with any kind of constitution but had no reason to think democracy preferable to others, and at his end regarded as one of the pillars in Europe of the ideals of freedom. The French Communist newspaper *L'Humanité* said that 'ears and hearts still re-echo the words that lashed at "stupid racialism" and "barbaric Hitlerism" '. The Nazi *Angriff* said that he started as a religious reformer and ended as

[26] AE, Santa Sede, 1939, Busta 44.   [27] *Tablet*, 1939/1/182.

[28] Extracts from the speech were quoted by Pope John XXIII; text in Pietro Scoppola, *La Chiesa e il fascismo* (Bari, 1971), which dissipated most of the legends which persisted about the contents of this speech.

a religious adventurer, who drew his Church into a crisis of conscience.[29]

The Italian journals sang the praises of the dead Pope. The French and British envoys at the Vatican found this extraordinary in view of the quarrels between Mussolini and the Vatican over racial laws and warlike speeches and Catholic Action. They were sure that the press must have received an order to represent Pius XI as 'a great Italian', and to sing the praises again of the Lateran Treaty, and to say how false was the opinion that the Pope disapproved the policy of Hitler and Mussolini. At the funeral ceremonies the Italian government behaved with perfect manners.

The *Giornale d'Italia* (11 February 1939) wrote: 'It is in vain that the French press tried to give to the dead Pope an interpretation as a liberal-democrat, and to make him a kind of Roosevelt-in-tiara.'

Osborne, as was his duty, wrote to the Foreign Office a summary of the Pope's career. The writing shows that he was moved:

He may be said to have died at his post, as he always said he would wish to do. His unfaltering courage in the face of prolonged and increasing physical and mental distress, his 'intrepid faith' and his resolute refusal to compromise with what he regarded as evil influences and forces had raised him at the end of his life to be one of the outstanding figures of the world and from whom even the most rabid anti-Catholic could not withhold a tribute of respect and admiration.[30]

The minutes on this letter were not so favourable:

A. N. Noble: 'I think that Mr Osborne should certainly be thanked for his despatch and that it should be printed and circulated.

I fear, however, that Mr Osborne in his review of the pontificate of Pius XI had overlooked one of its essential features. The Pope's experience as Nuncio in Warsaw increased his natural hatred of Bolshevism to such an extent that it blinded him to the scarcely lesser dangers of Fascism and Nazism. It was only in the last year or so that he came to see that Fascism and Catholicism are fundamentally opposed but that fact had been evident for all to see since the early days of the Fascist movement. It does not follow that the Pope ought to have got up and publicly denounced the Abyssinian war, but at least he ought from the very beginning to have put to the Italian people and to the world the inescapable conflict between the doctrine of absolute devotion to the State and Christianity.'

From the Foreign Office archives comes a last point of interest for the Legation at Rome under Pope Pius XI. For it reveals for the first time the possibility, in the British agents at the Vatican, of a new world of activity.

[29] *Tablet*, 1939/1/205–6; Ogilvie-Forbes (Berlin) to Foreign Office (telegram), 11 February 1939, FO 371/23789.   [30] FO 371/23810/450.

The document is unsigned and undated. When it came it was placed by the London recipient away from the main collection of documents and in the archive reserved for specially confidential papers. From the surrounding papers it looks as though its date must be March 1938; which if true is a surprisingly early date in view of the contents.

In this paper the writer, urging Osborne to complete secrecy, draws his attention to the Pope's secretary, the Jesuit Father Leiber. He begs him not to mention Leiber's name because Leiber has relatives in Germany and is known to Heinrich Brüning, the former German Chancellor.

In the light of what was to happen later this obscure fragment can only mean one thing. British Intelligence had already realized that Rome's links with the old Catholic Centre Party of Germany were not to be despised; that Rome was a capital where you might meet at cafés Monsignor Kaas, the leader of the Centre Party before Hitler suppressed it; and that here it was possible, perhaps, to establish links, very secret links, with Germans who were dedicated opponents of Hitler. If this document is placed in the right order in the archive, and has not been displaced from some other file (which is unlikely), then already, two years before anyone has supposed, the underground chain of information was beginning to be put together; and the Vatican Legation was beginning to have a utility which was neither ceremonial show, nor routine reporting, but one link, and not the least important link, in a secret plan for the overthrow of a tyranny.

It was not the only moment that year when Osborne touched the world of the secret services. On 6 July 1938 he passed a confidential report by a German ex-officer, who was a Catholic aristocrat, on the movement of German troops.[31]

[31] FO 380/40.

2

The Conclave of 1939

Pius XI wanted Cardinal Pacelli to be his successor. A week before he died he told Monsignor Tardini that he had sent Pacelli on a visit abroad to prepare him, and that 'he will make a fine Pope'.[1] At the consistory of cardinals in December 1937, when he expected soon to die, he spoke too meaningfully to the cardinals about his successor, using the words of the first chapter of St John's Gospel (the words of St John the Baptist about the coming Christ: 'Among you stands one whom you know not.') The Vatican newspaper *Osservatore Romano* made the text apply to all the cardinals; but only the five new cardinals were then in the room, with a sixth, who was his Secretary of State, Cardinal Pacelli.[2] But many Popes want their Secretary of State to succeed, and a dead Pope has no influence in a Conclave.

In February 1939 it mattered more to the Powers who the new Pope was than at any election since the earlier nineteenth century. When Pius XI died he was (in a political aspect) part of the alliance of democratic powers resisting Hitler; and especially resisting Hitler's growing influence over Italy. His ideals of peace and justice, his denunciation of racialism, supported the convictions of the democratic powers and helped to win American opinion to their side and caused scruples to many Italians and perhaps caused scruples even to a few Austrians and Bavarians. Accordingly it was important to Britain and France that they should get a Pope who would continue the same policy, the same utterances, if possible with the same boldness and trenchancy.

Conversely it was important to the Italian Foreign Office (though not personally important to Mussolini), that the next Pope should not be like Pius XI: should not be, as the newspaper said abusively, a Roosevelt-in-tiara; should not be a Pope in total breach with Germany and very near total breach in Italy. If they could not have an openly pro-German Pope, which even the Germans recognized to be impossible, then certainly a pro-Fascist Pope; or, if that proved to be impossible, then at least a neutral Pope, one who would not follow his

---

[1] D. Tardini, *Pio XII* (Rome, 1959), p. 105: *un bel Papa*.
[2] Ibid., pp. 105ff.; the five new cardinals were Piazza, Pizzardo, Hinsley of Westminster, Gerlier of Lyons, Pellegrinetti.

predecessors by taking sides, a Pope who would remain above the dust of the conflict – in short, a non-political Pope. This last was a very historical position among powers trying to interfere in papal Conclaves. And if you look round for someone with no politics, then find a remote man, an otherworldly man, a man of prayer, a man who has spent all his life in a monastery (but there is a prejudice in Conclaves against members of religious orders). If you want a non-political it is perhaps not wisest to try for a monk; but still, get a saint if you can. For if he is a saint he will have spent so much time at his prayers and at self-sacrificing care for the poor and needy, he cannot have the glimmer of an understanding what international politics are about. This is a very strong position for politicians trying to affect the outcome of a papal election. The cry *let us have a saint* echoed in the breasts of all the best cardinals: they want a vicar of Christ who shall be Christ-like. Descents into politics are corrupting the Church and making it worldly, so let us at all costs have a man of God whose eyes are set on heaven and not upon this ephemeral world – that argument has so much truth and right in it that it became a very historical argument in the history of Conclaves. If a State's representatives do not like the politics of the man whom the cardinals look like electing, then they should tell the cardinals that political Popes are undesirable, and that we must have a man of prayer.

The immuring of the cardinals in a Conclave was designed to exclude interference by the Powers in an election. To some extent the Conclave achieved this by withdrawing the cardinals from all human contact. But it never achieved it fully, and at times of European crisis, when attitudes of the new Pope mattered to all governments, it was impossible to make it secure, and the Powers had always been able to exert a certain amount of pressure on Conclaves, either through their national cardinals or through their ambassadors or through both.

Such interference continued openly and unashamedly until the Austro-Hungarian cardinal of 1903, on behalf of his emperor, vetoed the election of Cardinal Rampolla, partly because his politics were very friendly to the French and partly because he behaved so uncompromis-ingly over the suicide pact of the degenerate Habsburg prince at the hunting lodge of Mayerling. This veto shocked the Conclave, and the Pope excommunicated such interferers for the future. But this bull, which excommunicated users of the veto, was not the real reason for the lesser interferences of the twentieth century. The real reason was the relation to Italy. The Pope had a quarrel with Italy. He said that Italy had stolen all his lands and that he was not free, that he was the prisoner of the Vatican. The Italian government kept saying that this was untrue, that under Italian government the Pope was as free as he had ever been. Therefore at all costs the Italian government must not be seen to interfere in a papal election. The only sure way of being seen not to interfere was not to interfere. And if Italy was determined not to interfere herself, that made a powerful motive for preventing German or Frenchman or Spaniard from interfering. The election was free because Italy, in its own interest, held the ring.

But in February 1939 the Pope was no longer the prisoner of the Vatican. This was the first election since the Lateran Treaty. The Pope looked free because he was head of a neutral State. But it was a very little State, dependent even for water and electricity on the city of Rome. And the Italian government was no longer a weak government but dictatorial. In this situation the idea of a Fascist government holding the ring for a papal election gave discomfort both to London and to Paris.

It happened that a decision of Pope Pius XI made interference by outside powers in a Conclave marginally easier. At the last Conclave of 1922 the Cardinal of Boston, travelling as fast as he could, still arrived too late. He found a Pope already made and was displeased. He made one of those protests which are the icier for being cast in respectful language. In a world of that size the protest seemed sensible. And so Pius XI lengthened the time, between the death of the Pope and the immuring of the cardinals, to three weeks. This was to have an important effect in modern Conclaves. It meant that there was more time for discussions to take place between cardinals and groups of cardinals before they went into Conclave. They could enter the Conclave with much of the forming of parties, or discarding of possible names, already done. And since this process happened with no restriction, these discussions could be held with the ambassadors of the Powers. The cardinals could talk with Osborne or Charles-Roux or Bergen or Pignatti as freely as with each other.

The constitutional position of 1939 was thus. There were 62 cardinals. The two-thirds majority necessary to elect was 42. Of the cardinals 35 were Italian. If the Italians were unanimous they still needed seven votes from non-Italians. But it would be a miracle if the Italians were unanimous. Therefore no Pope could be elected who was unacceptable to the Italian majority but no Pope could be elected without substantial support from non-Italians.

The Italian government took extraordinary precautions in secret about the forthcoming election. It is hard to understand why. The quaestor who gave the orders (Francesco Argenti) was guilty of an excess of zeal. He ordered increased vigilance by all security agents, especially on railways; demanded increased supervision of all suspect persons, and reports on any unusual absences, and instant telegrams if any suspect left his usual place, and more officers on trains, and careful inspection of all trains before they started, and opening of luggage of suspects, interception of postal packets addressed to 'high personages', 'with the aim of discovering and destroying explosives sent for terroristic purposes'.[3] We can only account for these orders by remembering the ancient Italian tradition that the time of Conclave is a time for riot and murder, which still existed deep in a folk-memory. Before the ceremonies of S. Andrea della Valle the police checked the crypt, the pictures, the furniture, anything that could hide a bomb.

Some Italian prefects expected their government to take a hand. The prefect of Turin assumed that Cardinal Pacelli would be impossible as a Pope. For he heard the sermon of Cardinal Fossati at the requiem mass for Pope Pius XI, and disliked what he heard, and reported in a coded telegram as follows:

He did not fail to bring out with a polemical accent some contrasts, talking of the peace of Christ, the invulnerable rights of the family in the education of their children, Catholic Action. From his address of this morning you can infer that if Fossati were elected Pope, he would continue, with intransigence, the policy of Cardinal Pacelli.

Evidently the prefect took it for granted that the Italian government wished to stop the election of Pacelli and, after his report, would wish to stop any chance of the election of Cardinal Fossati.[4]

The files of the authorities of Public Security show that the Duce made special payments to a number of agents in connexion with the Conclave. Mostly these agents dealt with matters of public order or ceremonial. But part of their duty is recorded, as a way of showing their merit, in the file thus: 'penetration of and contact with the Vatican authorities, work which needed maximum delicacy'.[5]

But the Italians, outwardly and in general, behaved with perfect discretion. The newspaper *Il Telegrafo* of Leghorn caused them vexation when it wrote political comments on the leading cardinals. The swashbuckling arch-Fascist Farinacci wrote an article in his newspaper *Regime Fascista* to say that Fascism has no candidates to present to the Conclave because the religious sentiment is universal and is not limited by frontiers or nationality; and, though no one could any longer call Farinacci an official mouthpiece, this was felt by government, outwardly, to be the right line to take.[6]

So far as the evidence goes hitherto, the Italian government behaved

[3] Orders of Argenti, 10 February 1939; AC, PS, 1939, 38A.
[4] AC, PS, 1939, 38A, Tiengo to Ministry, 17 February 1939.
[5] AC, PS, 1939, 38A, Conclave: report of 29 April 1939.
[6] See the report of the Inspector-General of Public Security in Bari, 3 March 1939: AC, PS, 1939, 38A.

honourably. Before the remains of the dead Pope, which lay in state in the chapel of the Most Holy Sacrament in St Peter's, Borgongini Duca the nuncio to Italy found himself next to Count Pignatti the Italian ambassador to the Holy See. Borgongini Duca asked Pignatti to get the Italian press to refrain from prophecies about a winning candidate. Pignatti, though he thought the place and time unsuitable for the conversation, reassured him; but the reassurance was perhaps as much for the benefit of the French ambassador Charles-Roux, who stood two yards away; and was perhaps a dig at the flood of speculation in the French press.[7]

Pignatti, though he behaved scrupulously, did what he could. He asked Cardinal Pizzardo if he might come to see him. Pizzardo preferred not to be seen at Pignatti's and invited Pignatti to come to him; but when he arrived, 'Pizzardo said almost nothing worth hearing. I found him not at all forthcoming, in fact almost distant. I will see him again before the Conclave and will try to soften him up.' On 13 February Pignatti went to see Cardinal Pacelli. They talked of the famous speech which Pope Pius XI never delivered, and which was believed to be anti-Fascist. Cardinal Pacelli relieved Pignatti's mind. 'It will remain a dead letter. It will be put in the Secret Archives.' Pacelli expressed pleasure at the way the Italian government took a prominent part in the mourning for the dead Pope.

How honourably the Italian government was behaving – despite the suspicion of the French and British that they were behaving dishonourably – is shown by Pignatti's refusal even to mention the Conclave to Cardinal Pacelli. Here he had an interview with the Camerlengo, in charge of affairs during the vacancy, who was also the former Secretary of State and a possible Pope. Yet he did not dare to mention the subject uppermost in both their minds. Pignatti afterwards explained his reasoning to his government:

I did not talk expressly of the Conclave. I felt extreme caution, so as not to raise diffidence. It seemed to me good tactics to let the good impression, made on the Cardinals by the Italian government, do its work, and let them draw the conclusions.

The Sacred College . . . will have to think seriously on the grave repercussions of what it will decide. They could capsize the situation in Italy. The Sacred College cannot be unaware that if our country is happy because we have won religious peace, the Catholic Church cannot flourish in a hostile Italy.

I dare to hope that if we stay prudent to the end, the Conclave will not deceive us.[8]

[7] Pignatti to Foreign Affairs, 12 February 1939.
[8] AE, Santa Sede, 1939, Busta 45; Pignatti's report to Foreign Affairs.

The French government had instantly its candidate. On the very day that Pope Pius XI died, the French Foreign Minister Bonnet approached the British ambassador in Paris Sir Eric Phipps. He thought that the two powers should work together to get a Pope who would be favourable to British and French interests. He had his man. It was Cardinal Pacelli, the Secretary of State.

In one aspect this proposal of Bonnet was obvious. In another aspect it was not at all obvious.

Inasmuch as Britain and France have received glorious moral and political support from Pius XI, that support will be best continued if his closest collaborator is chosen, his Secretary of State, who has had the drafting of many of these documents which we admire.

The contrary argument: it is a law of history, though not of the constitution, that Secretaries of State are never elected Pope. Any elective system of this nature – the election of heads of Oxford colleges is a case in point – always looks to compensate for what is missing in the predecessor. Some qualities are good at one time, others at another. Never choose a man who will do nothing but what his predecessor has done.

It was not quite true that the Secretary of State had never been elected Pope. In the early days of the office, when it was still embryo, more than one Secretary of State was elected Pope. But since the days when the office rose to its full stature as the Pope's prime minister, it had never happened. When Bonnet proposed to the British that together they should try to get Pacelli elected, he marched against the laws of history and of elective constitutions.

This proposal made the British Foreign Office think furiously. The argument is best related in their minutes:

A. N. Noble: 'A good many people favour Cardinal Pacelli and it is quite possible that he will be elected despite the general tradition against the election of the Cardinal Secretary of State. But I am convinced that any attempt on our part, and still more on the part of the French, to work for him or in any way to intervene in the election would be highly dangerous. The 35 Italian Cardinals may not be greatly enamoured of Fascist Italy but they would surely be likely to resent any attempt at pressure from outside. The German press has already begun to exert such pressure and I think we should be well advised to leave it to German tactlessness to do our work for us.

The French assume that Cardinal Pacelli would as Pope continue the policy of Pius XI. It is likely that he would, but it must be remembered that Cardinal Pacelli has been rather overshadowed as Cardinal Secretary of State by an autocratic Pope. Pacelli as Pope might be a very different man from Pacelli as Cardinal Secretary of State.

On all counts, I think we should refrain from trying to meddle in this question and that the French should do the same.'

E. M. B. Ingram: 'Certainly and I should drop a hint to that effect to the French.'

At this point the more junior desks received communications which passed between Lord Halifax, the Foreign Secretary, and Sir Robert Vansittart:

Vansittart to Halifax: 11 February:

The death of the Pope at this juncture is disastrous. I am in whole-hearted agreement with the last paragraph of this telegram [i.e. Phipps' telegram on Bonnet's proposal suggesting Pacelli].

The question is how, if at all, we can contribute to the success of Cardinal Pacelli, whom M. Bonnet rightly considers our best man. I would like to discuss this at once. I think we *can* do something without detriment to our candidate – though we must of course act without connivance with the French. It is a matter of supreme importance that the right man – and not a man of totalitarian straw – should be elected.

Halifax to Vansittart, 13 February:

I agree, but I don't know how these things are worked. What would you suggest? or can we discuss. But there isn't much time.

Vansittart to Halifax, 14 February:

I would consult the leading English Catholics at once – Lord Fitzalan and Lord Howard for example. But they are both old. Therefore perhaps the Duke of Norfolk too. They could press Cardinal Hinsley who would need no pressing. I could suggest other ways of operating in Rome also. We have a sure approach available to the General of the Jesuits, for example.

These proposals from Vansittart for high-minded intrigue at Rome were passed by Halifax to the staff of the Foreign Office for reconsideration of their doctrine that it was far better not to try to interfere in the election of a Pope.

Orme Sargent did not change his mind:

Personally I cannot help feeling that it would be better for us not to try and influence the election. I can hardly believe that we have sufficient influence to affect the election one way or the other, and the knowledge that we are trying to exercise it will, I fear, only have the effect of arousing suspicion and resentment without producing any concrete result.

In any case, before we embark on this course I hope we will consult Mr Osborne on the subject. His views and advice are, I think, essential before any decision is taken.

Alexander Cadogan at the top of the Foreign Office, faced by all these minutes, felt himself in a mysterious world which he hardly understood. His minute ran:

I instinctively share Sir Orme Sargent's doubts, but I confess I know nothing of

Vatican procedure or intrigue, nor how we set about it. I do not know how Cardinal Hinsley or leading Catholics would react to any approach – nor what degree of influence they could exercise – nor what we should ask them to do. Who is the candidate we want to press?

Evidently Cadogan was not so familiar as his juniors with the name of Cardinal Pacelli.

All the papers went back to the Foreign Secretary, who decided that Osborne should be approached:

Halifax: 'Let us quickly put the problem to Mr Osborne, and ask him whether there is anything we can usefully do: and how: and on whose behalf. Lord Fitzalan is away: the Duke of Norfolk is not likely to have many views or contacts, but would no doubt do anything we asked: Lord Rankeillour would be available to help: and I could surely see him if I knew what to say to him.

I see no objection to an approach to the Superior-General of the Jesuits, if he is reliable and likely to be able to help. But I would rather hear what Osborne has to say first.

The resulting letter to Osborne in Rome was signed (20 February) by Ingram and reveals the internal uncertainties among the British.

Ingram to Osborne, Secret, 20 February 1939:
We entirely agree [with the French] that it would be very much to our advantage to have as the next Pope a man who would stand up to the dictator as boldly as did Pius XI, but we are not quite sure who would be able to exert sufficient influence to canvass a candidate of our own, and even if we had whether an attempt to do so might not do more harm than good. Perhaps the most that could be done would be in the negative sense of preventing the election of a pro-Fascist Pope, but is there any danger of such an election?

Assuming we do want to intervene, would you advise us discreetly to approach such men as Cardinal Hinsley, the Superior-General of the Jesuits, the Duke of Norfolk and Lord Rankeillour and get them to use their influence in our interest? Or should we do better to work through the French, who would presumably try to use French Cardinals?

To enable us to take a decision on this delicate question we should be grateful for your views on the following points:
(a) Whom should we back; or put negatively, whom should we oppose?
(b) How would such a man as Cardinal Hinsley react to our approach?
(c) Could we through him or through other channels exercise enough influence to have a reasonable chance of affecting the result one way or another, either positively or negatively?
(d) Would our intervention be likely to cause resentment and therefore to have the opposite effect to what we desire?
(e) Would it be better to leave it to German and Italian pressure and tactlessness to do our work for us?
If you can assuage our fears we shall have to work quickly and we should therefore be grateful if you would reply by telegraph.

You should destroy this letter after you have telegraphed your reply.

Noble in the Foreign Office consoled himself and his colleagues (17 February):

It must be remembered that most of the foreign Cardinals are unlikely to be much influenced by Nazi propaganda and that the 35 Italians are all men of a certain age who probably have not been won over by Fascist teaching and who have increasingly found it a menace to the fundamental principles of their own faith. It is significant in this connexion that even such a man as Cardinal Schuster of Milan, who during the Abyssinian crisis adopted an attitude that seemed to be unduly favourable to the Fascist cause, has recently condemned in public and in outspoken terms the racial doctrines of Signor Mussolini. There are one or two Cardinals who were thought to be rather pro-Fascist; whether they still are may be doubted; I think the worst we have to fear is a weak Pope, but even weak men have been known to show unexpected courage as Pope when Roman Catholic doctrines were at stake.

The worst we have to fear is a weak Pope – at least they could not conceive the election of a Fascist Pope still less a Nazi Pope.

Meanwhile, like all interested governments, they got out their list of possible candidates, with qualities and sketches of character. It numbered twenty-five.[9]

It took the British ten days of vacillation before they even decided to ask Osborne what to do; ten days while others were active in Rome; while Nevile Henderson reported from Berlin alarmingly but predictably that the Nazis expected a saintly Pope and report from Rome came that Mussolini wanted a religious Pope. The French press started the rumour that the Italians were trying to interfere in the election. The Italian consul at Chambéry reported the French press of the left to assert that Count Ciano had given 'tough directions' to the Vatican cardinals to veto the election of either Cardinal Maglione or Cardinal Pacelli – Maglione because he was the former nuncio in France and a friend of the French statesman Aristide Briand, Pacelli because he wanted to continue the policy of Pope Pius XI.[10]

In this intrigue the British were bound to play second fiddle to the French. For this there were several reasons.

First, the British were not a very Catholic people, and were brought up by the Church of England to think it improper for governments to interfere too much in the choice of high ecclesiastics of any church except the one to which many Englishmen belonged. The Foreign Office was perfectly willing to interfere, but was determined at all costs not to be seen to interfere. They thought the evil of being seen to interfere outweighed any good that might come from efforts to inter-

[9] FO 371/23789/404–38.
[10] Italian consul's letter to Foreign Affairs, 23 February 1939, in AE, Santa Sede, 1939, Busta 45.

fere. The French suffered not at all from these scruples. They were perfectly certain that the Italians would try to interfere and they must not be behind.

Secondly, the British had very little power whereas the French had a little army. The British had one cardinal only, Cardinal Hinsley of Westminster, and he was a good man and totally against racialism and dictatorships but he was a new cardinal and in any case very little known, a man of no following. For two years Osborne had hinted, suggested, or even demanded that they should be given a second cardinal, an Englishman inside the Curia, but all these requests or hints were met by Pius XI with less than encouragement.

The French had six cardinals but they also had Cardinal Villeneuve of Quebec, who counted as French; and Cardinal Tappouni a Syrian, who also counted as French; and with them went the Cardinal of Tarragona in Spain, who was a refugee from the Spanish Civil War. If the French could agree they were a formidable group of nine votes. This was not all. Among these nine were two men of international name. One was Cardinal Tisserant, the only non-Italian cardinal in the Curia and therefore a man who knew the Italian cardinals. The other was Cardinal Verdier, whose services to France and the Church had won him so wide a reputation that his name was bound to be weighty with other non-French cardinals.

Further, London sent Osborne to Rome not because he was a powerful man but because he was a delightful man. They had not yet confidence in his weight. Charles-Roux was a Catholic, a strong personality, and the most influential ambassador in the Vatican.

Meanwhile Osborne himself, before he was asked what the British should do, reported.[11] The report was sensitive: 'What does seem to be emerging as clear is that the issue overshadowing the election is that of the choice between a religious and a political Pope.' If this was pursued consistently, it excluded the Secretary of State Pacelli, and all the cardinals who had been nuncios. If then all the monks and members of religious orders are also excluded, because the cardinals were very unlikely to elect one of them, who was left? The leading man was the Archbishop of Florence, Cardinal Dalla Costa, who was very ascetic, and very much a man of prayer. But Osborne did not think Cardinal Dalla Costa much to be desired. 'I once called on him when I was in Florence, and found him of a rigid and forbidding austerity that precluded any human contact, but it may be that he does not care for heretics, or for the English.'[12]

[11] 17 February 1939, FO 371/23789/40.

[12] This was not everyone's impression of Dalla Costa. Attolico sent a report on him to Italian Foreign Affairs. Relations between the Church and the Fascist authorities in Florence were excellent. Dalla Costa was 'absolutely and purely religious . . . a true

Osborne admitted that Pacelli, though very desirable from the British point of view, was not a probable; because he was the Secretary of State; because he was a political cardinal; because he was too identified with Pius XI from whose policy there must be change; because the Italians did not seem to want him and the Italians were a majority in the Conclave. And yet, Osborne refused to regard Pacelli's prospects as so remote; for this reason: who else is there? 'There are today, apart from Cardinal Pacelli, no outstanding personalities.'

Secretaries of State could not be elected Pope because they wielded such power under the previous Pope. But this Secretary of State had not wielded such power. The Pope was an autocrat, his Secretary a shadow.

If the choice was for a religious rather than a political Pope it seemed to exclude Pacelli. But did it? The man had a reputation for being a saintly man. He fitted the character demanded of *pastor angelicus*. So much so, that, said Osborne, he 'has been a politician in spite of himself'.

This report by Osborne was very intelligent. The British and French governments wanted Cardinal Pacelli as Pope because Pius XI had stood strongly against the Rome–Berlin axis, and Pacelli was identified with Pius XI as his Secretary of State and therefore likely to continue his policy. They realized that it was difficult to get Pacelli because Secretaries of State were 'never' elected Pope, for the very reason that they were too identified with the policy of the predecessor, and because German and Italian cardinals must long for a man who would break with the policies of Pius XI. They would go for a non-politician, a holy man, a man like Dalla Costa of Florence, so austere as to be almost incapable of human contact. But Osborne had perceived a hint of two things. If the choice must fall on a holy man rather than a politician, was it so certain that Pacelli was excluded? Undoubtedly he was a religious man. He could not help being a politician, his whole life had been spent in politics. But Osborne wondered whether this was natural to him. He used the phrase *a politician in spite of himself*.

At this moment arrived the letter from London asking Osborne for his advice – whom shall we support? Whom shall we try to exclude? Is it safe or wise to try to do anything? Osborne was instantly decisive in his reply: 'I should like to back Pacelli if we were in a position to do so, but we are not . . . Cardinal Hinsley would react unfavourably.'[13]

apostle of Peace' – his person elicited reverence. 'He does not trouble himself with politics and does not encourage others to.' AE, Santa Sede, 1940, Busta 48, Attolico's report of 15 October 1940. And for a friendly memoir, see Giuliano Villani, *Il vescovo Elia Dalla Costa* (Florence, 1974). See also 'L'atteggiamento del cardinale Elia dalla Costa durante l'occupazione nazifascista di Firenze', in *Miscellanea Historiae Ecclesiasticae* (Brussels, 1984), pp. 174ff. [13] FO 371/23789/446.

The two Englishmen in Rome hardly dared to see each other. Cardinal Hinsley was staying at the English College. Osborne asked to see him, Hinsley invited Osborne to lunch at the English College. But in the invitation he made it perfectly plain that he thought this meeting dubious and that he had scruples of conscience whether he ought at this moment to meet the representative of the British government. He was afraid, as Osborne expressed it to Lord Halifax, that Osborne would 'endeavour to disturb the spirit of impartiality and of receptivity to divine guidance with which he will enter the Conclave'. What happened at this lunch conversation is not yet known. If we judge by the parallel French interviews, Osborne must have asked whether Hinsley did not think, in view of the centralization of the Fascist State, that the Roman Curia ought not, for the sake of the Church, to be made less Italian and more international – a proposition to which he could be confident of getting the answer Yes; and then have asked whether it was Cardinal Hinsley's opinion that in these tense days the diplomatic skill and the known anti-racialist views as well as the holiness of Cardinal Pacelli might make him a person whom the cardinals were likely to elect. But Osborne's manners were so perfect, his desire not to seem to intrude so fixed, his sense that Hinsley was embarrassed by any hint that the British government might be telling him what to do, that the conversation at that lunch is likely to have teetered round by circuitous routes.

Osborne had been told by London to do all he could to try to get Cardinal Pacelli as the next Pope and he was willing to do all that he could. But he did not think that he could do much, if anything. He went round to see the British ambassador to the Quirinal and found that he agreed. He told London: 'Since British influence at the Conclave is almost certainly nugatory, I see no purpose in incurring possible odium within and without the Vatican by endeavouring to exercise it.' He thought very little of this plan of Vansittart's to tell various Catholic English laymen or the General of the Jesuits to use their weight for Pacelli. The only things that could be done must be done in Rome. He would do all he could. It was not likely to be much.

He did not think that many cardinals would aspire to 'the appalling responsibilities, enforced retirement from the world and immolation on the altar of lonely unremitting labour. So the Conclave must have much of the anxiety of a mass meeting of patients in a dentist's waiting-room, dedicated to the selection of one of their number for the honour of occupying the chair.'[14]

The next question for the British was this: if Osborne advised them

---

[14] Osborne to Halifax, 24 February 1939, FO 371/23789/452.

that it was a mistake to try to influence the election, should they try to stop the French influencing the election? 'I am afraid,' said Ingram when the question was raised, 'nothing we can say will prevent the French from trying to influence the election.' They were not even sure that they liked the sentence of Osborne which said that he would do all he could, and wondered whether to warn him off but decided that they could trust his discretion.

They were right to think that they could not stop the French. The Quai d'Orsay archives show Charles-Roux hard at work in Rome.

Charles-Roux saw the French cardinals one by one (that included the French-Canadian and the Syrian and the Spaniard). He did not think the 'religious' candidate Dalla Costa at all possible. Dalla Costa was no democrat but learned in doctrine and respected as a holy man and strong – that is, too strong for Mussolini's government – 'perhaps he could be a more bitter adversary to governments with a totalitarian morality than a politique Pope with liberal and democratic ideas'.[15] With ears flapping for every rumour, Charles-Roux kept trying to hear of Italians – he needed fourteen or so – who could be brought to vote for Pacelli, and kept being discouraged. Putting even the most optimistic interpretation on the rumours he could not make it more than seven. It was borne in upon him that not many Italians wanted Pacelli. And the Italian who most flamboyantly wanted Pacelli discontented Charles-Roux for another reason. Pacelli had an ardent admirer and supporter, the vicar of Rome, Cardinal Marchetti-Selvaggiani. He was not merely an admirer, but a campaigner full of dash. But he was a disadvantage, probably, to the cause. He was too passionate to be persuasive, and was regarded by other cardinals as full of whimsy. He was gravely ill, perhaps dying. A nervous affliction troubled his legs. He was determined to enter the Conclave nevertheless. Yet it bothered Charles-Roux a little, not only that this oddity should be the leading Italian backer of Pacelli, but that his reasons for backing Pacelli were completely different from the reasons of the French and British governments.[16]

The French cardinals had none of Hinsley's scruples about having lunch with the envoy. The sardonic Cardinal Baudrillart came into his room saying, with an air of dry mischievous humour, 'I have come to learn how my government wants me to vote.' Charles-Roux reported that all the French but one would vote for Pacelli. He found that the Cardinal of Tarragona, who had been expelled from republican Spain and lived in exile at the Chartreuse at Lucca, would vote for Pacelli. He

---

[15] Charles-Roux to Bonnet, 16 February 1939.
[16] Apart from the evidence of Charles-Roux, see AE, Santa Sede, 1939, Busta 42, Pignatti to Foreign Affairs, 4 May 1939.

went round the ambassadors of all the anti-German powers – Poland, Belgium, Portugal, Hungary, Czechoslovakia and Great Britain. Osborne told him that he thought Hinsley likely to vote for Pacelli, so something must have passed at that luncheon. The other ambassadors said the same about their own cardinals. He could still find nothing like enough Italians. And he realized that far his best hope lay in Cardinal Verdier, whom many Italians greatly respected.

Nevertheless, the interviews with two of the French cardinals produced a little disquiet in Charles-Roux; Cardinal Baudrillart, for the reasons which he produced for voting for Pacelli; and Cardinal Tisserant, for the reasons which he produced for not voting for Pacelli. The reasons were almost the same.

Cardinal Tisserant was a scholar, one of the great bibliographers of the epoch, the man who modernized the Vatican Library; the only non-Italian cardinal in the Curia; a man of few nuances, who easily exploded and always said what he thought. He gave one of Osborne's friends the impression that in the Curia he was like an elephant in a china shop. He was a man totally unlike Cardinal Pacelli, who had so many nuances, so rare a finesse. He knew the other members of the Curia better than any of the foreign cardinals. He told Charles-Roux that he could not vote for Pacelli. Charles-Roux reported to Bonnet thus: Cardinal Tisserant recognizes Pacelli's merits, especially his wide culture and diplomatic skill. But he is afraid that he lacks decisiveness. He believes him to be by nature a hesitant man. Tisserant refused to say for whom he would vote (17 February). He would only say that whoever was elected was 'destined to reign in torment'.

Charles-Roux went back later to try again to work upon Tisserant and see whether he would not change his mind. It was no good. 'I find him still irreducible in his opposition to the election of Cardinal Pacelli. He judges him not to be the man for the situation. He says that he is indecisive, hesitant, a man more designed to obey orders than to give them. This judgment of Tisserant is obviously sincere; though it is influenced by a personal antipathy towards the former Secretary of State, an antipathy probably born of the relations during their careers' (to Bonnet, 1 March).

Cardinal Baudrillart, the other scholar among the French cardinals, talked of the past, as a historian. He discoursed on the traditional alternation between a Pope of action and a Pope who marked time; between a Pope who rules with a strong hand, and a Pope who rules with a gentle hand.[17] The implication was clear. Pius XI did much, Pacelli would not do much. Pius XI was a forcible character, Pacelli was

---

[17] F. Charles-Roux, *Huit Ans au Vatican* (Paris, 1947), p. 267.

not. Nevertheless, it was time for a gentle Pope who would not do much.

Something was ominous in Baudrillart's accession to Pacelli. Charles-Roux regarded him as the *enfant terrible* among the French. He was no man's disciple. The other French cardinals were impatient at his sallies and offended by his abruptness. Of all the foreign cardinals Baudrillart was nearest to being a Fascist. He was strong for France, approved of Mussolini, wanted good relations between France and Nazi Germany, and saw Hitler as the saviour of Europe from Bolshevism. Naturally he wanted détente between the Pope and the totalitarian governments and thought Pacelli his man. If Baudrillart wanted Pacelli, Pacelli had a real chance of being elected, though Secretaries of State are never elected; wanted by democrats because he would continue resistance to dictators, and by anti-democrats because he would bring détente with dictators.

The Polish government was in touch with its Cardinal Hlond. They did not identify Hlond with the 'foreign cardinals' who would be likely to support Pacelli because he would continue the anti-Hitler policy. Their view of the situation ran thus: the Italian cardinals are divided; the first group want a pastor, a bishop, a priest uninterested in politics and 'aloof' from politics; and this group would 'undoubtedly' be backed by Fascists and Nazis. The second group want an experienced politician, which means someone who has been a nuncio to one of the Powers, someone who will have the knowledge to be able to play his part in the international arena. Of the former nuncios, one stands out, the former nuncio in Paris, Cardinal Maglione; who is known to be a friend of the democratic powers. Between these two groups the Poles imagined a centre holding the balance and therefore influential; and in this centre party they put the Frenchman Cardinal Baudrillart and their own Cardinal Hlond. This group maintained a position between the Italian cardinals, who advocated a non-political Pope, and the former nuncios, who advocated a politically minded Pope.[18]

The people of Rome in their pasquinades often hit the mark at a time of Conclave. The saying of Pasquino ran thus:

If you want a holy Pope, Pacelli
if you want an intelligent Pope, Maglione
if you want a good-looking Pope, Tedeschini.

Tedeschini had a white head, was tall, slim, with regular features, a noble air, and beautiful hands.

Meanwhile, unknown to the French or British, Pignatti, the Italian

---

[18] A. J. Drexel Biddle to Secretary of State, Washington, after conversation with Beck, Warsaw, 13 February 1939; Hyde Park Papers, PSF Poland, Box 65.

ambassador to the Vatican, wanted to know what the Germans thought. His counsellor talked to Menshausen, the counsellor at the German Embassy. Menshausen 'repeatedly insisted' that the best thing for Germany would be Cardinal Pacelli as Pope and Cardinal Tedeschini as Secretary of State, for this election would bring détente between the Reich and the Holy See. He said that his ambassador (Diego von Bergen) had tried to get Berlin to silence or at least soften the SS journal *Schwarzes Korps*, so far without success. Menshausen said that Cardinal Pacelli believed in a policy of conciliation towards Germany, and told Diego von Bergen that this was what he thought.

The Italians wanted to know how the four German cardinals would vote. Menshausen said that Cardinal Schulte of Cologne was to be admired as a man and was favourable to Cardinal Pacelli; that Cardinal Faulhaber of Munich was a fine man but on certain questions intransigent against the Nazis; that Cardinal Bertram of Breslau was not thought a leading man, and that he had the attitudes of the Curia; and that Cardinal Innitzer of Vienna seemed 'very disorientated and frightened'. The Italians inferred from this conversation that the four German cardinals would vote for Cardinal Pacelli 'unless contrary orders reached von Bergen by 28 February'.

As Charles-Roux saw the French cardinals, and Osborne saw the only English cardinal, Diego von Bergen saw the German cardinals. He got an assurance out of both Cardinal Schulte and Cardinal Faulhaber that they would vote in the Conclave for a policy of conciliation. Cardinal Bertram talked 'more vivaciously', but von Bergen formed the impression that he would follow Schulte and Faulhaber. He could form no idea what Cardinal Innitzer would do. Schulte told von Bergen that he had three conversations with Cardinal Pacelli; and Pacelli expressed, unequivocally, plans for conciliation with Germany and also with Italy.

Diego von Bergen formed the impression, therefore, that Cardinal Pacelli was putting himself forward as a candidate.

Pignatti asked von Bergen whether the government in Berlin liked the idea of Pacelli as Pope. Von Bergen answered that he had kept the German government informed; that he had shown them his own clear opinion in favour of Cardinal Pacelli; that he had received no instructions to the contrary; and therefore he inferred that his government looked with a friendly eye on the candidature of Cardinal Pacelli.[19] (In fact the Germans had only a lukewarm attitude to Cardinal Pacelli.)

The cardinals entered the Conclave on 1 March at 6 p.m. They were

[19] AE to Alfieri in Berlin, 3 March 1939; AE, Germania, 1939, Busta 63.

all present. Never before in the history of the Papacy had all the cardinals entered a Conclave. It was, said Charles-Roux, 'the advance of medicine and transport'.[20]

There were only two rivals to Pacelli and both of them had strong arguments against. Dalla Costa of Florence had stature and was holy. But his holiness was cold, he was not warm with people, the non-Italians would never vote for someone who could not relate. Maglione was the ablest man in the Curia. But he was long nuncio in France, was identified with French politics, and was doubtful in an election which must satisfy Italy and not infuriate Germany.

Pacelli thus by the end had no serious competitors. As one of his supporters said when the Conclave was over: 'We had against us nothing but a handful of dust' ('nous n'avons en face de nous que de la poussière').

So Cardinal Pacelli, on the day of his 63rd birthday, was elected Pope as the French and British wanted and had striven to achieve – wanted by several foreign cardinals, backed by anti-German governments; wanted by some Italian cardinals tired of a dictatorial Pope and eager for a gentler person who would govern by consensus; wanted by some Italians who were afraid of Fascist reprisals and sought détente at all costs with Italy and possibly even with Germany, and knew that Pacelli was a reconciler by nature; wanted by the German ambassador because he had unequivocally stated his resolve for conciliation with Germany; wanted as a holy man and man of prayer; wanted by some afraid of the coming storm, who thought it essential not to have too strong a character at the helm when the ship might need to run before the gale; and finally, wanted because his wide education, his ability to speak languages fluently, and his charm of presence, made him stand out among the cardinals.

The press reported that the election was unanimous at the final ballot. Osborne soon knew that it was not. During the ballots the news spread that if Pacelli were elected he would have Maglione as his Secretary of State and this had a good effect among waverers. There is conflict of evidence about the behaviour of Cardinal Tisserant. According to an early account he wanted Cardinal Maglione, and later, seeing this to be impossible, rallied to Pacelli and so swung votes. But according to Charles-Roux's successor, who became a close friend of Tisserant, Tisserant told him that he steadily voted for the Jesuit cardinal of Genoa (Boetto), 'campaigned' (so he later said) against Pacelli and refused to the very last to vote for Pacelli, who he believed to be a mistaken choice.[21] To vote for Boetto was to throw away his vote. Boetto was a Jesuit. And no Jesuit had a chance.

[20] *Huit Ans*, p. 275.   [21] D'Ormesson, *Ambassade tragique*, p. 225.

The secret course of a Conclave is at first known only through gossip. Contemporary 'informed' gossip reported that by the time the cardinals entered the Conclave the possibility of a foreigner had disappeared – Villeneuve of Quebec was at the front. At the first ballot the three leaders were Pacelli (28 votes; 42 needed) Maglione and dalla Costa. Then dalla Costa's men swung to Pacelli, who had 35 votes. Finally Villeneuve's men came over, so that at the third ballot Pacelli was elected with 48 votes.[22] None of the information could be guaranteed. But probably fourteen people, twelve and Pacelli and Tisserant, went on voting against Pacelli to the end.

The British and French governments were delighted. Charles-Roux told Bonnet, 'This is the election which could best maintain the Papacy on the high moral level to which Pius XI had raised it' (2 March, telegram). Osborne waxed lyrical and he was not a lyrical man:

'impressively saintly character . . . keen intelligence . . . great political experience . . . fine gift of oratory . . . accomplished linguist . . . extraordinary personal charm . . . probably a disappointment to the German government . . . the sort of paragon that the Pastor Angelicus should be. With all these qualities I am not quite sure how strong a character he is; working, as he did, under an autocrat like Pius XI, it was difficult to tell. It might perhaps be a good thing if he were not so resolutely uncompromising as his predecessor, that is to say, if he were equally firm and courageous, but rather more tactful.

The Germans will be very indignant. I am not sure about the Italians . . .'

Osborne expected him to become 'a very great Pope'.[23]

It was put about that the Italians were discontented. Count Ciano said, 'Nothing could be more untrue. I am delighted with the election. I am on the best terms with Cardinal Pacelli . . . His election is a great success for Italy.'[24] Foreign ministers have a public duty to make the best of a situation which they cannot alter, and the British and French wondered how far this could be meant.

The French and British thought it an excellent omen that he took the name of his predecessor and became Pius XII.

The British got the Pope whom they wanted and for whom they worked. Even so, they suffered an occasional qualm, and we are not surprised to find it voiced by Sir Robert Vansittart. He lunched with the former German Chancellor Heinrich Brüning who was a Catholic of the Centre party, and asked him what he thought. Afterwards Vansittart sent a line to Lord Halifax. Brüning 'does *not* [the *not* is underlined

---

[22] For the numbers, derived from an involuntary leak by Cardinal Baudrillart, see Giancarlo Zizola, *Quale Papa?* (Rome, 1977), pp. 145–7; a reference which I owe to the kindness of Peter Hebblethwaite.

[23] FO 371/23789/21 and 500.

[24] Charles-Roux to Bonnet, 9 March 1939.

in the original] share the general optimism in regard to Cardinal Pacelli. Dr Brüning knows Cardinal Pacelli very well and considers that there is a great deal of naiveté in his make-up, particularly in the sense that he thinks Pacelli may still have in his mind the possibility of proceeding by way of treating with the present regime in Germany and Italy, whereas Dr Brüning himself is profoundly convinced of the contrary.'[25] Some of the press, and especially the French press, had no such qualms. Their tone was so exuberant that it started to cause anxiety among the diplomats. Phrases like *the Church will continue to struggle against totalitarian States side by side with the democracies* were thought to be unwise and in poor taste. Even the *Manchester Guardian* (3 March 1939) called the election a victory for western democracy and a serious setback for the dictators. The Foreign Office on the whole had no complaint against the truth of these statements, but thought it imprudent that they should be stated so baldly.[26]

In Rome, Osborne did not mind that attitude of appeasement about which Brüning and Vansittart were complaining. He was pleased that the new Pope at once received the German ambassador and the German cardinals, and rightly thought that he must be testing the ground for a possible reconciliation with Germany. 'I put nothing beyond his powers of achievement!'[27]

Not everyone in the British government was so pleased when the Vatican newspaper *Osservatore Romano* changed its tune overnight. During the last few months under Pius XI it had been the principal source of news about German persecution of or misbehaviour towards the Catholic Church of Germany and Austria. These reports ceased, almost startlingly.

The people who most hated the election were the Portuguese. They had been foolishly told by their press that the new Pope would be a non-Italian, and very likely their Patriarch of Lisbon, Cerejeira, who was the youngest of the cardinals. They saw the election of Pacelli as almost an offence to their national prestige. They had not been encouraged in this mirage by the nuncio in Lisbon (Ciriaci), who was one of the few men to realize that the election would be mostly settled before the Conclave began, and that the outcome could be Cardinal Pacelli, backed as he would be by a strong group of non-Italian and 'democratic' cardinals headed by Cardinal Verdier of Paris. The nuncio

---

[25] FO 371/23789/2. See also Brüning's letter of 23 May 1939 of which a copy was sent to Roosevelt and is in Hyde Park Papers, PSF, Germany, Box 44. 'For me of course, there can be no doubt that the leanings of the present Pope are very much pro-Italian and pro-Fascist.'

[26] Cf. FO 371/23789/495 and 497; cf. the *Manchester Guardian*'s supplementary article on 14 March 1939, correcting for diplomatic reasons.

[27] FO 371/23789/31.

in Lisbon had not liked the new system of Conclaves. He talked outspokenly to the Italian ambassador in Lisbon, who reported what he said to Rome. 'He greatly blamed the extension of time before a Conclave. Before the new arrangements, Cardinals had scarcely enough time to arrive, go through the ceremonies, and enter the Conclave. Now, the thing is done beforehand, in the middle of all sorts of outside influences . . . You ought to shut up the Cardinals the moment they arrive in Rome and make them tell their rosaries all day from morning to night.'[28]

General Franco's men at Burgos in Northern Spain were almost as displeased. They were cold, and did not hide their coldness. They had not liked the near-impartiality of Pope Pius XI during the Spanish Civil War, and blamed his Secretary of State Pacelli. Franco's Foreign Minister, Suñer, let out a phrase of disappointment which was unprintable. Franco's generals, and the political leaders of the Falange, felt the same, and young hothead Falangists could be heard talking of the need for a national Spanish Church. The feeling grew even stronger when they head the rumour that the new Pope would make Cardinal Tedeschini his Secretary of State; for Tedeschini had been nuncio in Spain, and was blamed for being one of the causes of the fall of the Spanish monarchy, and therefore a cause of the Spanish Civil War.

Otherwise the world was pleased. Pleasure was reported in Bogota, Smyrna, Brazil, even Prague. Copenhagen was said to exaggerate like the French and British press, with paeans of praise for a 'democratic' Pope. In Berlin the head of the German Foreign Office, Ernst von Weizsäcker, surprised the Italians by not being displeased, for he thought that the diplomatic experience of the Pope must be an advantage. Local Nazi organs could be unpleasant. In Graz (Austria) a rumour had spread that a new Pope would not be elected because the election would be too difficult amid the international tension; and therefore the Catholic people greeted the news of the election with the pleasure of relief. The Nazi Graz newspaper was very cool – the new Pope is a 'servile continuator of Pius XI's ill-fated policy . . . International politeness forces us to salute the new head of the Church . . . But for the German people it is of no importance whether a Pius XI or Pius XII sits in the Vatican.'[29]

Pacelli was born six years after the Pope became the 'prisoner' in the Vatican. He grew up in the shadow of the prisoner Popes. The atmosphere was always remote from the world. What was happening

[28] Lisbon Legation to Foreign Affairs, 23 February 1939; AE, Santa Sede, 1939, Busta 45.
[29] Reports and cuttings in AE, Santa Sede, 1939, Busta 49.

after the loss of the Papal States was the change in the Papacy from a partly political office to a fully spiritual office. This change took several decades. And for nearly ninety years this process needed an ever increasing sense of the sacred in the office of Pope. The walls of the Vatican grew higher. Pope Pius XI was more of a cult-figure than Pope Leo XIII. A French observer called it the business of enclosing the Pope as if in a tabernacle. Because the office was more inaccessible, it gained in sacredness. Pacelli grew up in this atmosphere. He carried the idea of a cultic Pope, a sacred personage, to its extreme point, whence it was impossible to come out at the world.

His thought was subtle. But he clothed it in an envelope of old-fashioned if not obsolete rhetoric, which had the effect of making every point that he made sound weaker. He grew up in a nineteenth-century tradition of Vatican circumlocution, fitted it naturally, and carried it to the ultimate. D'Ormesson, the Frenchman who knew both Pius XII and his successor John XXIII, once said that John's greatest service to the Church was to call things by their right name.[30]

Pius XII looked otherworldly and sounded otherworldly. His face was ascetic and pallid; his eyes were set deep in his head; his movements were controlled, his hands clasped.

The ambassadors respected the Pope; even revered him; his purity, his piety, his conscience. But as the tension mounted, they occasionally wished that his personality was stronger. They admitted him to have the quality of prudence and balance to an exceptional degree. Occasionally they wished that he had less of those qualities. The quality which they least admired was his eloquence; the baroque style, the flowery metaphors, the grandiloquence, the air rather of reciting than speaking. When they got him alone, in private audience, they were impressed by his conversation, but for curious reasons. He would never talk of large issues, always of little things, and with no sense of a breadth of outlook. They noticed his trick of repeating the same phrase, even several times, and going back over his own thought; as though, thought d'Ormesson, 'he is embarrassed to pass to a new question'. It was never the Pope who led these conversations. But always in conversation he was charming, natural, making them totally at ease, never anything but gentle.

Pius XII had only to write down a text to be able to speak it afterwards from memory. He had a prodigious memory. Being an excellent linguist he could even do this with tongues not his own. As he talked, he used his tapering aristocratic hands in big gesticulations. Something in the voice felt to the listeners artificial. He knew how to

---

[30] W. d'Ormesson, *De St Petersbourg à Rome* (Paris, 1969), pp. 306–8.

make the phrases sing musically, and yet they were conscious that he knew.

They also thought him a little too Italian for their comfort. At a homily during 1940 he was once heard to say 'Our Mazzini'. He was a monarchist who shuddered at demagogues; but with that care of the monarchist for the ordinary working people which issued later in famous encyclicals about the structure of society. They knew that he deeply disapproved of many things about Hitler, many things about Stalin, and at least a few things about Mussolini. But they could not say that he *passionately* disapproved, or that he *vehemently* disapproved, for he was far too self-controlled to show either passion or vehemence and they doubted whether he possessed these endowments. This explained the contrast that they knew him to dislike some of Mussolini's decisions as strongly as he could dislike anything, and yet heard few public words from him which hinted at this dislike.

They knew that he still felt Communism to be the ultimate enemy. Osborne did not agree with the French. The French suspected that this fear of Bolshevism made him willing to come to terms with any regime that was against the Russians. Osborne showed no sign of believing this credible.

The most sensitive and illuminating of portraits of Pope Pius XII is that by his assistant Domenico Tardini, who worked with him under Pope Pius XI and then through all the agonies of the Second World War and its aftermath.

Tardini's portrait of Pius XII was consistent: 'refined, amiable, obliging, affectionate'. He would seem often to doubt himself, saying 'Do you think?' or 'Is it not so?' He had a loud resonant laugh, with big mouth agape. He liked to tell silly stories. When Tardini served him as Cardinal Pacelli, he was with him every day and was not quite sure. The intelligence was quick, versatile, even brilliant. The memory was extraordinary. The dedication to duty was absolute. The Pope was capable of hours of work at a stretch. And yet the business took long to transact. Pacelli kept going again and again over ground already covered. He spent a lot of time on things that seemed trivialities. Tardini used to get bored by these meetings. After Pacelli became Pope, Tardini did not find the meetings boring. But the gentleness remained, in the sense that the Pope would refuse to over-ride opposition even when he was sure that he was right. He loved study, solitude, quietness. He read books, very rapidly. He was shy of people, especially perhaps of bishops. Pius XI never used a telephone, Pius XII was uncomfortable face to face and used a telephone regularly. He was a solitary, with very few intimates; with a touch of aloofness. And he was very gentle; so gentle that he hated a fight. He avoided controversial interviews. He postponed, and postponed, controversial decisions. He preferred to avoid rather than to confront battles. To decide anything important was suffering. Hard words, and rough phrases, and brusque manners were pain. He always seemed to be 'above' his company; never therefore formidable, but 'above' by otherworldliness; never off-putting, for everyone left his presence happy. His aloofness seemed a loneliness which elicited the protective instinct. He did not like to give orders. He would persuade. He found it difficult to say no. If he had to take an unpleasant decision, he would cut the strong words from the draft letter, or add a gentle phrase. And his style was so superabundant, with parentheses, amplifications, ornamentations. Even in conversation he might fancy that he had said something clearly and the hearer went away with a wrong impression of what he meant. In conversation he had a little stammer. In public utterances this vanished. But the effort to overcome it caused him to sound pontifical – a little too loud, a little note of declamation. Every movement was controlled. If he said mass, not a muscle was out of position. Tardini described him signing a letter, with a very fine nib and very black ink. He would take up the pen with certain attentive formality; look at the nib closely to see if it was dusty; if he suspected dust he cleaned it carefully with a little black cloth always on the desk; dipped it in an antiquated inkwell, but with the utmost caution, afraid of a blot on the paper or the table; and after signing would put everything back into their exact places. Altogether he was a very gentle, cultured, shy, very controlled, very prayerful, lonely man with a yearning Christian heart. And he was the last Pope to have the mentality of 'the prisoner in the Vatican'. He wanted to keep the office unspotted by the corruptions of the world, and therefore fenced in like a sanctuary, but fenced because close to God.

The new Pope chose Cardinal Maglione as his Secretary of State. Osborne reported enthusiastically to Lord Halifax. Personally the two men were not akin. Though not a monk, Pius XII gave everyone that sense of withdrawal which some men find in monks. Maglione well understood the world. The Pope was hesitant, Maglione knew that men must decide. The Pope's earlier diplomatic experience was German, and he commanded the German language. Maglione's main diplomatic experience was French. Observers agreed on a more intangible difference of personality, of such a nature that the relationship between the Pope and his chief minister could never grow into a friendship between intimates. Osborne heard a rumour that Pius XII would have liked one of his two former assistants at the Secretariat, Tardini and Montini – 'I should have thought Montini too junior to be considered, though he is first class and the Pope is very fond of him.'

When Maglione was appointed, the British and French were both pleased, precisely because they regarded him as pro-French. 'He and the Pope,' said Noble, 'should make a strong team.'[31] Osborne had rarely met him before but found him an unaffectedly friendly man.

Maglione was learned in the Napoleonic wars and had maps of the Napoleonic campaigns on the walls of his study. He was to follow the military movements of the Second World War with flags on pins, and could make severe comments on the strategy of generals. He could be very silent, which everyone thought remarkable in a Neapolitan. They thought of him as totally trustworthy and one who could keep a secret. We have opinions of him from several of the Italians, and they use warm language in his praise. One of the later ambassadors of Italy at the Holy See, Guariglia, said that he was 'a man of the highest gifts of mind and heart'.[32]

The ambassadors thought him stronger and more intelligent than the Pope. When they went to see him, they found that on some days they could extract hardly a word. On other days he would talk freely, and when he talked he was always fair. They found that they did best not to force. If they tried to badger him into talking, he said nothing. They had to wait for him to take his time.

He was an officially neutral person. But they were fully aware that he had good memories of France, and, though he could not say so, much preferred the French side to the German.

His weaknesses were two. The Fascist party suspected him. It mattered that Farinacci wrote hostile articles against him in *Regime Fascista*, even though by now Farinacci was a figure of less influence, and was suspected of being in the pay of Dr Goebbels. Maglione's record in France made him a doubtful character to Italians engaged in a quarrel with France. The second and more serious weakness was the lack of rapport with the Pope. Mostly this hardly mattered because the Pope agreed to what the Secretary of State wanted. But occasionally it mattered much. Occasionally the Pope did not even tell the Secretary of State a crucial piece of information. Part of the trouble was ritual. Maglione and Pacelli being friends of old, Maglione saw no reason to change his manners and continued to treat the new Pope as an equal.

[31] FO 371/23789/30 and 45. Maglione: born 2 March 1877, exactly a year younger than Pius XII. From a village near Naples; educated at a Jesuit school in Naples and Capranica College in Rome; trained for the diplomatic service, but acted for some years as a parish priest in Rome and the surrounding countryside; 1909 a secretary in the Congregation of Extraordinary Affairs; 1918 Nuncio in Switzerland; 1926 Nuncio in Paris; 1935 Cardinal, and President of the Congregation of the Council.

[32] R. Guariglia, *Ricordi, 1922–1946* (Naples, 1950), pp. 492–3; cf. G. Dalla Torre, *Memorie* (Verona, 1965), pp. 141–5 and the article in *Osservatore Romano* of 12 March 1944, *Defensor Civitatis*.

Something in Pius XII's sense of the majesty of the office was not sure that this could be right. And as time went on he felt that Maglione was not so much his secretary as a colleague. Like the ambassadors, the Pope felt that Maglione was the stronger of the two. 'I don't want collaborators', the Pope said finally, 'I want people who will do what I say.'[33] This must not be exaggerated. Extant evidence shows a conflict between Pope and Secretary of State where the Pope won.

During the war the Curia wanted to appoint an Italian to be chargé to the Polish government in exile in London. The British refused to let him come. The Pope said that it was a matter of principle, on which the Holy See could not yield. In London the Poles did not mind. They suggested that an Englishman be their chargé. The Pope thought this a good idea. Cardinal Maglione thought it a bad idea, because a principle was at stake. Thus the Pope was more flexible than the Secretary of State. The Pope pressed, more than once, that the Englishman be appointed. Nothing happened. Finally he insisted that it be done 'without delay'. It then took many days before Maglione did what the Pope ordered.[34]

Thus the Pope found it hard to make Maglione do what Maglione thought mistaken. But the Pope was not weak. Delay though there might be, he got what he thought right. And in the particular case, he was the more sensible and the more practical of the two.

The lack of rapport between Pope and Secretary of State increased the weight of Maglione's two assistants, Tardini and Montini. Tardini was in charge of 'Extraordinary Affairs', Montini in charge of 'Ordinary Affairs'. Extraordinary meant high policy, ordinary almost everything else. But the distinction had never been clear. Often the Pope simply decided whether he preferred Tardini or Montini to deal with the question.

The Pope had an unusually close friendship with, or affection for, Montini; they were almost on a relationship of father and son. Tardini and Montini were opposite types of character, and the ambassadors liked them enormously. Tardini was a stocky little man who came of modest origins from the Trastevere and had a touch of vulgarity and a lively mind without a lot of education. He had a humorous mouth and a strong jaw. But in this old and prudent and courtly world the utterances of his lips, strong, vehement, sardonic, and humorous, were a refreshment. He loathed Nazis and disliked Fascists and, even at times when he could hardly say so, was perfectly willing to make his revulsions evident. He gave them immense pleasure when he christened Hitler *that motorized Attila*. He also had a horror of protocol,

---

[33] 5 November 1944; Tardini, *Pio XII*, p. 79.
[34] See ADSS, 5, 646–7, 679; 7, 85 and 293ff.

ceremonies, pomp, and the cardinals of the Curia. They felt that he was the only person in the whole place to say things without the slightest precaution to cover himself. That could lead to battles, for he could make brutal comments on the behaviour of Britain and France. But the ambassadors found this frankness cleansing and warming in the atmosphere of nerves, caution, murmur, gossip and espionage which surrounded their every movement. In what one of the French once called 'the thousand détours of the Curia', it was a big thing to meet a responsible man who never used circumlocutions. Tardini came in the end to put a high value on the British Minister.[35]

Where Tardini was forcible and decisive, Montini was gentle, persuasive, and indecisive; very sincere and frank, likeable as a man and yet they found in him something elusive. Far more than Tardini he bore the stamp of the professional diplomat. He had the self-control and never-failing balance of the professional. He too had a horror of Nazism. They liked him greatly and were pleased at his views. But he would not speak with the élan of which Tardini was capable. He was always kind and they knew him to be on their side. He would bring them presents of delicious fish from the lake at Castel Gandolfo, or baskets of fruit from its orchards.

Everything about the pair contrasted. If Osborne went to see Montini he was greeted with a perfect courtesy. If he went to see Tardini he was greeted with a mocking rudeness so cheerful and so humorous that it could not give offence.

As they watched the three men at work – Maglione, Tardini, Montini – the ambassadors could not withhold their admiration. The machinery was archaic; the nuncios mediocre; the courier-service irregular; the supply of information inadequate; the money insufficient. They were not well-informed about events. Sometimes they knew less than any layman who listened to the radio. With all these disadvantages their judgment was superb. 'They have an extraordinary intuition about men and things.' One of the French wondered why. 'The experience of a thousand years; an inflexible tradition; a transcendent position which confers more serenity and more detachment.' And they are Italians, who see nuances more perceptively than any other people on the earth.[36]

---

[35] D'Ormesson, *Ambassade tragique*, p. 61; Giulio Nicolini, *Il Cardinale Domenico Tardini* (Padua, 1980), p. 124; for Montini's earlier career see especially Robert A. Graham, 'G. B. Montini Substitut Secretary of State', in *Paul VI et la modernité dans l'Eglise*, Actes du colloque, 1983 (Ecole française de Rome, 1984), pp. 67–84. Born 1897 near Brescia, drawn into the papal diplomatic service by the influence of Pizzardo, he served for a short time at Warsaw but was permanently in the Secretariat of State from 1924, Substitute from December 1937.

[36] D'Ormesson, *Ambassade tragique*, pp. 231–2.

Charles-Roux's successor as French ambassador put it thus:

When Pius XII succeeded Pius XI, almost everyone thought wrongly that they were the same. Pius XI's personality was so strong that everyone around him disappeared behind him. So when Cardinal Pacelli became Pope most people expected that nothing would change in the policy of the Vatican. The new Pope took the name of his predecessor and so confirmed this impression.

In fact, the two were very different men. To a robust Milanese mountaineer succeeded a Roman bourgeois, more passive in temperament. A diplomat took the place of a student.[37]

[37] D'Ormesson, *Final Report*, p. 8.

3
The peace plans of Pius XII

The new Pope's coronation was unprecedented in its grandeur. For it was the first coronation of a Pope since the Lateran Treaty and therefore the first in the open air for nearly a century, and the first which combined a ceremony in the open with the ability to travel easily from all parts of the world. The King of England had a representative in the Duke of Norfolk. For the first time, the President of the United States sent a representative, its ambassador in London Joseph Kennedy, who was a Catholic. The prime minister of Eire, Eamonn De Valera, came in person, France sent the poet Claudel, Italy its Crown Prince Umberto and its Foreign Secretary Count Ciano. Germany was content with its ambassador in the Vatican, von Bergen. Ciano was alleged to have made a scene when he found that he was placed below the Duke of Norfolk. After the coronation was an enormous reception at the Palazzo Colonna where Osborne introduced the Duke of Norfolk to Cardinal Maglione and other members of the Curia.

Pius XI's conflict with Hitler and Mussolini left a Papacy more popular in Britain than at any time since the Reformation, and more popular in France than at any time since the fall of Louis Napoleon.

On 13 March 1939, only a few days after the Pope's election, Hitler drove into Prague and dismembered Czechoslovakia. Since this occupation shattered the western policy of appeasement, and turned the flank of Poland, it made a European war probable within months unless a miracle happened.

Vatican policy changed overnight. It was in part a question of priority. Pius XI denounced the Nazi ill-treatment of the Churches, or countered Mussolini's anti-semitic provisions, and generally stood up for justice and liberty. All these good objectives were suddenly seen as secondary to one supreme quest, that of helping the European powers not to destroy each other.

To the Vatican, therefore, the need of the moment seemed to be not a Pope who would follow Pius XI in denouncing racialism and anti-semitism and the idolatry of the State. Denunciations increase tension.

This was the belief of the Pope and his close collaborators. It was also the belief of the British minister to the Holy See. But it was not everyone's belief. The French ambassador, Charles-Roux, disliked the doctrine. What ought the Papacy to do? Should it seek to be the moral guide to the nations and take its stand on absolute right? If so, it was its duty to condemn aggression, and treaty-breaking, whenever they occurred. Even some Italians longed for a Pope like Pius XI, who would call aggression brutal and not mind about the consequences. But these were people not responsible for the care of Churches. To make the Roman Catholic Churches of Germany and Austria still more hated by their half-persecuting government was not a plan to attract the pastors of a world-wide Church unless something could be achieved. And for the moment there was a higher moral cause – stop a world war.

Pope Pius XII and his advisers exaggerated what they might achieve. They knew that their influence with Hitler was nil. They made almost no attempt to influence Hitler. They knew that they had a certain influence with Mussolini, especially because they had a strong influence among Italians. They knew that they had a lesser influence, but not to be despised, among the Poles. They did not exaggerate this. Because Beck, the Polish Foreign Secretary, left the Church after a second marriage and turned Protestant, he was not on good terms with the Pope. Pius XI refused to receive him when he came to Rome. The Vatican knew that the chief maker of Polish policy did not think highly of the Vatican. Still, the Poles were a Catholic people. A word from Rome might help to make them less bellicose.

Therefore, if the Vatican could only get above the controversy; if they could only be seen by the dictatorships not to be the partisans of the democracies; they had the chance – or thought that they might have the chance – of bringing the two sides together to talk. It looked more important at this moment to diminish tension than to denounce injustice.

This great change of policy, which at bottom was due to the change in the plight of Europe, was also due to the change in the personality of the Pope. By temperament Pius XII had grounds for thinking courtesy better than attack. The Nazis persecuted the Churches. Pius XI denounced. Result: worse persecution. Let us try the opposite. Let us get on terms with the German government, and see what good can be done by persuasion. The new Pope said, in a sentence characteristically rich in metaphor, 'We grasp the tiller of St Peter's ship with the intention of steering it to the port of peace across so many waves.' He chose as his coat of arms a dove with an olive branch in its beak.[1]

On Good Friday 1939 Mussolini's armies invaded Albania. That was not much of a state. The Italians had long an interest on that side of the Adriatic. When Hitler swallowed Czecho-Slovakia Mussolini could see

---

[1] *The Pope Speaks* (London, 1940), pp. 61–3.

the German threat to the Balkans and wanted to forestall Hitler by strengthening Italian power. But the aggression was naked and on a sacred day. The act made it harder for a peaceable Pope to talk about Hitler's aggression. Under the Lateran Treaty the Pope could not condemn Italian aggression, for he was bound not to enter Italian politics. But Pius XII had no intention of condemning German aggression or Italian. His eyes looked to a more practical goal.

Charles-Roux and Osborne came to an argument. Osborne was persuaded that if the Pope expressed the least disapproval of Germany's aggression against the Czechs, it could do no good and could only hurt the Catholics in Germany. Charles-Roux said that the Papacy stood high in prestige and could help Europe to principles of justice – especially it could exercise influence on Italy. Osborne said that he was not disposed to advise the Vatican to speak, for the reasons which he had given. But he did not refuse the idea of getting the Secretariat of State to tell the Italian government that it regarded recent events in Central Europe as contrary to the interests of Italy.

Charles-Roux reported confidentially to his government: 'I don't want this known in London.' Both the English missions in Rome share this attitude. The strong language uttered at home sounds to them too strong. 'They have seen the spectre of Bolshevism. They want France to come nearer to Italy.'[2]

This new form of appeasement was not so unpalatable to all the British as was afterwards supposed. The British and French Foreign Services were both divided on what it was best to expect from Rome.

Both were agreed that if the Pope thought of himself as a mediator between the Great Powers he was under a wild illusion. The goal which to the Pope looked practicable looked to Whitehall and the Quai d'Orsay a dangerous dream. And if his form of mediation was to persuade them to sit down at a table with Hitler, they were not going to do any such thing. They had sat at a table in Munich and were betrayed. Therefore the Foreign Services were convinced that the policy of the old Pope was a better policy than the policy of the new Pope. Since the new policy had no chance, and since the old policy held up the cause of the democracies as the cause of justice, this was a natural feeling in Whitehall.

Nevertheless, not everyone in London or Paris was spoiling for a fight with Hitler. They expected it to be the destruction of their civilization. If anyone could find a way out of the impasse they would bless the proposal. The British and the French were in a situation where at all costs they must not tell the Poles to concede an inch to

---

[2] QO, Vatican, no. 39, 27.

Hitler. They were bound by every tie of honour, and by a less than wise guarantee of 31 March, to give the Poles their unconditional backing. But behind the scenes they were less unconditional. If the only way not to have a war was for the Poles to concede to Germany Danzig and a route through the Corridor, then this might be the least bad of all solutions. They could not tell the Poles to yield. But if the Poles decided to yield, some of the British would not be infinitely distressed. And in persuading the Poles to yield, they saw that the Pope had just a chance. The importance of the Legation in the Vatican was rising, as one instrument of a last desperate act of concealed appeasement.

Inside the Vatican were those who believed, and with reason, that the British and French governments, or some of their members, really wanted to concede more but could not dare to say so. Some of the cardinals accepted the Fascist proposition that the world had been left by the Treaty of Versailles divided into haves and have-nots and that the haves, who were Britain and France as the European victors of the First World War, refused to concede an inch to the have-nots. Some cardinals agreed that this was a form of international injustice which ought to be settled in a civilized way by concession. In his heart Neville Chamberlain, at times, still believed this also. His Foreign Secretary, Lord Halifax, was still apt to raise the hope of an adjustment over the former German colonies, as a wan way of persuading Hitler back to the negotiating table. To some in the Vatican – certainly for a time Tardini, probably also Cardinal Maglione – reason must support this course. If Britain had not wanted to shed the blood of its young men, or put its cities under bombs, for the sake of saving Czecho-Slovakia, why should it face the horror for a lesser thing, Danzig or German rights in the Polish Corridor? The Vatican thought that the British must want the chance of another Munich; not called Munich, nor at Munich, looking as unlike Munich as possible, but still a conference which would enable Britain to get out of fighting for Poland over certain 'lesser' matters in a situation where mere geography prevented the British from helping the Poles physically. Into early June 1939 Tardini believed that the British must want to negotiate if they could. And about some of them he was right. He did not yet see that Hitler's brutality to the Munich agreement, and his pogrom against the Jews in November 1938, made it impossible for them to negotiate ever again with a blackguard German government.

Therefore it was just possible that an appeal from the Pope could do good. The Poles were a Roman Catholic nation, the Pope had a little influence there, he might hint at concession. A lot of the French people were not so divided behind their government's strong words as appearance might suggest. The British had a vast empire, frail, too easily lost if they entered a European war, they could hardly defend its eastern provinces adequately in peace time; they must want the chance of coming to the negotiating table even if they could not say so aloud. And above all Cardinal Maglione was aware that Mussolini, who strutted and puffed and threw out his chest, had no desire whatever to go to war at Hitler's side, and his problem was how to avoid doing so now that Hitler was set on war. If the Vatican tried to push for negotiation, it would certainly have one ally, perhaps only one open ally, namely the Fascist dictator. Every word the Pope spoke in favour of peace must help to prevent Italy going to war at Hitler's side. Like the British Foreign Office, the cardinals saw that Mussolini was the only person in Europe with a chance of pushing Hitler to relent and negotiate. Like the Foreign Office, they did not rate Mussolini's chances high. But even if this idea of pushing Mussolini to push Hitler was an illusion, it could be tried; and the very effort must help Italy to stay out of the war, and would incidentally bring before the world that Catholic Europe stood for peace, and that the Pope was a man of peace, and Christianity a message of peace.

Thus the idea of a peace plan put forward by the Pope slowly grew. When in the days after his coronation the Pope identified himself before all the world as a Pope of peace, he started to receive many letters, especially from Americans, begging him to issue an appeal to the world for peace. George Lansbury, former leader of the Labour party, an Anglican and a pacifist, begged the Pope to summon an international conference in Jerusalem and send out an appeal from the Mount of Olives. The Pope also received more militant advice. In the House of Lords Archbishop Lang of Canterbury asked him to make a declaration against the exaltation of the State at the expense of human personality, and the new exaltation of force; and said that he would join. He did not ask for a neutral Pope, but a Pope who condemned aggression. About this the Italian ambassador to the Holy See took the trouble to ask Monsignor Montini; who said, reported Pignatti, that he had heard nothing. He added that he could at once exclude the idea that the Pope would participate in demonstrations of this kind. Then he told Pignatti of all the letters coming out of America, but evidently thought nothing likely to result. 'The Vatican has not replied. It intends always to remain outside rivalries between nations.'[3]

By the end of April 1939, however, the Pope had a plan for peace; or rather, for persuading the Powers in contention to meet at a negotiat-

---

[3] Pignatti to AE, 21 March 1939, AE, Santa Sede, Busta 43. Lang in *Hansard*, 20 March 1939, vol. 112, col. 324.

ing table. The first thing to do was to secure the consent and approval of Mussolini. The Vatican selected the normal instrument for messages from the Pope to Mussolini, the Jesuit Father Tacchi Venturi.

Mussolini liked and trusted Tacchi Venturi. He was a good historian who won Mussolini's respect in 1922, during the Fascist struggle for power. He was like a Jesuit born out of due time – a diplomat by the back stairs. The modern Society of Jesus suspected him as too political a clergyman. But his achievements on behalf of the Church, during the Fascist regime, had been signal.

Father Tacchi Venturi saw Mussolini on 1 and 2 May. 'I like the Pope's idea,' said Mussolini. 'So far as it rests with me, I approve.' He had no doubt that the Catholic world would approve. He talked of the Catholic majorities in three of the five countries, and the large Catholic minorities in the other two. 'An invitation, sent impartially to the heads of the five Powers, cannot offend and will be listened to.'

Father Tacchi Venturi gave the all-clear to the Pope and the next day Cardinal Maglione sent out a message to the three nuncios (Paris, Warsaw, Berlin) and to the Apostolic Delegate in London asking them to take soundings.

The British Foreign Office instantly suspected that Mussolini invented the plan for his nefarious purposes. They were wrong. The idea was the Pope's or Cardinal Maglione's. What was true, was that the Vatican took the trouble to sound Mussolini before anyone else. They knew that the country which they could influence was Italy, and that they could only influence Hitler through Mussolini. Therefore the plan was only useful if Mussolini approved. If he approved, it did not much matter whether the plan afterwards failed – though they hoped it would not fail. They would have given Mussolini an extra lever in his own quest to prevent embroilment in a German war which he did not want.

The Apostolic Delegate in London, Monsignor Godfrey, called (4 May 1939) to see the Foreign Secretary, Lord Halifax, and handed him a memorandum. Halifax saw him that day and the next. He regretted the omission of Russia from the list of Powers to be approached by the Pope. Godfrey said that he feared in no circumstances would it be possible for the Pope to consider such an approach to Russia.

Halifax then pointed out the crying difficulty. Was this to be another Munich, a compromise-peace in which Germany was given most of what it demanded so aggressively? He asked Godfrey where the Pope thought that the proposed conference should be held? and who would preside? 'Was it likely to be in the mind of His Holiness that it should be held in Rome under Vatican auspices?' Godfrey said that he did not think 'that the Vatican would suggest anything of the kind themselves but might no doubt be willing to consider it if suggested by the parties to the conference'.[4]

We possess the minutes of the 45th meeting of the Committee on Foreign Policy, held 5 May 1939, which show that the Pope's proposal was brought forward. At that meeting Halifax said that he thought that the Pope might possibly have ascertained first that the proposal was acceptable to Mussolini; and that if the invitation was refused, it should be refused by Germany and not by Great Britain. Neville Chamberlain said that the Pope would do better if he saw the representatives of each of the five Powers separately, and did not try to get a single conference.

The meeting preferred two conferences (Poland/Germany: France/Italy) to one and saw no need for Britain to be represented at either. But it agreed that Halifax should consult Warsaw and Paris.

In Berlin the nuncio Orsenigo asked the Foreign Ministry whether he could see Hitler, and cannot have been confident that he would be received. He did not tell them why he wished to come, and as they suspected he wanted to protest over the state of the Church in Germany, they were not at first hopeful or helpful. When they realized why he wanted to go, the tone changed at once. He was very gratified to find that an interview was arranged at Berchtesgaden for the afternoon of 5 May, and that they would fly him to Salzburg in a special aircraft and give him luncheon at the Grand Hotel in Berchtesgaden.

Hitler talked with him for an hour (4 p.m. to 5 p.m.) in the presence of two witnesses, Ribbentrop and his aide Hewel who took notes. Then Hitler offered tea. We have two different reports of the meeting, one from Orsenigo in the Vatican documents, the other from Hewel in the documents of the German Foreign Office. The two accounts say different things but are never incompatible.

Orsenigo said that the Pope proposed a conference of the five Powers. He said that 'the Pope was deeply concerned about the tension in Europe and wished to do everything that lay in his power to ward off the danger of war from mankind'. He did not specify the nature or form of the proposed conference, but its agenda would be the two most urgent questions, Germany and Poland, France and Italy.

Hitler listened, reported Orsenigo, 'very deferentially' (*molto deferentemente*) – the portrait startles the reader of the report. He asked Orsenigo to thank the Pope for his interest and care. He said that his links with Italy were so close that he could not decide without knowing what Mussolini thought, for he felt himself under deep, and lasting, obligation to Mussolini.

[4] FO 371/23790/110.

Then he went on more conversationally, as though he had finished with the official reply (the words are as reported by Orsenigo):

However, I don't see any danger of war. I don't see it between Italy and France, because Mussolini's demands – Tunisia, the Suez Canal, Djibouti – which I find reasonable demands and which I fully support – are not such as to lead to war but only to negotiation.

As for me, I have made no demand on France. I have made us impregnable against France. I have made no demand on England – except only colonies, and I have said that that is no motive for war. I have repudiated the 1934 Pact with Poland, not because she refused my demand, but only because of our mutual situations since the intervention of England. But even this does not mean war by me. As for Danzig, it is a free city, under the League of Nations. We can discuss and negotiate; but it is not said that it leads to war. My other demands may mature with time, in 1942, or possibly 1945. I'll wait. I don't see a reason for war – at least unless the Poles go mad and stir up their people to demand that the frontier of Poland should be the Elbe. So everything depends on the Poles keeping their heads and staying calm.

He then talked of the blessing of a mountain retreat and its healing power for nerves frayed by city life; and said that a conference of heads of State could bring a time of spiritual rest and make them all less excited.

Then he started to attack England. It pretended to want peace and encouraged war. It stirred up the Emperor of Abyssinia against Italy. It encouraged the Reds of Spain to resist Franco. It kept war going in China when there was a chance of agreement between Japan and Chiang Kai-shek. It stirred up trouble in Czechoslovakia after the Munich agreement; and he specially blamed the military attaché at the British Embassy in Berlin, who worked to these ends in harness with the British minister in Prague. And now, he ended, it is doing the same to Poland, putting spanners in the way of possible treaties and encouraging the Poles to fight.

'I listened,' reported Orsenigo, 'in silence.' Then he 'respectfully' said that he could not share the Chancellor's optimism, given the growing tension between Germany and Poland. He said that he could not subscribe to the complete sincerity of his prophecies of the future. (Hewel reported no such bold utterance.)

Hitler did not tell Orsenigo that he had already given his generals an order to prepare war against Poland.

Orsenigo advised his masters in the Vatican, nevertheless, that in the light of this conversation there was no imminent danger of war provided that the Poles would calm down and shut up. This must gain time, and so negotiations could be undertaken, for example, to get a German motor road across the Polish Corridor.[5]

[5] Orsenigo's report, ADSS, 1, nos. 28–9, pp. 128ff.; Hewel's report in ADAP, Series D, vol. VI, no. 331, pp. 352–4; Eng. trans. in DGFP, Series D, vol. VI, pp. 426–8.

Three days later, back in Berlin, Orsenigo saw one of Henderson's staff from the British Embassy. He described how well he had been received. But he would say nothing of the matter of the interview with Hitler because he had been requested to promise the strictest secrecy. He then made remarks for the benefit of Sir Nevile Henderson and the British government. In the context of the time the remarks sound curious. He 'hoped that His Majesty's Government would note that the present Pope since his accession had not in public uttered a single word of criticism of German policy towards the Church. His Holiness had moreover intervened specially to see that *Osservatore Romano* did likewise.'[6]

In Rome Osborne mentioned to Tardini that any conference would inevitably look like another Munich. Tardini said that this could not be helped. But he would draw the Pope's attention to the need that the conference should not look like Munich.[7]

The French were resolute not to confer with Italy at the Pope's or anyone else's invitation. They decided that Cardinal Maglione was a secret agent of Mussolini. The Foreign Office in London found this Machiavellian theory incredible, and were wryly amused that only two months before, the Quai d'Orsay 'were moving, if not heaven anyhow earth', 'to secure Cardinal Pacelli's election as Pope!'. All the same, they shared Léger's opinion that such a conference would look like another Munich in the sense, at least, that it would 'resound to the glorification of Mussolini'.

On 10 May Sir Alexander Cadogan formulated the difficulty. Neither British nor French could do with a conference. Neither British nor French dared to say so publicly. 'Who', asked Cadogan, 'is going to kill Cock Robin?'

I should strongly deprecate throwing the smallest drop of cold water on the proposal, and I should be sorry if M. Léger were to draft the reply for the French and to give a hearty cold douche.

I shouldn't want to embarrass the French by being too warm about it – if they don't like it – but I wouldn't share with them any of the onus of turning it down . . .

I only wonder whether the French need reminding of the harm they will do themselves by being bluntly non-cooperative, and whether we might say that *we* shan't turn the thing down, and express the hope that they won't take this upon themselves.[8]

In Berlin Sir Nevile Henderson reported to Halifax the view of Attolico, who was now Italian ambassador in Germany. Attolico regarded the Vatican proposal as premature. Henderson could not see any future in a meeting only between Poles and Germans. To have a

---

[6] Henderson to Foreign Office, FO 371/23790/139.
[7] FO 371/23790/128, cf. 126 and 148.   [8] FO 371/23790/133–4.

chance of bringing them together there must be a conference, and an arbitrator. 'Personally, I see no other possible arbitrator than the Pope, and it is a hopeful sign that Hitler apparently did not turn down the suggestion out of hand.'[9]

We see the problems if we list what the various governments at the moment wanted out of the Vatican.

Italy wanted not to go to war and therefore wanted Poland to concede, and therefore would like the Vatican to help in persuading Poland to concede.

Germany wanted the same, but not for the same reason, because its government liked the idea of war, and only preferred to get what it wanted by concession.

Poland wanted condemnation of aggressive attitudes.

Britain and France wanted to hear again the voice of Pius XI. They wanted the great principles of international morality sounding out whatever the consequences – which would make them appear to be in the right and the Axis powers in the wrong. But some of their officials also wanted Poland to concede.

In Rome, meanwhile, the French and British envoys took views entirely different from those of their superiors in Paris and London. Osborne was glad at the Pope's initiative and thought the moment propitious. Charles-Roux had a harder doctrine. He told Bonnet, 'The proposal . . . is not so naif as it looks. The Pope's interest in intervening does not depend entirely on his success in intervening. The Holy See knows that all the peoples want peace. The Vatican knows that it has nothing to lose, and everything to gain, by taking an initiative of which it will get the honour and merit in the eyes of the people whether it succeeds or fails.'[10] Both Osborne and Charles-Roux were anxious that their principals should not attribute the plan to secret machinations by any of the Powers. Yet on 10 May 1939, despite all this friendliness, or at least refusal to throw cold water, the Pope decided not to proceed with his plan.

The French press got hold of the plan. On 9 and 10 May the French newspapers were full of it, argued and criticized it. The right-wing newspapers were pleased that the Pope should try to use his influence, but hardly anyone liked the idea of a conference of five Powers. They felt that the omission of Russia was perhaps fatal. The Communist newspaper *Humanité* roundly declared that it was a proposal for a new Munich.

Cardinal Maglione was cross about these French acidities.[11]

---

[9] Henderson to Halifax, 11 May 1939: printed in DBFP, 1919–39, Third Series, vol. v, pp. 802ff.

[10] Charles-Roux to Bonnet, 18 May 1939.   [11] FO 371/23790/201.

Simultaneously a leakage occurred in Britain. On 10 May the *News Chronicle* published correct details of the Pope's proposal, and the Foreign Office were cross about the leakage. The press besieged the Vatican for information. Osborne was told that the plan was abandoned, though it might later be revived. The Secretariat said that the chief motive for abandonment consisted in assurances from Hitler and Mussolini that the German/Polish dispute and the French/Italian dispute carried 'no immediate menace of war' [!]. Everyone was very polite to the Pope.

All this did not stop a very anxious report from New Zealand (where the Prime Minister, Savage, was a Roman Catholic) that the Pope had proposed a plan for peace by holding a conference at the Vatican; that Germany, Italy and France were willing; but that the British were cool and tried to kill the plan[12] and influenced the Polish government to be lukewarm. (The source of this information was a Press Association report from Rome on 16 May.)

The circular letter of 10 May, written by Cardinal Maglione to nuncios to explain the cancellation of the plan, contains interesting wording. He said that the first objective – of making clear to the Powers the longing of the peoples for peace – had been attained; and that the second objective, a conference, did not now appear necessary owing to the improvement in the international system.

This last sentence looks brazen in view of the imminent 'Pact of Steel' between Hitler and Mussolini. It did not come out of Maglione's head but out of the head of the Italian Foreign Minister. Ciano met Ribbentrop at Milan on 7 May; the meeting which led towards the 'Pact of Steel'. The two Foreign Ministers discussed incidentally the Pope's plan, and then Ciano sent a message to Maglione: 'The Ministers were agreed in highly valuing the Pope's aim to propose a conference of the five Powers. But they agreed that the international situation had improved, and that a conference of the five Powers would be premature and at the moment is not necessary.'[13]

What had changed was the view of Mussolini, on whose assent the entire plan rested. Mussolini realized that he was not prepared to have his quarrel with France discussed by irrelevancies like Germany and Britain and Poland. So he told Ciano, and Ciano told Ribbentrop, and the Foreign Ministers agreed, and Ciano told the Pope, and Maglione

[12] *Evening Post* (New Zealand), 17 May 1939; *Dominion*, 17 May 1939; cf. FO 371/23790/194.
[13] ADSS, 1, no. 36, p. 138; Italian ambassador to Holy See, from Ciano to Maglione (note of 9 May): 'L'avvenuto miglioramento della situazione internazionale e ritenuto che una conferenza . . . sarebbe ora prematura e attualmente non necessaria.' Maglione to nuncios (10 May): 'La Conferenza non è apparsa sul momento necessaria in sequito al miglioramento della situazione generale avvenuto nel frattempo.'

told the nuncios, that the international situation was better and the conference was not necessary. And the 'Pact of Steel' was signed in Berlin on 22 May.

Even after the plan was scotched, the French continued to be suspicious, and their suspicions were shared by the British. On 15 May Sir Alexander Cadogan had a talk with the French ambassador in London, Corbin, and said that he 'could not imagine that the Vatican could have taken this initiative without a measure of connivance with the Fascist government'.[14] Both governments were still inclined to believe that the Pope's offer was only a mask for a ploy by Mussolini. More than one French cabinet minister went round saying that it was all due to Mussolini. Osborne assured London, and Charles-Roux assured Paris, that this theory could not possibly be true.

All the same, the texts prove something interesting. The idea came from the Vatican, not from Mussolini. But they felt the need to clear it with Mussolini before they tried it on anyone else. And when the circular went out cancelling the plan, the Secretary of State used words, and the formulation of an idea, derived from Count Ciano.

On 15 May Mr Sorensen, who was a Nonconformist minister, asked a question in the House of Commons about the Pope's proposals. For the Foreign Secretary, R. A. Butler replied that the Pope had made no formal proposal. 'I can assure the House that His Majesty's Government are naturally most sympathetic to any steps which His Holiness may think can usefully be taken with a view to furthering the interests of world peace.'[15]

Behind the scenes a point, little but of real importance, came from this argument.

Ever since the invasion of Abyssinia, the two western democracies had driven Mussolini into the embrace of Hitler. Since Hitler became a warmonger, Britain saw this policy as mistaken; and a fundamental plank in the programme of British appeasement policy, ever since Anthony Eden resigned as Foreign Secretary, was kindness to Mussolini, so that he might be drawn back into the western camp. Intellectually the French agreed. But actually they could not or would not help. They had a quarrel with Italy which they were not willing to discuss.

Thus there came to be a common interest between Britain and the Vatican. Britain wanted to persuade the French not to be so intransigent with Mussolini; at least they should be willing to talk with the Italians. The Pope had precisely the same wish, though for a different

---

[14] Corbin to Bonnet, 15 May 1939, QO, Vatican, no. 39, 80.
[15] *Hansard*, 15 May 1939, vol. 347, col. 964.

reason. As an Italian with an independent mind, who disliked German racialism and German aggression, he also wanted to prise Mussolini out of Hitler's arms. The only way in which this could be done was to satisfy Mussolini by other means. This satisfaction could only be obtained at the expense of France. Therefore the Pope also wanted to persuade the French not to be so intransigent; and, if that proved awkward, wanted to persuade the British that they should try again to persuade the French not to be so intransigent.

But this desire of the Pope touched very tender sores. If the Pope asked the French to be kinder to Mussolini, he only looked like a clergyman, pretending to be an international figure but really fulfilling the nationalist aspirations of his own Italian people.

When the British were asked by the Vatican if they could help with the French,[16] they had two reactions. The first was, that they had tried and failed, and that it would be ignominious to tell the Vatican how powerless they were to influence their own allies. The second was, the Pope was trying to shift the onus to their shoulders. Robert Vansittart wrote another of his astringent minutes: 'The Vatican, if not passing the buck, is at least passing the ball as quickly as possible – without having made any ground. This is bad and timid policy.'[17]

In the numerous letters which passed to and fro over the Pope's peace plan, one important change in the attitude of the British did not go unnoticed in the Vatican. You could not stop war from coming unless you were willing to sit round a table. A conference of some sort was absolutely necessary if peace was to be preserved. The Axis powers did not mind a conference, because they were the powers which wanted change; and a conference must mean the chance of peaceful change instead of warlike change. But the British would never sit down again at a German table. For they sat at Munich, and betrayed Czechoslovakia for the sake of peace, and afterwards were themselves betrayed. In the Pope's eyes concession was still better, far better, than war. Was it so awful if the Germans got Danzig, a German city, and German rights of way across the Corridor, itself an artificial creation of the peacemakers of Versailles? The Poles must if possible be persuaded to concede. Eight months before, Britain was determined that Czechoslovakia should concede, and so save Europe from a suicidal war. Now Britain was determined, or seemed to be determined, that the Poles should not concede, because any conces-

---

[16] Maglione made the suggestions verbally to Osborne on 10 June 1939; but no record of the conversation has been found in London or in the Vatican Archives. Cf. Osborne to Maglione, 17 June 1939, ADSS, 1, no. 65, p. 179; contents more easily seen in Osborne to Maglione, 21 June 1939, ibid., 1, no. 67, p. 181; cf. DBFP, 1919–39, Third Series, vol. VI, no. 32, p. 32. [17] FO 371/23790/222.

sion would be another Munich. Therefore, the Vatican perceived by 10 May 1939, Britain was ready for war. For it was no longer willing to contemplate the only alternative to war.

Osborne believed in the policy of appeasement. He thought it both necessary and right; necessary because Britain was not ready to fight; right because good men seek to avoid war for so long as they can with honour. He met Chamberlain, and gave him a luncheon, when Chamberlain came to Rome to visit Mussolini, and liked him very much. 'He seemed to be one of the few people I had met whose heart and head were geared to the same fly-wheel.'[18] Osborne liked the famous umbrella as a symbol of Europe's longing for peace (including the German people's longing) and was sure that no one ought to condemn Chamberlain for the policy of appeasement.

But now the age of appeasement was dead. The Vatican had not quite realized that until this moment. It was the dragging of the feet, the talk of *not another Munich,* which brought it home. Monsignor Tardini said to Charles-Roux, 'I understand that England is now ready for anything. Last September, the English took the initiative over Munich. Today, they say that under no circumstances would they do the same. What that proves is this: last summer they were not ready to fight, now they are ready.'[19]

On 22 May a lot of optimism in Rome was shattered by the signing of the 'Pact of Steel'. The Pope had believed that his influence with Mussolini, and with the Italian people, might keep Italy out of the war. The 'Pact of Steel' committed Mussolini to joining Hitler in war; with only one small saving clause about consultation.

On 4 June the Pope told Osborne that he was willing, if asked, to try to work out a basis for agreement between Germany and Poland.[20]

The Foreign Office did not like the sound of this interview. The Pope was trying to *conciliate* Hitler. Conciliation could not improve the lot of the Roman Catholic Church in Germany. It must make the Pope *a little*

---

[18] Osborne's *Diary,* 10 November 1940.

[19] Charles-Roux to Bonnet, 10 May 1939, QO, Vatican, no. 39, 51; cf. also Bonnet's conversation with the Dominican Father Gillet, reported by Gillet in ADSS, 1, no. 73, pp. 187ff.

[20] Osborne to Halifax, 5 June 1939, FO 371/23790/273. According to Tittmann's Papers (Brussels), III, 39, Halifax told Osborne on 26 May to urge the Pope to lend all assistance to German–Polish negotiations. Halifax suggested that he use the Jesuit general, Ledochowski (who was a Pole), as a mediator. Osborne replied that he discussed this with Cardinal Maglione. But Maglione replied that it was Britain that guaranteed Poland and so stopped the possibility of negotiation. Osborne reported to London that he did not believe that Ledochowski could help.

Tittmann was not yet close to Osborne. But he preserved a record of valuable documents. Halifax did something not in agreement with the general policy of the British government at that moment.

diffident in taking a lead which would displease Nazis and Fascists. 'We have no right,' commented Noble, 'to expect the Pope to interfere in international affairs in our interest and criticism of his reserve is too often based on a desire to see him having a whack at the totalitarians; but I think one may properly wish that the Pope would see his way to make clear to the world the incompatibility between the worship of God and the worship of the State.' Was it possible, asked Noble, that the Pope was being tempted to try to *exorcise the devil with soft words*?[21]

Orme Sargent wrote a perceptive minute:

I think it is fairly evident that the Pope intends to maintain a middle course between the 'Democracies' and the Fascist and Nazi dictatorships. He conceives such an attitude to be necessary if he is at the appropriate moment to play the part of mediator. But the trouble is that such an attitude of impartiality prevents him in large measure from exercising his moral authority in defence, as Sir A. Noble says, of Christianity as against the worship of the State. Personally, I feel that he would be able to influence events far more effectively as champion of certain moral principles in the world of today than he is likely to be able to as possible but improbable candidate for the post of mediator between the Axis and the Democracies.

A meeting between the nuncio in Poland, Cortesi and Beck, which was arranged so that Cortesi could take his leave, caused a flurry of speculation that the Vatican had worked out suggestions for a Polish settlement and that Cortesi gave the plan to Beck. *The Daily Telegraph* (17 June) adopted this theory and wondered whether – 'perhaps at the suggestion of Signor Mussolini' – the Pope was trying to get Poland to concede. The Foreign Office in London heard that the Pope had a plan for Danzig which the Germans liked and the Poles disliked. They asked Osborne whether this was true (21 June) and the next day Osborne asked Cardinal Maglione whether it was true, and got a denial. It later turned out that Cortesi got an assurance from Beck that the Poles, on any minor provocation, would exercise self-constraint to the utmost possible limit. It was not much of an assurance. Simultaneously the American ambassador in Warsaw, Biddle, sent a message to Roosevelt that the Poles were very critical of the Vatican; that they thought the Pope was acting more as an Italian than as the Holy See; and that one Pole had told him how Warsaw had long been aware of the Pope's pro-German leanings, and that he felt the Pope lacked a warm heart for any clear understanding of Poland. The same Pole told Biddle that Pius XI regarded Nazis and Fascists as a worse menace than Russians, but that Pius XII regarded Russians as a worse menace than Nazis and Fascists.

[21] FO 371/23790/283.

This report of Biddle[22] had no relation to the truth about the Vatican, but it showed what a number of leading Poles thought; and that Vatican intervention was not likely to force the Poles to concede unless they decided on other grounds to concede.

In early July London heard a rumour of another plan by the Pope to make the Poles concede. This rumour seems to have been started by the Russian agent in Rome. Osborne again asked Maglione. Maglione thought the rumour sufficiently dangerous to compel him to write a formal letter (in French) to Osborne, setting out the whole question of mediation as he saw it:

Very Confidential   Vatican, 15 July 1939
. . . I must make it clear to Lord Halifax that the Holy See has never thought it opportune – and does not now think it opportune – to take the initiative in proposing to the two governments a concrete solution of the problem. On the contrary, it has conceived its duty to be limited to recommending to the two leaders in the case that they treat it calmly and with moderation.

In this sense we made the démarches to Berlin and Warsaw in May. You and your government are well aware of those démarches. Afterwards the Holy See thought that it should underline what it recommended. Early in June the Pope told the head of the Italian government, Signor Mussolini, that for the sake of peace it would be very good if he could use his great influence with Hitler and the German government to ensure that the Danzig question was treated with that calmness which the delicate international situation made more than ever necessary.

A short time afterwards we received from a serious source of information the assurance that Germany had no intention of attacking Poland. So I thought it good to use the nuncio in Poland, Monsignor Cortesi, to renew to the Polish government privately our earlier pleas for prudence and moderation.

On 22 June Monsignor Cortesi replied to me that the minister Beck had told him, among other things, 'Poland will go on holding the line of prudence and moderation which it has followed up to now, despite the controversial and intentional provocations from the other party.'

On 1 July I wrote all this to Monsignor Orsenigo the nuncio in Berlin. In the same letter I added that the Holy See did not doubt that Germany on its side would maintain the prudence and moderation necessary in so delicate a situation.

On the firm attitude of the British government over Danzig, I am well-informed. When I was afraid that the situation would get worse, I made it clear to the Italian ambassador to the Holy See – for transmission to his government and the German government – that if Germany occupied Danzig, England and France were determined to go to war.

On 7 July, in obedience to the Pope, I repeated to the Italian ambassador that I was more than ever convinced that England and France would declare war on Germany at the first attempt by Germany to solve the Danzig question by

22 Biddle to Roosevelt, Warsaw, 23 June 1939, enclosing a memorandum of 20 June 1939.

violence. I said to him that in Hitler's circle there were still perhaps people with illusions about this. They risked repeating the mistake of 1914.

I am sure that the Italian ambassador passed this to his government.

Finally, I renew the prayer of all men of good will, which you and your government have surely at heart: may God bless the efforts to save peace, and spare the world a conflict which would have terrible and unforeseeable results.[23]

What was the 'serious source' by which Maglione learnt that Germany had no intention of attacking Poland? It could not be the German government, nor the German ambassador at the Vatican. Osborne was convinced that it was none other than Mussolini.[24] We know from the Vatican documents that it was Ciano.

On 18 August Cardinal Maglione, who was tired and overworked, went off on holiday and left the office in charge of Tardini. This departure, at such a moment of history, did not please the diplomats. It suggested at least a loss of the earlier faith that the Vatican might be able to achieve something.

By 22 August it was round the world that on the morrow Germany would sign a pact in Moscow with Russia. That is, that war was inevitable. That day Lord Halifax telephoned Osborne asking him to persuade the Pope to do what the Foreign Office had been trying to stop the Pope doing for three months – to try to bring Germany and Poland to the negotiating table, and to issue a 'last appeal to reason, with all the weight and influence that he commands'.[25] Probably Halifax really believed that there might be a last chance, and was not simply pursuing the hard-headed doctrine that a world appeal for peace on the highest moral grounds must make the aggressor look to be in the wrong when he attacked.

That same evening Osborne sat down with Tardini to discuss how a last appeal might be made on Vatican radio. Osborne tried to suggest phrases which might be useful – 'the necessity of settlements by negotiation', 'the immorality of forcibly imposed solutions', 'wars of aggression undertaken for forcibly imposed solutions were contrary to the law of God and man'. Osborne, who three months before thought it was not sensible for the Pope to condemn aggressors, was now engaged in trying to influence the draft which would turn into such a condemnation.[26] Tardini thought that the Pope would wish to appeal. He committed himself to none of these strong phrases.

Tardini and Montini supplied the Pope with four different drafts, of

[23] DBFP, 1919–39, Third Series, vol. VI, pp. 371–2; ADSS, 1, no. 90, pp. 209ff.
[24] Osborne to Halifax, 17 July 1939; DBFP, 1919–39, Third Series, vol. VI, p. 370.
[25] DBFP, 1919–39, Third Series, vol. VII, p. 117.
[26] Ibid., p. 183; cf. ADSS, 1, no. 111, p. 229.

varying degrees of outspokenness and strength of language. The Pope chose the draft which was least 'political', that is, which had the least strong language from the political point of view. He wished it to be a pastoral appeal. It has been proved that the substance of the appeal was drafted by Monsignor Montini. Osborne wished that the appeal could have been more specific in condemning aggression.[27] But the broadcast was moving, and phrases in it were not too far from phrases which Osborne had suggested:

. . . Standing above all public disputes and passions, I speak to all of you, leaders of the nations, in the name of God . . . I appeal again to governments and their peoples; to governments that they lay aside threats and accusations and try to settle their differences by agreement; to their peoples, that they may be calm and encourage the efforts of their government for peace.

It is by force of reason and not by force of arms that justice makes progress. Empires not founded on justice are not blessed by God. Immoral policy is not successful policy . . .

Nothing is lost by peace. Everything is lost by war . . . Let men start to negotiate again . . . I have with me the soul of this historic Europe, the child of faith and Christian genius. All humanity wants bread, freedom, justice; not weaponry. Christ made love the heart of his religion.[28]

Lord Halifax was moved, and quoted it in his own broadcast to the British people that same evening.

In Berlin Sir Nevile Henderson more than once, at this late hour, suggested that the Pope should put forward mediating proposals for Danzig. Henderson told Attolico of his idea. Attolico said that he would pass it to Mussolini. Henderson said to Attolico that they must gain time, and they needed *concrete proposals* before them, and only the Vatican could produce such proposals with a chance of being accepted as neutral. Attolico agreed. He said that he had been doing his utmost with Orsenigo. But, he said, 'the Catholic Church was afraid of intervention recoiling on itself'.[29]

Still the pressure on the Vatican continued. Sir Percy Loraine in Rome, himself under pressure to approach Mussolini to restrain Hitler, advised Halifax that the Pope would be more useful.[30] Henderson, confronted by German horror or simulated horror at Polish attacks on German citizens, asked his counsellor to suggest to Orsenigo that the Vatican should immediately appoint 'a local commission of ecclesiastics' to enquire into the alleged incidents in Poland. Orsenigo did not like the proposal. He said that it would look as

---

[27] Burkhart Schneider, 'Der Friedensappel Papst Pius XII vom 24 August 1939', in AHP, 6 (1968), 415ff. Full text, ADSS, 1, pp. 230ff.
[28] DBFP, 1919–39, Third Series, vol. VII, pp. 254–5.   [29] Ibid., p. 402.
[30] Loraine to Halifax, DBFP, 1919–39, Third Series, vol. VI, p. 633.

though the Vatican was taking sides. More sensible than Henderson, he knew that a commission of ecclesiastics had no chance and preferred a commission of laymen. But he consented to ask Rome to ask Warsaw and Berlin about the humane treatment of minorities; or else that Berlin and Warsaw should themselves appoint a commission of laymen to enquire. None of this had any chance.

The activities of the British government after 22 August 1939 show that the wish to have a war was not so whole-hearted as it seemed to be in the previous three months. They had supposed that they could stop a war by an iron front – saying that they would fight, making the Poles intransigent, and making a military alliance with Russia. For they were confident that Hitler would not dare to attack Poland if then he had to fight Russia and Britain and France at once. This was in part bluff. Hitler called the bluff because Stalin gave him the chance. The moment the bluff was called, the British stance was less iron. Halifax, whose men tried to stop the Vatican encouraging the Poles to negotiate, now wanted the Vatican to encourage the Poles. It was not the only change of the last minute. On 28 August the British Cabinet telegraphed direct to Beck asking him if he would allow them to tell Hitler that he was ready to negotiate.

The German pact with Russia had the small by-consolation that it helped those who wanted to stop Mussolini marching with Hitler. The Italians hated Stalin. Tardini said to Osborne (28 August), 'This dictator is the less mad of the two and this is the moment to influence him.' Tardini wanted Father Tacchi Venturi again to press Mussolini to do what he could with Hitler. To this suggestion Monsignor Montini added a crisp note: 'The Pope thinks this superfluous. It is clear that the Italian government is doing all it can without our prompting.'[31]

On 29 August Cardinal Maglione, back from his holiday, sent Father Tacchi Venturi to Mussolini. He told him to tell Mussolini that the Pope was very satisfied with all his efforts for peace, and begged him to do still more; and he talked of the need to keep Italy neutral if war came. Mussolini looked pleased at this congratulation from the Pope. He said that it was a duty to work for peace because war could destroy civilization. Germany, he said, was much stronger than in 1914 and harder to beat. But he thought a way out to be possible – and he wrote a little note which he gave to Tacchi Venturi: 'Poland does not oppose the return of Danzig to Germany and asks for direct negotiation with Germany on (1) Polish traffic in Danzig, (2) the Corridor, (3) the reciprocal minorities.' He asked Tacchi Venturi to ask the Pope to get a message via the nuncio to the President of Poland begging him to

[31] Ibid., vol. VII, p. 351; ADSS I, p. 246.

follow this line of action. He believed that Hitler ought to accept and would accept this solution. If he did not accept everyone would be against him and Poland would be in the best possible situation.[32]

Osborne and Charles-Roux had denied to their governments that the Vatican had any plan for such concession. Now the Pope not merely had a plan but pressed it upon Poland. (1) Would the Pope, Tardini asked Cardinal Maglione, seem to have played Hitler's game? Hitler will eat up another tasty mouthful, and next spring start again. (2) The Holy See will seem to have arranged a new Munich. (3) The Holy See will seem to be a little too close to Mussolini. Everyone will easily see that he suggested the plan.[33]

Maglione's message to the President of Poland, dated 30 August 1939, not merely adopted Mussolini's suggestion but used Mussolini's language. There is no word on the little piece of paper which Mussolini gave Tacchi Venturi, which does not appear in Maglione's letter to the Warsaw nuncio.[34] Maglione summoned Osborne and gave him a copy of the letter to transmit to Britain. He did not tell Osborne that the hand which drafted was the hand of Mussolini. To London Osborne expressed himself very pleased at the Pope's move.[35] He guessed that the information came from the Italian government but had no suspicion that they were Mussolini's own words.

In Warsaw Cortesi, moving in a very different atmosphere of warlike preparation, sent back a telegram doubting the wisdom of the Vatican suggesting these concessions, and wondering even whether it was practicable or sensible for him to pass on the suggestions.[36] Maglione dismissed the hesitations and wired him to act.

When Germany invaded Poland, both Charles-Roux and Osborne clamoured politely for a papal condemnation of aggression. They both asked, separately, that the Pope should express 'profound grief that, in less than 24 hours after the dispatch of his appeal, the German government should have assumed the terrible responsibility of plunging the world into war'. Cardinal Maglione rejected the plan. It would mean 'specific intervention in international politics'. He said that facts spoke. The world would condemn German aggression.

Osborne then asked whether the Pope could express his approval that the Italian Grand Council (1 September) announced that Italy would not initiate war against anyone. Maglione declined, for the same reason.

[32] Notes of Tardini, ADSS, 1, no. 148, pp. 258–9. Ciano telephoned Lord Halifax to tell him of the plan; cf. DBFP, 1919–39, Third Series, vol. VII, nos. 580 and 627.

[33] ADSS 1, no. 152, pp. 262–3.

[34] ADSS 1, no. 153, p. 263.

[35] DBFP, 1919–39, Third Series, vol. VII, no. 526, pp. 403–4.

[36] ADSS 1, no. 165, pp. 274–5.

Maglione in his turn asked Osborne something. Since the neutrality of Italy was now assured, he begged Osborne to get his government not to irritate Italy, and not to compromise it. Osborne said that he wholly agreed, and that both he and the ambassador at the Quirinal (Loraine) had advised London in this sense.[37] Maglione then said he hoped Osborne felt that in recent weeks the Vatican had done all they could for peace. Osborne said 'I thought they had, given the evident limitations on their actions.'[38]

These documents bring out points of interest:

1. Between the beginning of May and the end of August 1939 the Vatican was close to Mussolini, even to the extent of using Mussolini's drafting. The reason was simple. They had a common wish. The Vatican wanted no one to go to war. Mussolini, despite his military bombast, had no desire to march with Hitler and knew that to march in 1939 would be military folly. The Vatican used Mussolini's drafting because they believed that Mussolini could influence Hitler and was more likely to know his mind. Mussolini was happy to use the Vatican as a small extra aid to help him not to fight (yet) at Hitler's side.
2. The documents show that because of these common interests both the British and French Foreign Offices suspected the Pope of being a secret agent of Mussolini; and that the Polish leaders were little inclined to listen to a Pope whom they suspected, on his record as a nuncio in Germany, of being pro-German.
3. The documents show that the British and French leaders were still touched by wistful hopes of appeasement even to the last minute. Lord Halifax was a deeply Christian man who revered the Pope's spiritual mission. But his interest in stirring the Pope to act upon the Poles was more than Christian. The British people might seem to be offended if Germany swallowed the German city of Danzig, but would not in truth be displeased if in consequence they need not go to war. More important still because more practicable, the British must try to stop Mussolini fighting at Hitler's side and in this policy could see the Pope as no minor pawn upon their chessboard. It was not rhetoric that made Lord Halifax ask for his aid.
4. The Vatican had a special interest in the nature of the peace. It preferred a compromise. The only way to keep peace without compromise was a full scale military alliance between France, Britain, Poland, and Russia; for it was possible that such a powerful-

---

[37] ADSS 1, no. 171, p. 277.
[38] DBFP, 1919–39, Third Series, vol. VII, p. 495.

looking encirclement would stop Hitler for the moment. The Vatican regarded atheist Russia with repulsion. But they had no need as yet to worry. Poland would not let Russian armies into its lands, in the reasonable fear that once they were in they would not soon be got out. The British were frightened of a whole-hearted commitment to Russia. Though the Vatican did not know it, some of the British thought of the Russo–British negotiations not as a way to get a Russo–British alliance but as a way to hamper a Russo–German alliance. Stalin was cynical and brutal about saving Russia by releasing Hitler into western Poland and western Europe, and in time Russia would pay a terrible penalty for that cynicism. But crooked logic suggested that Stalin and Hitler ought to be friends. Both their countries lost the First World War. Both wanted to overturn the Versailles Treaty. Both made huge territorial gains from the Pact of August 1939.

Therefore the Vatican had no need as yet to fear a military alliance between atheist Russia and democratic Europe. Instead they had to endure the instant destruction of Catholic Poland by two dictators, between whom the cardinals found it hard to decide which was the worse.

4
The winter war, 1939–40

i. The conquest of Poland

Osborne had no doubt what the Curia thought. They had strong sympathy for Britain and France. At the Eucharistic Congress in Cirie near Turin, an English Roman Catholic priest received warm expressions of sympathy from the officials. Cardinal Fossati in a closing address laid all the blame for war on 'the arrogance and pride of one man' and urged his audience of several thousands to pray for the brave men now fighting in the trenches 'to re-establish the reign of truth and justice among the nations'.[1]

Charles-Roux kept assailing the Pope, the Secretary of State, and Tardini, to get a public condemnation of German aggression, especially the bombing of open cities, sinking without warning by submarines, and other inhuman methods of war. Osborne was much less pressing, as was the nature of the man, but wondered whether to do the same. He told Halifax, 'I shall not be deterred by the almost certain prospect of failure.'

Charles-Roux said to Osborne that the Vatican esteemed highly Lord Halifax, and wondered whether Osborne could not *mobilize* Halifax to bring this pressure to bear upon the Pope. Osborne advised Halifax against any such plan. He wrote to Halifax:

I agree with him that your influence at the Vatican is considerable, but for that very reason I should be disposed not to abuse it and to hold its exercise in reserve for vital occasions.

If, however, you considered a denunciation of the inhuman methods of warfare by the Pope a matter of vital importance and will send me a personal message for him I will deliver it, although I cannot vouch for its success.

My French colleague is always endeavouring to galvanise the Vatican into action, if only for the effect of such action on Italian Catholic opinion. I personally think he is inclined to under-estimate their difficulties and limitations. He complains that the present Pope lacks the courage and resolution of his predecessor and does not I think make due allowance for the fact that his Holiness has hardly had time to find his feet or to establish the measure of his authority. Moreover it is unquestionably true that while he may not be as open and uncompromising in public denunciation as Pius XI, whose censure in fact

---

[1] British Consul, Turin, to Sir Percy Loraine, 4 September 1939; FO 371/23791/11.

availed little, his personal influence particularly amongst Italians is enormous, whereas his predecessor's was very slight. There is no doubt that sermons in churches throughout Italy during the past month have done much to consolidate the prevalent Italian desire for peace and that many devout Catholics in Italy have placed their hopes for the preservation of peace upon the Pope. I believe therefore that he has directly or indirectly done more than my colleagues give him credit for. At any rate Italy is not at war and is generally speaking strongly anti-war.

His Holiness is and will always remain open to suggestions of helpful action, but I feel we should avoid any impression of exercising pressure on him and that we should be careful to dissipate neither our own influence at the Vatican nor the Vatican's own authority, but to reserve both for vital purposes and occasions.[2]

Charles-Roux wanted a Pope's condemnation but very soon saw that he would not get what he wanted, not even after the Russians invaded Poland. The Pope would not 'mix in politics'. He would not give any excuse, or any more excuse, for Catholics in Germany or Poland to be persecuted. He would talk in general principles; the wrongness of oppressing people, the need that treaties should conform to divine law and not rest upon naked force, the identity between the European idea and Christian civilization.

Meanwhile the British and French lifted the littlest of fingers to help the Poles in their war; the British because they could not, the French because they imagined that they could not, or saw that the only road to fight Germany lay through neutral Belgium which would not let them pass. They contemplated invading Belgium, saw that the plan was immoral, and let Poland vanish under superior forces. On 17 September the Russians occupied eastern Poland.

This last move filled the Vatican with care for eight million Catholics now under Russian rule. Tardini also half-expected that this was only the first stage of a Russian drive towards the Balkans.[3] He did not expect that Russo-German amity could last long, and wondered if they would quarrel even in the act of dividing Poland.

The Polish ambassador at the Vatican, Papée, asked the Polish government to send Cardinal Hlond to Rome to bring influence to bear upon the Vatican by disclosing the situation of Poland. The manoeuvre was astonishingly rewarded.

Cardinal Hlond arrived and on 21 September was received by Pius XII. He got little but compassion. But two days later Mussolini delivered an aggressive speech beginning 'Poland is liquidated.' At this speech, the Vatican was shocked. Five days later, on 28 September, Cardinal Hlond was given the free use of Radio Vaticana. Hlond

---

[2] FO 371/23791/3–4.   [3] ADSS, 3, 78.

held back nothing. To allow him to say what he said from a neutral station was almost an act of war by a neutral state:

Martyred Poland, you have fallen to violence while you fought for the sacred cause of freedom . . . Your tragedy rouses the conscience of the world . . . On these radio waves, which run across the world, carrying truth from the hill of the Vatican, I cry to you. Poland, you are not beaten! By the will of God you will rise with glory my beloved, my martyred Poland![4]

Charles-Roux was satisfied. If the Pope would not speak himself, he allowed (if he allowed, for the ambassadors were never sure how much control the Pope exercised over Radio Vaticana and knew that he left it a 'relative' independence) – he allowed, or his agents allowed, the Cardinal-archbishop of Poland to say in extreme emotional language what no Pope could say. Probably it was not the Pope's personal doing. The nearest person to a king of Radio Vaticana was the Jesuit general, Ledochowski, a Pole.

Two days later, on 30 September, Pius XII gave audience to a large group of Poles, headed by Cardinal Hlond, Papée the ambassador, and Ledochowski. He talked with affection and compassion; he uttered a faith in the resurrection of Poland; he praised the grandeur of their national history and their deep Catholic faith. He begged them not to despair of providence, and mentioned Lazarus rising from the dead.[5]

Charles-Roux was moderately pleased. He had wanted a condemnation of German and Russian aggression. He said so to Monsignor Montini, and left him a telegram from his leader Daladier in this sense. Daladier said that the Pope had abstained from condemning German aggression for fear of hurting Catholics in Germany. This could not apply to the Russian occupation, and Daladier said how surprised he was at the failure to condemn. He said how they had hoped that Pius XII would follow the example of his predecessor. He had in mind also the need to open the eyes of the Italian people. 'What will happen to the prestige of the Papacy', Charles-Roux asked Montini, 'if it does not react when injustice shouts so loud? What interests can take precedence of that?'

Monsignor Montini said that to condemn could only hurt Catholics in Russia and Germany; that the Pope had spoken the principles with perfect clarity; that the eyes of the Italian people were already open.

[4] Charles-Roux, *Huit Ans au Vatican 1932–1940* (Paris, 1947), pp. 344–5; *Nasza Przeszłość*, 42 (1974), 174ff., which is a biography of Hlond, though brief on the Rome episode. Hlond in Rome was closest to Charles-Roux after Papée and Ledochowski the Poles. His activity thereafter was much hampered by Nazi and Fascist pressure. Hans Frank, the Nazi governor of Poland, said in an interview of 6 February 1940 that if Hlond returned to Poland he would have him shot (*Tägebucher*, 108).

[5] AAS, 31 (1939), 393–6; cf. ADSS, 3, 84.

Papée and the Poles were not pleased. They expected an outright condemnation of both Germany and Russia. They not only expected, they were confident. Their disappointment was the more bitter, and they went round Rome talking angrily about the Pope's indifference to the fate of Poland. The result was an article in *Osservatore Romano* (14 October 1939) which strongly denied the Pope's indifference and cited his speeches. Monsignor Montini started to organize the press to prove that the Pope was 'far from indifferent' to Poland.

Nevertheless, the Pope expected that the rapid destruction of Poland meant the end of the war. On 6 October 1939 he told Cardinal Tisserant at Castel Gandolfo that they would have peace within a few days.[6] He had heard and believed a rumour that the Germans had invented an explosive that nothing could resist; and had heard of a reconsideration in British public opinion, and that some members of the French government hoped for peace. Tisserant denied all this; talked of the high morale in Great Britain and France, and of the question of moral right. Pius XII said 'You know which side my sympathies lie. But I cannot say so.'

Cardinal Hlond went round Rome interviewing the cardinals of the Curia and trying to interest them in the plight of Poland. Most of them were friendly. A few, especially Cardinal Marchetti-Selvaggiani, were unfriendly and taxed Poland with provoking its own destruction by imprudence. But Hlond found the common opinion to be that nothing could be done for Poland. They could not believe that France and Britain were able to beat Germany.

The Pope was hurt that the Poles, and the French after them, were so discontented with his address of 30 September. He said that he had expressed his grief and pity 'in the warmest terms, with all the eloquence of which I am capable'. But they wanted not blessings on themselves but curses on others. 'I could not say more than I said. There are in Germany fifty million Catholics and plenty of Poles, who would suffer in liberty or body for the curses which they asked me to pronounce.' His old memories of the iniquities of Beck rose to his mind. The criticisms of the Pope mounted, and the Poles were the source. Osborne reported it to London. It was being widely said, reported Osborne, that 'papal pronouncements since the outbreak of war have pusillanimously evaded the moral issues involved'.[7]

The eyes of Rome looked further than the eyes of Paris and London which at this time could see only as far as Berlin or Rome. For the Vatican the worst thing of all was the Russian conquest of half Poland.

[6] Charles-Roux to Bonnet, 6 October 1939, QO, Vatican, no. 40, 105.
[7] Charles-Roux to Bonnet, 14 October 1939, QO, Vatican, no. 40, 130; Osborne to Halifax, 1 November 1939, FO 371/23791/27.

This was bad in itself, a big loss to Catholicism. But it was also bad because it was heavy with future ills. Germany and Russia now had a common frontier. That meant, in the eyes of Monsignor Tardini inside the Vatican, war between Germany and Russia, sooner or later. Cardinal Hlond expressed the same opinion inside the Vatican; a Russian–German war must come. And when that war came, one side would win. If the Russians won, atheistic Communism would be all over Central Europe, and then what would happen to Italy and the Catholic Church? If the Germans won, Europe would be Nazi – and then what would happen to Italy and the Catholic Church?

In this mood of foreboding, Monsignor Tardini at least was inclined to encourage the forward Italian policy in the Balkans. For a moment the foreign policy of Italy and the needs of the Church were again in harmony. Since Poland was divided and Czechoslovakia dismembered, the Balkans were going to be dominated by one great Power or another; more likely the Germans, whose pressure on Slovakia was already overwhelming, and pressure on Hungary persistent. The only possible chance of averting this domination of the Balkans lay in Italian advance in the Balkans – the Italians were already in Albania, were looking towards Greece, had an influence already in Yugoslavia. A member of the Italian Foreign Office reported Tardini's opinions thus: 'The Holy See follows with a very lively interest Italian policy in the Balkans which . . . could bring notable gains, above all blocking the German drive into the Balkans, and create for Italy a hegemony. The Holy See holds that the present policy of Italy in the Balkans could much help Europe and especially Italy in the short term, and in the longer term still more.'[8]

On 20 October the Pope issued from Castel Gandolfo the encyclical *Summi Pontificatus*. It was not published in *Osservatore Romano* till 28 October.

The process of preparing the encyclical illustrated both the hesitancy and the care of the Pope. He often made life difficult for the press because he would insist on altering and altering till the last minute, and the media could not get in advance the copy which they needed. This important encyclical made a special example of this reluctance to reach a final form or decision; perhaps a fastidiousness; perhaps a perfectionism which constantly strove to improve; perhaps an innate quality of worry whether this or that phrase would be understood or misunderstood. The growth of this encyclical is best shown by recording the announcements of the *New York Times*: 20 July 1939, Pope to compose an encyclical; 4 August, Pope working on the encyclical; 28 September,

---

[8] AE, Santa Sede, Busta 48, report of 12 October 1939.

encyclical expected; 6 October, encyclical expected at the end of October; 7 October, Pope composing; 8 October, encyclical nearly ready; 18 October, encyclical delayed; 22 October, rumour of contents; 25 October, encyclical expected; 26 October, encyclical delayed; 27–8 October, issue of encyclical.

We possess the drafting changes in manuscript as well as the final text. He spoke of the anguish of his heart at human suffering through war; of the proof, given by war, that without Christian faith men cannot live in civilized society. He condemned the idea that the State has unlimited authority as a doctrine that brings death to the internal life of nations and to their prosperity, as well as the smashing of unity in international society, a unity which can only rest on agreement in the moral principles of the natural law. 'An authority which recognized no limits to its power, and abandoned itself seemingly[9] to an unrestrained expansionism, would tend to conceive the relations between peoples as a struggle, in which might would prevail; and the rule of force would take the place of the noble kingdom of law.' (But this admirable paragraph was suppressed before publication.) He condemned a unilateral breaking of treaties. He considered the idea of a promised New Order, bringing justice and prosperity, and asked whether it would be better. Victory brings external triumph, and very seldom that moderation in the victor which is needed for future justice. A New Order that lasts can only rest on natural law and God's revelation.

He mentioned specially Poland, with its glorious merits in Christian civilization, now receiving the sympathy of the world, and awaiting the hour of resurrection in justice and in peace (a strong sentence added in draft by the Pope's hand). He appealed for peace but a just peace.

Osborne thought the encyclical excellent. 'The Pope', he told Halifax on 3 November, 'has handsomely vindicated himself from the reproach of weakness and pusillanimity in facing the political problems of the day.' He asked that he be allowed to convey to the Pope an expression of appreciation. He thought it especially weighty because the Pope's doctrine of the State was a criticism not only of Hitler but of Mussolini.

The Foreign Office liked what the Pope said, and determined to give it wide publicity. Nichols minuted that it was 'perhaps, in some ways, the most important document the war has yet produced' and wanted Halifax to send a personal message of the government's appreciation. Orme Sargent was afraid that to express gratitude would drive a wedge

---

[9] The word 'seemingly' (*quasi*) was added by the Pope's own hand, just weakening the force of the sentence. ADSS, 1, 318.

between the Pope and Mussolini. Alexander Cadogan said that a *verbal* thanks from Osborne could do good; and Lord Halifax himself did not mind if it was written. Vansittart would not comment. So the mood of the Foreign Office was enthusiastic.[10] They were not alone. Cardinal Hlond was fervent in his gratitude.

The sentences about Poland were repeatedly quoted. In France Lebrun, President of the professed anticlerical republic, spoke of it with high praise. The prime minister Daladier spoke of it with an equal warmth in the Chamber. The French Air Force dropped 88,000 copies over Germany. Everywhere the western world sensed agreement between the principles of international morality asserted by the Pope, and the causes for which Britain and France fought. The Germans allowed it to be read from many pulpits but stopped its printing or distribution. Rosenberg's office accused it of being anti-racialist. The Gestapo ordered enquiries into people who read or tried to distribute the encyclical. The German Foreign Office told von Bergen that the Pope had ceased to be a neutral. Ribbentrop told von Bergen to use the French air drop to show the Pope how his words could help the enemies of Germany. In Poland the German authorities printed false editions of the encyclical, with Germany in the text instead of Poland, to lower the Pope's reputation among the Poles.[11] The encyclical was not the utterance of a weak Pope. In its way it was as strong an attack on Nazi policies as *Mit brennender Sorge* of Pius XI, two and a half years before. The Italians hesitated and then published it.

In December 1939 a Frenchman returned to Paris after an interview with the Pope. He claimed that the Pope warned him that France would be well-advised to distrust Mussolini.[12] It sounds an unlikely thing for that Pope to say. But the Pope's conduct bore out this sense of the Curia that Mussolini's neutrality was insecure. He kept sending private messages to Mussolini thanking him for what he had done to keep the peace. On 21 December the King and Queen of Italy, accompanied by Count Ciano, paid a formal visit to the Pope; and in receiving them the Pope talked of the wisdom and strength of this king-emperor who kept Italy peaceful, and so blessed the King and Queen. Osborne did not fail to observe and report on all these activities. He learnt, with no surprise, that Ciano was the instigator. Sir Andrew Noble in London took too optimistic a view of what was happening:

I think it quite likely that his [Ciano's] motive is in part to make it more difficult for Signor Mussolini to force Italy into war on Germany's side, by mobilizing

[10] FO 371/23791/37–9; ADSS, 3, 111–12.
[11] Robert A. Graham, 'L'enciclica *Summi Pontificatus* e i belligeranti nel 1939', *Civ. Catt.* (October 1984), 139–40; cf. Charles-Roux, *Huit Ans*, pp. 352–3.
[12] FO 371/23791/61.

the Pope and the Royal House to support a policy of moderation. Count Ciano does not agree with Signor Mussolini's policy and I have the impression that he is working to get the power into his own hands. It is not at all impossible that before long the control of Italian policy will pass to Count Ciano.

There is an obvious likelihood that we may be faced with peace proposals and certainly the Holy See and the Italian Government, though for very different reasons, would warmly support any peace proposals which seemed to offer a reasonable chance of acceptance. The Holy See, at least, would sponsor nothing outrageous though it might father some ill-considered proposals.

On the whole I am inclined to the view that internal considerations were the primary cause of this visit; other results may flow from it.[13]

On 6 December 1939 Cardinal Maglione summoned Charles-Roux and Bergen and Osborne and gave them the Pope's proposal for a truce of arms on Christmas Eve and Christmas Day. The Secretary of State thought it not impossible because no one was raiding anyone else at night and what meant most would be the feeling of civilians that they could safely go to mass at midnight. They had a little not very reliable information that public opinion in the three countries would approve, and received a frank request from Cardinal Faulhaber of Munich. All the Powers, of course, refused the plan as unpracticable. Charles-Roux was cross that the French were foolish enough to refuse first, and that the Germans were able to refuse last. Osborne at least said that Britain refused *dolentissimo*, very sadly.[14]

ii. The German conspiracy

Josef Müller was a Bavarian lawyer who at the outbreak of war was taken into the German intelligence, the Abwehr. He was a devout Catholic. The well known leader of the conspirators, Colonel Oster, spotted him and told him that his function was to strengthen the bonds between the Vatican and the German opposition. It was easy to send him to Rome on an Abwehr mission, to use his Vatican contacts to report on Italian and other defeatism, Italian relations to the democracies and whether Italy would enter the war. From Rome he made perfectly straight reports on these matters to Berlin.

In Rome lived the old leader of the Centre Party, Monsignor Kaas, whose role in making the party vote for Hitler's Enabling bill of March 1933 is still one of the most controversial acts of German history. Kaas was an exile in Rome. He earned his living as the Secretary of the Congregation which looked after St Peter's. Josef Müller knew Kaas.

[13] FO 371/23791/81; cf. Osborne to Halifax, 26 December 1939, FO 371/23935/29.
[14] Charles-Roux, *Huit Ans*, p. 355; ADSS, 1, 336 and 344.

He asked him for advice on how to use the Pope as an intermediary to the British.

The German conspirators started by thinking to use the Vatican as a safe place to meet western representatives and did not think of bringing in the Pope. But when the first news came from Rome that discussion in the Vatican might be profitable, someone in the German group asked what guarantee could be got that if the Germans overthrew Hitler the western Allies would not force a Carthaginian peace like Versailles upon Germany. From the widow of one of the conspirators, von Dohnanyi, we have evidence that her husband suggested a secret guarantee of the proposed conditions of peace by the Pope. This guarantee was to be got through Müller.

Early in November 1939 Müller came again to Monsignor Kaas, who put him into touch with Father Leiber the Pope's secretary. Not without doubts whether he was doing what was right, Father Leiber put the plan personally to the Pope. The Pope was to be asked to tell Osborne, for the British government, that the German opposition to Hitler existed in strength. He was asked to elicit honourable peace terms from London, to be negotiated with a new and upright German government after the overthrow of Hitler; and he was himself to be asked to guarantee certain articles of the peace terms beforehand, so as to make the overthrow of Hitler an easier work for the conspirators. Probably at least the Müller–Kaas proposal, which Father Leiber passed to the Pope, was couched in such general terms.

The Pope was being invited to engage in a conspiracy to overthrow a tyrant, and incidentally to put himself and his aides into those dire risks which attend conspirators. Not surprisingly, he took a day for quiet reflection. From many situations during the later life of Pius XII we have evidence that he found it difficult to make up his mind on any weighty decision. Therefore he astonished Father Leiber at the end of his day of meditation, by a decision cast (according to Leiber) in resolute form, to do what the German conspirators asked. He said 'The German opposition must be heard in Britain', and he was willing to do what he could to see that it was heard. On 6 November 1939 Father Leiber assured Josef Müller that the Pope was ready to do 'all he can' for peace.

It was not only typical of Pius XII that he found it hard to make up his mind, it was typical that he made up his own mind. His closest advisers were against or uneasy. Monsignor Kaas at that moment was sceptical about the whole plan. Father Leiber thought that the Pope was going much too far in committing the Papacy to such a risk. The Pope was not doing something because his entourage wanted him to do it. Cardinal Maglione knew nothing about it.

No doubt it made much difference to the Pope that from the time when he was nuncio in Germany he knew General Beck, the leader or at least the figure-head of the German conspirators.

Accordingly the secret chain of communication was set up through the Vatican: General Beck to Colonel Oster, Oster to Josef Müller, Müller to Leiber, Leiber to the Pope, the Pope to Osborne, Osborne to Halifax, Halifax to Chamberlain. Osborne had also a link which did not pass through the Pope or Leiber. He could meet Kaas, who could meet Müller.

From this secret chain of communication there were two astonishing omissions. The first was the French. Neither of the two French embassies in Rome had an inkling of what was going on under their noses, though the two countries were shoulder to shoulder and Osborne was now a close friend of Charles-Roux. A lot of other evidence shows that the German generals were not interested in the French. They wanted to extract undertakings only from Britain and believed that whatever Britain promised the French would have to allow.

The second astonishing omission is the office of Secretary of State. Cardinal Maglione knew nothing about it. His first assistant Monsignor Tardini knew nothing about it. His second assistant Monsignor Montini knew nothing about it. Maglione knew that a group of German generals wanted to get rid of Hitler, because he had a full though sceptical report to this effect from the nuncio in Switzerland.[15] But Leiber later gave evidence that Maglione, and the entire office of the Secretary of State, was excluded from all knowledge of the Vatican's part in the conspiracy. For this exclusion Leiber produced a very curious reason: the lack of rapport between the Pope and his Secretary of State. This is very improbable. There was a better reason. If secret work is afoot do not tell the responsible officials. They are the people who need to deny that anything is happening. Therefore it is better that they do not know anything to be happening. And perhaps there was another reason. The Pope and Father Leiber both knew that in the office of the Secretary of State worked a secret agent of the Axis Powers.

One other man in Rome got to know and was very disturbed by the knowledge. Leiber was a Jesuit. He probably thought himself under obedience to tell his superior. The Jesuit general Ledochowski was a Pole, deeply pro-British, passionately anti-Nazi, a strong and courageous man. In August 1939 the Italian ambassador at the Vatican, Pignatti, told his government that under Ledochowski the whole Jesuit

---

[15] ADSS, 1, 334; the nuncio's informant was a German Benedictine, the ex-Duke of Württemberg.

order was 'drawn up, with extreme decision' against Nazi Germany.[16] Ledochowski told Osborne[17] that the war was a crusade for civilization. But he was disturbed at this conspiracy and it was easy to see why. In the Counter-Reformation the Jesuits won a stinking reputation for secret political intrigue. Since the middle of the eighteenth century every Jesuit general tried to keep his people out of politics, so that no breath of the old smell might lower their name again. And here was one of his Jesuits doing that very thing, engaging in a secret conspiracy to overthrow a government.

He may have been disturbed for another reason. This was all too close to the Pope. Nominally the chain only ran through Leiber. This could perhaps be represented as private enterprise by a Jesuit in his spare time, who in his working day was secretary to the Pope. But no exclusion of Cardinal Maglione could get the Pope out of the chain. He was necessary to the German conspirators. Remembering 1918–19, conscious that they could not trust promises made by the other side, they wanted a mediator, who should be a man of honour and trusted by both sides. Leiber was only useful if he represented the Pope. Pius XII must be engaged. They could not dispense with his mediation.

Osborne's letters and telegrams show a little, but certainly not all, of what went on.

In the week before 1 December 1939 he lunched alone with Monsignor Kaas. Kaas said that he had been approached by Müller – he did not give Müller's name – about the possibility of using the Vatican as an intermediary to get a fair and honourable peace on condition that certain army officers would take over the government of Germany and be rid of the Nazis.[18] Osborne regarded all this as *very·nebulous* and pressed Kaas and found in him a *healthy scepticism*. Kaas said that the Vatican could hardly be involved, and he thought all the negotiation premature, and that some guarantee was needed that Müller's principals could do what they promised to do. Osborne said that he agreed. But he did not rule out the possibility of future contact through the Vatican. This was equal to a roundabout invitation to German conspirators to use the Vatican.

On 8 January Osborne met Kaas again. Osborne noted in his diary,

---

[16] AE, Germania, 1939, Busta 63, Pignatti to AE, 9 August 1939. He asked them not to spread this information so that Ledochowski would continue to have confidence in him and talk freely.

[17] *Diary*, 22 January 1940.

[18] P. Ludlow, 'Papst Pius XII, die britische Regierung und die deutsche Opposition im Winter 1939–40', in *Vierteljahreshefte für Zeitgeschichte* (1974), 328. Evidently Müller began his talks with Kaas and Leiber as early as 6–11 November 1939, and the first agendum was the effect on peace movements of the Encyclical *Summi Pontificatus*. Müller's report in the Bonn Archives is printed in an appendix to H. Grosscurth, *Tägebucher* (Stuttgart, 1970), pp. 506ff.

'At five to tea with Monsignor Kaas, who reported another impending visit.' Kaas said that Müller (he did not give the name) was back in Rome. He seemed to be irritated at the idea. He reasserted that all such negotiations were premature; doubted how anyone could know that the generals could carry out what they undertook or, even if they could, were to be trusted. Monsignor Kaas, reported Osborne, 'strongly resents this endeavour to involve the Vatican in dubious and nebulous intrigue'. At this interview Kaas appears to have asked Osborne that the British press should not speculate on the internal divisions of Germany.[19]

However this mood of scepticism changed on 12 January. The Pope summoned Osborne to a private audience. Pius XII said that he had received the visit of a German representing certain German army chiefs. The Pope said that he knew the names of the generals but preferred not to tell Osborne. They sent a message as follows: a violent offensive was planned in the west, in the month of February, and using Holland as a route. This offensive need never happen. If the German generals could be assured of an honourable peace which would not be *Wilsonian in nature* (i.e. not like the Versailles Treaty, hostile to Germany), they would overthrow Hitler and negotiate a reasonable settlement in eastern Europe – which would restore Poland and Czecho-Slovakia but keep the union with Austria.

The Pope was infinitely cautious. He

said that this communication had been made to him, but that he had not been asked to put it forward . . . At any rate he had felt that his conscience would not be quite easy unless he sent for me. He wished to pass the communication on to me purely for information. He did not wish in the slightest degree to endorse it or to recommend it.

Osborne made some critical comments – the hopeless vagueness of it – and the Pope then said, 'perhaps, after all, it was not worth proceeding with the matter and he would therefore ask me to regard his communication to me as not having been made'. Osborne refused this 'promptly'. He said, 'I refuse to have the responsibilities of His Holiness's conscience loaded on to my own.'

Osborne asked whether he could guarantee the good faith of the generals, and the Pope said that he could not. Osborne asked whether he could guarantee that the generals could carry out what they undertook and he said that he could not.

He begged Osborne to regard the matter as absolutely secret. 'If anything should become known,' he said, 'the lives of the unnamed

[19] Osborne to Halifax, 9 January 1940; printed in Ludlow, 'Papst Pius XII', pp. 329–30.

German generals would be forfeit.' He said that if Osborne ever had a message about it, he could ask to see him at any time.[20]

Never in all history had a Pope engaged so delicately in a conspiracy to overthrow a tyrant by force.

Osborne, who was not yet nervous that his diary might be burgled, dared to record:

12 January. Bad weather again. I saw the Pope at 11 and talked with him for half an hour. He was very well and charming. He gave me a personal message for Halifax and enjoined secrecy on me . . . Back to Chancery, and then to lunch at Embassy . . . Told Percy [Loraine] about my talk with His Holiness. After, back to Chancery to write private letter . . . [indecipherable] . . . to Halifax to go by Bag on Monday.

Charles-Roux was interested. What was happening between Osborne and the Pope? Osborne refused to say.

13 January (after playing golf) Back to tea, to which Charles-Roux came, and most indiscreetly tried to worm out the purpose of my audience yesterday . . .

Someone keen-sighted among the French observed the dry information that the Pope received Osborne, and realized that the French had uniquely been told nothing of what had happened. They demanded to be informed. William Strang at the Foreign Office gave the French ambassador the news that a German emissary approached the Pope with a suggestion of overthrowing Hitler and the Pope took no responsibility. He did not pass on the meat that followed.

On 25 January Osborne received an answer from Halifax. Halifax told him that they felt a duty to tell Daladier in Paris of the substance. Osborne's attention was almost diverted by another letter in the Bag from Sir Alexander Cadogan, offering him the post of ambassador at Santiago in Chile. He knew that he could not refuse if they insisted but would loathe to go.

I replied by same day's Bag that I would rather stay here and thought I could be more useful here; that I had no real ambassadorial ambition, except as regards pension; and that I thought I could do more good here and now than in Santiago.

He wrote a letter to the Pope, and delivered it to Cardinal Maglione for delivery to the Pope. Osborne's letter to the Pope has not yet been found.

Diary 6 February 1940: The strain of waiting for a decision on whether I am to go to Santiago (the idea is really hideous to me) is as severe as the strain of waiting for Hitler's offensive.

[20] Osborne to Halifax, 12 January 1940, Halifax Papers, FO 800/318; printed in Ludlow, 'Papst Pius XII', pp. 330ff.

Diary 7 February 1940: Interesting talk with Arborio Mella, the Pope's Maestro di Camera.

This entry was a marvellous understatement, and showed that Osborne dared not put more detail into his diary. That day the Pope summoned Osborne.

This time he took trouble to see that the audience could not be reported. Osborne was not to dress for an audience, and if he was asked as he came was to say that he had an interview with the Maestro di Camera. He was to go to the office of the Maestro di Camera and thence be conducted. Osborne felt the whole proceeding to be comically cloak-and-dagger.

The Pope said that he had been approached again by Müller. He would not give his name, nor the name of the German general whom he represented, though he would say that the general was well-known and sufficiently important to be taken seriously. He said that he withheld the name as he did not wish inadvertently to be the cause of the man's death if it should come out. Nothing could say more clearly that Pius XII was engaging in this affair though he had not absolute confidence in the secrecy.

The Pope had four pages of typescript which Osborne could see to be in German. He talked of Hitler's plans for an invasion of Belgium; of how Hitler boasted he would be in the Louvre by the summer and that one of his first cares would be to find a more worthy site for the Venus de Milo.

Then he talked of the planned coup in Germany. The coup might not succeed at once. There might even be civil war in Germany. The anti-Hitler government would have to start as a military dictatorship. But it would soon hand over power to a 'democratic' government, 'conservative', 'moderate', 'decentralized'. It would be a federation. Austria would be within the federation. Poland and non-German Czecho-Slovakia would be independent. This new democratic government would then negotiate for a reasonable peace. What it wanted the Pope to get was an assurance from Britain that a Germany which included Austria could be guaranteed as a basis for peace negotiations. That is, as Osborne saw, what was wanted was an assurance that the Germany of the Munich settlement would be maintained in a future peace.

Osborne attacked its vagueness as strongly as before: what guarantee of authenticity, how probable the German ability to do what was suggested, how likely the future German government to be less aggressive than the Nazis?

The Pope made no attempt to defend it or even to recommend serious consideration. He said he intensely disliked even having to pass it on and he would no more expect an answer than on the previous occasion; but his conscience would not allow him to ignore it altogether lest there might be conceivably one chance in a million of its serving the purpose of sparing lives.[21]

He told Osborne that he did not want Cardinal Maglione to know. If Osborne ever had anything to communicate he should do it through the Maestro di Camera. The Pope insisted that nothing be put on paper except Osborne's letter to Halifax. Osborne told London that this time he was much more strongly inclined, from the Pope's attitude, to believe the offer genuine.

This report went to Halifax and thence to Chamberlain and thence to King George VI, who cheerfully remarked that he already knew, through his cousin Queen Marie of Yugoslavia, that there was a plot to 'bump off Hitler'. But very few other people in London were told, not even the Cabinet; not Churchill, nor Butler, nor Vansittart. Apart from the King, the Prime Minister and the Foreign Secretary, the papers went only to the top professionals in the Foreign Office, Cadogan, Orme Sargent, Strang; and their immediate juniors, Kirkpatrick, Makins, Frank Roberts, and G. P. Young.[22]

The next document contains undated notes in Neville Chamberlain's hand. It sounds uncompromising;

1. Great Britain will do nothing without France.
2. Great Britain would be willing to discuss any conditions asked for with France if convinced that business was meant.
3. It would be impossible to enter in[to] discussions with France on the basis of such vague and unvouched-for proposals.
4. If progress is to be made a definite programme must be laid down and vouched for authoritatively.

That is, let us know who the people are and get them to put their proposals down in detail. Then we will consider it as long as we may bring in the French.

On 17 February Halifax wrote to Osborne asking him to keep open the line of communication. The Pope should be told that the British were ready to discuss; that the French must be brought in; that they must receive definite proposals. With regard to the guarantee of a Munich Germany, Osborne was to say that though they did not look to gain territory, they looked for future security. The plan of decentralization might help this. We thought that Austria should be given the free choice whether or not it went into the federation.

Thus Halifax's letter, though faithful to Chamberlain's notes, was

[21] Halifax Papers, FO 800/318; printed in Ludlow, 'Papst Pius XII', pp. 333–5.
[22] Ludlow, 'Papst Pius XII', p. 325.

less uncompromising by far in its tone. The British were taking the plan seriously. One thing is clear: if Hitler had vanished, both Chamberlain and Halifax were willing to return to the old policy of appeasement, because they could apply it to a reasonable Germany and not to Hitler.

The day before this letter went, Osborne 'in my footman's livery' took Lady Halifax and her son to see the Pope. The Pope was sad and austere at first, but later bloomed. He talked of a 'just peace, but a solid and durable one'. He said that all he wanted was 'the salvation of souls and the relieving of sorrow' (Osborne's Diary *ad diem*). Then he drew Osborne aside, away from Lady Halifax, for a private message. He said that the Germans confirmed their wish to change their government. Osborne said 'If they want a change of government, why don't they get on with it?'[23]

Osborne noted in his diary for 21 February 1940: 'Mgr Kaas to luncheon, and very interesting as usual.' Probably at this meal, where he dare not specify the talk, Osborne learnt a little more of what the Pope said, that the Germans 'wanted' to change their government. It must have been at this meeting that Osborne used Kaas as an agent to tell the German conspirators that the British were growing impatient because nothing happened.[24]

The Bag did not arrive till 26 February and then contained Halifax's letter of 17 February. Osborne was enjoying his role as a most secret mediator. He communicated the substance to the Pope the same day. Two days later (28 February) Cardinal Maglione went to lunch with Osborne. Probably Maglione still knew nothing. But we know very little of what now went on between the various agents engaged in this conspiracy. We know that the substance of the message, which Osborne gave the Pope, went from the Pope to Father Leiber, and from Father Leiber to Josef Müller, and thence to Germany. We know also that for more than a month the Pope heard no more from either side.

On 4 March Osborne had a long talk with an unknown whom he recorded under the pseudonym or translation of Goldpiece. He was a Jewish anti-Nazi, a doctor called Stückgold, who took refuge from Nazi rule in Rome and remained in touch with German groups critical of Hitler and henceforth passed his information quietly to Osborne.

After the war Father Leiber remembered that all through February and into March the few who knew anything inside the Vatican were tense, waiting for something to happen.[25] If the memory is right, they concealed it perfectly. Osborne's papers show no clear sign of tension.

About this date someone gave the Foreign Office cause to think that Monsignor Kaas was not to be trusted. This alleged conspiracy could

---

[23] Ibid., p. 337. [24] Cf. Müller's memory in 1952, ibid., p. 307.
[25] Ibid., p. 319.

be organized by Hitler. Someone suggested that Kaas was a secret agent of Hitler at the Vatican. The Foreign Office in London, besieged by Nazi peace feelers along various routes, had every reason to begin by distrusting what came out of Rome. They were more than ready to suspect that Monsignor Kaas played a double game, and to think it quite probable when someone told them that Kaas was in the service of the Gestapo. British intelligence had this reason for their suspicion of Kaas. Attached loosely to the office of the Vatican Secretariat of State was an employee who was also in the service of the Gestapo and his name began with the letter K. (Monsignor Kaas was not an employee in the Secretariat of State. For Kurtna, the spy in question, see p. 176.) Philip Nichols wrote from London to Osborne a *most secret* letter (12 March 1940) which has not survived because they required him to burn it and he obeyed. (The London draft is R 3237 G but this was not accessible to me.) The letter contained first, the suspicion of the British that Monsignor Kaas was under the control of the Gestapo and their anxiety that he had such easy access to the Pope; and secondly that German spies might be planted among the German seminarists in Rome.

Osborne's letter of reply came as near to contempt as was possible for so unscornful a man. The German seminarists, he told London, 'are dressed in the brightest possible scarlet from head to foot, which does not conduce to the work of secret agents. I doubt if they ever see anyone but other students of other nationalities, and the most they could do would be to seduce them from their loyalties.' As to Kaas: he was living quietly, an exile, working hard because he had charge of the repairs and the vestments of St Peter's. He had his own house in the Vatican, and Osborne saw him occasionally. He believed him to be 'strongly anti-Nazi but a good patriot'. He told London that if they had reliable information he must warn the Pope. He said humorously that he was willing to ask Kaas whether he was a German agent; but 'that seems too obvious to be desirable'.[26] All this Osborne played down delightfully in his diary:

17 March: I am very interested indeed in the information I am sending home, and glad to think that it justifies to some extent my refusal of promotion to Santiago.

18 March: Monsignor Montini to luncheon, wearing his squeaky shoes and charming, as always.

According to the German evidence (nothing in Osborne's extant papers corresponds) the Germans asked for no invasion immediately

[26] FO 371/24962/72.

after the coup. Chamberlain and Halifax greatly valued the Pope's role as mediator: that is, they put a high value on his willingness to act as a guarantor for the authenticity and respectability of the mysterious messages. The questions to the British included whether certain persons would be acceptable in a non-Nazi government – Schacht was mentioned.

There is evidence that no paper passed. Leiber said that he once saw a document in Osborne's hand. Osborne spoke to the Pope. The Pope made notes. The Pope talked to Leiber and may even have given him the notes. Leiber talked to Müller, and once wrote down a sheet on paper with the Vatican watermark. Osborne saw a typescript of four pages in the Pope's hand. But the Pope did not show Osborne the typescript, nor give him a copy.

Messages from government to conspirators passed orally through three intermediaries – between Osborne who had paper, and Beck who had paper though more concealed paper; the three being the Pope, Leiber, Müller. Still, more messages passed than we so far have in the papers of the Public Record Office.

On the German side were three documents, none of which now exists. Müller destroyed all his papers – except a visiting card of Leiber and a single sheet of paper, with the Vatican watermark, on which were written the British conditions. These two scraps of paper were used in Germany to prove to General Halder the genuineness of what was going on. The visiting card had writing on it. The writing said: 'Today O was with my chief. He told him something which will cause you to go home at once. We must have a talk about it today.'[27] Therefore the visiting card was written on 12 January or 7 February or (probably) 16 February. The single sheet of paper had the handwriting of Father Leiber.[28] It vanished. But it had the British conditions, for from it Dohnanyi made a fuller report, the report now known to historians as the X-report. This X document was laid before the commanding generals Halder and Brauchitsch in the spring of 1940. It looks as though the Gestapo discovered this X-report among the papers which they found in the safe when they raided the Abwehr office at Zossen on 22 September 1944. Halder saw it again during his imprisonment but that is the last trace of the document. It was probably burnt with other Gestapo papers in 1945.[29]

The best evidence for the contents of the X-report comes from Ulrich

---

[27] Kurt Sendtner, 'Die deutsche Militäropposition im ersten Kriegsjahr', in *Die Vollmacht des Gewissens* (Munich, 1956), p. 454.
[28] H. C. Deutsch, *The conspiracy against Hitler in the Twilight War* (Minneapolis, 1968), p. 289.
[29] P. Hoffmann, *Widerstand, Staatsstreich, Attentat*, 3rd edn (Munich, 1979), pp. 720–1, note 299.

von Hassell's Diary for 16 March 1940, when he was shown the papers. Hassell was impressed with the lengths to which the Pope was prepared to go for the sake of Germany. Halifax (Hassell learnt) had talked of 'the decentralization of Germany', and of a plebiscite for the Austrians to decide whether or not they continued to be united to Germany. The Pope (Hassell learnt) had told the Germans – that is, told Leiber to tell Müller to tell the Germans – that he did not believe these conditions to be an obstacle to agreement.

Osborne's Diary for 27 March notes: 'At 5 to tea with Monsignor Kaas who was not particularly interesting'. This is an understatement. At this tea party Kaas told Osborne that the German conspirators had laid aside their plans for the time being. He also said that the coming German offensive would be carried out with every form of horror, microbes, gas. Osborne doubted even Hitler's capacity to use microbes. Kaas was sure of it. Osborne thought that someone meant to curdle his blood. And Osborne was probably right. The Nazis were well capable of seeing that Kaas received information about the coming terror, so that he would tell the Pope, who would tell the French and the British and lower their morale in face of the coming onslaught.

When the Pope saw Osborne on 30 March he was almost aggrieved. He had learnt that the British had received other peace feelers by other routes, and was vexed. Osborne did not say why this should have vexed him but it is obvious. First it lowered the whole importance of the delicate manoeuvres on which they were engaged, and secondly he, Pius XII, had endangered the Papacy without necessity and in vain. But Osborne recorded no sense of grievance in his *Diary*:

30 March: Bad morning. Very worried over finance . . . Then John [May, Osborne's manservant] lost his temper and shouted at me which is intolerable. To Chancery and then to the Vatican where I had an audience with the Pope at 11. He was as enchanting as ever; as easy and friendly; and very interesting. After to see Maglione . . .

2 April: I am completely baffled over the stories of imminent German blitzkrieg and fall of Ciano. Anyway if latter materializes I shall pack up for the Vatican.

3 April: . . . I have sent no sensational telegrams for several days.

5 April: To Vatican. Met a friend who warned me that, for reasons, they could not see me these days. John [May] told me I have a plain-clothes policeman watching the house – I can only suppose for watching my visitors. Two things together intriguing and disagreeable.

6 April: To see Cardinal [Maglione] who was precariously optimistic. Also to see Montini, whom I like so much and who will be, in my opinion, next Pope but one, or possibly next.

On 8 April the one plain-clothes policeman on watch over him turned into two.

The British lost a chance. In a dictatorship like Hitler's they could hardly expect that conspirators should come out of their anonymity and give their ranks and dates of birth. This mediator was not a lightweight. But the fact was, they were not quite sure that what they were being offered was anything like enough. They were being offered a Germany minus Hitler, it was true; but they were also being offered the Germany of the Munich settlement, and furthermore a Germany with its armies intact. After what happened they could hardly bear the idea of returning only to the state of affairs of October 1938. Osborne told the Pope on 16 February: 'Even if the government [of Germany] was changed, I don't see how we could make peace as long as the German military machine remained intact.'[30]

They were, in retrospect, wrong. To get rid of obsessive anti-semites from a government and to restore Poland to independence would have averted the Final Solution even if bad things otherwise happened. But the British could not know beforehand of a Final Solution and would not have believed it if they had been told. At least, we may say that in retrospect they would have been absolutely wrong if they had confidence that the German generals would do what they promised. They had no confidence that the generals could even if they would. Their attitude resembled that of Bishop Preysing of Berlin when he later learnt of the conspiracy. He dismissed it contemptuously with the words, 'They'll dither about till the Russians reach Berlin.'[31] In this view of the matter there was an uncomfortable amount of truth.

These two conversations with Osborne, and the consent to be a mediator between Beck and Halifax, represent a crisis of moral decision in the career of Pius XII who was slowly passing into such moral torment. He was under no one's influence. The powerful Cardinal Maglione was excluded. The Pope risked the fate of the Church in Germany and Austria and Poland and perhaps he risked more. He probably risked the destruction of German Jesuits. He could not be absolutely certain that the principals were trustworthy. Patently it was crucial that when he was Cardinal Pacelli he had known Müller, for he could hardly have trusted the word of Kaas unsupported. But, even if Müller was trustworthy, he might be found out and tortured into talking. The Pope could prevent paper being passed but he could not prevent the risk of Germans intercepting Osborne's messages to Halifax or the danger of a spy in the Quai d'Orsay if Halifax insisted on telling Daladier. He disliked what he was doing intensely, and it is not

[30] Ludlow, 'Papst Pius XII', p. 357.   [31] Sendtner, 'Militäropposition', p. 472.

surprising that he disliked. He took this big risk solely because his political experience saw that, however unsuccessful this plan was likely to turn out, it was probably the one remaining chance of halting the coming invasion of Holland and France and Belgium, of saving untold bloodshed, and bringing peace back to Europe.

While these high matters were in train, rumours were passed of a new German willingness for peace. The British government feared lest the Pope lend himself to the plan of proposing peace, with or without the aid of President Roosevelt. In the first two months of 1940 even Osborne was apprehensive. A Polish refugee, Count Horodyski, who was a friend of Ledochowski, the Jesuit general, reported in London that Ledochowski was disturbed about a coming peace offensive by the Pope under German, Italian and neutral pressure. Horodyski wanted London to send Cardinal Hinsley to Rome for ten days to tell the Pope what Britain thought about a peace offensive. 'As his Eminence is not very intelligent, Count Horodyski thought it would be preferable that he should be accompanied by Bishop Mathew'; and the visit could be followed by other visits, from another English archbishop and perhaps from Cardinal Villeneuve of Quebec. 'The latter might possibly ginger up His Holiness as the French Canadians regard the present war as a holy crusade.'[32] Horodyski regarded Godfrey the Apostolic Delegate as useless for these purposes, because he 'had mentally lost his nationality, and . . . viewed matters just as much from the Vatican point of view as any Italian'. The Foreign Office did not agree with this view of Godfrey who seemed to them wholly British, and disliked the idea of sending out Cardinal Hinsley or any other cardinal. However, they consulted Osborne.

By then (13 February 1940) Osborne was persuaded that the Pope could not be 'inveigled' into a peace offensive, for the moment. He saw no merit in the sending of Cardinal Hinsley, and agreed with London on the Britishness of Monsignor Godfrey.

The intelligence agents were apt to pick up Vatican rumour, their heads in London reported it to the Foreign Office, the Foreign Office asked Osborne, and Osborne replied that it was very unlikely.

From an Austrian refugee at Stockholm they picked up the story, and told the Foreign Office, that Cardinal Pizzardo was secretly working for Count Ciano, and that he even worked behind Cardinal Pacelli's back while he was his Under-Secretary of State; and they suggested that the object of his intrigues was private ambition, to supplant Cardinal Maglione as Secretary of State. The Foreign Office was not likely to believe these stories but had formed the impression,

---

[32] FO 371/24959/213.

and stated, that this Pope was 'more open to influences than his predecessor'. They asked Osborne. To such enquiries Osborne had a direct approach:

the picture does not fit the Pizzardo I know. I will go and see him shortly and sound him about these stories.

I think it is probably true that the present Pope is more open to influence than his predecessor – at any rate in the best sense; that is to say, he is more ready to listen and to weigh opinions, and less rigid and uncompromising in his own views and actions. But it does not at all follow that he is unstable and easily swayed, and I do not think that this is the case.[33]

iii. American intervention

In February 1940 a new turn was given to the diplomatic game by the arrival of an American accredited to the Pope: Myron Taylor.

Ever since Pius XI made the Papacy so popular among democracies, men high in the American government argued whether it would be useful to have a diplomat attached to the Vatican. In the early summer of 1939 the common interest of Pope and President Roosevelt in keeping the peace, or even in mediating, strengthened Roosevelt's opinion that a diplomat in Rome was desirable. The despatch of Joseph Kennedy, US ambassador in London, to the funeral of Pope Pius XI had more than respect as its motive. It was part of the President's preparation for something more. Even as early as June 1939 the American press talked of the possibility.

It was not easy. Till 1867 the Americans were represented at the Vatican. The Pope of 1867 was very unpopular with democrats and liberals, and the American Senate cancelled the money to pay the stipend of a diplomat in Rome. Three years after that the Pope lost his state to the Italians. This created a new situation. The American constitution insisted on separation between Church and State, and no favour, even in ceremonial, to a particular denomination. If the Pope had a State, the State might receive an American diplomat. If he had no State, an American diplomat in Rome would be a way of favouring one religious denomination above others. Protestants in the United States pointed this out loudly and repeatedly.

The Lateran Treaty of 1929 recreated a State for the Pope. But the constitutional argument against a diplomat in Rome was established. If President Roosevelt tried to send an official diplomat to Rome, he

---

[33] FO 371/24935/64, Osborne to Nichols, 24 February 1940; cf. Randall to Nichols, 13 February 1940, FO 371/24935/56–8.

could hardly expect the Senate to provide the money. He would please a lot of Catholic voters but alienate more Protestant voters. The President discovered a way to overcome the difficulty. He would send, not an envoy of the US government, but a personal representative of himself. And he would find a man who needed no pay.

Myron Taylor started as a banker and became President (1932–8) of the United States Steel Corporation. Nevertheless he was a strong supporter of Roosevelt and his New Deal, a humanitarian and an ardent Democrat. He was also a godly episcopalian, with a keen interest in what Churches could do for moral order. He had experience of the refugee problem of Europe, and helped to devise an (abortive) scheme for getting German Jews allowed into Latin America. He was host to Cardinal Pacelli when he visited New York in 1936. He admired the earlier Mussolini, and thought the conquest of Abyssinia excellent, and believed in the civilizing mission of the Italian people. He had two estates of his own near Florence. Here was a man who was a friend of the President; knew the Pope; cared about what the Pope stood for; had experience of refugees; needed no pay; and had a chance of being trusted by the Italians.

The Vatican had every reason to want an American mission. For nearly three-quarters of a century it vainly wanted diplomatic relations with the United States. And it had strong present motives for encouraging the mission. Mussolini was not yet in the war. But he might join Hitler any week. If he joined Hitler the isolation of the Vatican inside Axis Europe would look terrifying. A formal link with the United States appeared to be one of the life-lines to a wider international world.

At Christmas time (23 December 1939) President Roosevelt sent a Christian message to the Pope and announced the despatch of his personal ambassador to the Vatican. The ostensible purpose was care of refugees. The President could not escape criticism from Protestant groups in America who claimed that this mission contradicted the separation between Church and State decreed in the American constitution. Roosevelt brushed off these protests with equanimity.

Myron Taylor was a rhadamanthine kind of man; not pompous, but he seemed to survey humanity as from a pedestal. One Italian observer, who sent to see him when he was ill in bed, had the impression that despite his prone position he was still sitting on a throne; and yet that beneath the august presence was a kindly person who was perfectly willing to listen.[34] After he arrived in Rome and was

[34] A. Tarchiani, *Dieci anni tra Roma e Washington* (Milan, 1955), pp. 15–17; cited Ennio di Nolfo, *Vaticano e Stati Uniti 1939–52* (Milan, 1978), pp. 9–10.

received by the Pope, Osborne and Charles-Roux both found him large in stature and generous in heart. Almost as important was his assistant Harold Tittman who had worked as a secretary at the American Embassy to the Quirinal and was an old friend of Osborne. Taylor instantly turned the pair into a trio. He kept in continuous communication with Osborne. His rooms in the Hotel Excelsior became a normal place for the three to meet. Charles-Roux and Osborne longed for the Americans to tell the Pope that the American army would intervene.

But Taylor was frank with Charles-Roux and Osborne that he was sent to advise Roosevelt (1) on whether he could usefully promote a negotiated peace; (2) on how he could help to restrain Mussolini from entering the war. To the relief of the French and British he soon satisfied himself that he could do nothing useful about a negotiated peace.

Taylor found it an advantage to be a personal envoy from Roosevelt and not the ambassador of the United States. He could do what he liked. He went through the wearisome protocol, like any other ambassador, of calling formally on all the other ambassadors. But he was exempt from the attentions of visiting Americans who wanted 'audiences, interviews, tickets, automobiles, bed, board, unlimited personal attention and the other favours expected, and exacted, of American diplomats abroad'.[35] His arrival had this additional importance, that henceforth his papers make a new source for the historian.

Roosevelt's original instructions to Taylor survived among Taylor's papers at Hyde Park. There was a generality, historic in the relations between the United States and Popes; the relation between liberalism and religious freedom with Catholic teaching; and there were particular points – the Fascist American priest Father Coughlin, the friendliness to Fascism of the Archbishop of Chicago, and how to find good men to appoint to sees. In short, Myron Taylor was sent to Rome for the domestic purposes of the United States. In the moment he linked with Osborne and Charles-Roux his duties and his perspectives were more international.

In the campaign to keep Italy out of the war, London used both its missions in Rome to make distinctions between dictators. They kept saying that Britain was only against bad dictators. They explained how they had friendships with authoritarian regimes. We 'regard it as no business of ours what kind of regime is chosen by other countries'. They mentioned British friendship with Salazar in Portugal, and with Turkey. They realized that Mussolini must think the fall of Nazism spelt the fall of Fascism thereafter, and wished to dispel his fear. They

[35] Osborne to Halifax, 3 April 1940, FO 371/24958/192.

sent messages through the embassy to the Quirinal, through Osborne, and through Monsignor Godfrey the Apostolic Delegate in London.[36]

The one thing that no one envisaged, in this optimistic endeavour to hold Mussolini in neutrality, was the collapse of the Allied forces in France.

[36] Cf. especially Foreign Office to Sir N. Charles in Rome, 18 April 1940, FO 371/24958/199–200.

5

The Italian entry into the war

i. The freedom of the Osservatore Romano

By early April 1940 everyone expected a German invasion of France soon and the real European war to begin; and everyone saw that if Hitler invaded France, and especially if he prospered in invading France, Mussolini could hardly fail to join the Germans. He was tied to Hitler by too many public commitments, and would seem to the world to be the sham that he was, all pugnacity of speech and no fight. Experts who knew something of Italian armour, who studied Italian industry, and were aware of the Italian economy, knew that Italy could only fight a war as a very junior partner and even then the war must be short. But everyone saw that unless the French, with British aid, defeated the German armies easily, Mussolini had to go to war. And dictators can only live from one resounding success to another. The Fascist dictator must be seen to win another war; or at least, to sit with the victors at the peace conference, so that he could gain what he wanted from the French – Savoy, Nice, Corsica, Tunis, Djibouti.

By March 1940, still more in April, the threat of Italy joining the war came nearer; in proportion as the German invasion of the West came nearer.[1]

A difference of view appeared between the British ambassador to the Quirinal and the British Minister to the Vatican. Sir Percy Loraine knew Italy less well than Osborne. But he had better opportunities of objective enquiries, and a bigger staff; and his staff told him that they observed a lot of bellicose Italian noise but almost no preparations for war and that these noises were still bluff and that the British government need not yet be too alarmed. Osborne, on the contrary, could sense the change in the atmosphere. It was not objective enquiries into preparation, but it was an unmistakably new Italian mood. 'Atmosphere very electric . . . in social contacts', he recorded in his diary on

---

[1] For the anxieties in March–April, see especially: DDI, 3, no. 536; no. 596 (Alfieri to Ciano, 20 March 1940 – the Vatican still trusts Mussolini's balance and realism); DDI, 4, no. 189 (the Pope to Mussolini, 24 April 1940); no. 195 (Mussolini's reply), cf. no. 276 (the informing of Hitler); FRUS, 1940, II, 686.

14 April. He began to burn papers, records in his files which – if the Italians entered the war and walked into the Vatican – would not only hurt the British. After the conspiracy of the winter war, the Italian discovery of his records would damage the Pope and his men very badly, and would probably lead to the execution of several German generals. Still he hoped that all this was unnecessary caution, but he was sufficiently pessimistic to think it prudent to burn.

I still believe it to be more likely that they [these precautions] are superfluous than not, but by a very narrow margin. In dealing with the modern dictator the laws of logic and common sense count no more than moral scruples and ethical principles and one has to be prepared for anything.

Afraid that London would think him alarmist and ridiculous, he was perfectly frank to the Foreign Office in explaining his burning of paper: 'In these blitzkrieging days I did not wish to run any risk of telegrams or despatches being found which could be used against either the Vatican or other sources of information.'[2]

These activities, and the reports that went with them, caused a minor quarrel between Osborne and Loraine. Osborne's burning of paper, and his talk of moving into the Vatican, showed that he feared Italian entry into the war at any moment. Since Loraine was reporting more optimistically, the two sources of information in Rome sang discordant tunes. Loraine told London (17 May) that in any case he mistrusted a situation where two independent agents reported from one place, and that he disliked what he took to be Osborne's main source of information.

Monsignor Pucci, that doubtful clergyman who made a living by selling information to embassies, was trusted by no one; but everyone bought his information. Loraine believed that Pucci was a German agent, and that the Germans thus fed Osborne with false information and alarm. Certainly Pucci was as willing to sell information to the Germans as to any other buyer.

Loraine had what he called a heart-to-heart talk with Osborne. 'I told him that I had an uneasy feeling that his principal and most frequent informant was, if not a tool, at least a dupe of the Germans. That would account for his occasionally getting some things right, so that the remainder should find credence with us.' Loraine asked only that he should be passed the information where it concerned the Fascist government. Osborne agreed.

In London the Foreign Office was more impressed with the pre-cautions of Osborne than with the sang-froid of Loraine. For they

---

[2] Osborne to Philip Nichols, FO 371/24963/16.

secretly asked Osborne whether he would like to take his own wireless transmitter with him if he had to move into the Vatican. Osborne refused the dangerous offer.[3]

The business of trying to keep Italy out of the war grew tenser as each day passed. Through Loraine the British government could make frantic efforts at the eleventh or twelfth hour to persuade the Italians that they would do better by staying out of the war; but since they could only look plausible if they persuaded the French to offer territory and the French had no such idea in their heads, these efforts were not promising. Meanwhile they had the Pope who was an Italian, wanted peace, was expected to want peace, could say that he wanted peace, and longed to stop Italy entering the war. Osborne had no need to encourage the Pope or the Curia in these sentiments. They could see, even more plainly than he could see, how an Italian war would hamper the work of the Church. They might be weak about Fascism but the quasi-persecution of Catholicism by the Nazis and then the terrible events in Poland made them loathe Nazis and they found it hard to bear the possibility that Italy, most Catholic-minded of countries, should ally itself with an anti-semitic and anti-Christian and murderous government.

Therefore Osborne's problem was not the opinions of the highest officers in the Vatican who wanted to keep Italy out of the war as ardently as the British or the French. His problem was different. Under the rising tension the Pope started to come under pressure, if not actual threats. How to protect, sustain or encourage him under German or Fascist threats, this was no easy task for the British and their minister.

For the purpose of influencing the Italian government, the Pope possessed four main instruments. First was Vatican radio, believed to be the direct mouthpiece of the Pope. Actually it had almost as much independence from the Pope as the BBC had of the British government. It was placed under the Jesuits.

Second, the Pope had the possibility of influencing Mussolini personally – officially, through Borgongini Duca, or privately through the Jesuit Father Tacchi Venturi. He knew that Mussolini's friendship with Catholicism was an important foundation for the Fascist regime, and that therefore the Duce ought to be touched if the head of the Catholic Church spoke of peace. In fact, the tenser the atmosphere and the nearer to war, the less influence of this type was possible. The best hope was to work on one or two of Mussolini's own circle who were still against the war – his son-in-law and Foreign Minister Count Ciano being the chief. But to encourage this secret and private influence Osborne could do nothing.

[3] FO 371/24935/89.

The Pope also had the possibility of formal pronouncements – bulls, briefs, excommunications, etc.; in the situation not real possibilities. If he declared openly for peace it must be in very general terms, for under the Lateran Treaty he was committed to refraining from interference in Italian politics, and a decision for war or peace was the ultimate political decision. Under the Treaty he kept the right to make the influence of the Holy See felt in matters of international peace and moral guidance. Such a right fully justified intervention in general terms. In general terms he continued to appeal, in briefs or sermons, for peace. He congratulated Mussolini on his efforts to keep the peace. Osborne had no need whatever to encourage the Pope in this, except by words of gratitude afterwards. But these papal endeavours to keep Italy out of the war affected the Pope's fourth and main instrument of influence, and here Osborne could not but be concerned.

The Pope had a newspaper, printed in Italian, the *Osservatore Romano*. Its circulation in normal times was modest, for the world does not always find ecclesiastical news exciting. As the war in the north proceeded, and the atmosphere in the south grew menacing, the subscribers to the *Osservatore* increased extraordinarily. It was the only newspaper in Italian outside the range of Mussolini's censorship. It contained attitudes to Germany, and reports from Allied sources, not found in any other newspaper in the Italian language.

If Italy entered the war, or even if Italy moved towards entering the war, this independence of the *Osservatore* would become intolerable to the Italian government. Thus to sustain the *Osservatore* became an aim of the British government.

The Germans had long hampered German Catholics from receiving the *Osservatore*. From early in April 1940 Italian pressure began. Dino Alfieri, the Italian ambassador to the Holy See, complained formally to Cardinal Maglione of the many sermons and 'manifestations' among the churches of Italy in favour of peace, pacifist manifestations at a time when the government was encouraging the military spirit. He complained officially of the attitude of *Osservatore Romano* and demanded that it behave more impartially. Maglione said that the Vatican had given no instructions to churches or bishops to 'intensify' their prayers for peace; that the Vatican had no need to persuade the people to pray for peace because they longed for peace without any persuasion; that the *Osservatore Romano* was different from the Italian newspapers because they took overheated attitudes. He said that he had always recommended the *Osservatore Romano* to be prudent and objective in reporting, and would repeat the advice.

On 25 April Mussolini said publicly: 'The Vatican is the chronic appendicitis of Italy', and was applauded by Farinacci and others.

Borgongini Duca, the nuncio to Italy, thought that this anger was caused by *Osservatore Romano*. Minister Bottai said to Borgongini Duca that the newspaper was well edited; but 'it needs to be careful how it is read and understood by men of the Left. Italy has plenty of them and they are the successors of Giordano Bruno.'[4] He accused it of looking at France and Britain through rose-tinted spectacles. Borgongini Duca said to the minister, 'The *Osservatore* cannot back Italian policy. The Holy See cannot be Fascist. The Pope cannot not talk about peace.' Bottai said, 'Of course.'

Alfieri, the new Italian ambassador to the Holy See, protested to Cardinal Maglione against the *Osservatore*; and Maglione replied uncompromisingly:[5]

The *Osservatore Romano*, though published in the Italian language, is not part of the Italian press. If, as you say, it is different in line, that is not because it has departed from its old line, but because the Italian press is inflamed to a white heat. I don't discuss this. I leave the responsibility where it belongs. But I must repeat that the *Osservatore Romano* cannot follow other newspapers in the way that they are forced to go. I have always recommended the *Osservatore Romano* to be prudent, objective and measured. I can easily repeat the advice. But it is good to reflect on this point: it is in the interests of Italy that the *Osservatore Romano* continues on its present line; for everywhere, especially abroad, it is seen to be truly the organ of the Holy See, impartial and serene. Only on this condition can it say a word of truth and justice about Italy.

Alfieri also talked to Montini. 'Monsignor Montini', reported Alfieri to his government, 'showed himself particularly understanding and repeated that he believes us to have the right to ask for an attitude in Catholic journals which does not hurt Italian public opinion at a particularly delicate time in the international situation. He added that the Holy See had never had the least intention of interfering in Italian business [*compagine*] . . . But he also said that we could not ask the Church to adopt an attitude contrary to its eternal principles of humanity and respect for the peoples . . .'[6]

The most Fascist of all Fascists was Roberto Farinacci of Cremona. In the early strike-breaking days of the Fascists of North Italy he led a squad of strong arm men; for a time was secretary of the Fascist party, where his thunderous anticlericalism and crudities hardly suited Mussolini when he tried to reconcile Italy; lost an arm in the Abyssinian war and therefore had the status of a hero; and alone in the Fascist Grand Council wanted Italy to go to war at the side of Germany

---

[4] ADSS, 1, 421 and 428. The reason for this outburst was an article in *Osservatore Romano* of 21 April 1940 entitled *L'Invito del Papa* (the Pope's Appeal).
[5] Charles-Roux, *Huit Ans*, p. 379; N. Padellaro, *Portrait of Pius XII*, Eng. trans. (London, 1956), p. 184.
[6] Alfieri to Ciano, 23 April 1940; AE, Santa Sede, 1940, Busta 49.

in September 1939. He now had no influence in the Italian government except as a gadfly, but much influence among old Fascists. He was an anti-semitic, which most Italians disliked, and very pro-Hitler, which many Italians disliked. But he had all the virtues of a swashbuckler, brave, amusing, unhesitant, and willing to fight to the death. He hated the efforts of the Vatican to repress obscenities in Italian cinemas or scanty costumes on Italian beaches. He hated it when the writings of totalitarian or anti-semitic authors were put upon the Index of Prohibited Books. The BBC called him Herr Farinacci. Osborne called him Farenazi.

Farinacci despised the *Osservatore Romano* as an international newspaper which aimed at Italian sacristans and bell-ringers. In Cremona he had his own paper, *Regime Fascista*. Nearly every number of the paper towards the end of April contained attacks on the *Osservatore Romano* and did not spare its editor, Count Dalla Torre. A leading article at the beginning of May accused the *Osservatore Romano*, and therefore the Vatican, of being on the side of France and Britain and against Italy, and was entitled *To the aid of the Jewish democracies*. Farinacci said that the majority of readers of this newspaper were Jews, Masons, and relics of the old Popular party (Sturzo's). The newspaper is 'the servant of the enemies of Italy and the evident mouthpiece of the Jews'. Osborne had heard with disbelief the story that Farinacci's reputation was low and that he counted for little. In fact he greatly feared that the *Osservatore* was at risk.[7]

On 4 May the southern newspaper *Calabria Fascista* urged its readers to beat up anyone found reading *Osservatore*.[8] Three days later the sellers of *Osservatore* in Naples were seized by the police and held, so that the newspaper could not be sold. A bicyclist with copies was knocked to the ground and hit on the head with wire. At which point the Pope provided the Fascists with the necessary provocation.

On 3 May the German agent Josef Müller told Father Leiber that the German attack on Holland and Belgium was imminent. Perhaps the attack would include Switzerland. Probably it would include a drop by parachutists on lines of communication. Father Leiber told Cardinal Maglione, who wired in code to the nuncio at Brussels and the internuncio at the Hague.[9] Italian counter-espionage knew the contents of the telegrams as soon as their recipients and told Mussolini. For once the Pope was guilty of imprudence. On 6 May he gave an audience to the Italian Crown Prince, and spoke of the imminent attack on Belgium. Umberto went straight to Mussolini who said that it was not true.

[7] Osborne to Halifax, 3 May 1940, FO 371/24935/69.
[8] Cf. Maglione to Alfieri, 8 and 10 May 1940; AE, Santa Sede, 1940, Busta 49.
[9] ADSS, 1, 436–7.

Through the officials of the Vatican Secretariat of State the information came to Osborne and Charles-Roux and the Belgian
Nieuwenhuys.

This passing of information about a coming invasion the German
government naturally found intolerable. They thought it the
equivalent of espionage. The days after 7 May were days of high risk
for the Papacy as an institution. The event helped to make inevitable
that Mussolini would enter the war. For the moment it destroyed the
Pope's influence for peace. After the passing of information Mussolini
could not do other than prove to the Germans that he totally rejected
the Pope.

On 10 May the German armies crossed the frontiers of Holland,
Belgium and Luxemburg.

The French government telegraphed Charles-Roux (who was
already pressing hard on his own initiative) to get the Pope to condemn
this 'abominable violation of law and morality'. Halifax telegraphed
Osborne to tell the Pope that this was the moment to condemn,
publicly and formally, German aggression; and simultaneously that he
should use all his influence to hinder Italy entering the war at
Germany's side.

Cardinal Maglione prepared a draft communiqué in which the Pope
deplored the violation of international law against neutral peoples and
expressed his horror. Monsignor Tardini prepared a draft letter from
the Pope to the Secretary of State. 'Today we see three hard-working
little peoples, at peace and peace-loving, attacked and invaded
without provocation or reason. Our fatherly heart bleeds . . .
Guardian of the teaching of the gospel which is the gospel of peace and
love, we have to raise our voice to lament wickedness and injustice
once again . . .'[10]

This language was felt by the Pope to be provocative. That evening
he sent the three famous telegrams to the sovereigns of Holland,
Belgium and Luxemburg. He sent King Leopold of the Belgians his
deep sympathy, and affection, and hoped for the re-establishment of
the full liberty and independence of Belgium. He sent Queen
Wilhelmina of Holland and Grand Duchess Charlotte of Luxemburg
messages in which he prayed for the re-establishment of justice and
liberty. All three sovereigns sent telegrams of gratitude. But nearly
everyone disliked the Pope's telegrams: Mussolini and the Germans
because they were sent at all, Osborne and Charles-Roux because they
failed to condemn the aggression.

In *Regime Fascista* Farinacci neither printed nor mentioned the

---

[10] ADSS, 1, 442–7.

telegrams, but on 11 May he came out with a cry of abuse. 'Judas sold Christ for 30 denarii. The gentlemen of the *Osservatore Romano* are ready to do worse. It is a pacifist paper. It is the faithful interpreter of masonic Jewish democratic thought. Its partisan politics are directed against Italy, which is not surprising as it is also a continuous outrage against religion; a heritage dear to our people.'

The predicament of the editors of the *Osservatore* was not helped by some in the British press, who praised *Osservatore* for its attitude to the invasion while they assailed the rest of the Italian press for not condemning aggression.

'In every generation', wrote Farinacci (16 May), 'the Vatican has been the ally of the foreigner against Italy.'

Osborne's Diary for 11 May spoke of 'Rome covered with foul anti-British manifestoes.'

Two days later (13 May) Charles-Roux was at the Secretariat of State again. He went on and on. He said that not only French Catholics but British, Belgian, Dutch and Luxemburger Catholics were waiting for the Pope to condemn the German crime. Tardini said that 'the Pope has already spoken, and with such clarity and sublimity and affection for the stricken countries'. 'I do not see that he can do anything more fitting, more sublime, or more effective.' Charles-Roux admitted that the telegrams were 'magnificent'. 'But', he said, 'sympathy is one thing, condemnation of crime is another.' Tardini looked astonished and said that anyone who knows how to read the telegrams finds there what Charles-Roux wanted. Charles-Roux said that he was not thinking about helping France but about the prestige of the Holy See.[11]

The same day the Italian ambassador Alfieri, who was about to become ambassador in Berlin and came to take his leave, protested at his audience with the Pope about the three telegrams. He said that Mussolini was angry and regarded the telegrams as a blow against his policy. The Pope said this was an error for the telegrams contained nothing directly hostile to Germany; he would have had the same duty to speak if the Allies violated neutrality. Alfieri added that the Fascist bands were tense and that something serious could happen.

The Pope was serene. He said he had no fear of ending in a concentration camp or in the power of the enemy if it was necessary. There are circumstances, he said, when a Pope cannot keep silent. He had been reading the letters of St Catherine of Siena, when she threatened the Pope of the fourteenth century with the judgment of God if he failed in his duty. How could he be so guilty as to say nothing

---

[11] ADSS, 1, 453.

when all the world expected him to speak? The Italian government could not claim that the Pope remained silent at the pressure of the Italian government. Where would then be the Pope's liberty? He spoke of the honour of the Italian people, only to be preserved if they refused to be associated with such acts. 'The Italians know well enough what horrible things happen in Poland. We ought to speak words of fire against things like that. The only reason we don't speak is the knowledge that it would make the lot of the Polish people still harder.'[12]

In France the story was put out that the Pope was utterly downcast and unable to do anything and that the three telegrams were only prised out of him by the indignant pressure of Charles-Roux. The Quai d'Orsay itself gave countenance to this gossip. Its origins lay in the constitutional inability of ambassadors to minimize their own 'success'.

These events caused the fiercest of all attacks upon the *Osservatore*. It had now become Italian interest to suppress or muzzle the *Osservatore*, British and French interest to keep the *Osservatore* as free and independent as possible.

The *Osservatore* of 12 May was issued on the evening of 11 May. It contained the text of the Pope's telegrams to the Belgian and Dutch sovereigns, which were not mentioned in the Italian press. On the evening of 12 May Fascists tried to prevent publication. When this failed, the police stopped all sales outside the frontiers of the Vatican. Sellers of the newspapers were beaten up, kiosks were damaged, priests walking on the streets were insulted, buyers were attacked, men seen publicly reading it were assaulted or insulted, bags containing it were turned away at the railway stations.[13] In provincial cities like L'Aquila the newspaper was seized at the station each day and destroyed. A couple who bought the paper at the kiosk by the Trevi fountain in Rome were thrown into the water. At the Via Marsala in Rome men armed with pistols stopped the Vatican mail-van, rummaged among the bags of letters without breaking them open, and ordered the two Vatican men to go with them. The two officials promptly resigned their Vatican posts. The blockage of the Vatican newspaper was broadening into a blockage of Vatican mail. At Messina 2,000 students from the university and the high schools went through the streets singing Fascist revolutionary hymns and burnt 50 copies of *Osservatore* found at a kiosk. The education authorities at Messina were ordered to stop their young misbehaving.[14]

On 15 May Cardinal Maglione protested by letter to the Italian

---

[12] ADSS, 1, 455.   [13] ADSS, 1, 456.
[14] AE, Santa Sede, 1940, Busta 49, report of 7 June 1940.

government. He said that the newspaper was always impartial and moderate. It published the 'high and noble messages' of the Pope. These messages were accused of damaging the honour and conscience of the Italian people. But this was not true. It was very harmful to Italy if it could be said at such a moment as this that the words of the Pope were prevented from reaching the people.[15]

The British Foreign Office unofficially approached Cardinal Hinsley about the *Osservatore Romano*. On 22 May 1940 Hinsley wrote to the Apostolic Delegate in the United States, Cicognani, suggesting that *Osservatore* be published in several languages, from a 'neutral and central Catholic country such as Portugal or Spain, the editing being done by wireless or wireless telephone from the Vatican, and asking American Catholics to pay for the printing press and the paper. The scheme was wild, but showed the value which the democratic world then placed on *Osservatore Romano*. Osborne begged London that while 'the future of the *Osservatore Romano* is at stake', its fate should not be discussed in the British press.[16]

By 20 May the *Osservatore Romano* was almost silenced. It no longer published comment in what Osborne called 'admirable leading articles'. It printed the official Italian war communiqué, and no other news of any interest. Count Dalla Torre, the editor, was convinced that this was due to German pressure. On 16 and 17 May the paper appeared in reduced form and without editorials. Osborne reported: 'Its columns are now almost entirely devoted to information of a religious nature . . . It has died an honourable death, or has at any rate honourably succumbed to temporary extinction . . . It is a tragedy, not only for Catholics but the world at large, that the German government and the Fascist extremists should have succeeded in suppressing the only source of impartial and reliable information open to Italians.' 'Most unfortunate' was the only note from a desk at the Foreign Office (Warner).

On 28 May the Vatican came to agreement with the Italian government. The *Osservatore* could be freely sold in Italy. In return, it would publish only the official war communiqués of the belligerents, without comment. This was a severe limitation. But Osborne began to notice a little more liberty in its texts, and lost his total pessimism about its

[15] AE, Santa Sede, 1940, Busta 49; Maglione to Italian ambassador, 15 May 1940.
[16] In England Monsignor Godfrey suggested to Lord Perth in the News Department of the Foreign Office that the Foreign Office should issue, as a communiqué, a statement issued by the Secretariat of State to all nuncios complaining about Fascist treatment of the *Osservatore Romano*. Perth was pleased at the idea and authorized the release of the communiqué to foreign diplomatic correspondents. Then he realized that it would have a bad effect and sought to cancel it. Only at this point did the Italian Department of the Foreign Office become aware. See the papers in FO 371/24935/72ff.

utility to the British. In August the Italian government protested that
the weather reports in *Osservatore* could help British aircraft, and
Cardinal Maglione agreed at once that such reports should not be
printed.[17]

During these tense days something unpleasant happened to the Pope.
The scarcity of censored reports make it uncertain what happened. The
Pope went in the papal car to celebrate mass at one of the churches in
Rome. At a crossroads the car was held up by traffic. Gangs of Fascist
youths rushed at it from different sides, screaming 'Death to the Pope',
'Down with the Pope', 'The Pope is loathsome.'[18]
Observers believed that this was a shock to him. The sacredness
with which the office had been surrounded since his childhood was
stripped away. It seemed to revive something of the attitudes of the
prisoner in the Vatican. And if his newspaper could not appear outside
the walls of the Vatican and his radio station was under threat, he
could not communicate with the Italian people. Osborne thought that
the experience affected his outlook. He knew himself to be what his
predecessors had been: a prisoner inside the Vatican. He could not
safely go out into the streets, to visit his own diocese. For the rest of the
war he could not go up to the summer residence at Castel Gandolfo,
and appeared again on the streets of Rome only after the fall of
Mussolini; even then in very dramatic circumstances.

ii. The rights of diplomats in war

On 15 May 1940 the German army broke through the French line near
Sedan and headed for the Channel ports. Italy announced its intention
to enter the war.
   The envoys to the Vatican discussed what they would do in case of
war, and where they could go.
   The Pope claimed a right to free diplomatic communication. In the
First World War the Italian government refused to allow the Austrian
and Prussian ambassadors to the Vatican to remain on Italian territory.
They were ejected to Switzerland, and from there tried to do their duty
from a distance. When Italy came into the war, would it allow enemy
aliens, like the British and French envoys, to remain on Italian soil,
from which they had the chance or even the duty of reporting
information?

---

[17] AE, Santa Sede, 1940, Busta 49, Stampa Cattolica, 3.
[18] Osborne's evidence, FO 380/46; d'Ormesson's evidence, told to a French friend who
   came to London, *Tablet*, 30 August 1941; A. Giovannetti's evidence, *Il Vaticano e la
   Guerra 1939–40* (Vatican, 1960), p. 171: 'Il Papa fa schifo.'

Since 1915 circumstances had changed. Mussolini and the Pope agreed a Lateran Treaty. Vatican City was now a neutral state, and like other neutral states could keep ambassadors on its territory even if in this case there would be standing room only. The Lateran Treaty had a clause on the subject, article 12, which both French and British lawyers found alarmingly vague:

The representatives of foreign governments to the Holy See shall continue to enjoy in the kingdom of Italy all the prerogatives of immunity belonging to diplomatic agents according to international law, and their seats shall continue to remain in Italian territory and enjoy the immunity due to them by international law, even when these states have no diplomatic relations with Italy.

Also article 19:

. . . the representatives of foreign governments to the Holy See . . . can without other formality come to the same across Italian territory.

Was it really conceivable that an Italy at war with Britain would allow Osborne to go on living in Rome and give him free communication with London?

Not long before the Munich Conference, when war over Czecho-Slovakia looked imminent, the then Cardinal Pacelli held a meeting with the Italian ambassador to the Holy See, Pignatti. Pacelli asked what would happen to the Pope's diplomats in time of war. Pignatti did not know. He asked what happened during the First World War. Pacelli said that the diplomats of States hostile to Italy retired to Switzerland, but that the Lateran Treaty changed the law.

Cardinal Pacelli then said that the Pope had at his disposal lodgings barely sufficient for the needs of his staff. He could not think of receiving the diplomats within the walls of Vatican City. 'Naturally,' said Pacelli, on the axiom that the Pope's diplomats would have to remain on Italian territory in Rome, and a little unrealistically, 'the Holy See would guarantee the absolute discretion of the diplomatic missions under discussion.'[19]

No one in Foreign Affairs knew what to do. But then war did not come in 1938. The Italians decided nothing because they had no need to decide.

When war threatened in the summer of 1939, Cardinal Maglione again pressed the Italians. He could get no answer. The Italians did not believe that Italy would go to war over Poland. They still hoped not to have to decide the question. The letters mounted, the files grew higher.

With war looming in August 1939, the Italian government asked

[19] Pignatti to Ciano, 12 September 1938, AE, Santa Sede, 1939, Busta 44, copy.

itself what should be done with the Pope's ambassadors in war. On 17 August the Ministry of War sent a memorandum to the other ministries concerned:

Situation of diplomatic representatives to the Holy See. Experience proves that diplomatic missions are centres of observation in all matters that touch the life of a nation (army, police, politics, economics, social life, etc.). Therefore it would be dangerous for a country to house within its borders diplomats who are citizens of enemy states and are kept there under special guarantees. This would be specially dangerous when they are housed in the capital. Therefore: though in normal times the Italian government, by long custom and for the sake of good relations between Church and State, allows the diplomatic representatives at the Vatican to live in the City of Rome, it insists that in case of war the concession ought as a matter of principle to cease, so far as it applies to diplomats from countries at war with Italy. The interests of national defence are overriding.

These diplomats must reside either in Vatican City or in some neutral country.[20]

A few days after the outbreak of war in September 1939, the Vatican asked Italy – though Italy was not in the war – to settle what the arrangements would be if Italy came into the war; that is, to assure freedom of action to its diplomats, and their right under the Concordat to go on living in Rome; to exempt from military service Italian superiors of ecclesiastical colleges in Rome and Italian members of other ecclesiastical bodies, like the Pontifical University, or representatives of religious orders; and to deal favourably with foreign religious institutes.

The lawyers from the Ministry of Justice gave the Italians a free hand. They ruled that the Concordat of 1929 did *not* bind Italy to allow the Pope's diplomats to stay inside Italy in the event of war and therefore Italy could do whatever was best. The War Office said that diplomats should not be allowed to stay in Rome but must live in Vatican City or a neutral country. The Ministry of the Interior could see no harm in doing what the Pope asked.

Mussolini himself was consulted.[21] At 5 p.m. on 20 September 1939 five representatives of the various ministries had a meeting to settle matters. From the War Office Colonel Cotronei said that the diplomats must go into the Vatican or into a neutral country; and since the Pope said that he could not take the diplomats into Vatican City for want of lodgings, 'and given the difficulties of a system of supervision and control . . .' only the second solution remained, to move out altogether.

[20] AE, Santa Sede, 1939, Busta 44.
[21] Maglione to Pignatti, 21 July 1941; memorandum by Ministry of Foreign Affairs, 12 September 1939; AE, Santa Sede, 1939, Busta 44.

This ruthless argument was not accepted by all present. From the Ministry of the Interior Caterbini argued that the Lateran Treaty bound Italy to allow the diplomats to remain in Rome. He was the only one of the five who took this line. But the Foreign Affairs man, Guarnaschelli, recommended a tactful approach. While they agreed that the Pope's diplomats must not be allowed to remain inside Italy, it would be wise not to return a flat refusal to the Pope's request. This they agreed; and Azzariti of the Ministry of Justice said that someone could quietly explain to the Vatican how impossible it was that anti-Italian Vatican diplomats should remain on Italian soil.

iii. The entry into the Vatican

Behind the scenes the Vatican was worried about more than the future of Osborne and his colleagues. It was worried about its own future. If Italy entered the war – and Mussolini had said it would – could the Vatican still buy food? And even if it assumed that Mussolini would honour the Lateran Treaty to the letter, was it safe to depend for currency on a Vatican lira tied to the Italian lira?

In those anxious days, when the sellers of *Osservatore Romano* were at physical risk, the Vatican in the utmost secrecy asked the Americans if it might transfer to the United States the gold bars which it held; and whether, if the Americans agreed to hold them, they would remain 'intact and free' for the use of Vatican City. They put the question, very privately and very urgently, to the American government. The US Treasury learnt of the request on 21 May and telegraphed its agreement on the following day. The Americans had an internal argument on how to avoid publicity. The gold was valued at $7,665,000. One portion of gold was not placed in the earmarked account, but was sold for dollars. The sum transferred consisted of nearly all the Vatican reserve.

The secret was amazingly well kept. There were rumours that when Italy entered the war the Pope would move to America. The Foreign Office in London even asked Osborne to tell them whether the Pope would welcome an invitation from President Roosevelt to seek asylum in a neutral United States. The Vatican denied a Swiss rumour that the Pope would soon move out of Italy.[22] Others heard a story that the Pope would move to Portugal. (This story, that the Pope would flee from Italy, was an advantage to Allied propaganda. From London the

[22] FO 371/24935/98; Morgenthau's Diary, Hyde Park Papers, 264/299; 265/120; 144, 162, 362; 366; 272/223; 285/409; and especially Cochrane of the US Treasury to Morgenthau, 22 May 1940; Cordell Hull to Myron Taylor, 22 May 1940; Morgenthau to Federal Reserve Bank, 24 May 1940. See also Robert Graham, *Civ. Catt.*, 129, 1 (1978), 123–4; *Guardian*, 6 January 1971.

Political Warfare Executive used it repeatedly in later years of the war. Usually the destination was alleged to be South America, in the later versions.)

Two years later this move of the gold helped to save the Vatican from a calamity in which it would have been at the mercy of Mussolini.

Osborne thought it almost certain that in the event of war the Pope would stay in Rome. His problem was whether he, accredited to the Pope, should try to stay in Rome if the Pope stayed. He was now destroying the draft of every letter which he sent, and asked London for guidance (20 May 1940).

If no attempt were made to set up a representation of the Secretariat of State on neutral territory, he suggested that he should go into the Vatican, taking his archivist Miss Tindall with him. But he thought it more likely that the Vatican would set up an office in Switzerland or elsewhere and 'would do their utmost to induce Missions to transfer' thither. Did London then want him to remain in Vatican City? If he were told that he could not go into Vatican City, should he go to Switzerland or elsewhere *under strong protest*, or go home? He thought that he should go to Switzerland under protest. But he believed that if the Vatican decided that it could not receive the diplomats, this 'will only be because the pressure of the Italian Government has proved irresistible'.[23] He would ask the nuncio in Rome (Borgongini Duca) to look after the property, and the safe would be empty.

At that moment London could see no practical advantage in an Osborne immured inside the walls of the Vatican surrounded by an enemy power. They did not see that he could do any work. But they saw the need to prove to the world that the Pope was truly a neutral, and not a crypto-Italian. If Osborne hid inside the Vatican he might have nothing to do. But by being there he proved that Vatican City was not part of Italy. And it still looked possible that the Pope in the Vatican might be something of a drag on a belligerent Italy.

On 30 May Orme Sargent telegraphed to Osborne that, especially as the French intended to stay, 'the balance of advantage lies in your remaining in Vatican City'.[24]

The pro-Italian members of the Curia, who were many, disliked sheltering enemies of Italy. The neutral or pro-Allied members of the Curia, who included the three leaders of the Secretariat of State, preferred them in Switzerland, because memories of the bad old days of war between Italy and the Papacy still lived, and they were afraid of demonstrating crowds in St Peter's Square or barricades outside the gates of the Vatican or stones thrown through the windows. Osborne

---

[23] FO 371/24964/52.   [24] FO 371/24964/55.

thought these fears unreal. But recent Italian history was not so alive to the non-Italians.

Osborne recorded in his Diary:

17 May 1940: I fear it [war] looks inevitable. The press attacks, the gang attacks, the blockade outside, the manifestoes – new ones today laying wreaths on the British navy. The people hate it.

18 May: Terrible night of gloom and anxiety and the fear of the morning paper – i.e. the damnable Italian version of the German lies. It is so horrible that I, who have loved Italy and Italians since I first came here exactly thirty years ago, can't help feeling my affection and loyalty sapped by present Italy. It isn't the people, I know – well, any how! To Vatican to see the Cardinal [Maglione], with a call on Charles-Roux en route to discuss instructions on matter of our position in case of war (*Is* Italy just watching, waiting, jackal- and vulture-like, the order of Berlin, or is it bluff, or is it fear of the German fifth column here?) Cardinal not very hopeful about prospects of diplomats in Vatican . . . Slept and walked – in some anxiety, since I hear that people talking French or English, or even looking English may be 'aggredito' [assaulted] – even babies in prams spat on for babbling an English word . . .

21 May: Bad news this morning. It is a horror to see the *Messagero* with its German propaganda exultation and its own joy in it . . . I slept (I do too much after luncheon now, but anxiety is terribly wearing.)

22 May: Went to see Montini about the question of being received in the Vatican . . . Found myself, on Via Veneto, being unpleasantly stared at by sinister individuals.

26 May, Sunday: Quite hot day for first time. I don't see how I shall stand a summer at the Vatican with no change of air or holiday . . . But I am so tired. To intercession service at English church . . . At 5.30 took Grace Charles to a Beatification at St Peter's. It was, as always, very beautiful and moving and there was great enthusiasm. It enabled me to pray today in both a Protestant and a Catholic Church that the Germans and all the horror they stand for, may be stopped.

On 26 May the British ordered the evacuation of their army from Dunkirk. On 29 May Osborne burnt more archives. On 2 June Mussolini decided to go to war on 10 June. On 7 June the German armour broke the French line between the Oise and the Somme.

7 June: Sent some Chancery furniture to Vatican. The rest, i.e. from the house, must await The Day . . . Bought some Flaubert, Dickens and Boswell for my internment reading and walked back across the Villa Borghese. Rome very lovely and very unwarlike. People in the streets look depressed, not belligerent.

8 June: It is a nightmarish world now. Chancery half empty of furniture . . .

John [May, the butler] furious because I said I had invited two people to dinner tomorrow and rather rude to me. I *do* wish he wouldn't.

9 June, Sunday: John's rudeness gave me a bad night. If he can't keep his temper now, what will it be in the Vatican?

10 June: The fatal day all right. Rather anxious morning and we finished packing up the Chancery. Cardinal [Maglione] sent for me to say that the Pope is worried by a ridiculous article for the *Giornale d'Italia* about an anonymous letter to the *Daily Telegraph*.

The *Giornale* threatened that bombing of Rome or Italian cities would be repaid tenfold by Italian planes over England. The Pope, said Cardinal Maglione, wished Osborne to telegraph London to say that he (the Pope) hoped the city of Rome would never be bombed. Osborne said to Maglione that writers of anonymous letters were utterly irresponsible and unimportant. But he promised to telegraph. He went back to draft the telegram but found that he could not send it because the Italians refused to transmit messages to London.

Osborne's Diary (10 June) continued:

The *adunata* [Fascist crowd-assembly] announced for this evening but still not known if it meant war. I didn't believe so . . . I rang up Noel Charles and asked them whether they had news of what the *adunata* meant. Like hell they did. Percy Loraine and François-Poncet had been told at 4.15 and 4.30 that the King-Emperor had decided on war as from midnight. So we finished our Chancery packing and got home before the adunatists started their return. I packed frenziedly. But nothing whatever happened except a complete black-out and there was no trouble at all at the Embassy. Noel and Grace Charles came to dinner . . . I have been told I must be within the Vatican within 36 hours . . . The French are fighting a grim retiring battle – superbly. I suppose the Italians will now attack them. It is a foul act for all Musso's talk of justice and injustice . . .

11 June: Up earlyish for more packing . . . The very nice and friendly Nuncio [Borgongini Duca] [came] accompanied by two lawyers, to draw up a sort of deed registering his taking over of the house and its contents and the Chancery and ditto. Also the English, Beda, Scots and Canadian Colleges and the Blue Nuns hospital. I got Serrao [the Embassy lawyer] to endorse it . . . Rome as usual under a brilliant sun, perhaps stunned and chastened rather than exhilarated. I believe very many Italians feel the vulture-like quality of the act . . . Home at 3 and stayed there as I hesitated to go out for a walk in the Villa Borghese though I longed to . . . Most of the furniture left by camion for the Vatican but there wasn't room for it all. It was all very dreary. Told by Belardo[25] we need not go to the Vatican till morning of the 13th . . . I had a last talk with Percy [Loraine] who is all in. Said a sad good-bye to him as the Nuncio had said I couldn't go to the station. The Italians bombed Malta at 4.10 [a.m.] . . . Nice for the irredentist Maltese.

The British coat of arms on the Legation was taken down, and only

[25] Commendatore Belardo was a lay officer of the Secretariat of State.

the papal arms remained. Two Italians remained in the Legation as caretakers. Osborne's Diary, 10 June:

Anyway it must be said that Ciano has behaved throughout with frankness and loyalty. For I have never accepted, and do still less now, the theory of those who held that his attitude was only calculated to hold the balance and keep us guessing until the moment for decision arrived. I am convinced that his professions were genuine.

11 June: It is strange to wake up an enemy to the country you are living in. And very distressing, if you are fond of it.

12 June: Packed most of morning . . . I did not like to go out being an enemy subject and perhaps recognizable as such, it seems unwise and provocative – to a small minority.

My Cairn terrier, Jeremy . . . doesn't like these goings-on at all [i.e. furniture removals] and fears the worst, i.e. my leaving him behind.

13 June: Finished packing and came to Vatican at twelve, with John, Miss Tindall having gone ahead. Said farewells, that made me nearly cry, to the old man of the *baracca* [lemonade kiosk] at the corner and a plain clothes policeman. Saw our rooms . . .

The Vatican informed the Italian government officially that it had prepared lodgings for the diplomatic representatives to be housed inside Vatican City. They would permit only two families for each embassy or legation. They asked whether on charitable grounds Italy would allow the Poles to go on living in Rome.[26] This last appeal the Italians refused. The Italians allowed 'one or two days' for the transfer of people and properties.

Three days after Italy entered the war Osborne moved from the Legation into Vatican City. He stored the Legation car in the Vatican garage. He could not use it but thought it safer. He took with him furniture, mostly his own, but some official, and he hoped the British government would not mind him moving their furniture about without asking their permission. Attached to the Convent of Santa Marta on the south side of St Peter's was a pilgrim hostel with little rooms for dormitories. This was to be the headquarters of the British envoy in the Vatican for the next four years.

He was not alone. He could not bring much, because the Vatican said there was no room. But he brought his typist, Miss Tindall, his butler John May and his Cairn terrier Jeremy, 'the first non-Catholic dog' to nose about Vatican City; the new French ambassador d'Ormesson and his wife came in, the French counsellor Rivière and his wife, the Polish ambassador Casimir Papée, his wife and son, and four other

[26] Italian Embassy to Foreign Affairs, 11 June 1940, AE, Santa Sede, 1940, Busta 49.

Poles; the Belgian ambassador Nieuwenhuys. Osborne never understood the presence of the Belgian ambassador since Italy was never at war with Belgium.

He felt suddenly remote. Diary:

14 June: The stupendous architecture of St Peter's, which is pure Michelangelo on this side, is like a safety curtain that shuts out the world. The effect is a little like living in an embalmed world.

28 June: It is like being suspended in mid-air, or isolated on an island or a liner.

To Osborne it was important that the French ambassador had changed. On the evening of 18 May the French Prime Minister Reynaud made Charles-Roux the new Secretary-General of Foreign Affairs. Charles-Roux left two days later. The reason for his promotion was too obvious. In the desperate quest to keep Italy out of the war though France was falling, Charles-Roux had a better experience and more levers than anyone else.

To succeed him Reynaud picked Wladimir d'Ormesson, of a diplomatic family – hence the name Wladimir, for he was born in St Petersburg – a writer and on the editorial board of *Figaro*. Reynaud was engaged in choosing non-professionals. 'I want to put fresh blood into a career service which has too many dried up men.' The Vatican was a good choice for d'Ormesson because he had been a close friend of Cardinal Maglione when Maglione was nuncio in France. He went off to Rome without any instructions except this from Daladier: 'Try to get the Pope to condemn German air bombing of the civilian population – on the roads it is specially abominable – the machine-gunning of refugees. The Pope ought to intervene – he ought to pronounce excommunications *ex cathedra.*' D'Ormesson did not think the instructions, or lack of them, very helpful. In Reynaud's salon to take his leave, he met the American ambassador Bullitt who said 'You are arriving too late at the Holy See. Nothing more can be done down there . . . The die is cast. I know from President Roosevelt that the Pope is terrorised and that one cannot count on him for any action.'

D'Ormesson's arrival meant a difference for Osborne and for our subject. Charles-Roux was the senior partner and Osborne the junior. Now the roles were reversed. Moreover, d'Ormesson's reports were not burnt by panicky officials of the Quai d'Orsay. And while this new ambassador might not understand all about diplomacy, he was a professional writer; so that when he wrote a report to Paris he knew how to make it fascinating. He was descended from a long line of French noblemen, the thirteenth generation in the same Château. And he and Osborne were at once *en rapport,* the same kind of people. They quickly became friends, for they were thrown into a physical proximity too close for comfort, by circumstances shortly to be related.

D'Ormesson kept a diary. He took this diary back to France. When the Germans occupied Vichy France, d'Ormesson went into hiding. He used three different hiding places and in one disguise he was a librarian monk at the Grand Chartreuse. In these hidings, sought by the Gestapo and Laval's police, he wrote from his diary a detailed narrative of his stay in Rome. Because it was written from the diary, and because the circumstances were tense, the narrative (which he called *Ambassade Tragique*) conveys the feelings of those months, and enables the reader to see inside the Vatican during the most tragic months of European history. He never finished it and he never published it. In quiet post-war reflexion he may have thought its judgments injudicious, or perhaps, from the circumstances of a book written on the run, likely to suffer from extremist points of view.

On 9 June 1940 d'Ormesson had his audience with Pius XII and presented his letters of credence. It was the day before Mussolini declared war on France: everyone in Rome knew that this was about to happen. Pius XII made the usual speech of welcome. This speech discontented d'Ormesson, and later Osborne when he heard what was said. D'Ormesson thought the Pope's sympathy too unemotional. It seemed to him a fault in tact; even an act contrary to charity. Was this the moment really to reproach the French of *laïcisme*, even in a veiled way? Osborne was blunter. He told London that the speech was 'a very parsimonious tribute to the fundamental principle at stake in this war' – though he admitted that the words would carry more weight to attuned ears in the Vatican.[27]

The local witnesses were agreed in observing a change in the Pope after the demonstration of 15 May and the threats to the *Osservatore Romano*. He realized how vulnerable he was to pressure, how powerless if Italy cut his communications with the outside world. It may be, however, that the real change came not with these mid-May events, but on 10 June 1940 when Italy entered the war on Hitler's side. A large part of his European importance, and especially his importance to the British and French governments, lay in his Italian influence, as the man who had far the best chance of keeping Italy out of the war. On 10 June that function ceased. And it was a question what other function was possible amid the strife of arms.

[27] Osborne to Halifax, 17 July 1940; FO 370/24962/R7235.

6

First months in the Vatican

i. Life in Vatican City

They all started temporarily in the small annexe to the Convent of Santa Marta, built for the use of pilgrims and known as the Palazzina. The building had no bath, nor even a hot tap. Osborne had four tiny cell-like rooms, two for himself, one for the typist, and one for the butler. The rooms were sordid. They dined in the refectory of the Convent, where meals were cooked by the French and Belgian sisters of Charity of St Vincent de Paul, odd but attractive in their huge white pointed coifs. Other foreign nationals of the Curia came to dine in the refectory. D'Ormesson said aloud, in such a way that he hoped to be overheard even in the highest quarter, that it was very extraordinary that, with the exception of the First World War, he should wait to be an ambassador before he found himself in a place where he could not wash. Osborne hardly missed the hot water. 'I quite enjoy the cross-word puzzle of washing from head to foot from a small basin with an inconveniently projecting tap.' Feeling absurd, he went over to the flat of Monsignor Montini to take a bath. He also left with Montini a lot of the Legation's money for safe-keeping. More than the tap, he minded the smell of mice and pilgrims in his bedroom, and the cloud of dust and flies which flew in if he opened a window. In the hot summer he went round slaughtering the flies with a swatter before he went to bed, and once found inside his bed a colony of well-nourished fleas.

Unknown to Osborne, the Italians insisted at first that the Vatican treat the diplomats 'rigorously'; that is, make them feel uncomfortable. The cold water was partly due to the pressure of the Italian government. The weakness of the Vatican's position was shown by an 'application' (of which Osborne and d'Ormesson knew nothing) from the Secretariat of State of the Holy See to the Italians asking that, in view of the armistice with France, they might now treat the diplomats less rigorously.

They looked with curious eyes at empty spaces elsewhere in the Vatican. Pius XI, whose taste was lamentable, built a massive and unsightly building not far from the nave of St Peter's, called the Governatorato, the seat of the government of Vatican City. D'Ormes-

124

son thought that it looked like a hotel on a beach in Brazil. On the first floor were rooms intended to receive the Pope's honoured guests. They had never been opened.

Osborne and d'Ormesson might reasonably claim to be honoured guests, but to open these doors needed the assent of the head of the Vatican administration, Cardinal Canali, who was dedicated to the Fascist government and had no wish to provide comfort for its British and French enemies. He was corpulent and bewigged and his temperament cantankerous. They thought his manner sly. He was said to be the intimate friend of Dr Petacci, whose daughter was to end her career hung upside down with Mussolini in Milan.

A tribe of workmen descended on a block in the main building of the Convent and modernized it totally, at vast expenditure. They installed bathrooms and lavatories, kitchens and gas rings, and new floors. Their guests puzzled over the expense and decided that after the war prelates would probably occupy the flats. Osborne and d'Ormesson tipped the workmen 2,000 lire each – with the aim of getting a little credit among the people of Rome. Osborne moved on 21 June. It was much more comfortable. In two rooms he had a Chancery. It had no safe, but he bought steel cupboards from the Rome Chancery and the robust butler was not only a waiter at table but a watchdog. In his rooms he plastered the furniture with photographs of Queen Elizabeth and the walls with maps of western Europe, which he used with guests as a way to make them speculate when and where the British would invade. They now had plenty of hot water, and a splendid view over Rome. They were deafened by the bells of St Peter's, 'particularly as my bedroom might be in the belfry.' In his little salon Osborne hung his pictures, including two Brangwyns and a Walcott, and a reproduction of a portrait of the Queen.

Osborne did not know whether he should pay rent. 'I am not sure whether we are tenants or guests of the Vatican.'[1] If the diplomats were not sure whether they were guests or tenants, they were even less sure whether they were prisoners of Italy and therefore helpless to serve their governments. They received the worst news daily. They could not at first communicate with the outside world. An American friend who visited Osborne at that time thought his plight heart-rending, 'most trying', and admired his calm and philosophical patience.[2] That may have been the impression which he gave to a visitor, but inside he had a feeling of total uselessness. 'We are pretty effectually isolated and insulated,' he wrote home.[3] The envoys felt aggrieved that some of their old friends and associates in the Curia kept away from them because they thought that they would be

[1] FO 371/24964.   [2] FO 371/24963/31.   [3] FO 371/24964/103.

Hospice of Santa Marta, August 1940

access to roof
|

Osborne	Nieuwenhuys
May, Tindall	wife, two daughters
	Nieuwenhuys had breakdown and got leave
	to move into Rome. Then Osborne took
	rest of this floor.

d'Ormesson: (after November 1940 Bérard)
d'Ormesson had wife, and after September two sons. Bérard had wife.

Papée
plus wife and son (until he left), counsellor, counsellor's father
(Meysztowicz)

	Rivière
later de Blesson and wife	later (1941) Zoukitch (Yugoslav)
plus two young girls	and wife
and child of 4	

Dispensary and chapel used by nuns;   refectory

compromised if they visited – the most grievous being Osborne's 'silky' friend Cardinal Pizzardo who kept away too pointedly.

Osborne felt not only useless, but embusqué, a shirker, hidden in a safe billet when all his friends were in danger. He tried to reassure himself that as he lived on the top floor of Santa Marta, and as Italian anti-aircraft fire was so inefficient, he was exposed to a consoling amount of personal danger.

At first sight all that had happened was that three Britons had been sent to a rather large and luxurious concentration camp inside Italy, and that they might as well go home, if they were allowed to go home, for all the good that they could achieve. Osborne asked himself the question. They helped the international status of the Pope by being a visible symbol of the independence achieved by the Vatican treaty. But their purpose in being there was not to help the Pope but to help Britain. Until 10 June 1940 they helped Britain because they were helping the Pope who was helping Italy to keep out of the German–French war. But now Italy was at war, the Pope had failed. He had no longer influence with Mussolini, he was isolated also, perhaps anyone who had influence with him had no longer any important influence.

These doubts and hesitations, felt behind the high walls of the Vatican, were not now felt in London. The Foreign Office did not doubt that they wanted Osborne in Rome. It might be difficult for him to do anything at the moment. But probably the time would come again. It was weighty, to bolster up the Pope's independent rights within an Italy at war. The Pope stood for peace, justice, humane methods of fighting. There at the heart of Italy was an Italian who could not help making more Italians wonder about the justice of this war and cause them to doubt whether it could be right to fight at the side of a power which behaved as Germany had behaved and was behaving in Poland. The existence of the neutral Vatican might weaken the Italian will to fight. Therefore its independence must be bolstered. Osborne's presence was the symbol of that independence. Even if he did nothing else but be there, he mattered to the Foreign Office.

The Foreign Office, when at last it got a letter through to Osborne (written 31 August 1940, by Philip Nichols),[4] tried to console him: 'We consider it of great importance to maintain a representative in the Vatican, if only in order to support the Pope's authority. Nor should you be subject to the faintest sensation of being embusqué. Nobody is embusqué in belligerent countries in these days of aerial warfare.'

On 17 August 1940 Lord Halifax ordered Osborne to protest the regret of the British government that the Lateran Treaty had been broken by his forced withdrawal into Vatican City. He did not mind if Osborne also thanked them for their hospitality, but if he did so he must only thank for a necessity which ought not to have arisen. Halifax was irritated that the Vatican protested to Osborne and d'Ormesson about the flight of Allied aircraft over Vatican City. Osborne was to assure the Vatican that the British intended to respect their neutrality, and might mention Italian aircraft flying over Vatican City, if it was the case that they flew over.[5] Osborne delivered this protest on 11 September, but left out the part about Italian aircraft flying over Vatican City because he had observed none lately.

The move into the Vatican seemed to Osborne at first to deprive him of any chance of doing good. But he had this advantage. He was now nearer physically, and soon nearer in friendship, to the men – or rather to three of the men – who counted inside the Vatican. He used Monsignor Montini's bath while his own was being put in. He began to use Montini's safe for storing valuables. They had lunches (which Osborne hardly ever failed to call luncheons) or teas together. The intimacy grew. Osborne recorded in his Diary:

---

[4] FO 371/24964/147.   [5] Halifax to Osborne, FO 371/24963/28–9.

8 July 1940: (Montini at tea). I like him enormously and greatly admire his qualities and his character. Among other things he has vision, courage, and a very nice dry wit. How he can work as hard and unceasingly as he does I cannot conceive.

11 July 1940: I have loved Rome and Italy so much and for so long. I wonder if I shall hate them now.

When he saw the Pope or Cardinal Maglione he spoke French, the official language of diplomacy. When he saw Monsignor Tardini or Monsignor Montini he spoke Italian, as the language of informal conversation.

Discomforts continued but they were those which were shared by the Italian people – rationing of oil and butter, then of bread and pasta. The worst was the refusal of the Vatican to turn on the central heating until almost the end of November. Osborne felt the cold bitterly, for he had no warm underclothes. Another discomfort lay in the waves of depression brought on by an excess of solitude. His prison had more acres and much more freedom than most prisons, but it was still a prison. He was cut off from friends; he could not cross the wall. The severance from friends hurt most, for he was a man of warm affections. If he went to St Peter's, he had to check an urge not to walk out with the congregation into the Piazza. The atmosphere inside the Vatican was monastic. By nature Osborne was not a monk, and enjoyed the sight of pretty women. The work was very hard. Cyphering and decyphering bored him, and he was forced to work at it for hours at a stretch. Visions of himself on some green golf-course, or fishing in the Kennet in Wiltshire, would dart unexpectedly into his mind. He would blame himself that the war of nerves got him down. Sometimes the worst was the sensation that he paddled in a backwater, that nothing that he did mattered. 'I reached the grave conclusion during the mass[6] that I am nothing but a pencilled marginal note in the Book of Life. I am not in the text at all . . .' When he appeared at a public occasion in St Peter's or the Sistine Chapel – especially on the very frequent occasions when there was news of some disaster to British arms – he screwed up beforehand an air of cheerfulness. No one must think the King's representative depressed by the course of the war.

The monotony kept recurring. 'Days and weeks', he wrote home, 'pass like telegraph poles and stations from an express train window and the station one is going to get out at (an end to the war) recedes faster than one approaches it' (6 February 1942). In winters he suffered epidemically from rheumatism. In the depth of one winter two and a

6 The mass was a requiem at Santa Anna for Meysztowicz, a Pole, who died on 14 February 1943 and whose courage and cheerfulness Osborne admired.

half years later, he reached the nadir. 'Life in Vatican City is like a combination of stickjaw and blanc-mange, combining the stodginess of the first with the insipidity of the second' (6 January 1943). In October 1943 he noticed that his hair was falling out and his face falling in. At moments, as the months dragged on, he had a half-fear that if the isolation continued his sanity would be at risk.

These were moods. Most of the time he knew that his work was important and enjoyed what he did and how he lived.

They managed to keep him supplied with cigarettes like Balkan Sobranje. John May was a first-class scrounger, and though he could not go out of the Vatican he tipped Italians to buy for him on the black market. Osborne did not know and fondly supposed that he had an honourable principle not to patronize the black market. Even at the worst time Osborne was able to astonish his guests with a never-failing supply of whisky. Myron Taylor sent him an electric razor. When the summers came he went up on his roof to sunbathe, and took elaborate precautions not to offend the canons of St. Peter's or 'their women attendants of canonical age'. Occasionally he got a friend to pour cans of cold water over him, to give him an illusion of bathing in the sea. 'Henri Papée', he wrote once, 'kindly watered me with watering cans. We had put some seasalt in the water to heighten the sea-bathing disillusion' (9 July 1941). To avert an excess of sunburn he had to use shaving cream.

The want of exercise troubled his spirits as well as his health. Near the top of the hill the Abyssinian College had a tennis-court. The students played a vigorous game in their long soutanes. The surface was pocked with bits of glass and old nails; to fall was unwise. Osborne played tennis badly but longed to play something, and tried to arrange a game three times a week. Delicately he negotiated through cardinals and won leave from a 'rather reluctant' Cardinal Canali to use the Abyssinian court on condition that no ladies might play, and no spectators might watch: Osborne preferred that no one should see his incompetence. The net was in shreds, but by the court stood a little pavilion to change clothes. The Abyssinian students always surrendered the court at their approach.

In his room Osborne kept a rowing-machine, where he would row a course with energy. He found that it helped to close the eyes and imagine the scenery of a pleasant river floating by. He tantalized himself with the memory of trout-streams, or of fresh green hills in the south of Ireland. He would dream of having money at last and buying Glengariff Castle even though it had no salmon in the stream. With the rowing-machine, and his electric razor, and the sword-stick, he would entertain memorably the occasional children of other diplomats, French, or later, American.

Osborne had been a golfer, and craved for the wide green spaces now denied. Attending a populous ceremony in St Peter's he experienced a longing to get out on a course. His nocturnal meditations included golf; as is proved by a letter to Philip Nichols: 'Trying to make the Vatican do something that they don't want to do and that they think would be ill-advised is (to use a metaphor that came to my mind in the night) like trying to sink a long putt using a live eel as a putter.'[7]

In the mornings till 1 p.m. and after 6 p.m. they were allowed the use of the Vatican gardens. Between those hours it was reserved for the use of the Pope. But the Pope's movements were perfectly timed and totally predictable. Every day, summer and winter, he came out at 2 p.m. and rode in a huge archaic car, a ride of two minutes, to the grotto of Lourdes. Then he walked round the Vatican garden, six times, rapidly, so that each circuit took ten minutes. Despite the speed he usually read a book as he walked. Then he climbed back into the majestic car and was driven back along his ride of two minutes. Once Osborne was amusedly indignant to find that he was excluded from the gardens because the Pope had decided to walk at an unusual time. 'It is too much that he should monopolize them morning and afternoon, his own though they be . . . What is he doing, gadding about the gardens all day? Has he no work to do?'

The garden was Osborne's chief refreshment. At first he thought it too tidy, too manicured, but with war conditions and fewer gardeners it fell into a genteel shabbiness. It always seemed to him, even when shabby, like the gardens of some English hydro for the elderly rich, like a hotel at Scarborough or Ilfracombe; a half-hearted attempt at a garden. Everywhere were roads and paths, and formal borders were few and ill-kept. There he breathed fresh air. He loved to watch the cherry tree and the peach in blossom. He would seek out the first violets or daffodils or hyacinths. He followed the hawks on the dome of St Peter's or on the masts of the radio station. He listened ecstatically to the chorus of birds. In summer he revelled in the bougainvillea and plumbago and everywhere in the gardens, oleander. He could rejoice even in a hot breeze. 'I am very grateful for my power of sensuous appreciation, devoid of all need of cerebration.' Once he obtained cineraria from the Pope's greenhouse and hoped that the transaction was above board. Once he feigned indignation that someone else stole the Pope's narcissi before he could steal them himself. Once he stole ten of the Pope's roses to decorate his rooms. He watched for the bees and lizards and red admirals. He so loved it that he asked himself

[7] Osborne to Nichols, 13 March 1941, on the Malta Archbishopric, FO 371/30179.

whether worship needed a congregation. When he was solitary in the garden he could feel it 'a cross between going to church and taking a bath – both forms of thanksgiving'.

He could not walk there in the mornings because he had to work, or in the afternoons because the Pope walked. Therefore he must walk in the later afternoon, or early evening; lovely in summer, black in winter. On his way round he would throw the dog Jeremy into one of the many rococo fountains with their goldfish. He longed to bathe, like his dog, in one of the fountains, but shrank from the indecorum. Sometimes, but rarely, he painted watercolours. John May was bolder, and in the heat would surreptitiously fish the fountains. When they came into the Vatican, cats strayed in the gardens, but as rationing grew more stringent the cats vanished.

To Osborne it was a great comfort that his relations with those to whom he was accredited were so happy; the quiet and dignity of the atmosphere in Vatican City while all the world outside was unquiet; the friendliness of the Pope; the near-affection between himself and Cardinal Maglione; his liking for both Tardini and Montini, in Montini's case more than liking, a 'fondness'. Unlike quite a number of people in the Vatican, he did not even dislike the chairman of its governing commission, Cardinal Canali.

The legal situation of the diplomats was not secure. Everyone confessed the wording of the Lateran Treaty to be vague. The French government consulted its lawyers and was disturbed to find them holding that the Holy See's right to keep belligerent diplomats at a time when Italy was at war was doubtful. In November 1940, after the French in Rome ceased to matter, the Foreign Office was still afraid that Osborne could be turned out legally and consulted the Master of the Rolls (Sir Wilfrid Greene); and was really worried when Greene advised that the Lateran Treaty did *not* compel Italy to allow diplomats to remain in the Vatican in time of war. Neither the British nor the French knew, but the Italian lawyers of Foreign Affairs advised the Italian government that the Pope had a legal right to house his diplomats, belligerent or not, in time of war.

Everyone knew that what was legal could easily be overturned by a coup de main, and that the Vatican and its diplomats must behave. A legal right to be there, if they had such a legal right, gave them no right to interfere in Italy's war. The Vatican must be seen by the Italian government to be useful to Italy, at the least not harmful to Italy's war effort, or the legal right would count for nothing.

Pressure on the Vatican took three forms. First, the majority of the members of the Curia were patriotic Italians by birth and family. The Pope had an international duty to be neutral. Cardinal Maglione and

his two assistants Tardini and Montini had the same duty. But the
Italian government could easily find willing helpers inside the Vatican,
from cardinals or canons of St Peter's to porters or policemen or
chauffeurs. The external pressure of Italy was also an internal
pressure.

A second pressure was the physical dependence of Vatican City on
Italy. The Italian government could switch off its electric light, or its
water supply, or even its food. It could refuse it banking facilities and
bankrupt the Pope's government. Whether such acts were in
accordance with the spirit of the Lateran Treaty would not matter. In
time of war the 'spirit' of a treaty had negligible force. If the Vatican
broke its side of the treaty by interfering in Italian politics, Italy had an
easy and instant answer.

A third form of pressure came from Italian intelligence. When
therefore the question arose, how the diplomats inside the Vatican
should behave, and how far they were free to do what they liked, in
theory the Vatican could decide freely and make its own rules. But in
reality it must within reason play along with whatever Italy insisted on
as necessary.

The man whom Osborne feared was the Italian ambassador to the
Holy See, Attolico.[8] He was aided by his wife who was dangerous
because she was a devout Catholic and therefore commanded Vatican
respect. Osborne and d'Ormesson thought Attolico cunning, subtle,
and unscrupulous. They were not pleased that Cardinal Maglione
liked and respected him, or that the Attolicos were frequent acquain-
tances of the Pope's two Pacelli nephews, who (wrote d'Ormesson to
his government) 'are not exempt from ambition'. They believed that
Attolico kept pressing the Pope to confine himself to his religious
mission and to keep away from politics. They suspected him of
exercising pressure on Vatican Radio and the *Osservatore Romano*. Their
suspicions were perfectly correct. The Italian ambassador to the Holy
See was given the secret duty of ensuring that the Vatican supervised
its diplomats tightly. This became the function which took the largest
part of Attolico's time, and that of his successors.

ii. The French armistice

The first months in the Vatican were emotional. D'Ormesson was
liable to weep in Osborne's arms at the tragedy of France. On the same

[8] Bernardo Attolico (1880–1942). Career in home civil service; then to Peace Conference
1919 and so into diplomatic service – ending at Moscow 1930 and Berlin 1935. A
believer, in 1938–9, that the alliance gave Italy a right to restrain Germany, he worked
hard to keep Italy out of the 1939 war and the Nazis began to isolate him. Recalled in

floor the Belgian, Nieuwenhuys, could not sleep for thinking of his country, and in the small hours could be heard walking ceaselessly round and round his room, and in the day time was poor company because of his crisis of depression. He admired British resistance and though he said nothing against France, d'Ormesson could sense that he reproached the French for their failure.

Communications hardly existed. The diplomats listened to French broadcasts on a crackling radio and so could follow the German advance. At the beatification of a Lazarist father in St Peter's (15 June 1940) d'Ormesson found himself sitting next to the Italian ambassador Attolico. They said nothing to each other. But d'Ormesson saw nothing of the ceremonies. His mind's eye saw only the tramp of German troops through the streets of Paris, filing under the Arc de Triomphe, marching down the Champs-Elysées. He almost had to go out in tears.

Four days after Osborne entered his imprisonment in the Vatican, the French asked for an armistice and so caused a breach with the British. Osborne and the new French ambassador had only known each other for two weeks. It might have been expected that they would quarrel, over France letting down Britain, or Britain letting down France, whichever it was. German and Italian newspapers reported that they quarrelled. The rumour went round Rome that, forced to use the same staircase at Santa Marta, they met, and argued, and came to blows.

On 4 July happened Mers-el-Kebir, when the French fleet in North Africa was sunk by Force H under Admiral Somerville. The British got by negotiation very nearly what they wanted. Then under orders from London they opened fire and the fleet was sunk with the loss of 1,297 French lives. All France, free or occupied, was filled with fury and the French ambassador to the Holy See was no exception. D'Ormesson thought the sinkings a failure of nerve and phlegm on which the British prided themselves. He did not conceal his opinion, and spoke to Osborne of rising anti-British feeling in France. On 5 July the government of Pétain broke off relations with the British, and Osborne was relieved that nevertheless d'Ormesson came to luncheon with him shortly afterwards.

We discussed the Oran tragedy without any recrimination, except that she [Madame d'Ormesson] complained mildly of the jeers at the Pétain government in the French broadcasts of the BBC. I had not heard them but I agree with

---

April 1940, he was made a count and ambassador at the Holy See, passing as he said 'from the devil to holy water'. Objective evidence suggests that Maglione's higher opinion of him was more just than Osborne's and d'Ormesson's. Cf. DBI *s.v.* Attolico.

her. We have no justification for jeers or reproaches. If we had been able to help more, things might have been different, though it was not our fault.

Osborne thought the action at Mers-el-Kebir detestable but justified. D'Ormesson had the sensation, nevertheless, that underneath his defence of his own government Osborne agreed with the French. At one point, probably at this luncheon, d'Ormesson fell into Osborne's arms and wept. If Osborne was embarrassed, we are not told. D'Ormesson surprised himself by his affection for this Englishman who ought now to be his enemy and was not. Everyone else blamed France for her defeat and surrender. Osborne said no word of reproach. He made excuses for France. He spoke of Britain's lack of preparation, of its inadequate army and air force, of its carelessness and improvidence.

Two years later, in hiding from the Gestapo, d'Ormesson wrote down a reverent portrait of Osborne; of his moral resistance in his dignified variety of prison; of the 'perfect gentleman'; of his love of Italy and the Italians; of how this Protestant was beloved by 'everyone' in the Vatican, persona grata to the Pope and Cardinal Maglione, bound in intimate friendship with Monsignor Montini. 'His nobleness of character was his best diplomatic trump . . . Like all Englishmen, he was very idle.'

This judgment was untrue in two respects. Osborne was a hard worker who no doubt learnt at an English school that every wise man gives the impression of being idle. And it was not at all true that 'everybody' inside the Vatican admired and loved him. We shall find a lot of people inside the Vatican who hated his presence.

The French armistice changed Osborne's situation. Until June he and d'Ormesson and Myron Taylor worked as a threesome. But now the French were out of the war and d'Ormesson's interests, as the representative of Vichy, were in part contrary to Osborne's. Myron Taylor ate bad lobster at a party and fell gravely ill, and after a time was invalided home. Suspicious minds in the British Foreign Office suspected this of being a diplomatic illness, to help Roosevelt gain Protestant votes at the coming American election. There was no truth in the suspicion, but the divergence of d'Ormesson and the departure of Myron Taylor left Osborne the solitary representative of the democracies. He was the only representative of the anti-Axis governments to whom, for the moment, the Pope could talk. From this moment until 6 June 1944 he was always the weightiest non-Italian influence in the Vatican.

Osborne begged London to ask Washington to send another envoy to replace Myron Taylor. Lord Halifax sent a message to this effect to the British ambassador at Washington. He said that the British were 'anxious to do all we can to fortify the Pope in the very difficult position in which he is placed'.[9] President Roosevelt preferred to hope that at some time Myron Taylor might go back and perhaps preferred not to be seen by American Protestants to appoint a successor in the year of an election. And at this very moment the Vatican was much troubled, unknown to the British, because the Italian police had caught red-handed an American prelate engaged in smuggling dollars and gold.[10]

D'Ormesson asked the Pope for a blessing on Pétain's government and got it. Pétain passed several laws in favour of the Catholic Church (laws against freemasons, re-introduction of religious teaching in schools, divorce to be more difficult). It looked like a return to old Catholic France. The group in Santa Marta was surprised to find that the Vatican received this news with such little warmth, almost, it seemed, with indifference. D'Ormesson worked to stir them to gratitude, but they saw the problem elsewhere. Europe was becoming a pagan empire under Hitler. In that shadow nothing else mattered, not even laws favourable to the Church in France.

Italian intelligence reported that Cardinal Tisserant was the person who prevented the Pope committing himself to the new Catholic ruler of France.[11] Certainly Cardinal Tisserant made no secret of his opinions. He often lunched in Santa Marta. He had no use for Marshal Pétain. D'Ormesson's children christened him Cardinal de Gaulle, and the name caught on with some inside the Vatican. He was a resolute person. But it is not likely that Italian intelligence was right, for Tisserant and the Pope were still far apart. Tisserant was not able to influence the Pope. And even he needed to be discreet. Osborne and d'Ormesson preferred him to be discreet. He was the head of the Congregation of Oriental Affairs, and still might be important to Syria or Indo-China. They did not want him to fulminate lest the Axis ambassadors found an excuse to make the Pope replace him with a more Vichyite prelate or a pro-Fascist cardinal.

But nearer the Pope was a prelate equally resolute and sceptical about Pétain: Monsignor Tardini. The one thing certain about Pétain was that he was too old to last. Tardini called him a superannuated dodderer. Tardini infected the other members of the Secretariat. If Pétain's regime could not last, the Catholic Church must not be seen to be entangled with a regime which one day was bound to fall, perhaps in blood.

[9] Halifax to Lothian, 31 August 1940, FO 371/24958/216.
[10] AE, Santa Sede, 1940, Busta 47, 25 August 1940.
[11] AE, Francia, 1943, Busta 80/10, memorandum for Mussolini on the history of the Holy See's attitude to the Vichy government, 24 June 1943.

Frenchmen meditate more than Englishmen about first principles. D'Ormesson settled down to do what the practical Osborne never did, think out the predicament of the institution of the Papacy in its new and menacing surroundings.

Why could not the Pope say more? Because he was bound by the Lateran Treaty, especially article 24 which banned him from mixing in the politics of the nation. But not only by this article. When the Pope was a prisoner in the Vatican he could say what he liked. After the Lateran Treaty he was tied. And when he was prisoner of the Vatican Italy had a series of weak governments. Now it had a strong government. The Fascist regime successfully persuaded the Pope not to interfere in politics and then drove him further heavenwards. 'It tends to chase the Pope and the Curia away from this world to the world above.' The Fascists wanted the Pope to be a mystical personage, 'wrapt in psalms, litanies and incense, to whom pilgrims can come from all over the world, bringing with them heaps of foreign currency'. They needed the Pope as an ornament to Italy, not as a counter-weight.[12]

But if the democracies – that is the enemies of Fascism – were fighting for Christian civilization, what then? Osborne and d'Ormesson were both sure that they were fighting for Christian civilization. D'Ormesson was the more ardent in this faith because he was a Roman Catholic and watched his country repressed by Nazis. It discontented him that he could not make the Pope more ardent in this faith. He kept finding the Pope cool, unemotional, unemphatic. He bled for France himself and thought that the Pope's heart ought to bleed more visibly for France. He seemed to himself to receive a sympathy which was wholly sincere, and yet a sympathy more of the lips than of the soul. He had an impression that the colours of the Pope were half-toned. He remembered the vigorous Lombard who preceded and wished that the temperament of the Romans were less passive. And all this went with the recognition that the man was good, and holy.

All the envoys thought the Curia too Italian. From time to time Osborne asked for a British cardinal in the Curia. He expected not to succeed. D'Ormesson told his government that the Italianity of the Curia was acceptable only so long as Italy did not exist or was weak in Europe. It was acceptable no longer.

They also suspected a few of the members of the Curia. They did not doubt that the great majority of ecclesiastics in the Vatican were honourable men with good Christian consciences. But even they had a

---

[12] D'Ormesson's *Final Report*.

subconscious Italianity. And, said d'Ormesson mysteriously, 'as well as the men of good faith, there are others . . .'.

These suspicions were well-founded. Osborne was aware that a majority of the members of the Curia were against him. But he had comforting sensations. He saw how Tardini and Montini hated the way in which Mussolini carried their country into an unnecessary war. He knew that their attitude to Nazi methods of warfare was all that he could desire. He saw how (at first) they admired the humane and generous aspects of the British conduct of early war.[13] They were full of respect for the courage of the British people under bombing.

Inside the Vatican everyone expected Hitler to invade Britain during the first week of July 1940. And everyone but Osborne, who had public confidence and secret doubts, expected him to succeed. The Pope thought that he would succeed.[14] On their radio they listened to the news of barges preparing on the Channel coast. They listened with agony to the Battle of Britain. When Buckingham Palace was bombed, Osborne went wild with rage (the only time in all these events, though not the only time when he was angry) and persuaded the Pope to send to the King and Queen a telegram of congratulation on their escape. Events which Rome could not influence were deciding the fate of the world. Osborne looked at the Holy See and saw that it was as helpless as himself – 'temporarily somewhat in abeyance as an active and important influence in international politics. But what decent influence is not in abeyance?' (Diary, 23 August 1940). He would turn on the BBC with a sense of suspense or at times a haunting anxiety, 'sick with anxiety' at the attacks on London. While the Spitfires fought over Kent, the Pope was quiet, Cardinal Maglione on holiday, Monsignor Montini exhausted and near breakdown. Osborne was irritated, in the midst of one of the decisive battles of the world, to receive an enormous telegram from the Foreign Office, which took several hours to decypher, and ordered him what to do about the filling of the archbishopric of Malta; a subject which at that moment he found infinitely boring, and worse because he thought the Vatican right and the British wrong over the archbishopric and could not say so too loudly except to himself.

Three days after the French armistice, the Vatican wanted Britain to seek peace terms.

The reason was not simply that the raison d'être of the Vatican was to persuade people not to make war. They could see the danger of a Germany invading Britain and winning; and into that foreboding came

[13] Osborne to Nichols, 13 March 1941, FO 371/30179.
[14] E. Di Nolfo, *Vaticano e Stati Uniti 1939–52* (Milan, 1978), p. 37.

fear for themselves, a fear which Osborne and d'Ormesson both perceived. Britain could still negotiate. Its fleet was intact, its empire at its back, it could still stand for the fundamental principles of European civilization. But if Britain fought on alone, it risked going under – as it looked like going under – and then Hitler would absorb western civilization – a prospect which Cardinal Maglione found too horrible to contemplate. Therefore, liquidate the war now, while one of the Powers was still intact. The Vatican was urged to this course by John Cudahy, the American ambassador to Belgium, who visited Rome and was convinced that Britain could not stop an invasion and must go under.

Could Rome say this to the British, when Churchill spoke about fighting on the beaches? If the Pope said any such thing would he look like a crypto-Italian doing the best for Mussolini and pretending not to be an Italian?

D'Ormesson suggested that Franco of Spain or Salazar of Portugal would be the best intermediaries. According to d'Ormesson, Cardinal Maglione thought this a promising idea and approached the Iberian dictators. Among the Vatican documents is no sign of such an approach. Nor has any trace of it yet been found among the British documents. What exists in the papers is a more direct approach; a revival of the old plan: ask the Powers whether they will not now negotiate.

Five days after the French armistice a telegram went out from Cardinal Maglione – it was from the Cardinal though the draft had corrections in the Pope's own hand – to Germany and Italy, and to Britain via the Apostolic Delegate in London, begging the three Powers to engage in negotiation, and saying that his sole motive was to save humanity and civilization.

It was not promising. A week later the British had not replied. Maglione again telegraphed London asking for information. He got it the same day, in a communication from the Foreign Office forwarded by Godfrey:

The British government appreciates highly the motives of the Pope. Its position has been made clear. It went to war because of a promise to help a friendly country to defend its independence. The British government has never had a quarrel with Italy. The Italian government declared war on Britain without the slightest excuse. The British government cannot abandon its allies. It has no wish to destroy Germany, but is determined not to allow Europe or itself to fall under Nazi domination and to that purpose will fight to the end. It is up to the Pope to decide whether to make his appeal. The Foreign Office is astonished that he does not also appeal to France.[15]

15 ADSS, 1, 500–1.

Undiscouraged and further pushed by one or two outsiders, including peaceable noises made by Hitler, Cardinal Maglione tried again at the end of July (26 July).

In London Monsignor Godfrey went to see Cardinal Hinsley and the two English Roman Catholic leaders agreed that this whole plan was a mistake. They told the Vatican their opinion. Osborne was not pleased. He thought it true, but the British government ought not to give the impression that it was letting fall a chance of an honourable peace. It is easy to imagine the reaction in London. By 2 August Cardinal Maglione had resigned himself to a long war. He saw that Britain meant to fight, whatever the consequences.

Nevertheless, on 1 October 1940 Monsignor Godfrey again went to the Foreign Office, under orders from Cardinal Maglione. He said that the Pope had another appeal to Britain and Germany in mind and he asked what would be the attitude of Britain. Vansittart handed him a memorandum which gave this short shrift.[16]

The Papacy was persuaded (like most of the world) that since the British refused Hitler's offer of peace they would be conquered because the island was not defensible. When or if the Germans occupied London they would seize the archives. And in time they would find the record of a correspondence in which the Pope helped German conspirators against Hitler. What then would happen to the German conspirators? And what would happen to the Roman Catholic Church?

Participants with long memories testified that in the course of this long summer the Pope asked the British government to destroy those dangerous archives. The Berlin conspirators appear first to have had the idea that they were themselves at risk if the German army occupied London. At the time of the Dunkirk evacuation Josef Müller, as he afterwards testified, passed a Berlin request to Father Leiber that the Vatican ask the British to destroy the records. Father Leiber confirmed that the request came from Berlin. And late in life Osborne himself was asked about it and said that he passed the request to London but had no idea whether London took action.[17] No such request, and no reply to any such request, appear among the documents now available. If Osborne later did not know whether anything was done, there can have been no reply. If the British in London agreed to do something about it, several at least of the documents the British paper-burners failed to destroy. But the documents which survive are curiously bitty. Someone perhaps destroyed something. That at least is the most

[16] FO 380/61.
[17] See the evidence of H. C. Deutsch, *The Conspiracy against Hitler in the Twilight War* (Minneapolis, 1968), p. ix.

probable explanation. At least someone removed, from Osborne's normal file, the letter in which he passed on the request.

On 4 October the message came that Pétain had recalled d'Ormesson. The Germans and Italians knew that d'Ormesson was a friend of Osborne. Italian newspapers and then the French radio gave out that d'Ormesson was removed because of his relations with 'British circles'. Osborne asked himself whether one Briton could make a circle (Diary, 10 October 1940). He said goodbye to d'Ormesson on 31 October. He knew that he would miss him greatly. D'Ormesson stood for democratic France. Despite the anger between Vichy and Britain the two envoys in the Vatican were at one in their attitudes. He had found d'Ormesson a brilliant talker and a likeable man, the one friend during the dark months of 1940. D'Ormesson's going was also a loss to the historian: his reports are far more informative than those of his successor.

Not all the Curia was displeased at the going of d'Ormesson. They had not liked his freedom with professional protocol. They resented his journalist's instinct to get to the bottom of things. They watched him go without regret.

Towards the end of November 1940 Osborne met Léon Bérard, d'Ormesson's successor; a distinguished man; a member of the French Academy; a friend of Pierre Laval who had wanted to find him a post. Osborne met him at the lift. Bérard shook his hand and bolted into the lift as though Osborne was a leper (Diary, 26 November 1940). The next time they met Bérard pointedly greeted everyone but Osborne. Next day they found themselves sharing the lift. 'We exchanged polite conversation on the bloodiness of the weather, and we were about to embark on the climate of Rome – at least I was – when our ways parted' (Diary, 4 December 1940). Bérard was very little trouble to Osborne except for social embarrassments.

By December Osborne was losing the fear that any day his country might be conquered. He was still liable to moods of fear, especially at night:

Diary – 5 January 1941: Spent a rather depressing night under the influence of claustrophobic-depressive melancholia. I pictured England slowly succumbing as her cities one by one are battered to death and her seaborne supplies grow more and more precarious. And against that hideous background I painted in a kaleidoscopic tragedy of the future, including my own, until I began to feel like a trapped animal.

iii. Radio Vaticana

The radio station stood at the only high point of Vatican City. It was new, and transmitted weakly. It was built by Marconi in 1931 and improved by German equipment six years later. It was easily jammed, more easily interfered with. Outside Italy the best place for listening was Marseilles. The BBC picked it up, at least partially. From the outbreak of war Germans were forbidden to listen to all foreign broadcasts, under a draconian decree which threatened death.

Its object was the same as that of the *Osservatore Romano*: to propagate the special utterances of the Pope, from speeches to encyclicals. Pope Pius XI made it more 'personal' to the Pope than most Vatican organs. He refused to place it in the obvious office where policy was interpreted, the office of the Secretariat of State. Instead, he retained a more direct interest by putting it under the control of the Jesuits. This meant that the ultimate controller of Radio Vaticana, under the Pope, was the Jesuit general Ledochowski, a stalwart and patriotic Pole, who was shocked at what he heard of Nazi activities in Poland from the many refugees from Poland in Rome. He was also a personal friend of Osborne, who admired his character.

Under the general of the Jesuits, Radio Vaticana had a Jesuit director, Father Filippo Soccorsi, who also taught physics at the Gregorian university. He was an intimate of Ledochowski. The Fascist police did not approve of his attitudes. They noted that he hated Hitler and Germany. They observed that he liked to talk with Italian youths, and believed that he tried to alienate them from their Fascist duty. They also noted, a little sadly, that a charge of homosexuality would not stick against him. They noted that he thought Nazism and Fascism the worst enemies of the Catholic priesthood; that he often talked politics outspokenly with his staff; that his character was 'indefinite, cautious, unstable, willing to do evil unwittingly because his conscience tells him that it is good'. Altogether Italian intelligence did not think much of the director of Vatican Radio.

Under Father Soccorsi served five lay technicians, an usher, a chauffeur, and three servants. Two of these laymen were members of OVRA, the Fascist Secret Police.

At the outbreak of war Radio Vaticana was still partly experimental. They prepared during the autumn of 1939 a system of transmission in various languages, which became effective during January 1940. Therefore Father Soccorsi needed various Jesuit assistants. He had a Swiss for the German transmissions (but the Germans could not listen); two Spaniards; two Poles; two English-speakers, one of whom was Irish, the other American; and two French-speakers, one French, the other Belgian. Of the two French-speakers, Father Boubée was important because he was multilingual and because he was quite close to the Pope. The Belgian Father Emmanuel Mistiaen became for Osborne the most important person at Radio Vaticana and one of the most important in all the Vatican.

What his general Ledochowski felt about Poland, Mistiaen felt after June 1940 about Belgium and France. He burned with anti-Nazi courage and conviction. Before the war he was at Jesuit headquarters in Rome. When Italy came into the war he disappeared into Santa Marta, where he got to know Osborne well. He liked to be given luncheon or tea in Santa Marta. He was totally committed to Allied victory, and made no pretence of neutrality. Then he went to live in a high-ceilinged room at the radio station, with a fine view. But he still saw Osborne very often. He was also a close friend of the French canon of St Peter's Monsignor Fontenelle, and they often visited each other, and walked in the woods together, and spies following them discreetly reported that their discussions were 'animated'. Father Mistiaen seemed to the spies to spend a puzzling amount of time gazing through binoculars at the hill of the Janiculum. Mistiaen's humour was such that he is quite likely to have done this to puzzle the watchers. To their superiors they accused him of being 'sly' and 'sanctimonious'. But nothing could be further from the opinion of Mistiaen held by Osborne. To him Mistiaen was a fine and courageous priest, who tried to insert into his French-language broadcasts little pro-Allied turns of phrase whenever he saw the chance.

The speakers on Radio Vaticana were not foolish. They knew that their master needed, and wished, to appear before the world as impartial and neutral in the battle between the nations. They knew that they were under a binding agreement not to interfere in the politics of Italy; and after Italy entered the war they knew that not to interfere in the politics of Italy was not to interfere in the politics of most of Europe. When the Italians protested that their news about prisoners-of-war could help the Royal Navy to infer the whereabouts of ships, they instantly gave way. When the Italians protested that their weather reports could help the RAF, they stopped the weather reports instantly. If they pushed the text of a broadcast towards sympathy with Britain, or towards criticism of Germany, they must frame it by nuance, by turn of phrase, even by pauses or intonations, so that if some Fascist or Nazi ambassador demanded the text it would look more impartial than it sounded. For transmissions in French the combination Ledochowski–Mistiaen was very strong on the anti-German side. For transmissions in English the combination Ledochowski–McCormick (an American Jesuit) was nearly as strong, at least in underlying attitudes. And so long as they worked with reasonable good sense, they were fairly free. No Fascist thugs could smash their kiosks, or beat their messengers. But they must seek not to provoke if possible, because they could so easily be jammed.

We have seen Cardinal Hlond, on 28 September 1939, issuing a clarion call to Poland, which in effect was a call to the world against Germany. Nothing like this broadcast was ever allowed to happen again. Its effect was lessened because it was delivered in Polish, and because the inhabitants of Poland seldom picked up Vatican Radio. But in September 1939 *Osservatore Romano* was still free, and could publish an Italian version. And Radio Vaticana was still able, that autumn, to tell the truth about Poland. Exiled priests came out of Poland with information of atrocity and murder, and ended up in Rome. One such was the vicar-general of the diocese of Katowice, Thomas Reginek, who was received in audience by the Pope and handed him a memorandum of evidence. A few days later the information went out in Polish over Radio Vaticana.[18]

But in January 1940 when the transmissions were better organized the Germans realized what damage the Polish news inflicted upon them in world opinion, and what help in propaganda was being given to the British and the French.

On 19 January the Pope told Monsignor Montini to arrange for a transmission in German on the situation of the Church in Poland. It also transmitted in English and French. The BBC picked it up and put it out. It was printed in English books or pamphlets, English newspaper articles appeared. The American press took it up. All the world was full of Nazi iniquities in Poland.

Radio Vaticana was not the only route by which the news of villainy in Poland reached the West. Swedish travellers passed information through Stockholm. Cardinal Hlond collected two reports of the Polish dioceses and presented them personally to the Pope, and they were translated and printed in English as *The Persecution of the Catholic Church in German-Occupied Poland* (Burns Oates, 1941). But the book included Vatican broadcasts in translation and was given a fiery anti-Nazi preface by Cardinal Hinsley of Westminster.

These accounts of what happened in Poland were important during the winter war of 1939–40. They helped to nauseate the British and French with the Nazis. They contributed to the inability of Britain to contemplate peace after the fall of France in June 1940.

Between the outbreak of war and the end of April 1941 the Foreign Office in London valued Radio Vaticana as one of the most useful

---

[18] *Civ. Catt.*, 1, 139 (1976), note 13.

instruments on their side in the struggle to influence European and American opinion, and in raising scruples about the Nazis in the propaganda war. Just as they valued *Osservatore Romano* so highly till May 1940, as a drag on Mussolini's entry into the war, so now they valued Radio Vaticana as a brake on the European acceptance of a Nazi New Order.

From the moment the foreign broadcasts were given a system, the German government began to threaten. Menshausen, who was counsellor at the German embassy, and acted while von Bergen was ill, arrived to see Monsignor Montini on 27 January 1940. He said that the broadcasts affected public opinion and made it anti-German. They could bring retaliation by the German press and the German government.

Monsignor Montini asked Father Soccorsi for the text of the broadcasts. He provided them. He also told Montini that the BBC had broadcast them with 'additions'. Montini pointed out to Menshausen that the cruder utterances of which he complained were not the fault of Radio Vaticana. On 29 January Cardinal Maglione (note that though the radio station was not under the Secretary of State, it did not make much difference) asked Father Soccorsi to suspend broadcasts on the state of Poland. Soccorsi must have doubted the authority of the Secretary of State in the matter, for the Pope had personally to confirm the suspension two days later. The division of responsibility was awkward. On 1 October 1940 the Pope ordered Radio Vaticana to send over to the Secretary of State the text of transmissions on the morning before the evening when they were due to go out.[19]

Perforce Radio Vaticana was silent for a time on Poland. When Italy came into the war, its situation was more delicate. But two things its transmitters could do. The first was the encouragement of the French after their defeat and occupation. Father Mistiaen was a master at putting the most general principles of the Christian religion in such a way that they raised the morale of the few French who heard them, and of the many more French who received cyclostyled copies from those who heard them.

For example, on 15 June 1940, we only possess the minute made by the Nazi listener to the French transmission: 'God created nature without sin. The brutalities and barbarities committed by man are the morbid excrescences of human personality . . . I believe that the sick phenomena that appear in Nazism, lie in going counter to the laws of nature.'[20]

If Mistiaen really mentioned Nazism by name, it was probably

[19] ADSS, 4, 208–10.   [20] ADSS, 3, 273.

unique among Vatican utterances during the war. The use of such a word in such a context would be a glaring breach of neutrality. It might just have happened. For this was the moment when France fell, and a French speaker on Radio Vaticana might become carried away. The Germans complained to Monsignor Orsenigo; Orsenigo to the Pope; the Pope to Father Soccorsi; Father Soccorsi to Father Mistiaen, who denied that he spoke the words complained of.

Therefore he probably did not say precisely what was reported. The then French ambassador d'Ormesson not only admired Mistiaen for his courage, he thought that the *delicate* way in which he sent out his messages was beyond praise. D'Ormesson said to Mistiaen, 'You have done well to talk in filigree, it is the only way not to be suppressed.' Mistiaen afterwards said that he dared not go too far, as Mussolini would switch off the electricity.

Father Mistiaen again (Radio Vaticana in French, 12 January 1941): 'Men must be free. Therefore the Church will never submit to the claim that might is right . . . She will always protest against the principles of morality being suppressed by the vast mechanism of war.' Or again, on Hitler's New Order for Europe (in French, 14 January 1941): 'There is an order of slavery and death, quite unsuitable for the whole of humanity. Is that what those who talk about *new orders* mean?' It was not surprising that the Fascist police kept a close eye on Father Mistiaen.

The second thing which Radio Vaticana could do, after the ban on broadcasts about Polish atrocities, was to report the condition of the Catholic Church in Germany. This was a historic function of the radio during the last two years of the reign of Pius XI. Its then German expert, Father Mariaux, had to leave for South America early in the war but left much of his material on the subject to be published in English. When Pope Pius XII succeeded, his policy was at first reconciliation with Germany, and as with the *Osservatore Romano* so with the radio, there was a pause in the recording of this information. But with the coming of war, and the still greater Nazi power in the German State, the pressure on Catholicism (and on Protestantism) grew; the closure of religious schools, the ejection of monks, the confiscation of their monasteries, the shutdown of youth clubs, the ending of publications down to parish magazines. Radio Vaticana continued, though not frequently and usually with prudence, to document what was happening to the Churches in Germany and Austria.

In October 1940 the Germans protested again. The cause was a transmission of Radio Vaticana in the English language, by Father Vincent McCormick, in which he documented the expansion of the Nazi acts against the Church to the newly annexed areas of Alsace-

Lorraine.[21] Menshausen came again to the Secretariat of State and said that McCormick spoke of 'the tragic and inhuman' influence of Nazism in Alsace-Lorraine, and of 'the immoral principles of Nazism'. The paper which he had was not the record of what Radio Vaticana said, nor even of what the BBC said that Radio Vaticana had said, but of what 'the Americans' broadcast in English. Nevertheless, after a few days of search both by Germans and by the Vatican for the authentic text it was found to contain phrases strong enough; and Menshausen knew that the author was Father Vincent McCormick. On 27 October, there was a clamp-down. Ledochowski told Soccorsi to confine himself to facts and not add comments; and afterwards the Pope himself saw Soccorsi and made the same order. He added a heavier one: Soccorsi was to reduce the actual number of transmissions from Radio Vaticana.

Ledochowski was upset at what had happened, and appealed against the decision to reduce the programme. He had evidence of the interest of the world; they had announced their programme for three months ahead and to change it now would cause comment; for nearly a month now the Secretary of State had had the chance to comment on the text before it went out; it was essential that the Americans be informed about the persecution of the Church; the Pope himself was known to want this and to have given orders to this effect. Ledochowski ended his appeal with a threat to resign on behalf of the Jesuits if their work was not found satisfactory. Ledochowski saw the Pope personally on 29 October, who agreed that the programme could be continued without any reduction in the number of transmissions. Ledochowski kept showing the Pope the numerous letters of gratitude from listeners who had heard Radio Vaticana.

Britain was very pleased with Radio Vaticana. These neutral attacks on Nazi religious or irreligious policy made excellent British propaganda. And it pleased the BBC to be able to record such a transmission of Vatican Radio as this (9 February 1941): 'We beg our listeners to excuse us if we speak too slowly and repeat all the time, but for some weeks now Radio Vaticana has been jammed by an unknown source.'[22] The BBC quoted extensively from the Vatican. The newspapers took it from the BBC. Robert Speaight, a Catholic actor, published a pamphlet-study of Radio Vaticana, called *Voice of the Vatican* (1942).

The BBC was not just pleased with Radio Vaticana. It was too pleased. The makers of transmissions to Europe were makers of propaganda. They could not be content with the truth. They could not resist the temptation to touch up what was strong untouched. They

---

[21] ADSS, 4, 189–90, 205.   [22] Cf. *Tablet*, 1941, 130.

made points more pointed. Occasionally they inserted an invention. These exaggerations would surely lead to the end of the usefulness of Radio Vaticana. But probably Radio Vaticana would have been silenced without the help of the BBC.

The attacks on Nazi neo-paganism culminated in March–April 1941. If Spanish newspapers declared that Nazism was a form of Christianity, it was hard for the Vatican to bear. When Spanish journalism was picked up by Italian newspapers, it had to be contradicted. For this reason, at the end of March 1941, Radio Vaticana issued several transmissions on the state of religion in Germany. German anger mounted.

The climax came in a message by the Pope. His Easter message (13 April 1941) was at first sight like all his messages: good, unspecific, rhetorical, above the world rather than in the world. It said that this war had gone beyond the limits of a just war; that we are all to pray for a peace of justice and not a peace of oppression, a peace in which the rights of all the peoples are satisfied; that we need to build anew the brotherhood of nations. He sent out a message of greetings to the victims of war, prisoners and their families, refugees. And then

To the occupying powers . . . govern with humanity; the treatment of prisoners and of a people under occupation is the truest sign of civilization. The blessing or the curse of God for your own country could hang upon the way in which you use your power over these peoples.[23]

The only powers occupying other countries in Europe were Germany and Italy and Russia. Von Bergen reported the Pope's lack of impartiality to Berlin. The Gestapo confiscated the printing of the Easter message. Four days later Goebbels said that Radio Vaticana was more dangerous than a Communist transmitter and must be silenced.

Now the Germans and Italians acted together. During the last week of April 1941 the Pope summoned Ledochowski and told him that Radio Vaticana was not to mention the religious persecution in Germany; more, no mention of Germany, till further notice. From Ledochowski or from Mistiaen Osborne learnt the news the same day, and sent off a message to London.

Osborne was deeply hurt by the silencing of Radio Vaticana. He thought that the Pope should have refused to give way, and implied in conversation that the Pope was wrong. Under instructions from the Foreign Office he presented the Pope with a formal protest at an audience of 10 June 1941. It used strong language. 'It is hard to understand how the Vatican can take a step which fatally tends to

promote Herr Hitler's ambitions . . . What will be the feeling of
Catholics of the world if it may be said of their Church that, after at first
standing courageously against Nazi paganism, it subsequently consented, by surrender and silence, to discredit the principles on which it
is based and by which it lives?'[24]

Osborne wrote a description of his audience to London: 'I was
completely disarmed by his charm, as usual'; and three days later,
when he was as much indignant about the Pope giving an audience to
the Croat leader Pavelic as about Vatican radio, 'Although one
approaches him with indignation in one's soul and protests on one's
lips, it is impossible not to be disarmed by his simplicity, humanity,
friendliness and sincerity, and by his devastating combination of
saintliness and charm. One talks so easily to him, he listens so readily,
responds so frankly, and smiles so enchantingly and easily that one's
carefully prepared attitude of dignified disapprobation just evapor-
ates.' The Foreign Office thought little of the Pope's charm, when they
received this, and much about his audience to Pavelic, whom they
regarded, not without reason, as a murderer.[25] The Pope did not
believe the stories about Pavelic.

The German ambassador von Bergen was not quite content. He told
Berlin that the attitude of Radio Vaticana was obstinate and
unpleasant. He presented the Pope with a private memorandum
which refuted the truths and inaccuracies put out by Radio Vaticana
about the persecution of the Church in Germany, and which accused
the radio of playing propaganda still on behalf of the Allies. Someone
gave him a reply – of the Pope's warm sympathy for Germany, of his
desire not to complicate the situation, of how this sympathy and this
desire drove him into a deep reserve. Nevertheless it is impossible to
leave unanswered German propaganda in Spain which asserts that all
is well with the Catholic Church in Germany, and which will go out
from Spain to the Americas. Silence will be interpreted as agreement
by the Pope. The spokesman assured von Bergen that from the
beginning Radio Vaticana was not allowed to enter politics.

Von Bergen's letter showed that even after the British were crying at
the silencing of Radio Vaticana, the Germans and the Vatican still
argued, and that the Vatican was not quite lying down.[26]

The Holy See replied formally to the British protest. Cardinal
Maglione wrote (28 June 1941) that the broadcasts were often altered
when they were quoted; that they were quoted out of context; and so
they caused the Holy See to lose its reputation for impartiality. The

---

[24] ADSS, 4, 542.   [25] FO 30174/155 and 159.
[26] Von Bergen to Weizsäcker, 22 June 1941; printed in DGFP, 1941, vol. I, p. 1082.

Vatican denied to Osborne that there was any agreement between the Pope and Germany and Italy.

Osborne kept lamenting the silencing of Radio Vaticana. Anthony Eden thought it outrageous. But it was not quite silenced. It was forced to be still more cautious. But even in the month of June 1941, after Osborne's protest was lodged, a broadcast in Polish (11 June) was of interest to the Poles and the Pope did not know that it went out till after the transmission.

That Osborne, despite his lamentations, still thought Radio Vaticana valuable, was proved by his attitude to Father Mistiaen. He was still afraid that any moment the Italians would succeed in getting Mistiaen dismissed from Radio Vaticana. He could see that despite everything that had happened, something could be achieved. During 1943 the Vatican acquired better equipment and could go out on medium wave. The Germans still thought it necessary to jam broadcasts to Poland, even as late as 1943. The Italians worked hard to get rid of Mistiaen; Osborne called it *gunning* for him. He was protected by Ledochowski. Osborne was very grieved when Ledochowski died at the end of 1942. He was afraid lest the result would be the instant dismissal of Mistiaen. In the event Father Mistiaen stayed; with a still narrower liberty. Mistiaen said that the broadcasts became pallid.

In March 1943 Mistiaen, who had to send all proposed transmissions to a censor, resented the censor bitterly and resigned. He asked leave for a passport to go away from Italy. The Pope heard of the resignation. The censor was changed and Mistiaen withdrew his resignation. He still thought the broadcasts pallid.

When the Germans occupied Rome in September 1943, the office of the Secretariat of State got wind that the Gestapo kept a special watch on Father Mistiaen. They begged him to be very discreet. And they used to him a new kind of argument in favour of discretion. It was useful to the Pope to be seen to be under the heel of the Nazis.[27]

[27] For Britain and Radio Vaticana, FO 371/30173–4, 30176; also the indispensable article by Robert A. Graham, 'La Radio Vaticana tra Londra e Berlino', in *Civ. Catt.* (1976), 1, 132ff. For Mistiaen, d'Ormesson was very close to him during the summer of 1940 and he often appears in the d'Ormesson papers. For the view of the Fascist police, AC, Min. Int., PS, 1943, Busta 71, file Radio Vaticana. Father Mistiaen after the war talked to P. Duclos, who reported what he said in *Le Vatican et la Seconde Guerre Mondiale* (Paris, 1955), pp. 34–7. Mistiaen appears frequently in Osborne's *Diary*.

7
Surveillance I

i. The watchers

All the guests in the Vatican had the sensation of being watched. If they went out, they were escorted. Men in plain clothes lounged about the courtyard of the hospice. They suspected men in cassocks of being secret agents of Mussolini rather than the Pope. The name of every visitor was taken down and reported to the Italian police. All this was a breach of the Lateran Treaty. But it amused rather than offended. They were much more offended because of what happened when one of the French crossed St Peter's Square (unostentatiously, keeping within the columns of Bernini). The square is inside the territory of Vatican City, and the passage caused instant protest from Italian police to the Vatican and a ban by the Vatican on any of the diplomats crossing the Square.

It was wearisome, the ritual Vatican saluting by gendarmes, bowing from the waist or hips or neck; especially when the spies watching them on behalf of the Fascist police were the most punctilious in these courtesies.

Winston Churchill would have felt uncomfortable if an educated and patriotic German, aided by an equally patriotic ex-soldier as a butler and a secretary, had been installed during the war on neutral territory amid the precincts of Lambeth Palace, almost immediately across the river from the House of Commons. The situation would have seemed intolerable, and we may guess that though Chamberlain and Halifax would nevertheless have tolerated, Churchill and Eden would not. But although Mussolini tolerated, and never did to the neutral state what the Germans did so ruthlessly with Belgium and Holland, the air was as full of suspicions as the courtyard was full of plain clothes detectives. One of Monsignor Tardini's secretaries drafted a minute for a letter to the Apostolic Delegate in London which Tardini erased from the draft, not because it was untrue but because it was inexpedient to state. It ran: 'It is easy to imagine how the mere presence of the British Minister in the Vatican makes difficulties and embarrassments for the Holy See. Outside the Vatican plenty of people suspect, and insinuate that, ringed as he is at close quarters by an enemy country, he can do whatever he can to hurt Italy. But the Holy See has never lent its ear to such rumours and would not even examine them unless proven evidence were brought; and is sure that such evidence will never come to light.'[1]

From the first the Italian police were sure that they must watch the diplomats with vigilance, and if possible surreptitious vigilance. Their experience grew with time. At first they thought it enough to record their movements and visitors and to check their communications. That was a lot to achieve, when the persons to be supervised were supposedly free guests within a neutral state. As time passed, they began to suspect that even these forms of surveillance were not enough.

Even during the summer of 1939 the Italian police recorded the visitors to the Pope. Part of their attention was simply security against bombs and madmen. They were quite tough with the Pope, saying (for example) that if he went to Castel Gandolfo by any route other than that specified, they washed their hands of responsibility. They would not let him *stop* at the Gesù to receive the homage of the Jesuits, and all he did was to *slow down* for that purpose. But they had also the habit of watching the diplomats. During the intense diplomatic activity of the few days before the outbreak of war (29 August–31 August, 1939) the comings and goings of Osborne or Charles-Roux were noted by the Italian police.[2]

When Italy entered the war, and Osborne and d'Ormesson and Papée moved inside Vatican City, this supervision was strengthened. Frequent reports went to the Questura of Rome listing Osborne's engagements, those with whom he had meals, people whom he met on his walks, people who called at his flat.

A copy of one of these police reports to the Questura has survived (in Osborne's *Diary*, 5 March 1943). It was not very helpful:

Vatican 1.12.1941

12.10 p.m. Yugoslav and lady [= Zoukitch] went out, came back 14.45
12.20 p.m. Lady and daughter of French Embassy [= Bérard] went out, came back 12.50
12.50 p.m. French ambassador came in
12.50 p.m. British ambassador went out, came back 13.25
12.55 p.m. French counsellor and lady [= de Blesson] went out, came back 13.25
14.30 p.m. 'The French blonde' went out
14.40 p.m. The Yugoslav went out, came back 15.45
14.45 p.m. The French counsellor and lady, went out, came back 15.30
14.55 p.m. The Yugoslav lady went out, came back 15.30
15.30 p.m. The French ambassador went out.

[1] ADSS, 7, 86, note.
[2] File, Villegiatura di SS Summo Pontifice: AC, PS, 1939, 38A.

Osborne eventually got hold of a copy of this useless document. 'It would immensely amuse me to show copies to His Holiness and everyone else here. What possible interest can this sort of nonsense offer to the Italian Secret Police?'

Or again, Osborne's *Diary*, 14 March 1941:

I learned today of another spy in our midst. But what, I ask myself, do they ever find to report?

The Italian police laid down the following rules:

1. The enemy diplomats must reside inside the Vatican and not cross the border into Italy.

    But for exceptional reasons they may ask permission to go into Rome. If this is granted they will be escorted by a police officer continuously. If outside the Vatican they may not use a telephone.

2. They may send no telegrams in code. They may send no private or unofficial telegrams.

    They may send official telegrams if in clear.

    'They are censored by our censors but naturally we do not tell this to the enemy diplomats.'

3. They may send official letters by post. These are not subject to censorship.

    'Naturally we exercise a discreet surveillance on the contents.'

    They may send and receive private letters from their families. These come under official censorship.

4. No diplomatic couriers ran between the enemy diplomats and their governments.

5. In their official communications they may only communicate what concerns their work as envoys accredited to the Vatican and may insert no other news.

Osborne once asked leave to go into Rome. He thought it right to go to the funeral of the ex-King of Spain. His request was refused. He asked to go to pay his condolences to the ex-Queen. His request was refused. He did not ask again, even on occasions when his colleagues asked. If those colleagues represented States not strictly at war with Italy – Vichy France, Belgium – their wives asked leave to go out to shop; a leave which was easily conceded, though a policeman must trail them from shop to shop. Osborne had no wife. His shopping was done by his maid or cook who were Italian citizens. Later on in the war he once went into Rome to see the Vatican film on the Pope's life, *Pastor Angelicus*.

Once the Portuguese ambassador, without asking Osborne, got

Italian leave for Osborne to go out into Rome for a celebration of a miracle and the anniversary of the Pope's consecration as bishop. Osborne refused to go. 'I didn't explain that I didn't care for the idea of being told that permission had been obtained for me to be let out for once, as though I was somebody's dog being taken out on a chain' (Osborne's *Diary*, 11 May 1942). 'I have no desire', he wrote a year later 'to go out into Rome. As one looks at it, it seems an utterly remote and alien city, but I suppose I shouldn't feel that if I did go out.'

The Italian chief of police, Senise, and his advisers considered (August 1940) what restrictions they should place on the diplomats' communications. If they were neutral diplomats, we should let them communicate freely with enemy countries or neutral countries; for if we refuse to transmit, they will find other routes and we shall lose the chance of knowing the contents. We aim to allow the diplomatic representatives in the Vatican to communicate by telegraph with their own countries, provided it is in clear, because then we shall get to know the contents.[3]

In January 1941 and again in February 1942 the Italians discussed telephones. They asked themselves whether they were adequately controlling calls going out of the Vatican. They agreed that all outgoing or incoming calls must be tapped; but to achieve this fully they would have to change some of the mechanisms from automatic to manual. No one in the Vatican could talk directly to Britain because no open line existed. No one there could talk to France because it needed the leave of the Armistice Commission sitting in Turin. On 16 January 1941 the Minister of War ordered that all telephones used by diplomats who represented enemy powers inside the Vatican were to be made unusable.[4] But the order was not executed because it could not be executed without a glaring and public breach of the Lateran Treaty.

The Italian censors worried over letters between the Vatican and neutral countries. Osborne, they feared, might find a Vatican official of British sympathies, and use him as a messenger to an official in a neutral country but in British pay. On 4 February 1941 the Director-General at the Italian Ministry of Communications laid down that there was no need (and under the Lateran Treaty no right) to censor Vatican messages to neutral countries or vice versa. But in March 1941 they refused to apply this to territories in Italian Africa. They would not allow article 12 of the Lateran Treaty to apply to the Italian colonies. And they continually held before their minds the principle that even

---

[3] AC, Dir. Gen. PS (Dir. Polizia 1927–44), Busta 204, file Città del Vaticano; request of 22 August 1940; restrictions listed in a memorandum for the Ministry of the Interior, 10 June 1942, in AE, Santa Sede, 1943, Busta 67.
[4] AE, Santa Sede, 1942, Busta 58.

though all official Vatican correspondence to Italy or neutral countries went uncensored, there were those who would exercise over it what they kept calling 'discreet surveillance'.[5] These were SIM, that is Servizio di Informazione Militare, military intelligence.

The police noted expressions of joy at Allied progress in the war. On 17 March 1941 the police reported that when the Italians released to the press the loss of a warship, the diplomats in the Vatican were openly pleased; especially the Polish ambassador, his son Henri, Rivière's wife and mother-in-law, and Father Emmanuel Mistiaen. They were seen walking 'happily' in the Vatican gardens, and some also expressed pleasure at the American release of ships (Lend-Lease) to the British.[6]

Osborne could do nothing himself that was unobserved. But might he do something through someone else who was not observed?

This was easy to stop, simply by threats against the friends. Osborne's old friends in Rome were prevented from calling at his flat. Osborne minded the loss of friends ('*How bloody it all is!*' *Diary*, 30 May 1943) but accepted the situation stoically as part of the tactics or miseries of war.

If the friend was a Vatican citizen, that was harder for the police. Nevertheless they did not shrink from approaching the Secretariat of State. Count Dalla Torre, editor of the *Osservatore Romano*, was a friend of Osborne and was seen to be paying him visits in the evening (February 1941). The Italian ambassador to the Vatican, Attolico, approached Cardinal Maglione; and Cardinal Maglione said that he would have a private word with Count Dalla Torre.[7]

ii. Ecclesiastics in the Vatican

The police had a fair idea which ecclesiastics at the Vatican were not on the side of Italy. They kept their ears open.

Just as they recorded 'anti-Fascist' utterances by Italian citizens or in Italian pulpits or Italian parish magazines, so they recorded such utterances when they heard of them inside the Vatican. A British submarine penetrated the bay of Savona (October 1940). Cardinal Tisserant was outspoken in his criticism of Italian defences. He met the Vatican Librarian, another scholar, Giovanni Mercati; and the police informers judged that Cardinal Tisserant must have inspired Cardinal

---

[5] Memorandum of 27 December 1940 signed by Ciano; AE, Santa Sede, 1941, Busta 54. For the work of SIM, see C. de Risio, *Generali, Servizi Segreti e Fascismo* (Milan, 1978); C. Amè, *Guerra Segreta in Italia 1940–3* (Rome, 1954); Robert A. Graham, 'L'occhio del SIM sulla Città del Vaticano', *Civ. Catt.* (1978), 4, 44ff.

[6] AE, Santa Sede, 1940 (*sic*), Busta 49; AE report of 28 March 1941.

[7] AE, Santa Sede, 1941, Busta 57.

Mercati with 'anti-fascist sentiments'. For Cardinal Mercati was reported as talking to his cook, and telling her that the Italian government had played the wrong card; that in some parts of Italy the people were already hungry; and that if the war did not end by the spring, revolution would break out in Italy. If a parish priest spoke such sentiments in a pulpit the local police could do something. The Roman quaestor could do nothing about Cardinal Mercati inside the Vatican. But they could try to block Italian honours being bestowed upon such a man. They noted that Cardinal Mercati was likely to be proposed as a member of the Academy.[8]

They also recorded, optimistically, the contrary, 'Vatican circles lament the recent student demonstration at Rome University, because it helps the enemy' (10 May 1941); 'In Vatican circles Hitler's speech has made a good impression. He recognized the sacrifices made by Italy, and guaranteed to Italy our living space' (8 May, 1941); 'in Vatican circles the setting up of the province of Ljubljana and its annexation to Italy has produced the best impression' (4 May 1941) (because the annexation would remove Slovenes from 'persecution by the Orthodox Church'),[9] 'we learn secretly that many Vatican prelates are full of confidence about the next offensive in Tripolitania – and in Albania too' (22 March 1941). 'Vatican circles fully share Archbishop Boetto's patriotic words after the bombing of Genoa' (15 February 1941). 'Yesterday morning the procurator-general of the Salesians, Francesco Tomasetti, an old friend of the Pope, talked with the Pope, who showed a lively appreciation of the good relations between the Italian State and the Holy See; and afterwards Father Tomasetti declared his faith in the victory of the Axis over Great Britain' (8 January 1941).

They recorded even bizarre messages (we find American and British Intelligence as bad; every item of news made the reporter important). They intercepted a personal message to the Pope (12 April 1941) from the President of the Consolidated Lithograph Corporation in the United States, who said that he employed 500 Italians and adored Italy, and who suggested that the Pope in his Easter message should invite the King of Italy to set an example by laying down his arms as an example for others to follow. 'It is practically impossible to ask all countries at once to stop fighting, but if Italy which is close to your heart, were to stop, in the spirit of humanity and religion, it cannot help but show the strength of your Catholic leadership. God be with you.' All this was solemnly vetted by the interceptors in counter-espionage.

[8] In the place of Papini, AC, PS, 1940, 35B; AE report of 15 October 1940.
[9] AC, PS, 1941, 35.

The Italian police had a clear idea which ecclesiastics inside the Vatican wanted British victory. Cardinal Tisserant said so, but despite his very forthright character was not wanting in discretion. A French canon of St Peter's, Monsignor Fontenelle, was known wholly to approve of de Gaulle and disapprove of Marshal Pétain, and this made a prima facie case for believing that he wanted Britain to win. Father Mistiaen shared some of these opinions; and the police noted that he and Osborne sometimes met. On present evidence the police paid not much attention to the German canon of St Peter's, Monsignor Kaas, whom Osborne thought it dangerous, after the conspiracy of the winter war, to meet; and this although Farinacci proclaimed to all Italy the unsoundness of Kaas. But Diego von Bergen and the Germans woke up when they heard a rumour that Monsignor Kaas would be made a cardinal.[10]

On present evidence the police took little notice of that dubious supplier of information, Monsignor Pucci; and this although Farinacci publicly accused Monsignor Pucci of being 'still another Vatican rat', though 'not so poisonous as Fontenelle and Gonella' (*Regime Fascista*, 1 September 1940. Gonella was after Dalla Torre the chief writer of leaders on *Osservatore Romano*.) On present evidence the police took little notice of the charge against Monsignor Pucci, because they knew him as one of their hired informants. There is evidence that he was a leading person in the Vatican in the pay of OVRA, the Italian Secret Police. Monsignor Pucci was in close touch with the German ambassador and kept away from Osborne. But he had a smooth and friendly manner and liked to keep in touch with Monsignor Montini. One witness said that he liked to be thought well of by Monsignor Montini because he hoped that Montini would get him a bishopric.

The attention of the police did not yet swing towards one of the Irish Monsignori, Monsignor O'Flaherty, who in the end was to justify their suspicions.

On present evidence the police paid hardly more than occasional attention to Montini. In his newspaper *Regime Fascista*, Farinacci told all Italy that Montini was the friend of the enemies of Italy. Cardinal Maglione held that Farinacci's attacks on Montini were subtle attacks on himself and the Pope, and could not disregard them. Several times he approached the Italian government, right up to Mussolini himself, to silence attacks on Montini which were attacks on those higher than Montini.[11]

The Lateran Treaty banned such attacks on the Pope, and Maglione

---

[10] ADSS, 5, 449.

[11] Maglione to Attolico, 30 August 1940; ADSS, 4, 127–8, referring to *Regime Fascista*, 25 August 1940.

appealed to its clauses (article 8). The nuncio Borgongini Duca went to Count Ciano who promised to talk to Mussolini. Monsignor Tardini summoned Attolico's counsellor Babuscio Rizzo to the Secretariat and denounced the articles of the *Regime Fascista* as scandalous, and found that Babuscio Rizzo agreed. *Regime Fascista* of 31 August 1940 had a column of abuse against the Vatican as on the side of the Jews in America, and pilloried Count Dalla Torre, Archbishop Spellman of New York, and Monsignor Fontenelle. Cardinal Maglione penned another formal protest[12] and asked how it was possible in a country where government controlled the press. Mussolini told the Minister of Popular Culture, Pavolini, to quieten Farinacci; and for a time the articles ceased. The Italian government told the Vatican officially that it had nothing to do with Farinacci's attacks (Attolico to Cardinal Maglione, 13 September 1940), and that Pavolini had intervened. Nevertheless, to shut Farinacci's mouth totally was beyond the power of Mussolini's government. Farinacci was a hero of Fascism and was revered or respected by all the more extreme Fascists, not least by Pavolini who had the duty of suppressing him, and who one day would be murdered almost at the same time as the murdering of Farinacci. So little could they control Farinacci that eventually Count Ciano said wearily to Borgongini Duca, after flipping through newspaper cuttings put in front of him, 'I recommend you to do what I do – don't read *Regime Fascista*'.[13] Only Mussolini could bring Farinacci to heel, even Mussolini perhaps not fully. And though Mussolini had deep in his child-memory a soft spot for the Catholic religion, he had also inside him, though now mostly concealed, a streak of anticlerical ferocity which liked what Farinacci said about the Vatican.

Monsignor Fontenelle had written a much-read life of Pope Pius XI, which sufficiently interested the Italian government to persuade them to buy an official copy. Like Cardinal Tisserant, he was well known to be strong on the side of Britain and of General de Gaulle. In *Regime Fascista* Farinacci (27 August 1940) accused Fontenelle of spending 24 hours a day plotting against Italy, and printed Vatican scandal that Fontenelle was known inside the Vatican as Grey Eminence; elsewhere (31 August) he called Fontenelle the 'silent serpent', an agent of France and not of Jesus Christ. In February 1941 formal complaints were made to Cardinal Maglione that Fontenelle was anti-Italian and misused his cloth to political ends. Cardinal Maglione told Attolico that he would tell Fontenelle not to write, not to go out of the Vatican, and to behave like a canon of St Peter's, and not like a politician. Fontenelle rejected

---

[12] Maglione to Attolico, 6 September 1940, ADSS, 4, 138–9.
[13] ADSS, 5, 474.

the charge absolutely. He said that he never touched politics, and had sympathy and respect for Italy.

Fontenelle was a man who talked a lot, but was not important to Osborne.

If the police watched every move of a Gaullist like Monsignor Fontenelle, they recorded sounds of an opposite timbre. Monsignor Raffaele Acernese, who had been a chaplain in the Italian army, was always being rude to the French at St Peter's and talking politics in the canons' house; he loved to attack the blockade, and call France and Britain 'the great starvers of the peoples'; and once in the Sacristy of St Peter's could be heard chanting 'I've been warned so I won't talk politics in here but when I get outside I shall cry a plague and vituperation upon France.' The police recorded him as a patriotic clergyman.

The Vichy Ambassador Léon Bérard protested to Cardinal Maglione about such rudeness to the French prelates. The vicar of St Peter's, Monsignor Vicentini, was summoned to the office of the Secretary of State and told to get the canons not to talk politics, and to be courteous to their French colleagues. Monsignor Acernese, when he was warned, said that after what had happened he could never say a good word about France. He put the blame for these fracas on Fontenelle.

Just before Christmas 1942 Italian counter-espionage said that it had information that Archbishop Gerlier of Lyons sent messages to Fontenelle, and that Fontenelle sent Gerlier 'very improbable' information on discontent among the Italian people.[14] The Italian Embassy took it up officially with Cardinal Maglione, who asked Fontenelle, who said that he had written Cardinal Gerlier one letter only as a Christmas greeting.

The canons of St Peter's were not always quarrelling in the political tension. Monsignor Kaas did not quarrel. Early in 1942 he was busy lying in ambush for some unknown who prised open collection-boxes and took the money; and after several ambushes caught the culprit in the act.[15] But the Vatican authorities were a little doubtful about the canons of St Peter's, under these tense conditions. In the spring of 1941 a trivial storm blew up because some old lottery tickets were found in the dust-bin of the canons' residence, and for a moment the Vatican authorities fussed unduly.[16]

The acting head of the Dominican Order, Father Gillet, who was French, puzzled Italian counter-espionage. A spy told them that in Dominican headquarters at Santa Sabina on the Aventine he kept a

[14] AE, Santa Sede, 1942, Busta 60: Ministry of Interior to AE, 21 December 1942.
[15] AC, PS, 1941, Busta 35, report of 1 May 1942.
[16] Osborne's *Diary*, 20 March 1941.

radio receiver, listened to hostile broadcasts, and then started conversations hostile to Italy. More seriously the police noted that he received visits from a woman whom they had good reasons for suspecting to be an Allied spy. But Gillet's behaviour and conversation satisfied them – he kept away from Fontenelle, and was a friend of Bérard, he praised the House of Savoy in a public speech, welcomed the German invasion of Russia, kept away from Osborne, and regretted that Vichy could not send troops to fight the British in Syria. Italian counter-espionage noted all these things and decided to acquit Father Gillet; though they kept on him what they called 'an opportune surveillance'.[17] They asked themselves whether to deport him, more for safety than because they had any proof, and were told by lawyers that under the Lateran Treaty they could not deport the head of an international religious order.

Early in 1941 the French embassy acquired a new counsellor, de Blesson. He made a contrast with his ambassador, Léon Bérard. The ambassador kept himself very retired. Though he lived in Santa Marta, he had nothing to do with the other occupants. He avoided Osborne sedulously. De Blesson was outgoing and sociable. His wife quickly caused the police anxiety because they lost her trail on a shopping expedition. He soon became a friend of Osborne, and often went to see him. He joined Osborne for walks in the Vatican garden. The Italian police began to suspect him. They discovered that he came from Holland where he lost all his property to the Germans, and was outspokenly anti-German. By the summer of 1941 the Italian police noted that relations between de Blesson and his ambassador and superior Bérard were icy.[18]

Then the Americans and British invaded French North Africa and the Germans invaded unoccupied France. At the mass in the French church or St Luigi dei Francesi, Bérard the Vichy ambassador met Monsignor Fontenelle. A very unedifying quarrel in church was the result. The voices were loud. Fontenelle said that in these new circumstances Marshal Pétain should leave France. Bérard went so far as to accuse Fontenelle of being a traitor to his country. Bérard became very isolated. His counsellor de Blesson was a Gaullist and they could only speak together on business. Now there came this total and public breach between the ambassador and the French canon of St Peter's.[19] Osborne enjoyed de Blesson much, but he tried, though not systemati-

---

[17] AE, Santa Sede, 1941, Busta 55. Then Father Gillet published a book, *Le réveil de l'âme française* (Paris, 1942), which he dedicated to Pétain, and paid the Marshal homage for having roused the soul of France.

[18] AE, Santa Sede, 1941, Busta 53, report of 10 August 1941.

[19] AE, Santa Sede, 1942, Busta 57, report of Italian embassy, 14 November 1942.

cally, to keep away from him in order not to compromise him with the Vichy government.

In these ways the not timeless politics of warring Europe intruded into what Osborne called the timeless atmosphere of Vatican City. But Osborne could not use Fontenelle if he wanted. Fontenelle lay under almost as close surveillance as himself.

One public place gave headaches to the police: church. An Italian could hardly be stopped from entering St Peter's to say his prayers, and might there find himself saying prayers in the row next to Osborne's butler, John May. In every church where such meetings could occur the police kept their agents. For a time they suspected St Anna. They always had someone at services in the French church of St Luigi. They suspected one of the Poles, Monsignor Meysztowicz. He was not difficult to watch because he spent most of his time reading in the Vatican Library. But they observed him going to St Anna, and decided that this was the place where he exchanged messages. The suspicion was unfounded. Meysztowicz went to St Anna to say his prayers.[20]

iii. Swiss Guards

The Swiss Guards were nearly all Swiss, but their sympathies in the war were various. Italian intelligence reported anti-Axis utterances by Swiss Guards. In December 1940 the Vatican was forced by Italy to take stern measures that Swiss Guards talk neither about politics nor about the war.[21] Nevertheless, the surveillance of Swiss Guards proved in the end to be a problem almost beyond the wit of the Fascist police.

The police saw no evidence that Osborne attempted to use the Swiss for any improper purpose.

iv. Neutral ambassadors

Unable to communicate with London except in clear or via the papal diplomatic bag which the police knew (though Osborne did not at first know) that they could check, might Osborne use a colleague who had more freedom because his country was not at war?

Counter-intelligence found it necessary to check, at least by spot checks, the messages from neutral ambassadors to the Vatican. They were not satisfied with what they found.

For example, on 28 March 1941 the Yugoslav Minister to the Vatican called on Osborne, and next day the Pole Casimir Papée had a visit

[20] AE, Santa Sede, 1943, Busta 66, report of 22 March 1943.
[21] Attolico's report, 30 December 1940; AE, Santa Sede, 1941, Busta 54.

from the Minister of the Republic of Slovakia. It might not have been expected that anyone would think important a meeting between a helpless Polish ambassador inside the Vatican, who could only write letters to the exiled Polish government in London, and the Minister of a very satellite Germanophile republic. But Mussolini heard of the meetings and was angry. We shall see reasons why the meeting between Osborne and the Yugoslav might make him angry. He demanded that the War Office and the police so limit and control traffic with the Vatican that such meetings were impossible.[22]

Early in 1941 Italian counter-espionage began to suspect the Portuguese ambassador to the Vatican, Carneiro Pacheco, of being a spy in the interests of the Allies. German intelligence told them 'on very good authority' that Pacheco went to Lisbon and gave his government a secret report. The contents of this alleged report disturbed the Italians. For Pacheco reported to Portugal strange things about Osborne. He told them that great Italian industrialists went to see Osborne; that members of the Italian General Staff went to see him; that men who called themselves 'monarchists' went to see him. They had meetings in the Vatican to discuss a separate peace for Italy. Even the conditions of such a separate peace were described (cession to Italy of Nice and Djibouti; agreement on Tunisia; Italian representation on the Suez Canal company; independence of Ethiopia, and restoration of Haile Selassie). For a moment Osborne was at risk, accused of being the centre of an Italian conspiracy against Mussolini.

Attolico confronted Cardinal Maglione with the Portuguese information. Maglione was not perturbed. 'The information is proved improbable by internal evidence.' If all these high Italians really visited Osborne, the news 'would have reached the Italian government before it reached Signor Pacheco. For your Commissar of the Borgo would have reported it. We all know that the Commissar has his agents inside the Vatican and gets a list of everyone who visits the English Minister.' Maglione said that he thought the information 'completely and absolutely absurd'.

Attolico reported the clearance to his government and said that he believed it. But he thought that he could use it: 'While I too hold the information to have no foundation, I mean to profit by it. Tomorrow I go to a meeting with Monsignor Montini. At that meeting I intend to insist that the Vatican supervise the English minister more closely.'[23]

---

[22] Report of Guzzoni in Ministry of Interior, 7 April 1941.

[23] Attolico to Ciano, 28 January 1941: AE, Santa Sede, 1941, Busta 53; for the Vatican side, ADSS, 4, 377–8, Maglione to the nuncio in Lisbon, Ciriaci, 6 February 1941. Robert A. Graham (*Civ. Catt.*, 129, 1 (1978), 122) thinks the source of all this must be the secret British propaganda machine SIB, but it is difficult to see what motive SIB would have had.

The Italians did not like the Secretary to the Portuguese Embassy to the Holy See, Dr Vaz Sarafana. He was pro-Allied and said so. Count Ciano complained to Attolico, Attolico spoke to the Portuguese ambassador Carneiro Pacheco, who promised to have his subordinate recalled if necessary.[24]

Between 6 April and 12 April 1941 Hitler's armies destroyed the government of Yugoslavia. The British removed King Peter, who swelled the number of exiled sovereigns in England. Italy occupied Dalmatia and the islands. On 10 April Croatia proclaimed itself an independent state. Suddenly the Yugoslav Minister to the Vatican was either an enemy or the representative of a non-existent government. His name was Niko Mirosevic Sorgo. He had worked for a reasonable harmony between Italy and Yugoslavia, and had in January 1941 proposed to Monsignor Montini the need for a peace of compromise. When calamity struck Yugoslavia, must Mirosevic move inside the Vatican? Italian Foreign Affairs (Buti) said (14 April) that he must, as soon as possible, and said that they had already cut his telephone and provided for his surveillance. Buti said that if the Minister and his Counsellor acceded to the new State of Croatia, all would be happy.

In Santa Marta they were gloomy. How would they fit Mirosevic, his family and his staff, into the rooms? Osborne foresaw that Mirosevic would need to move into the former room of the Belgian ambassador, where surplus British furniture was now stored, and five of Osborne's rooms (including kitchen, laundry, bedrooms of two Italian servants). 'A great bore, especially as they have to come in and out by my front door' (Osborne's *Diary*, 9 April 1941). Then Mirosevic was allotted the house across the courtyard where Osborne had started. But Osborne also found Zoukitch and his wife with Galeazzi and the Vatican engineers poking about his ex-Belgian rooms. He had hoped to keep the rooms for an American if America came into the war, and said so to Galeazzi; and afterwards had qualms of conscience about being a dog-in-the-manger.

But on 28 April the nuncio Borgongini Duca appealed above the heads of the permanent Foreign Service to Count Ciano; and he cited the leave won by the Belgian Nieuwenhuys to live inside Rome and outside the Vatican, and a similar leave accorded to the Lithuanian. He mentioned the Lateran Treaty, and asked leave for the Yugoslavs to go on living in Rome. Borgongini Duca gave Ciano a memorandum on the subject, and Ciano said that next day he would talk to Mussolini. Mussolini gave the permission – that Mirosevic, his counsellor Zoukitch, and Zoukitch's charming wife, need not go into the Vatican.

[24] AE, Santa Sede, 1942, Busta 61.

Osborne and everyone else in Santa Marta were relieved to hear the news. They would mind if anyone else came to share their space.[25]

But Mirosevic was not pleased. He told Monsignor Montini that he was going into the Vatican, whatever permission Mussolini might give, that he had already stripped his Roman apartment of furniture and put various things into the Vatican. Montini said that he had no reason to move into the Vatican. Mirosevic appealed to Cardinal Maglione, who upheld Montini's refusal. Mirosevic demanded an assurance from the Vatican that his diplomatic rights would be respected if he lived in Rome. The Italians gave him the assurance, and Cardinal Canali gave orders that he was not to be admitted to the Vatican (Osborne's *Diary*, 6 May 1941).

This did not last. The exiled Yugoslav Foreign Secretary Nimcic escaped to Jerusalem. Thence he tried to keep in touch with Serbians inside Yugoslavia. He started using, as one of his routes for secret messages, Mirosevic in Rome. In June 1941 Italian counter-espionage intercepted several telegrams, and found ample evidence that the Legation passed information which it regarded as harmful to Italian interests.

Mirosevic could not take lying down the new relation between Italy and Croatia. He could not like the new state of Croatia at all. He minded that the Yugoslav College in Rome displayed the Croatian flag. He minded the new boundary between Italy and Croatia. He minded the dictator of Croatia, Pavelic, who embarked on a slaughter of Serbs, coming to Rome. He minded a rumour that the Bulgarians would appoint a blood-thirsty blackguard as governor of the Macedonian bit of Yugoslavia which they annexed. He made his discontents plain to Cardinal Maglione; and though the Cardinal kept secrets, his discontents soon became plain to the Fascist police. Attolico verbally demanded from Cardinal Maglione that he make Mirosevic behave courteously to Italy.[26]

On 24 July 1941 Attolico told the Vatican that Mirosevic was a spy. He demanded that the Vatican get rid of him and send him out of Italy. Cardinal Maglione refused. He had no proof of the charge. He did not think the charge probable. Mussolini intervened. On 25 July the Italian police put Mirosevic under house arrest and ordered him out of Italy. The fact was, Italy could not tell the Vatican what it knew about Mirosevic without simultaneously telling the Vatican that it secretly tapped Vatican correspondence. They said that this act was due to the

---

[25] The Fascist police recorded John May's opinions on the subject: Questura to AE, 12 April 1941, AE, Santa Sede, 1941, Busta 53, where John May is described as 'il noto maggiordomo inglese'.

[26] ADSS, 5, 110. S. K. Pavlowitch, *Balkan Studies* (1978), 105ff.

emergency of the times and they intended to observe the Lateran Treaty.

This shocked the Vatican; force applied to one of its accredited ambassadors. Osborne reflected the shock in his diary for 25 July:

Madam Mirosevic came to see me this morning in great distress, saying that their Legation was picketed yesterday and today Italian police have entered it, forbidden Mirosevic to leave the house, even to go to the Vatican, and have informed him that he must leave Italy at once, but that he may not go into Vatican City. On hearing this I at once went to the Cardinal [Maglione] and urged him to resist this blatant violation of the Lateran Treaties and of diplomatic rights. He said that he was already investigating and doing all possible, but that in the last resort the Holy See could not resist force . . .

Madame Mirosevic told Osborne that she was afraid that her husband would be fetched in the night and shot. 'I tried to assure her that it was not so bad as that.'

Cardinal Maglione protested formally (26 July 1941). He demanded proof of the charge. He had no reason to doubt Mirosevic's honour or correctness. The expulsion of Mirosevic was a glaring breach of the Lateran Treaty.

On 31 July Mirosevic was put across the Swiss border. Zoukitch and his wife were allowed to stay if they moved inside the Vatican. Osborne found them both a delightful asset to the little company of foreigners in the Vatican. Mirosevic went to Lisbon, where he remained an ambassador-in-exile of a government-in-exile.

Osborne was worried. If the Italians could expel one Vatican ambassador on charges which they refused to prove, they could easily expel him. On the day of Mirosevic's arrest he talked with Cardinal Maglione. He called it 'a flagrant violation of the Lateran Treaty' (which it was). He demanded a vigorous protest, and that the Cardinal 'insist' on Mirosevic's right to move inside the Vatican. He did not think, or pretended not to think, the protests made by Cardinal Maglione to be strong enough to meet the case. 'While admitting the inability of the Vatican to meet violence with force, I remain of the opinion that the Holy See should have been better able to defend the person and interests of Monsieur Mirosevic, the accepted principle of diplomatic immunity and its own indisputable treaty rights by a more forcible and effective exploitation of the great moral authority of the Vatican.'[27]

---

[27] Osborne to Maglione, 10 September 1941, ADSS, 5, 199; cf. 417. Chile and Colombia sent notes. Even after several months the Brazilian ambassador Accioly made a solemn protest (9 February 1942) against all the breaches of diplomatic immunity. The Holy See had to issue to every diplomat an assurance of its intention to observe and get observed the Lateran Treaty. Cardinal Maglione passed Accioly's protest to Italian

v. *Italian servants*

Several of the diplomats had Italian servants. Apart from his secretary, Miss Tindall, and his butler, John May, Osborne had four Italians: an usher or footman, who commuted from Frascati; a footman Livio Moratti, who was the youngest (28 in 1940) and slept at the Vatican; a chambermaid Giuseppina who lived in Rome; and a male cook who lived in Rome.

The police began to think about them. Might they be bribed, though Italian citizens, to work for the British – e.g. to carry messages from Osborne to unknowns in Italy? Alternatively might they be bribed, or rather, might their pay be duly supplemented, if they were part of the observer-corps that watched over Osborne? Or even, might one of them be disloyal enough to Osborne, or patriotic enough to Italy, to be still more effective – e.g. by secretly photographing his papers? On the one hand they were possible suspects. On the other hand they could be got at. The difficulty of the police consisted in the inability to plant servants. Most of them worked for the diplomats before the war. But the police succeeded in planting a footman inside the French embassy during the summer of 1940. D'Ormesson was perfectly aware.[28]

Osborne's Italian housemaid, Giuseppina, who had served him for four years, was in the habit of shopping in Rome once a week. She went out one morning (6 May 1941) to buy at the chemist's and other odds and ends, and never came back. Osborne besieged the Secretariat which approached the Italian police. They said that she was in the Regina Coeli prison charged with espionage. For one of the three times observable in these sources, Osborne exploded with rage: 'a superlatively nice and decent woman', not interested in politics and without the brains to discuss politics. 'It is perfectly damnable' (*Diary* 7 May). He told Cardinal Maglione angrily that a charge of spying against his maid was a charge of spying against himself and even the whole Vatican. He talked of approaching even Count Ciano directly. 'To begin with, and above all, I don't deal in espionage. But there's something mysterious.' 'It is a farce, but a foul farce. Her arrest clearly derives from a desire to satisfy a grudge against her, or me, or my household' (*Diary*, 9 May, 11 May 1941).

Actually, the Italian police had dubious reason to believe that John May used Giuseppina as his mistress, and therefore that she was sure to be pro-British.

Foreign Affairs, which automatically rejected it; cf. AE, Santa Sede, 1942, Busta 60.
There is no evidence that Osborne used Mirosevic as a way of communication between Britain and the Yugoslav underground. That is very improbable. There is no evidence that he was aware of what Nimcic in Jerusalem tried to communicate to the Yugoslav underground.   [28] Osborne's *Diary*, 19 October 1940.

In London the Foreign Office thought that Osborne reacted to excess about the arrest of Giuseppina.

Orme Sargent said that the idea of approaching Ciano was 'silly and dangerous'. Sargent thought it obvious that the Italians removed the maid because she refused to spy on Osborne and would now plant another maid who would not refuse. They thought that Osborne's ferocity was a sign of the lowering of his morale by too many months immersed inside Vatican City. They did not realize that this was an old-fashioned English aristocrat caring passionately about injustice to one of his tenants. He did not think much of the Foreign Office comments but promised to be on the look-out for efforts to plant a spy. She went to house-arrest at Pistoia, so that he never got her back. Eventually[29] her only fault turned out to be that she was heard to say how glad she was to work for the British because they treated and paid her well. She was not freed finally till 9 May 1942, that is, after an arrest of just over a year.

Frightened also of being arrested, Osborne's Italian cook resigned and left, and Livio, the footman, talked of leaving. Osborne wondered whether this was the object in arresting Giuseppina. 'It looks like a deliberate attempt to deprive me of servants. I suppose, if necessary, I shall have to return to eating downstairs in the refectory' (Osborne's *Diary*, 29 May 1941).

Livio remained, but his fears were not groundless. On a Sunday in January 1942 he was suddenly seized, taken to a carabinieri barracks, stripped, searched for letters, and held for six hours (Osborne's *Diary*, 19 January 1942). He was believed by the Fascists to carry news out of the Vatican. They found nothing. When they released him they threatened that he must stick to his work 'and not concern himself with anything else, or it would be the worse for him'.

The problem of Osborne's Italian servants hit the Italian police hardest in the spring of 1943. They decided to try, if they could, to change all the servants, in the effort to get more reliable, and more useful, and more informing servants. The Italians decided that they wanted to control, far more tightly, the Italian servants of the diplomats. They restricted the diplomats, but not their staff. The Ministry of the Interior suggested that they could only cross the border if armed with a special permit from the Ministry of the Interior, and that the Questura should have a right to object against their employment.[30]

---

[29] FO 371/30195.
[30] Ministry of Interior to AE and High Command, 29 March 1943; AE, Santa Sede, 1943, Busta 66.

But how? The Italian embassy talked about it to Monsignor Montini. Montini said that for the servants to sleep in the Vatican was impossible, that the Vatican had no room for any more people. The embassy advised Foreign Affairs that what the Ministry of Interior proposed would be a gift of propaganda to the Allies – Italy cannot trust its own Italian citizens; and that the Vatican would strongly resist the plan.

Osborne's footman, Livio, was young enough to fight. The Italians called him up. Osborne pleaded to the Vatican Secretariat of State that they get him exempted. The Secretariat of State pleaded with the Italian embassy that Livio be exempted. Livio was allowed to stay, but about this time he accepted the duty of being the spy of the Italian government inside Osborne's flat at Santa Marta. Probably the exemption from call-up as well as money had something to do with this betrayal of his master.

At this point we have a strange story. Livio, according to this story, was given the charge of getting Osborne's cypher. He succeeded in May or early June 1943. Opposite the safe there was a duct for hot air. During Osborne's afternoon walk from Santa Marta Livio passed the bulky book out of the duct to an agent of Italian intelligence who photographed it. Because the material was bulky, this operation took three days.[31]

If this happened in May or June 1943, it must have happened after 18 June when Osborne returned from London – if, that is, Osborne was really out walking when it happened. But the story has two difficulties. Sam Derry, the British officer who later, as we shall see, slept in Osborne's flat and saw the arrangements of the flat perfectly, said that this operation was impossible to perform. And it would not be very sensible for Italian intelligence to go to lengths to steal Osborne's cyphers when, as we shall see, they already possessed them.

John May, the butler, was as closely watched as Osborne. In his cockney accent he was outspoken, and there were those in the Vatican who thought this risky. On 15 February 1941 Cardinal Maglione went so far as to warn Osborne to tell May to be careful; for May had a fierce argument with the chef, and everything he said was reported to the Questura, who reported it to the Embassy, and the Embassy complained (verbally) to the Secretary of State. Osborne was angry. 'It really is a disgusting state of affairs,' he wrote in his diary, 'but it is certainly due to the encroachment of the New Order and the Hitler system into Italy.' Nevertheless, the friends of Osborne inside the Vatican wished that May could be better trusted to keep his mouth shut.

---

[31] See Robert A. Graham, in *Civ. Catt.* (1978), 4, 47–8.

vi. The Vatican police

These were the police of a neutral State. But many of them had come from the Italian police. The relation between the Questura of Rome and the Vatican police seemed at times to be as close as the relation between the Questura and the Italian police. This made the watch upon Osborne and his colleagues easy.

We have the documents to show us the attitudes of both sides to this matter. The Ministry of Popular Culture under Pavolini was a far more important ministry than it sounds because it was not only a ministry of propaganda but a mechanism for the control of opinion, and therefore had functions in intelligence or counter-espionage. In February 1943 it received a report on the successful way in which the Lateran Treaty stood up to the stresses of war; and this was due (it said) largely to the equable way in which both sides have interpreted the treaty. Naturally there have been differences, especially over some particularly delicate matters. But they have been settled 'in a spirit of sincere and trusting collaboration'.

In this spirit have been resolved all the complex and delicate questions over enemy diplomats in Rome . . . On its side the Holy See has always met our wishes and has adopted restrictive measures which made it possible to adapt our pledges under the Lateran Treaty to the exceptional necessities of war.[32]

Osborne described the situation for his own benefit, differently:

I believe that daily reports are sent out on our doings. They must be damned dull reading. The precise connection between the Italian police outside and the Vatican plain clothes police and gendarmerie inside defies precise definition, but it very definitely exists. In its subtlety it is both very Italian and very Vatican. So that, while guests of the Pope, we are at the same time to some extent prisoners of the Italian government.

The normal Vatican policeman at the gate of the Santa Marta flats was named Anton Call. He had served eight years in the Vatican gendarmerie. Unlike several other policemen he was always courteous to the diplomats. As the months passed he got to know them and exchange greetings. Osborne discovered Anton Call to be a friendly person; and found his supervision of the diplomats to be 'unobtrusive and amiable'. He grew so friendly that, with John May, he operated on the hernia of Osborne's dog Jeremy.

This could not last. The fact was, Monsignor Montini had taken a very bold decision, almost out of keeping with his cautious character. Aware that the Fascist police and the Italian Secret Police OVRA had

---

[32] AE, Santa Sede, 1943, Busta 65, file Italia e Santa Sede.

their secret (or not-so-secret) agents inside the Vatican, he did not see how the diplomats could be protected in their 'rights' given by the Lateran Treaty, if the policeman in charge of their surveillance reported directly to his supervisors who would pass the information to the Fascist police. Therefore he ordered that Anton Call should report directly to himself, and not to his superiors in the Vatican police force. Consequently the supervision of Santa Marta was accused by the Fascist police of being a separate enclave, not subject to routine procedures. Of course they put in other observers, who adopted procedures that were not routine. OVRA men had been watching Anton Call, both at his flat in Rome and inside the Vatican. Being a policeman himself, Call knew that he was being watched and found the experience tense. His Vatican superiors resented that he did not give them reports. Twice his immediate superior said angrily, 'You never give us news.' Call answered simply that he had orders from Monsignor Montini.

The fall of Anton Call was brought nearer by a change in the command of the Vatican gendarmerie. The commander was Colonel de Mandato, an officer of the old school and not a Fascist. The arrangement between Anton Call and Monsignor Montini could only work with the complaisance of Colonel de Mandato. Under pressure de Mandato resigned. It was easy because he was elderly. Age was pretext enough. The governor of Vatican City, Cardinal Canali, who disapproved of Monsignor Montini, nominated as his acting successor Soletto, who happened also to be a member of OVRA, the Italian Secret Police.

Under the commander of the Vatican gendarmerie came two sections – ordinary police, for traffic, crowd-control, normal patrolling; and secret or 'Special' police for political purposes. The head of the section of Special police was the son-in-law of Colonel de Mandato, by name Giovanni Fazio. An early member of the Fascist party, Fazio founded a Fascist group in 1921, took part in the March on Rome, and led violent squads to smash strikes. At one time he was believed to be a confidant of Farinacci. He was thought to be very elegant and have plenty of money. By way of being an officer in the Bersaglieri, he moved into the Vatican police and served there from 1929. His job was to collect information; make sure that the surviving members of the old Popular party (like de Gasperi) conducted themselves harmlessly; see that Count Dalla Torre and the group running the *Osservatore Romano* behaved. He had a wide range of informants inside the Vatican and compiled a sheet (*Notiziario*) every morning. This sheet did not go to his official master, who was Cardinal Canali, chairman of the commission that governed Vatican City.

During 1942 Fazio was dismissed. It is not clear why. A document of September 1941 shows that Italian counter-espionage began to suspect him of being on the wrong side, and accused him of being a friend of Osborne. They had evidence that his surveillance of Count Dalla Torre had turned into a friendship. They believed that he had also grown close to Fontenelle. They said that he had discovered the German espionage system in Rome. In short, they privately suspected this long-standing Fascist of now being anti-Fascist.[33]

The archives of the Italian government disagree. Foreign Affairs attributed the dismissal to a protest by Osborne, seconded by Papée. Most of the time the diplomats accepted resignedly the endless petty harassments of a tight surveillance. In March 1941 Foreign Affairs told a suspicious High Command that the papal police exercised 'due vigilance' over the diplomats and that they all observed the restrictions precisely, except the daughters of the ambassadors of Bolivia and Peru, and except the chargé d'affaires of Uruguay, who resented the restrictions and found them intolerable.[34] But in the spring of 1942 the tightening drove Osborne to protest against harassment, as unworthy of an independent and neutral State.

The Secretariat of State passed the protest to Cardinal Canali, as chairman of the governing commission. Cardinal Canali told Giovanni Fazio. Fazio retorted that he only did his duty. He said 'The activity of these enemy diplomats is a form of disloyalty to the Holy See, because it explicitly aims to hurt Italy.' For this attitude (according to the document in the archives of Foreign Affairs) Fazio was dismissed with a pension and went into business.[35]

But the Ministry of the Interior, with its organs of public security, had a different attitude. They registered the dismissal of Fazio as necessary, not because he was so unkind to Osborne and his colleagues, but because he was too friendly.[36]

The resignation of Colonel de Mandato, and then perhaps the dismissal of Giovanni Fazio, put at risk the guardian of Santa Marta, Anton Call. The first effort of the police to get rid of Anton Call was to frame him. A man employed in OVRA asked to meet him privately in the church of Santa Anna. Call went to the meeting. There the OVRA man produced a packet of money and asked Call if he would pass it to Osborne. This would have been evidence against Osborne as well as Call, and probably Osborne was the quarry. Call realized that this was a trap and left the church.

[33] AC, PS, 1941, Busta 55, Città del Vaticano – Ufficio di Polizia.
[34] AE, Santa Sede, 1943, Busta 66.
[35] AE, Santa Sede, 1942, Busta 57, report of Embassy, 17 April 1942.
[36] AC, PS, Busta 55, reports of 31 March 1942 and 13 April 1942. The office of the Special Police was suppressed.

Even in November 1941 Osborne heard the news that Call was being replaced because he was friendly. He lodged a complaint instantly with Cardinal Maglione. On 13 November Monsignor Montini came to luncheon with Osborne.

I complained bitterly about our new surveillance arrangements . . . I told Montini I had considered myself a guest of Vatican City, but I was being made to feel like a prisoner in a concentration camp. He was very nice about it, but I don't know if he can, or will, do anything.

But an unpredictable event made it easy for the police to get rid of Anton Call.

A British leading seaman, Albert Penny, escaped from a camp for prisoners-of-war near Viterbo. He got himself a bicycle and a work-man's overalls and pedalled hard for Rome. Then he pushed his way into the Vatican at a moment when the eyes of the Swiss Guards strayed, went straight ahead, was not challenged, and found himself in the Vatican gardens. He came round the back of St Peter's and in front of Santa Marta was challenged for the first time, by none other than Anton Call; who was astonished to discover that he had caught an escaped prisoner-of-war.

For his private comfort Call should have taken Albert Penny to the frontier and handed him to the Italian police. But he knew something vague about international law, and the rights of an escaped prisoner in a neutral country. He sent up a message to Osborne that Penny was downstairs.

Osborne ('I take off my hat to him') was astonished at Penny's feat. But he did not at first see how the Vatican could resist an Italian demand that he be handed back. And no one saw more clearly that the Vatican could not afford to be a refuge for escaped British prisoners-of-war. Nevertheless he decided to try an appeal to international law.

Diary, 5 October 1942
At 3.30 I went to Montini and said that Penny had come here confident in the protection of the Pope and in obtaining liberty in the Vatican City and I demanded that protection for him though I foresaw and admitted the likeli-hood of his having to go back to his camp, poor chap. This evening I am not quite so sure.

6 October
The Italians know that he is here, or that a British prisoner is here, but do not know who he is. They have demanded his surrender but the Vatican have stalled for time. I think the only hope is an appeal to the Pope's charity.

On 8 October Osborne went to see Cardinal Maglione and appealed to the Lateran Treaty and to the Pope's charity. 'I pointed out to the

Cardinal that a principle of great importance for the Vatican City was at stake and that Vatican rights to the neutrality and inviolability recognized in the Lateran Treaty should be defended.' He caused the Brazilian ambassador Accioly, an international lawyer by profession, to prepare a paper on the legal rights of an escaped prisoner.

Eventually he won. Penny was exchanged for an Italian prisoner. Until the exchange the Vatican insisted that he live in Osborne's flat. *Diary,* 22 October 1942: 'He ought really to be free in Vatican City, but I am complying with this request as I would not exclude a kidnapping.'

The Italians blamed Anton Call for the case. Any other Vatican policeman would have handed Penny back to the Italian police. Osborne would never have known that he walked so brazenly into the Vatican gardens. No question of international law would have arisen. It was enough to doom Call.

At that moment Monsignor Montini's father died in Brescia. He said to Call that while he was away the reports should go to his lay assistant Belardo. The day after Monsignor Montini went to Brescia the Vatican police arrested Call.

Under the lamentable Cardinal Canali they examined Call on a trumped up charge and expelled him from the Vatican, which was to deliver him to the Italian police, who threw him into the prison Regina Coeli. For eight days he was interrogated with a searing hostility. He was released on 28 January 1943 and given a minor post as German interpreter with the carabinieri. Osborne was angry. 'It all makes me, against my will, very anti-Vatican and anti-Italian' (21 January 1943). Anti-Vatican because Call was an employee of a neutral State who had done nothing but his duty. He had committed no offence. For being polite to visitors he was thrown out of his career. And the Vatican authorities cooperated in ridding themselves of a faithful servant so unjustly. At many moments Osborne recognized that the Vatican administration could not resist Italian pressure if it pressed very hard. Nothing made him like it. He did not fail to point out to the Secretariat of State his view of the morality of the question.

Osborne did not know, but before Anton Call was taken away to prison he did something to help the Secretariat of State directly, and indirectly Osborne. He saw Montini; and at that last meeting gave him a list of the employees of OVRA who were working inside the Vatican. His list was headed by Monsignor Pucci. It included Soletto, the new head of the Vatican police. On the list stood the names of two lay members of the staff at the radio station. Probably Montini would have known some at least, perhaps all of this before Call gave him the list.

Not all the Vatican policemen were as humane as Call. John May once complained bitterly to Osborne about his 'persecution' by the gendarmerie (Osborne's *Diary* 25 July 1942) and Osborne had no doubt that they treated him unpleasantly. It must be said that John May liked to provoke 'persecution'. He liked to be offensive to Fascists if he saw the chance. He would pull the legs of supervising policemen. He called himself Professor of Domestic Economy and pretended to be furious when they failed to call him Professor May. This was one of the aspects of John May's behaviour which Osborne's friends inside the Vatican regretted.

vii. Rumours among Fascists

The immuring of the diplomats; the restrictions upon their acts and movements; the spasmodic tightening of the border-crossings; the escorts if any of their families went shopping – all helped to create the legend, in popular opinion, that this was 'a nest of spies'. Blame then washed, in the people's gossip, not over the Pope but over his high officials in the Vatican, whom rumour supposed to be protecting these pseudo-diplomats. One of the Italian ambassadors, Guariglia, thought that the life of some of the higher Vatican officials was 'embittered' by the constant suspicion under which they laboured, as men who were in touch with enemy spies: Fontenelle, Kaas, Montini.

Cardinal Canali was powerful as the head of the Vatican administration and nearly everyone was his man. Montini was not his man. Canali disapproved of Montini, and Montini regretted Canali. The Pope was fond of both and supported both. That helped Montini to protect Osborne. But the situation made Montini's life hard. He was unpopular among the Vatican staff. And outside the Vatican Rome heard rumours that Osborne and Montini were in the habit of going together up to Vatican radio and broadcasting information to help London. For this reason Anton Call, when in charge of surveillance, disliked Osborne's walks in the Vatican gardens. Call privately begged Osborne not to extend his walk towards the radio station. Osborne was bad at obeying this request because his exercise was already restricted. Call approached Monsignor Montini, when he went on his way to tea with Osborne, and begged him to tell Osborne not to go near the radio station.

Call blamed Cardinal Maglione, at least a little. Monsignor Montini needed backing. The Pope was known to back him but he needed backing at a lower level, from the pressures of Cardinal Canali and the administration. Call believed that the Secretary of State could have helped Montini more.

Montini and his humane attitudes were indispensable to the protection of Osborne and the diplomats. Yet he was hesitant and was distrusted inside the Vatican administration for his liberal outlook. Osborne could sense the insecurity of the situation.

The worst was the sense of danger. The more Fascists believed the Vatican to be a nest of spies, the more the Italian government would come under pressure to occupy Vatican City. It was fortunate for everyone that Mussolini himself never seems to have believed the diplomats to be dangerous.[37]

When Guariglia arrived as ambassador in February 1942, he discovered that he had another job besides that of being ambassador. He had the duty of a gaoler. He was expected to organize supervision of Osborne and Papée and the other diplomats. This took a lot of time, in petty detail; and he must constantly listen to fantasies of plots, intrigues, secret messages. A single example suffices. A spy brought to Guariglia the story of a plot concocted between Osborne, Tittmann the American, and Monsignor Montini. The spy had observed them meeting by night on the Cortile Borgia to hatch their plans. When Guariglia pursued this evidence, he discovered that this particular spy was famous for inventing.[38] The story had improbability on its face, for the three 'plotters' did not need a cortile by night, they could use any one of a hundred rooms in comfort and safety.

The spring of 1941 was an anxious time. The suspicion of the Yugoslav and the Portuguese spilled over into heightened suspicion of the British.

On 11 February the Italian War Office sent out a warning. 'Counter-espionage has been able to establish that some of the diplomats in the Vatican do things not easy to explain; and others, representatives of nations at war with Italy, engage in military spying against us. It is obvious that these activities greatly endanger our armed forces; which cannot move without the movement being known. In view of the situation in the war at the moment, this Ministry holds it necessary and urgent to complete the earlier provisions by further special measures to neutralize the spying of the diplomats.' They suggested[39] that no one enter or leave the Vatican without a special passport and that they carefully watch anyone who visited one of the diplomats.

This was not popular with Foreign Affairs who saw that two facts made it hard to implement fully. The first was that special passports required the cooperation of the Vatican, who must refuse to place obstacles between themselves and the Curial offices still within the city of Rome. The second was St Peter's. How should you insist on a special passport if a good Italian Catholic wanted to say his prayers?[40] Besides,

[37] So Guariglia thought, *Ricordi*, p. 500. [38] Guariglia, *Ricordi*, pp. 501–2.
[39] Report of Ministry of War, 11 February 1941. [40] Report by Anfuso, 2 March 1941.

all this was unnecessary. Counter-espionage already had better methods of control.

This did not satisfy the Fascists.

Osborne's *Diary*, 5 May 1941:

There are signs of anti-Vatican propaganda in Rome, the purpose of which would be to excuse any action taken against the Vatican! For example, it is being put about that the Pope is conducting an espionage service for the British! How vile it all is.

Strange rumours about Osborne came from remote places. The Italian naval attaché in Belgrade had information of gatherings, to spread defeatist propaganda, in Rome, Milan and Turin; probably also in Trieste and Naples. He alleged that these gatherings paid large sums to priests who in turn paid people to spread alarmist rumours. He further alleged that the coordinator of all this activity was Osborne.[41]

More ominously, Mussolini himself was said to have said at a meeting, 'The church is our irreconcilable enemy.'

The Pope was disturbed by such reports or rumours. A Redemptorist, Father Salza, who was an army chaplain and approved by Mussolini, took it up with Mussolini (4 February 1942). He told Mussolini the stories of what was said. Mussolini was in one of his churchy moods. 'Father, the Conciliation of 1929 proves that the Vatican and Fascism are not irreconcilable.' He hammered out the words: 'I am in Rome, and while I am here no one will touch the Vatican. The Vatican has had 2000 years of life, and will have at least 2000 years more. I am sure of it – naturally as a human being . . .'[42]

Mussolini went up and down. Later the same month he spoke strongly against the Vatican. The Pope and Cardinal Maglione hoped it was not true. Count Ciano officially denied the story but privately admitted its truth.[43]

On 30 May 1942 Cardinal Maglione told Osborne privately that the Italian military authorities particularly suspected him as a source of information about conditions in Italy. He also said that he was well aware that Osborne 'scrupulously' observed his 'pledge not to send any such information'. The very next day Osborne heard that in Rome he was accused of successfully fostering anti-Fascist sentiments in 'several' government offices, though how an immured man could achieve this was a mystery. 'In wartime hysterical suspicion exceeds all bounds of sanity. Also excuses must be found' (Osborne's *Diary*, 30 May and 1 June 1942).

[41] AE, Santa Sede, 1942, Busta 61, report of 14 May 1941.   [42] ADSS, 5, 410–11.
[43] Ciano, *Diario (1939–43)*, 5th edn (2 vols., Milan, 1948), vol. 2, p. 130; ADSS, 5, 443; cf. 656.

The Vatican recognized that its neutral territory was full of Italian spies; that no one, whether papal or diplomatic, could do anything without the Italian government knowing. Monsignor Montini had a more sinister anxiety. All these spies had nothing to do, and nothing to report. What if they fabricated evidence of espionage by foreign diplomats? Montini held this to be not only probable but in a few cases actually to be proven; and the object would be to prove that the Holy See was the enemy of Italy, and to force the expulsion of the foreign diplomats. He imagined a situation where a bomb was planted and evidence framed to implicate the diplomats. He took the trouble to talk to the Italian Ambassador (then Guariglia) about this worry in case something like it were to happen.

viii. Rumour and German intelligence

The Italians were likely to be sceptical about false information when manufactured. The Germans, being further away and less familiar with what went on, were more likely to be deceived. This could add to the danger for the Vatican and for Osborne.

The Gestapo had an agent inside the Secretariat of State as early as 1939–40. The Pope was aware of his existence. But his duty at that time was primarily the behaviour of the German bishops, and correspondence concerning them vanished mysteriously from the Vatican desk. Since all the senior members of the Secretariat of State knew that he had these responsibilities to Germany he was largely ineffective.

This mysterious German agent whose name began with a K was almost certainly Alexander Kurtna. This was an Estonian seminarist who was a student at the Russian college until 1940 when, because they found no sign of a vocation, he remained a layman and did translation work for the various Vatican offices. His connexion with the Gestapo was proved after July 1942 when Italian intelligence arrested him on the suspicion that he was a spy for the Russians and found that he was also, or instead, a spy for the Gestapo.[44]

During the summer of 1941 a discontented Italian journalist, Virgilio Scattolini, who was dismissed from the *Osservatore Romano* in 1939, started selling information to the Germans. It was sometimes quite lurid, and sometimes had a slim foundation in Vatican gossip. An SS Standartenführer in Berlin, Rudolf Likus, who had a special duty to observe Monsignor Orsenigo, thought Scattolini's 'news' valuable, and laid some of it on Hitler's desk. The Italian police considered

---

[44] For Kurtna, see de Risio, *Servizi Segreti*.

imprisoning Scattolini for spreading false information to the discredit, for example, of Monsignor Montini. But Scattolini was protected in Italy by Farinacci, who told the police that this was 'a faithful and laudable informant'.[45] The Germans might not be able to do anything from a distance but if they believed Scattolini they had a duty to bring pressure to bear both on the Vatican and on the Italians.

On 22 October 1941 the head of the Sicherheitsdienst, Heydrich, ordered various measures about the Catholic Church, one of which was to get trustworthy informers, if possible, into 'the system' – by which he meant communications with the German bishops – and another was to get spy-students among the German theological students in Rome. The Gestapo obtained a series of reports on Germans in the papal service, including Father Leiber. They had of course a report on Cardinal Tisserant. They suspected the office for prisoners-of-war (not without reason).

During the winter of 1941–2 German hostility started to seep into the Vatican through Italian sources. Prince Bismarck was reported to have spoken contemptuously in a Rome hospital of the Vatican as a mere museum that you would buy a 10 lire ticket to get inside; and other Germans were alleged to have talked in the same way, of soon turning the Vatican into nothing but a museum; even Kurt von Tannstein, who was von Bergen's attaché in the German embassy to the Holy See. The German threat was passed over all Rome. Maglione approached von Bergen who denied the truth of the story. A German official, who attended a liturgy in the Sistine chapel, was reported as saying that the ceremonies were very interesting, especially as this was the last time when they would be celebrated. Some German was reported to have said, 'Nazism can never be reconciled with Christianity. Christianity will have to go to the wall.'[46]

Early in March 1942 some Germans made the gravest possible accusation against Osborne. Von Bergen, who hardly ever did anything, told Cardinal Maglione that Germany had information of spy-

---

[45] U. A. Grimaldi and G. Bozzetti, *Farinacci il più fascista* (Milan, 1972), p. 99. For Scattolini, see Robert A. Graham in *New York Times*, 13 September 1973, and in 'Il Vaticanisto Falsario', in *Civ. Catt.* (1973), 3, 467ff. For the whole question, Graham's article 'Spie naziste attorno al Vaticano durante la seconda guerra mondiale', in *Civ. Catt.* (1970), 1, 21ff. Scattolini was another employee of OVRA. He was first a freelance writer of plays and pornography. During 1935–6 he was taken into service by the Vatican as a publicist. From 1939 he imagined plausible stories and wove them into an authentic context of audiences or interviews. Sometimes the audiences or interviews were also imaginary. His power to persuade uncritical editors depended partly on the plausibility and the skill of the weaving, but more on the impenetrability of the Vatican world which made editors, desperate for news, grasp at anyone who said that he knew something. Scattolini's reports misled scholarly men, like A. C. F. Beales, *The Catholic Church and International Order* (Penguin Special, 1941) and N. Micklem, *Papalism and Politics* (1955).　　　[46] ADSS, 5, 214–15; 396–7 note; 411.

ing; to the effect that from the Vatican the news was passed to London that the city of Mannheim had no anti-aircraft guns, and that this information caused the British bombing of Mannheim in December 1940. Von Bergen also said that the Germans had information to show how from the Vatican news of the sailing of Axis ships reached London.

Cardinal Maglione was not moved. He told the Italian ambassador Guariglia what von Bergen said, but thought it mere tales by ignorant Nazis.[47] Menshausen said that the German government and the Nazi party did not believe the story. Nevertheless the German security services sent a Gestapo officer named Heymann to Rome, to examine whether Italian counter-espionage was doing all it should to supervise Osborne and the diplomats and to stop them from any chance of being spies.[48]

Late in July 1942 the Vatican buzzed with the story that a German officer told one of the Pope's entourage, that Germany would win the war within a few weeks (the German army was just approaching Stalingrad and the Caucasus); would then 'more or less' take over Italy; would lodge Mussolini in a castle, and expel from Italy both the King of Italy and the Pope. The Pope would be allowed to take refuge in the United States or South America. Osborne believed not a word (*Diary*, 23 July 1942). He was incapable in any case of believing that Germany would win the war, in however many weeks.

That summer the American Magic codebreakers picked up a report that among the German students at the Angelicum in Rome were spy-students in the employ of the Gestapo, and that 'Gestapo agents' were inside Vatican City.

During 11–13 October 1942 the head of the Gestapo, Heinrich Himmler, was in Rome. He asked questions about many things, and did not fail to ask about the diplomats in the Vatican. He pressed Count Ciano on the subject.[49] Afterwards a story reached the Vatican that he demanded the expulsion of the diplomats, and that this did not happen only because the Italian ambassador to the Holy See, Guariglia, protested. This story must have contained a measure of truth; for we have a brief note on the subject in the hand of Cardinal Maglione: 'This is not accurate.'[50]

German pressure upon the Italians mounted. The Italian counsellor Babuscio Rizzo came to see Monsignor Tardini (30 October 1942) and told him that one or two of the diplomats were suspected of spying.

---

[47] Maglione to Guariglia, 6 March 1942; Guariglia to AE, 10 March 1943; AE, Santa Sede, 1943, Busta 65; Secretariat of State to German Embassy, 6 March 1943, ADSS, 5, 465; Gröber of Freiburg in ADSS, 2, 259.   [48] AE, Santa Sede, 1942, Busta 60.
[49] Ciano, *Diario*, vol. 2, p. 205.   [50] ADSS, 5, 753.

Tardini asked *which*?, but Babuscio Rizzo would not say. There was a clamp-down on the shopping expeditions, and the leaves to go out, for which Osborne never asked. Mussolini was known, in these weeks, to speak menacingly about the Vatican.[51] The bombing of Italian cities was worsening, and hatred of the British grew in Italy, and the presence of Osborne grew even more offensive. Montini (4 November 1942) made a private note of the Italian discussion, how they were to rid Rome of the diplomats inside the Vatican. On 15 November Buffarini summoned the nuncio Borgongini Duca, raged about the bombings, and said that Rome had become 'the great centre of espionage'. He accused ecclesiastics of carrying secret news about the movement of troops and ships, and accused the enemy diplomats of having secret radios with which they sent home information. Borgongini Duca said that this was all fancy.[52] Nevertheless, in Santa Marta Osborne heard a resulting rumour, that German troops would shortly surround the frontier of Vatican City and control all access (*Diary*, 19 November 1942). Diego von Bergen heard the same story and reported it to Berlin. Cardinal Maglione warned the nuncio in Spain of a story that German forces would bombard the Vatican, seize the archives and expel the diplomats.[53]

Early in May 1943 Count Ciano had a conversation with Mussolini about the need to reduce the chance of illicit contacts between the diplomats and Italian traitors. The Holy See, he said, was likely to cooperate because it could not please the Vatican, at a time when women and children in Italian cities were being killed by bombs, to be called by some Italians a 'den of spies' (*un covo di spie*). Ciano said that he had talked to Montini; who recognized 'with grief' that some Italians told such stories and the stories were believed by people who do not know what precautions were taken, for example that the diplomats could not send messages in code; precautions, said Montini, 'which render practically impossible any spying of a military character of any real use to the enemies of Italy'. Montini worried about the effect of a still stricter surveillance over the private lives of the diplomats. He said that they were already suffering from claustrophobia.

Montini then made a prediction that was almost a threat. He told Ciano that 'this state of mind among the diplomats would result, at the end of the war, in strengthening the move to internationalize the Catholic Church' and make it less Italian. 'Monsignor Montini said,' reported Ciano, 'that he talked from the heart as an Italian and as a

---

[51] Ciano, *Diario*, vol. 2, pp. 212–3; Guariglia, *Ricordi, 1922–46* (Naples, 1950), pp. 528ff.
[52] ADSS, 7, 73–4, 94.
[53] Von Bergen to Berlin, in AA Inland II.g.n. 330; cited Robert A. Graham in *Civ. Catt.* (1972), 1, 324.

priest; and he inferred that such an internationalization was not in the interests of the Church'; and therefore it would be best if Italy did nothing, that was not strictly necessary, to give the appearance of an excessive Italian control over the Apostolic See.[54]

Gestapo agents with long ears; Fascist police with agents in post; Vatican police working for the Fascists; a Vatican government with its own methods of private control; telephones tapped by counter-espionage; telephones tapped by normal Italian censorship; fakers of false evidence – surveillance showed an obsessed determination to stop Osborne and his colleagues from lifting a little finger that might hurt Italy. And events were to prove that even such obsessiveness was not quite enough. The ecclesiastics of the Curia who passed the frontier on the business of their dicasteries; the tradesmen who crossed the frontier to supply the Vatican with food or fuel; the barracks of the Swiss Guards sited at the frontier; the men who happened to meet at a service in St Peter's – Osborne could not be made a total nonentity without the total shutting of the frontier. And to close the frontier totally was equivalent to occupying Vatican City and destroying the Papacy.

[54] Embassy memorandum, 10 May 1943; AE, Santa Sede, 1943, Busta 66.

8
Surveillance II: the bag

i. The usefulness of the bag

Under the Lateran Treaty the ambassadors accredited to the Vatican had a free right to communicate with their countries. Warring Italy refused to keep this clause of the Treaty. The Pope had a moral obligation to secure free communication between Osborne and London. Therefore the Vatican offered Osborne and his colleagues the privilege of using the papal diplomatic bag. They made the condition that into the bag Osborne should put only material which concerned his mission as envoy at the Holy See. Osborne perforce gave this undertaking. He scrupulously kept the undertaking to report only on what concerned his mission to the Vatican. 'Discussion of any point at the Secretariat of State brings it within the purview of my official activities, and consequently enables me to report on it without violating my undertaking. So Jesuitical am I becoming!'[1] From about this time (November 1940) he started to say nearly anything he liked that helped the British government. Once we even find him trying to provoke the Secretariat of State into confirming unconsciously that the Germans had set up an air base at Frascati. If it were asked whether this was 'espionage', or intelligent observation from a neutral state, or a breach of the undertaking given to Monsignor Montini, he could reply that everything of this sort concerned his mission; for a German base at Frascati could affect the security of the Vatican from British bombers.

He began at once to use the courier system.

Osborne wrote a letter; cyphered it; gave it to the Secretariat of State. The bag went out alternatively by papal courier to Berne, or by papal courier to Lisbon. In Berne or Lisbon the nuncio handed it over to the British, who put it in their diplomatic bag for London. When the bags would go, could not be quite predicted. This often meant rush at the last moment. From December 1942 the Berne–Lisbon courier route was blocked. The Berne courier still came twice a week, but to Lisbon a courier now went by air, only once a month.

The British asked themselves whether the diplomatic bags were secure; that is, whether the nuncios through whose hands they

[1] Osborne to Nichols, 12 November 1940: FO 371/24964/96 and 173.

181

passed, were trustworthy, or whether a corrupt ecclesiastic or his servant might be bribed or bullied into breaking the British seals.[2] These suspicions were proved in the event to be prudent.

They dare not send to Osborne truly confidential matter in the diplomatic bags because they felt that they could not be absolutely certain of the nuncios. They thought tampering 'very unlikely'. They could not think it impossible. They argued with those responsible for Political Intelligence, and then with the Admiralty over their intelligence; but they saw no way out, and decided that they could trust nothing very important to their avenues of communication with Osborne in Berne or Lisbon. And they were right, because by March 1941 they had evidence of extensive tampering with the bags.[3]

Osborne was even more nervous than London about the security of the bags. And this bears upon the quality and picture of the evidence which lies there so massively in our public archives. He dare not say what he wanted. Especially he could not tell London what good the Vatican did for the Allies in the war because he was confident that the other side would get to know.

This situation is described with complete frankness in a letter from Osborne to Anthony Eden dated 11 February 1941.[4]

My dear Secretary of State,

I am afraid that my communications about Vatican policy (if any) and sentiments are so cautious and reticent as to confirm what I expect is your bad opinion of the general attitude of the Holy See.

The fact is that there are things I would like to say that would mitigate, I think, to some extent this opinion, but I dare not either write or telegraph them for I have not entire faith in my communications by either Bag or cypher telegram. The Bags I send by Vatican courier go a long way round via Berne and thence Barcelona, Madrid and Lisbon. I have entire faith in the Vatican authorities here and elsewhere, but I cannot entirely exclude the possibility on so long and complicated a journey of misfortune or carelessness. And the Germans are diabolically ingenious and would be pleased to get anything against the Vatican or the diplomats in the Vatican City. As to cypher telegrams, the most able American diplomat I know, Alexander Kirk, who was Chargé d'Affaires in Berlin during most of last year and part of the preceding year, has told me that he believes that the German experts can break down any cypher system in a short time and that they probably have all of our cyphers – British and American. This seems incredible to me, but he knows what he is talking about . . .

Nor do I exclude the possibility that one day the Germans might walk in on me here and seize my cypher before I can destroy it.

For all these reasons I am careful not to say anything of sentiments or

---

[2] FO 371/24964/127.
[3] FO 371/30190.   [4] CAB 954/31A/06875; cf. FO 371/30179.

expressions of opinion here that might be incriminating. And my style is consequently somewhat cramped in representing the Vatican attitude.

I hope that you will bear this in mind if you are inclined to condemn me for lack of precision or the Vatican for lack of understanding of what is at stake in the war.

As early as March 1941 Osborne was refusing to put candid information into his reports because he could not trust the diplomatic bag: 'I won't discuss the war because I am never quite sure of the courier service.' The Italian archives show how justified were these suspicions.

At the end of June 1940 the Vatican found that the Italian censors opened letters and telegrams, addressed to the Vatican, even addressed to the Cardinal Secretary of State. They protested verbally. They followed this with a formal letter (2 July 1940): 'the Secretariat of State is sure that this is a mere oversight. But we should be grateful if the Italian embassy could make representations to those responsible.'[5] Attolico thought this a well-justified reproach and said so not uncertainly. He told the Vatican that precise orders had been given to avoid this 'inconvenience'. Nevertheless, the Vatican protested again, and then again, and then again; at least five times by 24 September 1940.

So started a stream of protests from the Vatican about tampered mail. The protests were always supported by the Italian ambassador to the Holy See. Sometimes the Vatican produced on demand actual envelopes which had obviously been opened. Occasionally (February 1941) the Vatican even threatened Italy with publicity, to show the world its misbehaviour over mail – but did not mean the threat. They provided proof that people inside the censorship system forged the seals of the Holy See. Cardinal Maglione never ceased to grumble.

The Ministry of the Interior was determined not to give way. In a state of war and the crisis of a nation, the clauses of the Lateran Treaty must give away. They did not say so to the Vatican, they kept saying so to themselves. Occasionally to satisfy the Vatican they would dismiss an employee whose censoring methods were too patent or too clumsy, for example the censor at Turin. But they had no intention of ceasing to check on Vatican mail, at least by spot checks. And they were quite successful. Files of ambassadors' letters can still be found in the archives of the Italian government – e.g. the Peruvian ambassador's reports to his government during September 1941.

They had plenty of ways of keeping the file going; or denying that they knew anything about it; or asking for proof of what was alleged in

---

[5] AE, Santa Sede, 1940, Busta 52.

a Vatican complaint. The police would say that distinguishing one envelope from another was very difficult, and that these things could happen unintentionally. In March 1941 the Ministry of the Interior disclosed to Foreign Affairs that it had perfect equipment for all these operations – but refrained from any check on Vatican despatches *in view of the delicacy of relations with the Holy See and to avoid harmful duplication with the controls by the organs of counter-espionage.*[6] In March 1943 they picked up a breach of the rule that all telegrams must be in clear. The Chilean ambassador sent two telegrams in a language which was obviously coded. A formal protest went to Santiago.[7]

None of this fierce argument between the Vatican and Italy over tampered mail was visible to London. But London had enough suspicion. One example out of several: 29 May 1941, M. M. Dunlop to Pierson Dixon: 'I am afraid our cypher to Osborne is not sufficiently secure to make this telegram in complete safety.'[8]

The second volume of Sir Harry Hinsley's work on the secret war of codes, has at page 642 a remarkable footnote. After the end of the Second World War was discovered in the archives of the German Ministry of Foreign Affairs a volume of 90 pages, containing British diplomatic signals for the years immediately before the war. This discovery caused an enquiry, though not until the year 1968. The enquiry showed:

1. that a number of signals were sent *en clair* – which we in any case can see easily from the diplomatic archives and which we know to have been one of the Italian conditions.
2. that in 1935 the Italians got hold of the cyphers of the Rome embassy and photographed them – that is, not the Vatican legation but the embassy to the Quirinal.
3. that they had fairly regular access to the cyphers at the Mission to the Holy See during the war.

Therefore the enquiry believed they might have read all telegrams to the Rome embassy between 1935 and June 1940; and they might have read many of Osborne's reports from Rome between 1940 and June 1944 when the Allies occupied Rome.

But Osborne cannot be blamed, either for carelessness or for naiveté. Like London, he instinctively suspected the bag. And, linked as he was in friendship and almost daily association with Montini, he quickly became aware, in general though not in detail, of the secret argument over tampering between the Vatican and Italy.

Once, Monsignor Tardini, privately to himself and in a fury, accused

[6] AE, Santa Sede, 1941, Busta 52, Rapporti; Busta 54.
[7] AE, Santa Sede, 1943, Busta 67, File, Censura.   [8] FO 380/74.

Osborne of being 'simple-minded' (*ingenuo*) for thinking that he could trust his cyphers.[9] Osborne had no such simplicity. From April 1941 he was aware that every word which he put into the diplomatic bag was read by the Italian police.

This meant that he could not send London the most important of all messages, and he knew it.

It also meant that a new chance of helping had unexpectedly appeared. If the Italians read his secret despatches to London, and did not know that he knew, he could begin to feed information into the diplomatic bag which was aimed not only at London but at influencing Italian authorities. The information which he sent could not be false. That would instantly be perceived. But at times it might, at least, mislead.

From the first, he found this rewarding but awkward. He had to misrepresent the Vatican to make it appear helpful to Italy in the eyes of the secret Italian readers. But if he misrepresented it too grossly, he would make London, which was already very critical of the Vatican's behaviour, wild with rage at the Vatican. 'Knowing the present sentiments at the Foreign Office, I have to be very careful in representing the views of the Vatican. That is to say, I have to steer between the Scylla of compromising the Vatican, on the assumption that the Germans read all cypher telegrams, and the Charybdis of arousing the Foreign Office's worst suspicions of the Vatican as being nothing but an appanage of the Axis. It is tricky work!' (*Diary*, 15 November 1942).

Nevertheless Osborne, while he consciously misled the Italians on the utility of the Pope to the Italian cause, could not help but mislead his own Foreign Office. He wrote them one general warning, but never dared to repeat it until he had opened a second channel of communication; unless one of the messages not yet released to historians by the Foreign Office, and almost certainly dated in the late summer of 1941, contained more explicit information on codes.[10]

As soon as Osborne knew that he was being read by Italian intelligence – and he was sure enough by the late spring of 1941 – he had a chance to help both the Pope and the Allied cause. That is, provided that the Italians had not guessed that he knew how they read his reports. He could draft his reports to inform London and to mislead SIM or the Gestapo. To inform and misinform simultaneously was not easy.

Tittmann once made a note[11] that Cardinal Maglione had on several occasions expressed to Osborne his sympathy for the Allies 'in no

[9] ADSS, 5, 460.
[10] Osborne to Eden, FO 954/31A; VA/41/4; one sheet closed till 2017.
[11] Tittmann Papers, Brussels, Atroc., 13 June 1942.

uncertain terms'. Tittmann found Osborne 'very unhappy' about his dilemma. He could not tell London because his code was broken. But if he said nothing about these feelings, London would think the Vatican nothing more than an appanage of the Axis. 'What is a diplomat to do when confronted with such a problem?'

The key aim was to keep the Vatican in being. It was helpless before the Fascists. It could be taken over, as Mussolini said, by a few hundred men, and at any minute. The Fascist government was frequently hostile. Fascist extremists like Farinacci loathed it and said so publicly. It was known to be pro-peace, and suspected of being pro-British. Inside its walls it housed enemies like Osborne who had to be watched continuously lest they hurt Italy. No one could think it whole-heartedly behind the Italian war effort, and yet it was an Italian institution with an influence on the Italian people; 'a cancer' as it was said among Fascists, at the heart of Italy. Even without being occupied it could lose all its water, or power, or food, or money.

Therefore the Italians must be made to think that the existence of the Vatican was no help to the Allies. And it was not enough to show the Vatican as no help to the Allies. It must be shown to be – on balance – of advantage to Italy in its war effort.

This utility was what Osborne could suggest by reports.

Some rules were obvious. No conspiracy like that of 1939–40 could be allowed to appear. If an Italian approached the Vatican with the object of getting Italy out of the war, Osborne could not say so to London. Then, he must always speak the truth. If he told untruth he deceived London and made the Italians suspicious. If he told untruth he must tell it only by omission, by nuance, by implication, or by suggestion. The reports to London must be real reports on the business of the Legation; even if they failed to tell all the business of the Legation.

Another obvious rule was to avoid abuse of Mussolini or of the Italian people. He could attack the Germans (in moderation) for the Germans were not popular with many Italian officials. He could attack Farinacci, also disliked by Italian officials. He could attack the Vatican as freely as he liked. The more ferociously he criticized the Vatican the better if his aim was the safety of the Vatican. The more acidly he criticized the Pope and the Pope's men, the more useful to Italy would the Pope seem to the Italians. This had the disadvantage that he could lead London to imagine the Vatican as dedicated to the Italian cause. He could cause London to be very acid indeed in its comments on the Pope's behaviour. And he could not compensate by telling the ways in which the Vatican helped the Allied cause.

He did not say everything that was true. But everything that he said was true.

ii. *The Italian Curia*

On 29 December 1942 there were 42 cardinals. Twenty-nine of them were Italian, more than double the number of non-Italians. Of the 22 cardinals of the Curia all but one were Italian, and the one was Cardinal Tisserant, the Gaullist shut away inside the Vatican. All the chairmen of the Roman Congregations but one were Italians. For centuries the Papacy had not been so Italian.

The Brazilian ambassador Accioly wrote for Osborne's benefit a frank memorandum, to the effect that Italianization of the Curia was due chiefly to the political and territorial situation of Vatican City 'which has left it in a state of half dependence on the Italian State – as one sees today very clearly'. He suggested an international guarantee for Vatican City; more non-Italian cardinals; more non-Italians in the civil service of the Curia. 'Vatican press and radio are vigorously controlled and supervised by the Italian government, and cannot express their opinions, even when it comes to denouncing religious persecution.'[12]

The Foreign Office in London was not impressed with this memorandum. The only practicable objective seemed to them to be to get an English cardinal into the Curia, which Osborne anyway suggested from time to time.

It was a good point to complain about. It happened to be true. And to complain about it told the unseen Italian tappers how Italian was the Pope.

The British Legation did not mention that the Pope had a German secretary, Father Leiber, whom he saw every day; that in appointments the Jesuit General, Father Ledochowski, a Pole, was believed to have more influence with him than any of the Italian Cardinals; that his housekeeper, Sister Pasqualina, was a German; that a former member of the Secretariat, now Archbishop Spellman, was believed to be influential and was an American; etc. The Curia must be made international. It was true.

iii. *Vatican citizenship*

Vatican City had few citizens. But the Curia claimed that a member of the Pope's diplomatic corps had the status of an Italian citizen.

[12] FO 371/37554.

Therefore they claimed that Vatican representatives of Italian origin were neutrals and had free movement in time of war.

The British would not tolerate this claim. They expelled Monsignor Mozzoni (January 1941) from the secretariat of the Apostolic Delegate in London. They expelled Monsignor Riberi, Apostolic Delegate and head of the African missions, from Mombasa; Monsignor Nuti, vicar-apostolic in Egypt since 1921; Monsignor Testa, Apostolic Delegate in Jerusalem; Monsignor Castellani, Apostolic Delegate in Addis Ababa.

Here was useful friction between Britain and the Vatican. It did no harm to Britain, and not much harm to the Vatican, which, however, cared about its missions and unlike the British refused to regard them as expendable in time of war. The more friction, the more Italian appeared the Vatican. Osborne could afford to be totally on the side of the Vatican. He could afford to be seen by the unseen watchers to be doing all he could to see that Italians, or at least Vaticanized Italians, remained free on British territory. He earned a sharp rebuke from London, and told Monsignor Tardini, 'I came into bad odour with my government on account of my refusal hitherto to carry out their instructions.'[13] Riberi was recalled from Africa and Cardinal Maglione gave Osborne a very powerful protest.

In February 1942 London ordered Osborne to demand the recall of all Italians in the Middle East, and Osborne found this a very disagreeable communication to make. London (he said) discovered the Catholic Church in the Middle East and East Africa to be pro-Fascist and pro-Axis; 'the political activities of most Italian ecclesiastics in the Middle East are inconsistent with their spiritual functions, and are as harmful to their religion as they are to British interests'. Osborne gave his covering note to Cardinal Maglione a wry little twist, which is the more amusing when we realize that it was written for more eyes than Cardinal Maglione's: 'His Majesty's Government are not responsible for the failure of Italian ecclesiastics to resist the temptation to indulge their patriotic instincts.'[14]

Cardinal Maglione (23 February 1942) denied altogether that the Catholic Church in the Middle East and in East Africa was generally Fascist and pro-Axis. London and Osborne reiterated the charge (24 March 1942).

Osborne could therefore be seen by Italy to be doing all he could personally; for example, to stop the British expelling all the Italian missionaries from Abyssinia; the Vatican and all its overseas services were seen to be accused by Britain of being pro-Fascist.

The Vatican found the British action shocking. Four hundred and

---

[13] ADSS, 4, 164; cf. 99–100.   [14] ADSS, 5, 428–30.

fifty men and women to be turned out of their godly work in Egypt and Palestine by the British – men and women above politics, some of them citizens not of Italy but of Vatican City, doing moral good, teaching in schools, nursing in hospitals, and harmless to the occupying authority. Monsignor Tardini could only account for it by the supposition that Anthony Eden was 'a ferocious enemy of Catholicism', 'however much he wraps it up'. Britain, noted Tardini (4 August 1942), 'is waging war on the Catholic Church.'[15] He metaphorically shrugged his shoulders. 'It's historic British policy. The history of Malta is enough to prove it.'

Monsignor Tardini wrote a curious little private memorandum on Osborne's manner.

He is jumpy, and suspicious; has been for a time. Perhaps he is being influenced by others. But the fact is, he is sure that in one way or another the Vatican helps Italy, and gives way to Italian pressure without protest.

The British Government is already hostile to the Holy See without any prodding. The only person who can soften it a little is Signor Osborne. Hence it might help to work a bit on him – it cannot hurt to try.[16]

That summer they kept worrying about Osborne's health:

Osborne's *Diary* 4 July. The Cardinal shocked me by asking if I was all right and why was I so thin? 20 August 1942. [Osborne spent most of the morning at the office of the Secretary of State.] I had a long talk with Tardini who was perfectly calm and good-humoured over our present wrangles, and begged me to do my best to comb them out.

Not quite the same picture of that meeting appeared in Tardini's notes:

I told the Minister that the Holy See would never decide to recall all missionaries of a particular nationality. On principle, obviously. If a government expels them all, that is its responsibility. The Holy See reserves the right to protest. The Holy See may investigate charges against individuals of undue interference in politics. The British charge against all the missionaries is too vast to have any probability.

So Britain will expel. The Holy See will protest. All the world's Catholics will be grieved. 'Does the Minister think that this would help Britain? Does he believe that it would be in accord with the usual cordial relations between Britain and the Holy See? The Minister said that he agreed with me; that would be neither opportune nor useful'. But he repeated that some have Fascist opinions; that the army command is preoccupied with security; that none of this is against the Holy See. 'I said that if the British did this, the Italians would do the same to British monks and nuns in Italy (reprisals are in fashion). The Holy See would protest – but those poor religious would suffer. Is this the moment to let loose such a storm?' The Minister said, It is not.

[15] ADSS, 5, 630.   [16] ADSS, 5, 549.

The British did not tell the Vatican, until much later, that when they searched Monsignor Castellani's house in Addis Ababa they found a wireless transmitter and a large store of arms and ammunition.[17]

So the British ejected the head of the Church in Ethiopia, although he was not an Italian citizen, and although he was the Pope's personal representative, because he was Italian by birth and had an Italian name. The event caused a little exchange between those two close friends, Montini and Osborne. On the evening of 1 December 1942, Montini gave a present of the annual medal of the Pope but talked sadly of the griefs of the Holy See with the British government, and almost reproached Osborne because of the kindness and consideration which he had received in the Vatican although his presence there spelt danger to the Pope's State. When he got back to Santa Marta, Osborne wrote a brief letter of thanks and friendship, that he would add the medal to his collection:

You reminded me of the great kindness and consideration with which I have always been treated in Vatican City. That is very true and I assure you that I cannot be more sensible of it. But I thought this evening as I went back in the impenetrable darkness, that I could have replied that I've always tried to make a return by causing you the least bother and difficulty in my role as involuntary guest; and above all by doing all I can to avoid or diminish every source of malentendu and of damage to the interests of the Holy See. I believe you know it, and that I don't need to insist on it. I may not always have succeeded to the extent I wished, that doesn't mean that I haven't from time to time had a success.

I tell you this only because I might have sensed some little personal reproach in your words. I assure you, it is not deserved.

2 December 1942: Montini to Osborne:

. . . I explained myself badly if I could be taken to blame you or your attitude . . . If so, it is contrary to my intention.

iv. Greek famine

Greece, conquered by the Germans, was in a famine. The occupying power had the duty of seeing that the people had enough to eat. Under international law Britain could argue that if it allowed food into Greece it helped the war effort of Italy and Germany and allowed the Axis governments to neglect their duty. The Germans argued that the Greeks lived by the sea and that the British blockade was what caused the famine. In the midst of these legal arguments the Greeks died. A similar argument over starvation in Belgium was more easily won by

[17] ADSS, 7, 327: Montgomery to Secretariat, 10 May 1943.

the British because they could argue that the troubles of the Belgian economy were due to dislocations caused by the German army. Queen Elizabeth of the Belgians (23 October 1941) wrote a heart-rending appeal to the Pope on behalf of starving Belgian children. The Vatican got some clothes and drugs into Belgium but little enough, and allocated some of the Belgian Peter's Pence to the bishops for the relief of sufferers.

In the case of Greek famine the problem was special. In the Suez Canal lay 350,000 tonnes of Australian grain which the Greek government had bought. Here was food for starving Greeks lying unused and within a day's voyage if the blockade could be lifted. The idea that the Pope was the only person who could persuade the raising of the blockade first came to the mind of Angelo Roncalli, the nuncio in Turkey who had also a responsibility for Athens. On 20 September 1941 the Vatican appealed to Osborne, who in conversation was an optimist. On 17 October he gave them the British answer, which was that Greece was the responsibility of the occupying power who were the Italians. The British even accused the Italians of allowing the Germans to rob Greece by pillage and extortion. They were content that the Greek government should be able to buy food across its land frontier with Turkey. They refused to lift the blockade. They asked the Vatican to draw the attention of the Italians to their duty towards the Greeks. This reply was very uncompromising and the 350,000 tonnes of wheat still lay in the Suez Canal. Osborne had to put up with a terrible verbal reproach from Cardinal Maglione. 'Here are the Greeks starving. Italy has done all it can. I believe that it cannot do any more. The British ought to remember that the Greeks were their allies. Their refusal is bringing horror to Greece.'[18]

Osborne said that he would tell his government. But the Vatican could see that the British, not for the first time, believed the Pope to be playing Italy's game, and indeed to suspect that the appeal for Greece was inspired by the Italian government. On 21 October the Vatican tried another appeal to Osborne about the wheat in the Canal. They told London that they had done all they could to persuade the Italian government to do what it could to relieve the Greeks. They asked if the British could stop thinking about the law of the situation and think more about the Greek people. They told the British that Roncalli had come from Turkey to Rome to appeal for the Greeks. They talked of going even beyond Anthony Eden at the Foreign Office and wondered whether the Pope should make a personal appeal to King George VI. The British budged not an inch. On 11 November 1941 Osborne gave

[18] ADSS, 8, 314.

his government's formal answer. And in Berlin the Under-Secretary von Weizsäcker told Orsenigo that they were sending some help to Greece but the responsibility lay with the occupying power, which was Italy.

A third time the Vatican went hard at Osborne (24 November). Tardini talked to him pathetically. The Vatican pleaded that the Greeks were suffering. All the British did was to say that a lot of other people are suffering, and to hint that the cause of papal anguish is the prompting of the Italian government. The Vatican was trying to help a people who were not Catholics, who were friends of Britain. Tardini told Osborne that if the Foreign Secretary had still been Halifax instead of Eden the tone of the British replies would have been gentler. 'That's only an impression,' he said to Osborne. But he added a note that he thought it to be also Osborne's impression.[19] And Osborne openly told Tardini that he thought the British should lift the blockade a little for purposes of relief, and said that so he would urge his government.

In mid-January 1942 Roncalli in Turkey reported a news item on the British wireless that announced the lifting of the blockade for the sake of the Greeks. The Vatican demanded information. They were told that the British had agreed to let in 8,000 tonnes of grain arranged by the Red Cross. Hugh Dalton, as Minister for Economic Warfare, announced it to the House of Commons on 27 January 1942. It was arranged that one ship should make three voyages from Haifa to the Piraeus.

And still the 350,000 tonnes lay in the Suez Canal. The British estimated, and told Osborne, that half a million people died in Greece during the winter of 1941–2, but the evidence was not scientific and they had a motive to inflate the numbers. They now said that the Germans stole the harvest of 1942. Osborne told the Vatican, 'After the war the story of Greece will be an indelible blot on the good name of Italy, at any rate of Fascist Italy.'[20] Tardini was not content with the statistics. He asked Roncalli in Turkey, and the nuncio in Switzerland, whether they could get information. Roncalli reported it as totally false that the occupying powers had stolen the 1942 harvest, and said that the Red Cross was in a good position to observe what happened. He said that Swedish vessels had brought in grain under the auspices of the Red Cross, that with the aid of Italian milk and food a minimum supply was ensured for the winter of 1942–3, and that the Swedes seemed to have got hold of a lot of the grain from the Suez Canal. He consulted a local doctor in whom he had confidence and who made statistical enquiries about deaths due to famine. For the city of Athens—

[19] ADSS, 8, 358.   [20] ADSS, 8, 671.

Piraeus he reached the figure of 34,622 deaths (approximately) due to famine, this being the number of deaths greater than the deaths in the same district for the previous year. 'In any case,' said Monsignor Roncalli, 'the true figure is far below that of half a million.'[21]

Here again Osborne's reports showed how useful was the Vatican to Italy. Italy was technically responsible for the Greek famine but had no food to help, and the Germans who had food would not help. If Britain let food into Greece the act helped Italy, and even gave a little help to Germany. The Vatican could plead the suffering of the innocent. And the Italians could see, as they read Osborne's reports, how the Vatican, supported by Osborne, touched stony British hearts with compassion. Of course, others were at work, elsewhere in the world, trying to get help to the starving Greeks – the Red Cross, Bishop George Bell of Chichester, Herbert Hoover. But here was a point where the existence of the Vatican, and of the British Legation inside the Vatican, helped Italy, could be seen to help Italy, and marginally helped the war-effort of the Italians against Britain. For the interest of Italy in Greece happened to coincide with the interests of Christian charity.

v. The German invasion of Russia

The summer of 1941 was a specially tense time for the Vatican. (It cannot be said that the time was ever not tense, between June 1940 and June 1944 and perhaps after.) The reason for this was the invasion of Russia by the Germans on 22 June 1941.

Some Catholics in the democratic states were disturbed at an alliance with an atheist power. The Roman Catholic bishops of England, except Cardinal Hinsley, were at first very uneasy.[22] In America, President Roosevelt at once said that aid could go to Russia, but a majority of the American bishops were opposed. Roosevelt tried to get a Russian undertaking on religious liberty, was pleased to see the Russian government behave less tyrannically towards its Churches; astounded those who knew anything by declaring at a press conference that the Soviet Constitution guaranteed a religious liberty analogous to the liberty guaranteed by the American Constitution; and asked Myron Taylor to get the Pope to 'interpret' the encyclical of 1937, *Divini Redemptoris*, which condemned atheistic Communism. In his private letters to Taylor, Roosevelt was optimistic that this alliance would lead to religious liberty in Russia. This optimism infected Taylor, who sought to persuade the Pope and Tardini and utterly failed to persuade

---

[21] ADSS, 8, 721.
[22] The Apostolic Delegate Godfrey to Nichols, FO 371/30174/180; E. di Nolfo, *Vaticano e Stati Uniti 1939–52* (Milan, 1978), p. 40.

either. A *private* letter from the Vatican to the Apostolic Delegate in Washington allowed a sufficiently narrow interpretation of the condemnation of Communism in *Divini Redemptoris*. The argument became academic after Pearl Harbor in December 1941, for America plainly needed Russian aid.

But meanwhile the Vatican came under strong pressure from Italy, the strongest pressure of all the war. Bolshevism was not only the enemy of Germany and Italy. Popes had repeatedly condemned it in hot language. Now western and Christian powers, one partly Catholic and the other almost wholly Catholic, assailed Bolshevism in its fastness. This was as clear a crusade as any that in former centuries Popes blessed. Let Pius XII speak out and call it a crusade. He cannot want the Russians to win, or Bolshevism will be all over Central Europe and perhaps over Western Europe. Catholicism would not have a happy time in a Bolshevik Europe. Therefore he must want Germany, aided by Italy, to win. Let him say so.

If the Nazis were less nasty, the Vatican might even have felt attracted. As things were, Europe would be a dreadful place, in the eyes of the Vatican, if Stalin's Russia won; it would be just as dreadful if Hitler's Germany won; yet to hope for the third possibility, that Russians and Germans should destroy each other, was not a moral hope possible for the Vatican. Only Tardini, as was his way, had the bluntness to express it brutally. Since victory by either side would have dreadful consequences, he hoped that 'in the providence of God' the war would end both Nazism and Communism.[23] To say it that way, instead of saying that Nazis and Communists should destroy each other, stayed within the borders of morality.

Italy had two views of Barbarossa. Italy wanted to win the war in Africa, and some Italians had little enthusiasm for so vast a distraction to the German army. They wanted to win Italy's war, which they only entered because they thought it already won, and had no desire to help win Germany's war. But others – some Fascists, including Mussolini, some Catholics, including some Italian bishops – felt that it was indeed a crusade; to lift at last the threat of atheist Bolshevism and international revolution, and to right the injustices of 1917–18. The Belgian ambassador Nieuwenhuys reported to Brussels (3 July 1941) that Italians showed no enthusiasm for the Russian war. But at Concordia Monsignor Costantini, who was Secretary of Propaganda and therefore a member of the Curia, preached strong for the crusade against Russia, calling the blessing of God upon the Italian soldiers who defended the ideal of Italian liberty from red barbarism ('Vatican

---

[23] ADSS, 5, 208; cf. 218.

Quisling' noted the Foreign Office in London). The Vatican correspondent of the *Gazetta del Popolo* reported that Catholics 'everywhere'
showed the utmost satisfaction at the attack on Russia.[24] Mussolini and
several round him were angry at the silence of the Pope. As late as
September 1941 the Italian ambassador to the Holy See, Attolico, still
pushed hard at the Pope to speak out against Bolshevism.

Tardini was very firm with Attolico. 'It is sad that the Vatican has
been placed in such a situation that it can only keep silence. But the
persecutions in Germany have been so severe that if the Pope had
talked about Bolshevism, he could not, in conscience, have kept
silence on Nazism. He preferred to say nothing.' This was what
Attolico reported to his superiors. Tardini's note of the conversation
was fuller. The Pope condemned Bolshevism when he could not be
accused of playing politics. If he condemned it again at this moment,
he could be thought to play politics. To talk now could be understood
as bowing down to Farinacci. Communism is the sworn enemy of the
Church but not the only enemy. 'The swastika can hardly be presented
as a crusader's cross.'[25]

The refusal to speak enabled Farinacci to browbeat the Vatican – the
weakness of the Pope, the silence of the Pope, the contrast with his
predecessors, the pro-Allied quality of the *Osservatore Romano* and of
some of his advisers, the presence of Osborne in the Vatican. For
almost the only time in this history, members of the Foreign Office in
London were enthusiastic about the Pope – 'his attitude as regards the
anti-Bolshevist Crusade leaves nothing to be desired' – they read
Farinacci with interest and for a moment almost admired the Pope –
'When we feel as we sometimes do, that we have reason to be
disappointed with the Vatican, we may console ourselves with the
reflexion that our enemies have much less reason to be satisfied with
it.'[26]

This silence of the Pope carried danger. One intelligent observer
(Guariglia) believed that it marked a turning-point in Mussolini's
personal attitude to the Pope and the Vatican. Mussolini never forgave
the Vatican for its attitude to Barbarossa. He liked Farinacci's
onslaught. This was to have later consequences.

Of course, Osborne did all that he could to keep the Pope silent over
Barbarossa, and was pleased at the outcome. But the Pope needed no
prodding from Osborne. He knew too much about Nazi persecution of
the Church in Germany.

---

[24] FO 371/30174/108; 30175/11.
[25] Attolico to AE, 13 September 1941, in AE, Santa Sede, 1941, Busta 52; Tardini in ADSS,
5, 182ff.
[26] W. L. C. Knight, FO 371/30175/17.

Osborne could help him just a little, by reporting to the unseen Italians what might help some of them. Eight days after Barbarossa began, he had an audience with Pius XII. The Pope said to him, Osborne reported to London and therefore to the Italians, that the war was being accepted as a crusade in many countries, especially in Italy; and Osborne added Spain and South America.[27]

Simultaneously, Diego von Bergen helped to relieve German pressure. The Pope keeps silent, he told Berlin, because he does not wish to condemn German persecution at such a crisis in German fortunes. 'But the Pope's heart, they tell me, is always on the side of the Axis.'[28]

vi. Prisoners-of-war

The Vatican sent its representatives to visit the camps of prisoners-of-war – except in German and German-occupied and Russian lands where it was not allowed; that is, it could visit in Italy and in the democracies. (Orsenigo once got leave to visit one camp under the Germans.) They visited prisoners in camps in Australia and Egypt and Canada as well as Britain and Italy. And the Lateran Treaty enabled them to do more for prisoners than was possible during the First World War.

Vatican radio disseminated news of prisoners. The better Red Cross conventions, now embedded in international law, were helpful. The Vatican had an Information Office, directly under Montini, and run by a Russian Monsignor Alexander Evreinoff, where nuns and young priests sat all day with filing cards and typewriters and cabinets. It was designed to bring families information about prisoners who had vanished. It also transmitted messages from families to the prisoners. The service was very effective, so far as British prisoners of the Italians – captured for the most part in North Africa – were concerned. The Germans refused to give the Vatican lists on the pretext that it was not sensible to duplicate the work of the Red Cross. The British made the same refusal on the same ground. They regarded the Vatican service of information as more an Italian than a neutral institution. But here the Vatican could be seen to be helpful to Italy, and Osborne had no need to pretend. It was a charitable work, and no one could accuse it of playing politics.

Because Germany refused information to the Vatican, the British followed the German example. British feeling that the Vatican was

---

[27] FO 371/30174; Osborne to FO, 30 June 1941 (telegram); cf. A. Rhodes, *The Vatican in the Age of the Dictators* (London, 1973), p. 256.

[28] Von Bergen to Weizsäcker, cited ADSS, 5, 11; cf. the Pope's radio message of 29 June 1941 as cited by Rhodes, *Vatican*, p. 258.

Italian, and Italians enemies, contributed to this reluctance to help. Britain allowed papal representatives to visit prisoners' camps but kept on refusing information. Osborne finally helped the Vatican to extract leave from a still reluctant London that prisoners' messages might be transmitted. Britain continued to refuse lists of prisoners.

The Red Cross had far better credit with governments; a more historic place in this work; more money; a fleet to transport necessities; a staff across the world; dumps for parcels; and the backing of the Swiss government. The Vatican could not grow to be an equal colleague. But the Red Cross was happy to accept its assistance, in transmitting messages, and in paying for parcels.

Osborne had no need to tell the watching Italians that the Vatican helped Italian prisoners-of-war. The Italian government knew more about it than Osborne. But perhaps it helped Osborne's safety a little that he was known to be on the side of the Vatican in persuading the British to release those lists of prisoners which they refused to release.

What helped even more was the part which the Vatican and Osborne played in trying to discourage the RAF from bombing the city of Rome. Nothing could be more useful to the Italian war-effort than to exempt its capital and headquarters from attack. Nothing did more to preserve the Vatican City in the face of Mussolini's anger. But the question of the bombing of Rome was so tangled, and so anxious, and so prolonged, that it will require a separate chapter.

In Osborne's reports we find, when we look at them in this light, a lot of interesting information. He realized that the situation was of an exceptional insecurity. At all costs he must protect the Vatican. He must never report the more extreme utterances of Monsignor Tardini, or of Cardinal Tisserant. He must keep saying how much good the Pope's relief operations do for Italians. He must keep stressing the absolute neutrality of the Pope amid the warring nations. He must keep saying how useless are the Pope's utterances to the Allied cause. At any minute the Vatican could be taken over and the Pope become a real prisoner. That might be a calamity for the Allies. The Pope could not say much, if anything, but he was a symbol of justice and peace and civilized ways of waging war. He was revered by many Italians who did not want to be in this war. At all costs the Pope must be protected from a take-over. Osborne realized that his peculiar situation – where he wrote reports for London in cypher, and knew that they were read by enemy eyes, and believed that those enemy eyes did not know that he knew that they were reading them – gave him an unusually advantageous position for protecting the Pope.

9

The Jews in 1942

i. The use in war of moral condemnation

Every warring state wants its cause to be seen as moral. Men will fight better for a cause which they think moral. Neutral states will be readier to befriend a state which they believe to be engaged in a righteous fight. The Pope was in theory useful to the belligerents as he stood for moral right. His stand could affect the opinion or morale of their people and the benevolence of neutral states. No one expected a Pope to declare one side to have all justice, or to say that for one side this was a just war. Just occasionally they hoped to persuade him to assert that a particular course of action was just, or at least justified. When the Germans invaded Russia in June 1941, they hoped to persuade the Pope to say that this was a crusade on behalf of European Christendom. Popes had so often condemned atheistic Communism and its materialistic philosophy of life. Germany was the bulwark of Europe, and set out to free Europe for ever from the menace of atheistic Communism. This was not a promising endeavour. We have seen why it was unthinkable inside the Vatican. The Pope's failure to declare the invasion a crusade did not surprise Hitler, who had a low opinion of Popes, but vexed Mussolini, who really thought it a crusade and was hurt that the Church refused to say so; and it pleased the British who were afraid that the Vatican might think it a crusade.

But mostly the Powers did not expect the Pope to say that one of their own acts was good. They hoped that he would say that an act by the other side was bad. And if they could persuade him to say this, it would be of political advantage. Therefore the ambassadors to the Holy See, whether German, Italian, British, or (at first) French had the duty of drawing the attention of the Pope to immoralities perpetrated by the other side. They had the further duty of suggesting that he condemn them publicly. They did not usually expect to succeed in this task.

They knew that from June 1940 the Pope adopted a policy of strict neutrality as the only way of standing above an impossible situation. Italy entered the war; and Italy not only had the Vatican State at its mercy, but had a treaty which prevented the Pope from criticizing its policies. If he could not criticize Mussolini publicly he would not criticize any other war leader publicly. And neutrality had merits. It lifted the Church above political entanglement, and retained the remote possibility of a future mediation between the warrior nations. The ambassadors liked this mentality very much when it helped their own side, disliked it very much when it failed to condemn what was obviously immoral in the other side. Osborne once called the policy of neutrality 'the abnegation of moral leadership in the interests of a strict neutrality'. This was in a report to London.[1] An earlier chapter has shown that Osborne had a good reason in reports to London to complain of the Pope's neutrality, because secret Italian tappers would be pleased with the Pope. But in his private diary he had not the same motive. At the Pope's jubilee address in May 1942 (for which Osborne elicited with much difficulty a congratulation from King George VI) the Pope said that he was impartial between the belligerents. And Osborne commented to himself, 'But is there not a moral issue at stake which does not admit of neutrality?'

On the other side, as the war developed, the Italians and even the Germans saw the policy of area bombing by British and Americans to be outrageously immoral, the purposeful slaughter of innocent women and children. The Pope must condemn! They pressed him again and again. But for the sake of neutrality between the warriors, he would only enunciate the general principles which implied condemnation, rather than utter condemnations of particular acts – 'not a word' wrote Farinacci in his newspaper (14 June 1944) 'to condemn this criminal and barbarous banditry'.

Therefore the ambassadors did not expect to succeed in their persuasions, but it was their duty to try. And they tried very often. The Italians wanted to make him condemn area bombing, or the particular immorality of the destruction of churches or hospitals or historic monuments, or the alliance of the Christian democrats of the West with tyrannical atheists from the East, or the British maltreatment of Italian missionaries in Ethiopia and the Middle East. On his side Osborne tried to make him condemn aggression against Poland, or aggression against the Low Countries or France, or the maltreatment of the citizens of the occupied countries.

Guariglia, Italian ambassador from February 1942 to February 1943, was in somewhat the stronger position actually, Osborne in somewhat the stronger position morally. Guariglia was strong because area bombing, with its terror for civilians on both sides, could come down upon Rome and even the Vatican. The Pope had a motive besides that

[1] FO 371/30175/93.

of general morality for protesting at area bombing. Nevertheless Osborne's position had a deeper hold. The government of Germany happened not only to behave immorally in certain areas of war, but to assert principles which justified their immorality. Osborne might not expect from the Pope particular condemnations of particular acts. But he could expect clear enunciations of Christian principle, about the sacredness of human life, or the value of the individual, which did not so easily marry to the totalitarian theory of the State. And declarations of generalized Christian principle were not political – or, if they were, could at least be argued not to be political – and were what Popes were good at, and were what this Pope was specially good at; even if the clarity of his enunciations left much to be desired. It had to be confessed that democracy and liberalism were easier to reconcile with high Christian principle than tyranny and racialism. On the whole Osborne respected the content, though not the baroque style, of the Pope's general speeches on peace, disarmament, a just social order.

The Foreign Office in London kept a close eye on these general proclamations and sometimes saw that however general they could be used. 'This speech [the Pope's Christmas broadcast of 1940] contains admirable propaganda material, and it should not be difficult taking the Pope's points one by one, to show how perfectly the cap fits the head of our enemies and how we are striving to establish in practice the very principles enunciated by the Pope.'[2]

But just as in two main areas – area bombing and the crusade against Russia – the Axis Powers hoped to make the Pope speak on their side, the Allied Powers were not content with general principles which sounded too general, and hoped to prod to a more particular condemnation.

Once the Pope gave them a particular condemnation unasked. On 10 December 1940 Osborne transmitted to London a 'curious' decree of the Inquisition about the killing of mental defectives. He reported a strong rumour in the Vatican, not only that Germany practised such killings, but that patients were made to serve the cause of the German race by becoming 'experimental material for poison gases'. London found such specific information useful.[3]

Osborne had a duty to persuade the Pope to speak out, if he could. But sometimes he did not try hard, partly because he knew that it would have no effect, and partly because he did not quite believe in the utility to the people who mattered, the victims. If the Pope condemned

[2] FO 371/30173.
[3] Decree of the Holy Office, 27 November 1940. It was published in the *Osservatore Romano*. FO 380/59.

publicly the machine-gunning of refugees on French roads, it might help the British government as propaganda but did not help the refugees. He did his duty by the British government, in making representations that such-and-such conduct was immoral and ought to be condemned. But he was never surprised when this failed, and sometimes he was lukewarm about the task.

But at other times his own moral sense was aroused. And then he would engage in a determined quest to make the Pope go public, at least on the moral principle, and if possible on the particular events which trampled on morality. The most important events of this nature were the early months of the Final Solution, when what was happening to the Jews was slowly beginning to be known.

ii. Vatican information

Modern scholars, as well as modern propagandists, have sometimes fancied that the Pope, with a priest in so many parishes across Europe, must quickly have known what was happening. But the diplomats in the Vatican kept being surprised by how little the Vatican knew, and what poor services of information it possessed. Orsenigo in Berlin had a diplomatic bag, but both the Vatican and Orsenigo knew that it was checked by the Gestapo. Madrid and Lisbon had diplomatic bags but the Vatican at least, and later Lisbon, knew that they were opened, perhaps in Berne, perhaps by Italian counter-espionage. The nuncios or apostolic delegates in Bratislava, or Ankara, or London, or Washington, or Vichy, wrote letters and occasionally they contained scraps of important information not obtainable in the newspapers. The Polish ambassador in the Vatican, Casimir Papée, communicated with the Polish government in London, though his communications were checked by Italian counter-espionage; and the Polish government in London had secret links via Sweden with the underground in Poland. Little information, and no reliable information otherwise obtainable from easier sources, seems to have reached the Vatican by this route. Mostly the Pope depended on newspapers; that is, the newspapers of Rome like *Il Messaggero*. The only newspapers which he read till two or three weeks after their publication were the newspapers of Axis Powers, and the Swiss newspapers.

When d'Ormesson arrived in Rome to be French ambassador to the Holy See, he was shocked at the inadequacy of the information which the Vatican commanded for its international duties.

The effective suppression of the *Osservatore Romano* during May–June 1940 made Osborne realize that the Pope could not be allowed to depend only on Axis news. He offered the Secretariat of State, for the

Pope's eyes, a service of news, derived from the news broadcast by the BBC.

Twice a day he took down the BBC news on his personal typewriter. He organized these into his personal diary, and the diary therefore makes a good source for what he passed to the Pope. Every other morning (at least) he dictated a compendium of the previous day's news to his secretary, Miss Tindall, and by noon copies went to the Pope, the Secretariat of State and to the *Osservatore Romano*, though the last could not use them. As at first he had not much to do, it was easy to find the time. As his other duties multiplied in the pressure of war, the work exhausted him. During 1941 he suggested to the Pope that he might stop doing this summary because the Pope 'might' now have other sources of Allied news. The Pope thanked him warmly and begged him to continue. The Pope assured him, more than once, that he read every word. He therefore continued the grinding labour until he went on 'leave' during 1943. To take his place some American monsignori organized a way to get American broadcast news daily to the Pope. That it became very burdensome to Osborne was shown by his later attitudes to the radio. He refused to own a set for the rest of his life.

Osborne's news summaries thus became the Pope's chief, usually his only, access to news not slanted by Axis commentators. Valuable though the Vatican found this service, they did not believe quite a lot of what the BBC said, any more than they believed all that Axis communiqués said. An Italian spy at the Vatican reported that 'a Very High Personage' talked of war bulletins and said that he believed 75% of the Axis bulletins and 35% of the Russian and the British bulletins.[4]

iii. The coming of Tittmann

Now a new influence entered the Vatican, and a new source for the historian. In December 1941 the Japanese bombed Pearl Harbor and the Americans entered the war. The counsellor at the Rome embassy of the Americans asked leave to take up residence inside the Vatican. Cardinal Maglione and his men much disliked this. They pressed the Americans not to add another to the immured ambassadors inside Vatican City but to send their man to Switzerland and there be accredited to the nuncio. The Americans were determined to have their man inside the Vatican; and, the Lateran Treaty being in existence, the Pope could hardly refuse. Harold Tittmann took up residence inside the Vatican on 16 December 1941.

[4] AC, PS, 1941, Busta 35, report of 23 August 1941.

He was a pilot in the First World War and suffered such terrible injuries in a crash that the doctors regarded his survival as miraculous; the physical effects could still be seen, especially by an artificial leg and a crippled hand.

His legal position was insecure. The Lateran Treaty assured the Pope of the right to have diplomats accredited from other nations. But the American Constitution seemed to forbid that nation to accredit a representative. Technically Tittmann was unofficially helping a personal friend of the President of the United States, and if that was his position the Italians could expel him from the Vatican tomorrow. The State Department hardly knew how to protect him. They persuaded Roosevelt at once that he had the title Chargé d'Affaires. But when precisely defined it was described by the strange title, Chargé d'Affaires of the United States near the Holy See.[5] His wife asked what she should put on the envelope when she wrote to him, and was told 'American Foreign Service Office, Santa Marta'. Meanwhile Cardinal Maglione did better in the way of protection. The *Osservatore Romano* (20–30 December 1941) listed Tittmann as 'Chargé d'Affaires of the United States of America', and so recognized him in a public document as in an official post. But the matter was still insecure. He and his wife both needed an identity card issued to prove that their diplomatic status was recognized by the Italian government. This was not only a question whether he was an accredited envoy within the meaning of the Lateran Treaty. A bigger question loomed in the background. Did the United States recognize the Vatican City as an independent State? The Lateran Treaty was an agreement between the Pope and Italy and no one else. If the Germans or the British occupied Rome nothing in international law stopped them from occupying the Vatican City with the rest of Rome. Was Tittmann not merely no proper envoy of a State, but put into a place which his State believed to be part of Italy? The American lawyers asked themselves the question and produced the thin but respectable evidence that in 1938 an Act of Congress provided that copies of documents of the State of Vatican City were admissible as evidence in court; and so 'it appears from this that the Congress has recognized the existence of the Vatican City State'.[6]

Tittmann had several months of anxiety. He finally got his identity card on 2 May 1942 via the Secretariat of State.[7]

For fourteen months, since the expulsion of Wladimir d'Ormesson, Osborne had no close friend, other than Montini, inside the Vatican. He had been getting to know the Irish Monsignor with an anti-British

[5] NAW 123/T53/206ff.; cf. FRUS, 1944, Europe, IV, 1307, 1319.
[6] NAW 866A, 01/32.
[7] NAW, SD, 123T, 53/244; cf. FRUS, 1942, 3/791–2.

background of the name of O'Flaherty, because they had a common interest in golf, which Osborne longed to be able to go out to play and of which O'Flaherty, who could still go out to play, was a champion. Osborne gave O'Flaherty his unusable golf balls. But among the diplomats no one had taken d'Ormesson's place. Tittmann had not d'Ormesson's range of literary interest, nor his French charm, nor his aristocratic descent. But Osborne found him a good friend. And Tittmann on his side was not the first nor the last man to find Osborne enchanting. It was not only their common interests which brought them into close friendship. Not immediately but slowly, Tittmann filled the gap left by the sacking of d'Ormesson.

The United States had many more Catholics than had Britain. The interests of its government in Rome were therefore greater. Nevertheless Tittmann recognized that Osborne had carved out for himself a unique place at the Vatican. Throughout their time together he looked on Osborne as the senior partner in their common work.

iv. The Jewish deportations

Let us be clear on one thing: everyone knew in 1941 that many Jews from Germany were being deported eastward. They were believed to be destined to supply a labour force. Germany made no secret of the plan. By late October 1941 the terrible drama began; Jews moving eastward to already overcrowded and filthy eastern ghettos; sanitation designed for five coping with five hundred; epidemics and squalid air; little official bosses strutting in ghettos; suspicion by Germany that Jews spirited away their valuables into ghettos; governors and mayors protesting; bureaucrats tearing their hair; trains dumping their human cargo – and what then? Everybody longed for the peace treaty with Britain and France and so the opening of Madagascar as the future Jewish homeland. By the end of the year 1941 everyone knew that to be deported was a bad fate; that the conditions of work and of rations in the camps were killing. No one knew much about it but everyone wanted to avoid deportation and with more fear than just fear of a compulsion to leave one's historic home.

The Final Solution was planned on 20 January 1942 at the Wannsee Conference. On the very day of the Conference, the Jesuit Father Tacchi Venturi wrote a letter to the Secretary of State in the Vatican, Cardinal Maglione, saying that his efforts for the Jewish children in Croatia had failed to keep them from *orribile deportazione*.[8]

So the deportations to Poland were already known to be *orribile*, and

[8] ADSS, 8, 416. I have used passages in this section from my article 'The Pope and the Jews in 1942', in *Persecution and Toleration*, ed. Sheils (Oxford, 1984).

those who endured them to be wretched. No one believed that they were sent to Poland to be murdered. They were sent to Poland to work. That very month the authorities in the Vatican still struggled to get passports and permits for Jews to emigrate to Latin America, or to prise the Lithuanian rabbi and his family out to Lisbon.

Everyone knew that the fate of Jews in Poland was not likely to be happy. In a screaming voice Hitler said so on the radio. Ten days after the Wannsee Conference, on 30 January 1942, Hitler made such a screech. Osborne, immured behind the Vatican walls, read the speech next morning in the Italian translation printed in the *Messaggero* newspaper. The sentence of Hitler which caught his eye was this: 'The Jews will be liquidated for at least a thousand years!'

On a foul cold wet day Osborne walked to see Cardinal Maglione; and Maglione had also taken the phrase, because he remarked to Osborne on 'Hitler's new outburst against the Jews.'[9] Everyone knew that it was bad to be a Jew and deported to Poland. They knew that in the Vatican just as clearly as anywhere else. Hitler said so. No one knew how bad.

During January 1941 Maglione took the trouble to extract a pledge from the Italian government that Italian Jews should not be subjected to any new restrictions.

In March 1942 the Vatican received news from its nuncio in Bratislava that Slovak Jews were sent to work camps in Poland, and that the deportation of 80,000 people to Poland 'at the mercy of the Germans' was the equivalent of sending a large number to certain death. But Osborne's *Diary* shows that this hardly touched him yet. He worried about the agonies of war, but at this time they were the Greek famine, or Japanese atrocities in Malaysia ('I don't care for the idea of a Japanese colleague' at the Vatican), or the shooting of hostages in Serbia or in France or in Warsaw for the deaths of German soldiers or policemen. These shootings of hostages made Osborne passionate enough to wear a black tie on Hitler's birthday (20 April) in memory of all the innocent victims whom he had killed. 'Perhaps Hitler is the great expiation of the German people, the eternalized sloughing off of the barbarian residue in the depths of their souls . . . Hitler, in fact, may be the devil in process of being cast out of the German sub-conscious.'

Grimly he went on recording the slaying of hostages, for himself as well as for the Pope. (21 April 'To see the Cardinal to talk about the Malta archbishopric question. Is this the moment?') There was no need for the BBC to tell Osborne, the German radio told everyone. They needed the publicity; as an inadequate way of diminishing the

[9] Osborne's *Diary*, 31 January 1942.

impossible German problem, how to keep reasonable order as a power occupying vast tracts of country where the people were hostile. Such an occupation was bound to be accompanied by savagery in France, Holland, Belgium, Poland, Western Russia, Yugoslavia and Greece and Czecho-Slovakia. With the entry of Russia and the United States into the war, the hostile population knew that Germany had a chance of being defeated, and they had a little less resignation in their sullenness. During these months the resistance began to organize, ineffectively and sporadically, but with those occasional shootings of straggling soldiers which, in the eyes of international law, were not war but murder. Even if the occupying government had been good, they would still have met the problem of murder by guerrillas. But the occupying power, specially in the East – the one place where they had a chance to reconcile a people, Ukrainians and Russians who hated Stalin – was as bad a government as could be. And even in the West the power of police over courts, and the system of martial law, turned the shooting of hostages into an instrument of government. Under such conditions government was bound not only to be a tyranny, and to appear a tyranny to the subjects under its heel, but – *pour encourager* – to proclaim its tyranny over the radio and so be hated through the world.

The British regarded the lives of the occupied peoples as expendable. They took the view that the only worthwhile help to Europe was to win the war. Therefore, if they could arm a peasant who would slay a German soldier, they thought that they had done good; and if the result was the slaughter of a hundred innocent peasants or the destruction of a village, they knew that their effort to win the war was helped, because the slaughter of innocent women and children by one side was a victory in propaganda for the other.

Gestapo chief Heydrich was wounded by assassins sent from England on 27 May and died on 4 June. The systematic shooting of Czech hostages thereafter was announced in German news bulletins. Osborne grimly recorded and added the numbers. On 10 June Daluege wiped out a whole Czech village for sheltering Heydrich's assailants, executing all the men and seizing all the women and children. Osborne had been gently chiding since the beginning of hostilities. The desks at the Foreign Office, at least since Eden succeeded Halifax as Foreign Secretary, were not displeased with his criticisms, and turned them, *moribus suis*, into fierce reproaches. But these Czech murders outraged Osborne in Rome. He said he wanted to strangle Germans with his bare hands. On 13 June he visited Maglione and afterwards recorded his feelings:

The courtyard of San Damaso was full of little First Communion boys and girls, an appealing sight. But unfortunately the moral leadership of the world is not retained by mass reception of Italian first communicants and all the others. The Führerprinzip demands more than the benevolence of the Pastor Angelicus and moral leadership is not assured by the unapplied recital of the Commandments.

On 12 June 1942 Tittmann sent Sumner Welles a personal letter telling him of a conversation with Osborne. Osborne had said how unpopular was the Pope in England at the moment, how unlike the Pope of 1939 and earlier months of 1940. The British government believed that the Pope was insuring against an Axis victory; thought that the whole Curia was at bottom Italianate; that this could hardly be other in so tiny a state, nominally independent but actually dependent. 'This unpopularity', Tittmann recorded Osborne as saying, 'had reached such proportions that it was only with the greatest difficulty that Osborne was able to elicit a message of felicitation from His Majesty the King of England to the Pope for his Jubilee . . .'[10]

Four days later Tittmann sent a report to the State Department. He said that a stream of criticism was directed at the Pope from pro-Allied sources. It was felt that the Holy Father was occupying himself with spiritual matters, charitable acts and rhetoric, while adopting at the same time an ostrich-like policy towards atrocities that were obvious to everyone. People think that the great moral authority won for the Papacy by his predecessor Pope Pius XI, was being dissipated. In Poland they have reserves about him, some are even hostile. The criticisms are particularly violent over the treatment of hostages in Poland and Czechoslovakia. Tittmann had asked Maglione whether the Holy See could not say something about the massacres that happened every day in Bohemia and Moravia (as a reprisal for Heydrich's murder). Maglione had shaken his head sadly and said that an intervention by the Pope could only make things worse.

Why, asked Tittmann, does the Pope take this attitude? Is it a policy of appeasement, resting on a conviction that the Axis is bound to win the war? Others say that he really believes that in the long run the Allies are bound to win; if the Nazis are going to be destroyed there is no point in subjecting antiNazis to more severe persecution.

Others say that his silence is caused by a fear of immediate reprisals. Those who want him to be bold admit that the result might be the seizure of the Vatican and himself by the Gestapo. But they were happy that this fate should befall because the moral stock of the Papacy would rise startlingly.

The impression is growing that the Pope still hopes to play the part of a mediator between the enemies. Therefore he has to refuse to say

[10] Tittmann Papers, Brussels, Atroc., p. 13.

anything which could compromise his impartiality. He probably thinks it is better to displease his friends than his enemies; they are more likely to forgive, in the end, his sins of omission.[11]

So wrote Harold Tittmann (16 June 1942). Still no information about the Jews. All Europe was in travail over hostages, not Jews.

Three days later (19 June 1942) Casimir Papée talked with Maglione on the same question. Maglione said 'The Holy Father cannot always be explicit; but all his public utterances about persecution where the victims are the Catholics and their families, are to be applied to Poland. Everyone really knows that the Holy Father is always referring to Poland.'[12]

On 25 June and 30 June the *Daily Telegraph* began to mount publicity on the extermination of Jews. The material was provided by Ziegelboim, one of the Polish National Council; who later committed suicide because of what he felt to be western indifference.

This was only newspaper material. Most people received it with a large touch of scepticism. But it was broadcast on the BBC and therefore included in Osborne's reports of European news for the Pope's eye. For example:

25 June In recent months the Germans have been carrying out a new and systematic pogrom against the Jews. In Vilna alone 60,000 have been killed during the past few months.
27 June It is announced that since October 1939 the Germans have killed 700,000 Jews in Poland as part of their deliberate extermination policy; . . . mass shooting, drowning and gas.

Osborne said he was quite prepared to believe this. But by saying that he was quite prepared to believe this he showed that some people did not believe a word of it and that he had to work hard to screw it up to credibility.

30 June The Germans have killed over a million Jews in all, of whom 700,000 in Poland. Seven million more have been deported or confined in concentration camps.

Osborne liked to remind the Vatican what other ecclesiastics were saying.

9 July Cardinal Hinsley has delivered an eloquent address in condemnation of the German terror in Poland and the other occupied countries, in which he referred to 'the utter bestiality of German methods'.
10 July According to an official report of the Polish government the Germans

---

[11] Tittmann, paraphrased in E. di Nolfo, *Vaticano e Stati Uniti 1939–52* (Milan, 1978), p. 170. Full text in NAW, 866A, 001/112.
[12] Casimir Papée, *Pius XII e Polska* (Rome, 1954); Carlo Falconi, *The Silence of Pius XII*, Eng. trans. (London, 1970), p. 207.

have exterminated, by execution and otherwise, 900,000 Poles . . . women and children have been hanged and gassed.

On 15 July Osborne got hold of the *Tablet* for 20 June and found in it an article called *The Slaughtering of Europe*. This was really on the massacre of Czechs after Heydrich's murder. Osborne drew marks on the article and gave the copy to Maglione and expressed the hope that it might be shown to the Pope. He had a talk with Maglione and complained, though gently as was his way. 'The reaction', Osborne told London,

was unsatisfactory. He [Maglione] said that the Germans would say that the stories of alleged atrocities were untrue. To this I replied that their own wireless retailed their threats to exterminate whole populations and announced mass executions and deportations. He also said that the Pope had already spoken clearly. I agreed he had, for instance, declared that the blessing or curse of God upon an occupying Power would depend upon its treatment of the population of the occupied country, but pointed out that this was over a year ago and that something more strong and specific was called for by the mounting score of massacres of individuals and of whole peoples. But nothing further emerged except that the Cardinal reminded me of his own representations to the Italian, Hungarian, Slovakian and other authorities. I think that it is true that he does all he can himself. But he has to defend the policy of the Pope, whether he approves of it or not.[13]

When this letter came into the Foreign Office more than a month later R. G. Meade commented on it (12 August 1942): 'Papal timidity becomes ever more blatantly despicable.' But this was not fair because by mid-August everyone knew or suspected more than in early July.

The one government which the Vatican really could influence was the Italian. And the Italians were the occupying power in parts of Croatia and elsewhere in the Balkans. In July and onward Maglione and Monsignor Tardini did what they could for the Croat Jews.

On 21 July there was a mass rally for the Jews in Madison Square in New York. The rumour of millions dead was incredible, it looked like one of those atrocity stories for the sake of propaganda, which the First World War made ridiculous. And it was sometimes accompanied by stories which were incredible and untrue – but which happened to be no more untrue than things which happened. The evidence of massacre might also tell of Jewish girls as harlots for German soldiers, which was absurd; or it might tell of Jewish bodies being used to make soap or fertilizers, which was absurd and happened to be untrue but not more absurd than what was true, feminine Jewish hair being used to make

---

[13] Osborne to Howard, 12 July 1942, FO 371/33426.

felt. But such stories were felt to be impossible and helped to discredit the witnesses. But then mere numbers tended to discredit the witnesses. If someone said that two million Jews were killed he was met by a wall of scepticism. How could any witness know about two million? There was strong propaganda reason to exaggerate, or invent. After a time the secret agents of the Polish underground, who began to know quite a lot, found that they were not believed if they told what they thought was truth. So, absurdly, they started to record numbers which were much fewer than they thought to be truth, in the hope that these numbers at least would be believed.

Osborne's *Diary*, 25 July:

I had a very pleasant lot of letters by Bag today, including a most admirable one from Bridget [McEwen] on the Pope's attitude – or lack of attitude – towards the German wholesale massacres in Europe. I am thinking of showing it to His Holiness, as the views of one of the faithful in England.

We have no evidence that he did show the letter to the Pope. He wrote a letter about it to London on 22 July, and R. G. Meade noted on the letter his pleasure that Osborne should give the Pope 'some indication of what we think about his silence'.[14] We notice that it is still the general suffering of the subject peoples of Europe, not the particular agony of the Jews.

Osborne's *Diary*, 31 July:

When I went for my evening walk I found the band of the Palatine Guard marching round and round the little path surrounding the bronze statue of St Peter on the top of the hill looking down on the back of St Peter's and the Vatican. I suspect that it was for a film which I heard today is being made, for world distribution, entitled *Pastor Angelicus*.[15] I find this very regrettable and much too reminiscent of Hollywood publicity. It is a great pity that the Irish monk – Malachi, I think, though maybe he never existed – selected the name Pastor Angelicus for the 262nd Pope.[16] Had he chosen *Leo Furibondus* or

[14] FO 371/33417.
[15] The film was not successful. The Italians said that too many different monsignori took a hand in insisting on cuts; report of 13 February 1943 in AC, Min. Pop. Cult., Busta 29, fasc. 426. But perhaps the Italians wanted it to fail. Father McCormick had evidence that the Italian police thought it made the Pope popular and weakened the war effort, and therefore stopped the showing.
[16] St Malachy was a legend made up by, or accepted uncritically from a faker by, Arnold Wion, a Belgian Benedictine of Douai. In 1595 he published at Venice *Lignum Vitae*, a catalogue of Popes and others. He said (vol. 1, p. 307) that he had only seen of St Malachy's works his prophecies on the Popes (St Malachy died c. 1148). He then printed the prophecy. At each Conclave someone would talk about the prophecy. Pius XII fitted the number, and this name Pastor Angelicus, in Wion's fake list. The Pope's consent to this title for this film suggests that he had a high devotional aspiration not to be unworthy of such a name, and that his judgment on personal matters was not unerring.

something of the sort the position of the Papacy in world estimation might be higher than it at present is. For I fear that His Holiness sublimates his frustration in overdoing the *Pastor Angelicus*, thereby, incidentally, weakening his health and his morale, and also reducing the Papacy to the role of Patriarchate of Rome. Though this is not his fault, for I have no doubt that, if it were possible, he would expend his sympathies on other peoples. Only why, then, does he not denounce the German atrocities against the populations of the Occupied Countries?

Two days before he recorded this about the Palatine band and the film, he went down to have a meeting with the Brazilian ambassador Accioly and Harold Tittmann. They agreed on a plan to make the Pope speak about atrocities, but it would take time to mature.

And now Jews again hit the headlines of the world, with the rounding up of Jews in Occupied France and then in Unoccupied France and in Holland. Unlike what happened in Poland this could not be hidden.

On 27 August Rabbi Wise wrote to the American State Department about extermination. The State Department took the line that this news was unconfirmed, and they believed that the Jews were put to labour. On 2 September there was a great meeting of protest in Caxton Hall, Westminster.

That September Mr Mander, a Liberal MP, drafted a question to ask the Secretary of State in the House of Commons whether he had any statement to make about the use by the German government of gas to murder a large number of Jews in Poland in mobile gas chambers? and if steps could be taken to interview the three grave-diggers who escaped? Early in January 1942 three Jews ran away successfully from Chelmno and in Warsaw told what they saw happen to Jews in touch with the Polish underground. The information was brought to the West by courier, doubtless through the Swedish travellers whom the Polish underground could use until the summer of 1942. American newspapers had it in late July. The Foreign Office asked the Polish government in exile to check. The Pole of whom they enquired was sceptical, and said that he could not check the authenticity. The Poles preferred nothing to be said in the House of Commons, lest it risk lives in Poland. The Foreign Office officials asked Mander to withdraw the question on 'humanitarian grounds'. The British government, like the Pope, preferred silence for the sake of the Jews.

The Vatican diplomats' idea to make the Pope say something went back to the end of July. It started with the Brazilian ambassador Accioly, who was the senior ambassador immured inside the Vatican. He was not influential because Brazil was not influential in the war. But he was liked, and respected. He started to approach his colleagues to

persuade them to approach their governments to allow them to join in
the united démarche. All the diplomats consulted their governments
and got a favourable response. They all agreed that they would leave
their démarche with Cardinal Maglione in mid-September. Most of the
démarches did not mention the Jews. But the British included it – 'the
merciless persecution of the Jews throughout Europe'. At that moment
Osborne's new assistant, Hugh Montgomery, arrived and presented
his credentials (11 September). He also joined the pressure. He said to
the Pope that 'the Poles had hoped for some further expression of
sympathy from the Holy See'. The Pope looked very concerned, and
said 'But I have already done so much!' He mentioned his broadcast of
Easter 1941. He said that this broadcast was suppressed in Germany –
which showed that the Germans knew what it meant. The Poles, he
said, did 'not know what difficulties faced the Vatican'. Messages to
Poland from the Vatican were stopped by the Germans. If he were to
go into details and mention names, it would only harm the victims.[17]
   On 11 September, then, the Pope's attitude was:

1. I have already spoken generally, and the Germans understand
   what I mean (as is proved because they suppressed what I said);
2. I cannot speak particularly because it would hurt the people I am
   trying to help;
3. I cannot get much through the barriers of censorship; and
4. in private we do real work for some of the victims and do not want to
   block this chance of helping.

   The Curia was angry at the common démarche. They thought that it
was a plot. They believed, and continued to believe, that public protest
must make the lot of the Poles and Jews worse, and that a public
protest must cancel the effectiveness of what they could now do by
private protest; that if they were required to denounce all the immoralities committed in a Great War the job would be a major industry and
would touch others besides the Germans; that it was still widespread
rumour rather than hard fact; that already the Pope had condemned
such immoralities in general terms and everyone will understand to
what these generalities refer in particular.
   'It may perhaps be objected' said Osborne in his démarche, 'that His
Holiness has already publicly denounced moral crimes arising out of
the war. But such occasional declarations in general terms do not have
the lasting force and validity that, in the timeless atmosphere of the
Vatican, they might perhaps be expected to retain . . . A policy of
silence in regard to such offences against the conscience of the world

---

[17] FO 371/33414; cited by A. Rhodes, *The Vatican in the Age of the Dictators* (London, 1973),
   p. 291.

must necessarily involve a renunciation of moral leadership and a consequent atrophy of the influence and authority of the Vatican; and it is upon the maintenance and assertion of such authority that must depend any prospect of a Papal contribution to the reestablishment of world peace.'[18]

On 17 September arrived in Rome Myron Taylor, Roosevelt's personal representative to the Pope, on a visit of a few days. He drove through Rome in a closed car. It was extraordinary that Mussolini let him come. The German government thought it extraordinary and made its vexation plain to the Italians. His principal mission was to persuade the Pope that the Americans could not lose the war and that they meant to win and that their determination to win had a moral basis against villainy and that this moral basis the Pope could not help but approve. Therefore he wanted to stop the Pope making proposals for a compromise peace (though of this there was at that moment no danger whatever). But he also, almost as a side-issue, gave the Pope American information about the maltreatment of the populations of occupied Europe. The information told of the French deportations, with very reasonable statistics though a little out of date.

In this personal interview with the Pope he made only a suggestion of a papal utterance. In an interview with Tardini (22 September 1942) he was more outspoken. Tardini's notes of the meeting heave a sigh thus: 'Mr Taylor talked of the opportunity and the necessity of a word from the Pope against such huge atrocities by the Germans. He said that from all sides people are calling for such a word. I assented with a sigh, as one who knows the truth of this all too well! I said in reply that the Pope has already spoken several times to condemn crimes by whomsoever they are committed. I added that some people want the Pope to condemn by name Hitler and Germany, which is an impossibility. Taylor said to me "I don't ask this. I have not asked that he condemn Hitler by name". I said again, "The Pope has already spoken". Taylor said, "He can repeat". And I could not but agree.'

Three days later Myron Taylor had a last interview with Cardinal Maglione, and we have the record of the interview made by the American priest Carroll, though his record was made from notes after the conversation. This ranged over the various subjects discussed by Myron Taylor when in Rome; and among them the atrocities. 'Mr Taylor said that there was a general impression both in America and Europe – and he said that he could not be wrong in reporting this impression – that it was necessary now for the Pope again to denounce the inhuman treatment of refugees, hostages, and above all the Jews in

---

[18] Cf. Tittmann Papers, Brussels, s.v. Atrocities, p. 22; Osborne to Eden, 3 October 1942, in FO 380/86; and ADSS, 5, 676.

the Occupied countries. Not only Catholics want the Pope to speak but also Protestants. Cardinal Maglione replied that the Holy See is continually at work trying to help the sufferers . . . In the different countries various representatives of the Church have openly denounced the maltreatment of the people and have done everything they can to help the oppressed. The Pope has condemned the oppressors of the peoples and has said that governments will be blest or curst by God according to the way they treat the occupied countries. That is a pretty strong statement; as strong as is possible without descending to the particulars which would involve the Pope in political questions and have to be supported by documentation, reports, etc. Obviously the Pope cannot do this. Mr Taylor showed that he agreed but insisted on the opportunity for an appeal of a high character. The earlier declarations were some time ago. It is time for another. Certainly it would please everyone. Individuals as well as peoples have poor memories. Many want the Pope today to denounce these evils. Cardinal Maglione assured Mr Taylor that at the first possible opportunity the Pope would not fail to express anew his thought with clarity.'[19]

Here then Myron Taylor extracted from the Secretary of State a promise; the Pope shall speak, as soon as he gets the chance, and shall speak clearly.

While Myron Taylor was in Rome, real news about the emptying of the Warsaw ghetto and the killing of its inmates reached the West. The news got out to the Jewish agency in Palestine; which reported to Geneva (30 August) that they had two eye-witnesses. From Geneva it came to Washington. On 24 September Washington sent off the evidence to Myron Taylor in Rome. Myron Taylor laid it before Cardinal Maglione; the liquidation of the Warsaw ghetto. Some of the evidence was still vague – 'it is said', 'one story says'.

No one was any longer in doubt. In August a telegram came from Ribbentrop to the German embassy to the Italian government asking the Italians to hand over to the Germans the Croatian Jews under Italian occupation. Bismarck from the German embassy read out the telegram to the Italians and said confidentially, 'This would mean, in practice, their dispersion and complete elimination.' The Italians were embarrassed. They felt a moral commitment to protect these Jews. An unknown hand drafted a note for Mussolini's eye, and it shows how much the Italians took for granted as true:

Deportation to Poland could have tragic consequences. It is a plan not in line with Italian racial policy . . . which does not believe in persecution. We have

---

[19] ADSS, 5, 705, 721.

maintained groups of Italian Jews in Tunisia, Algeria, Greece, the Levant. Our policy differs totally from what has happened in France.

The Italians were resolute not to cooperate with the Nazis. They kept the file going. They said it was under consideration. They said that they had no efficient transport. They said that the roads in Croatia were infested by partisans and it was unsafe to move. From the Second Army in Croatia General Roatta protested that the plight of the Jews harmed Italian prestige and helped the guerrillas. On 23 October the Germans asked that all the Croatian Jews be handed over, not to the Germans, but to the Croatian army working closely with 'special organs of the German police'. And the counsellor of the German embassy to Italy quietly told the Italians that this would mean shooting of Jews on the spot. 'Our policy,' noted Foreign Affairs for Mussolini, 'is based on fairness to minorities.' The Italians made an offer to the Germans, that they would put the Jews in camps and so 'keep them from all harmful activity'. More than occasionally the Vatican asked the Italians to do what they could. The Italians needed no prompting, at least so far as concerned Italian Jews.[20]

Osborne recorded for the Pope (29 October) how big a meeting was held in London to protest against the extermination of the Jews, and how the Archbishop of Canterbury spoke and Cardinal Hinsley was represented.

Meanwhile the news began to change. Stalingrad held; everyone still expected its fall to be only a matter of time; but incredibly, the siege went on, seventy days, eighty days, a hundred days. There began to be faint signs of Allied morale rising, visible even in Rome. Then the news of El Alamein began to come in; and then the American landing in North Africa.

Osborne did not yet expect this dramatic change to make a difference to what it might be possible for the Pope to say.

Osborne to Eden, 9 November: 'The Pope is still considering: I doubt myself if he is going to say anything'.[21] If the Germans were going to win the war, that made a difference to what it is prudent to say; and if the Allies had after all a chance of winning the war, the motives for prudence might at least shift in balance. That was not at first seen. All Osborne was still doing was to record for the Pope the Jewish atrocities as reported by the BBC; especially on 30 November when the deputy Polish Minister gave details. And Osborne commented:

[20] AE, Yugoslavia, 1943, Busta 138, file of deportation of Croatian Jews. For Vatican pressure, see the evidence in *Civ. Catt.*, (1964), 2, 452.   [21] FO 380/86.

From all I hear it is quite true that Jews are crowded into trains, the floors of the carriages being covered with disinfectant in the form of chlorine or chloride or whatever it may be. The heat from the sun and the overcrowding results in a poison gas. They are hermetically sealed goods wagons. The result is that after a long journey the great majority of the unfortunate Jews are dead. Those who survive are finished off on arrival. Italians have seen this. There seems every reason to credit the incredible report that Hitler and Himmler have decreed the extermination of the Jews in Poland if not in all Europe . . .

Notice that the report is still called *incredible*, only there is reason to credit it.

Meanwhile the Pope and Maglione were working hard to prevent Rome being bombed. They tried every sort of diplomatic channel to extract an undertaking from the British. The British could not see why they should refrain from bombing an enemy capital and in any case, even if they never bombed Rome, were determined not to tell the Italians that they were not bombing Rome. This problem had given Osborne much work for months and months. But it was only in this December 1942 that the battle at last got him down; and what got him down was the ardent activity of the Vatican to prevent an 'atrocity' in Rome while it showed small signs of activity about atrocities in the rest of Europe.

Sunday, 13 December 1942: 'The more I think of it, the more I am revolted by Hitler's massacre of the Jewish race on the one hand, and, on the other, the Vatican's apparently exclusive preoccupation with the effects of the war on Italy and the possibilities of the bombardment of Rome. The whole outfit seems to have become Italian.'

This almost became Osborne's normal defence against pleas that the British should promise not to bomb Rome. 'I urged,' he wrote of a talk with Maglione on 14 December, 'that the Vatican, instead of thinking of nothing but the bombing of Rome should consider their duties in respect of the unprecedented crime against humanity of Hitler's campaign of extermination of the Jews, in which I said that Italy was an accomplice as the partner and ally of Germany.'

He collected all the factual information he could about the pogrom and handed it to Monsignor Tardini on 18 December, in the effort to make the Pope say something about it in his Christmas Eve broadcast. He asked Tardini, when he handed him the dossier, whether the Pope was not going to say something. 'But he said that the Pope could not take sides! It is very unfortunate. The fact is, I think, that His Holiness is clinging at all costs to what he considers to be a policy of neutrality, even in the face of the worst outrages against God and man, because he hopes to be able to play a part in restoring peace. He does not see that his silence is highly damaging to the Holy See and is entirely destructive of any prospects of his being listened to.'

19 December: 'I went to see the Cardinal and had a quiet and amiable talk with him. I didn't want to go back again to my aggressive talks about Vatican policy and the Jews etc. He seemed deeply moved by my only reference to the Jewish atrocities.'

From early in December telegrams began to flow into the Vatican from Jewish communities all over the world; the Jews of Costa Rica first; mostly from Central America, but also from Egypt and from Canada. The Chief Rabbi in London besought the Pope, invoking the Fatherhood of God and the brotherhood of man, to save a suffering people; and Montini took orders from the Pope that they were quietly to reply that the Holy See is doing all that it can.

By 3 December the British Foreign Office possessed at last information that must be substantially true; descriptions of the emptying of the Warsaw ghetto; the report of a Polish policeman inside the ghetto; a more doubtful report on Belzec. They had nothing on Chelmno or Auschwitz. It is extraordinary that no one yet had anything on Auschwitz. What they knew about was the Warsaw ghetto. Not for another two months did anyone report anything about Auschwitz.

A day or two later Count Raczynski laid before Anthony Eden some of the Polish evidence. Churchill saw the note and asked for more. There was talk of a common declaration by the Allied Powers on behalf of the Jews. The State Department was not friendly: the reports are unconfirmed, we can do no good, the only way to help Jews is to win the war. The London Foreign Office drafted a joint statement, with a phrase[22] which the Russian ambassador Maisky added, that the number of victims was 'many hundreds of thousands of entirely innocent men, women, and children'.

On 17 December the Allies issued from London, Washington and Moscow their joint declaration on the German persecution of the Jews; and Osborne brought it to the Pope, suggesting that the Pope might endorse it in a public statement.

Cardinal Maglione gave his negative a little more clearly, with reasons. The Holy See could not mention particular atrocities. It had frequently condemned atrocities in general. Privately it had done everything possible to help. He deplored the cruelties. He said that they could not verify Allied reports on the number of Jews exterminated.

The diplomats were beginning to watch this Christmas broadcast, but in their different ways pessimistically.

[22] R. B. Reams, in Walter Laqueur, *The Terrible Secret* (London, 1980), pp. 225–6.

22 *December*   Harold Tittmann, telegram to Washington, no. 212: 'It is rumoured that the Pope, in his Christmas message, will take a strong line on the subject. Any deviation from the generalities of his previous messages is unlikely, I am afraid'.

22 *December*   Osborne's Diary: 'Having been reliably assured that the Pope was going to speak out this Christmas, I am now equally reliably assured that he is not. The Vatican will be the only State which has not condemned the persecution of the Jews'.

The Pope said something at last in clear. He appealed to all good men to make a vow to bring back society under the rule of God; it is a duty we owe to those who lie dead on the battlefields; to the mothers and widows and orphans who have lost their men; to the exiles torn from their homes by war, to 'the hundreds of thousands of innocent people put to death or doomed to slow extinction, sometimes merely because of their race or descent'; to the many thousands of noncombatants who have lost life and everything else by those air raids which we have never ceased to denounce from the beginning.[23]

Even in this utterance the Pope was very careful to guard against exaggeration. The story was, two million Jews killed for their race. The Allied Declaration had not believed it, and said hundreds of thousands. The Pope says, some hundreds of thousands. The story was that they were all killed just for their race and this was true. The Pope says they were sometimes killed only for their race, *talora*, on occasion. Like the minds of most of western Europe, the mind of the Pope was not bad enough to believe the truth. Like the high officials of the British Foreign Office he thought that the Poles and the Jews exaggerated for the sake of helping the war effort.

The phrase was not trivial. It displeased Mussolini. 'The Vicar of God . . .' he said contemptuously, 'ought never to open his mouth. He ought to stay in the clouds. This is a speech of platitudes . . . a speech worthy of the parish priest of Predappio.'[24] Some people said that it was made possible by the changing war – El Alamein, the Americans in North Africa, the German failure in the Caucasus, and Stalingrad – it really looked as though the Germans might not win the war. Ribbentrop wondered whether the Pope was deserting his neutrality and ordered Diego von Bergen, his ambassador in Rome, to threaten retaliation. Von Bergen obeyed. The Pope stayed quite silent. Then, very calmly, he said that he did not care what happened to him; that if there were a struggle between Church and State, the State would lose. 'Pacelli,' reported Bergen to Ribbentrop, 'is no more sensible to threats than we are.' German security studied the broadcast and defined it as

[23] Text in ADSS, 7, 161.
[24] Ciano, *Diario (1939–43)*, 5th edn (2 vols., Milan, 1948), vol. 2, p. 232.

'one long attack on everything we stand for' . . . 'God, he says, regards all peoples and races as worthy of the same consideration. Here he is clearly speaking on behalf of the Jews . . . He is virtually accusing the German people of injustice towards the Jews, and makes himself the mouthpiece of the Jewish war criminals.'[25]

Harold Tittmann's telegram to Washington of 28 December took a more moderate line. 'The message does not satisfy those circles which had hoped that the Pope would this time call a spade a spade and discard his usual practice of speaking in generalities. The message is described in Vatican circles however, as "candid and forceful".' The French ambassador, the Vichy man Léon Bérard, asked the Pope directly why he had not used the word Nazi in his condemnation. The Pope replied to Bérard that if he had mentioned the Nazis by name he would have also had to mention the Communists by name.

In Poland Archbishop Sapieha heard the broadcast and welcomed the speech as what he had waited for.

The Pope himself told several ambassadors that his speech was the condemnation which they had all been demanding. He took this for granted when he talked to Tittmann. He seemed surprised when Tittmann told him that not everyone thought the same. Tittmann reported to Washington what he said:

He said, that in his opinion, it was obvious in the eyes of all that when he spoke of hundreds of thousands of innocent people killed or tortured, and at times solely because of their racial or national origins, he had in mind the Poles, the Jews, and the hostages.

He told me that, in speaking of atrocities, he could not have mentioned the Nazis without also mentioning the Bolsheviks, and this would surely not have pleased the Allies.

He also said that he feared that Allied information on atrocities was, alas, only too true, though he gave me to understand from his attitude that, as he saw things, they contained a small element of exaggeration for the sake of propaganda. Taken as a whole, he said that he thought that his message would be well received by the American people and I said that I agreed with him.

The American Jesuit Father McCormick discussed the message with Father Leiber and told him that the talk had been 'much too heavy, ideas not clean-cut, and obscurely expressed'.[26]

Listening to the broadcast, Osborne also thought it useless. ('He has produced the inevitable Five Points, this year on the special social

[25] Ribbentrop to von Bergen, 24 January 1943; von Bergen to Ribbentrop, 26 January 1943, RSHA report on the broadcast; Rhodes, *Vatican*, pp. 272–4.

[26] James Hennesey, 'An American Jesuit in War-Time Rome: the Diary of Vincent A. McCormick, S. J., 1942–45', in *Mid-America*, 56 (1974), 36.

problem or social problems.') When he had his New Year audience on 29 December he spoke very frankly about the Jews and the Pope listened with kindness and understanding. To London, after reflexion, Osborne began to make the best of it. On 5 January he reported to London that the Pope considered his broadcast 'clear and comprehensive' and that it 'satisfied all demands recently made upon him to speak out'. But he also reported (31 December) that this was not the opinion of all his colleagues, and that the reaction of some at least of the other diplomats 'was anything but enthusiastic. To me he claimed that he had condemned the Jewish persecution. I could not dissent from this, though the condemnation is inferential and not specific, and comes at the end of a long dissertation on social problems.'[27]

Papée admitted that 'stripped of verbiage and rhetoric' the address denounced totalitarian doctrines in general and Nazi practice in particular. But he knew that his exiled Polish government in London would never be satisfied until the Pope used the actual word *Nazi* in a condemnation. He told Harold Tittmann that he would do his best to persuade his government that the Pope could not have spoken more clearly.[28] Papée did not succeed in this endeavour.

That month of February 1943 Cardinal Hinsley of Westminster fell gravely ill. He died on 16 March. He had denounced the Nazis repeatedly, in tough language. Winston Churchill, who disapproved of Archbishop Lang of Canterbury as a former appeaser, is said to have suggested Hinsley for Lang's successor at Canterbury when Lang retired. Osborne (27 February 1943) wrote of his courageous and outspoken patriotism. Farinacci called him a philobolshevist. When Osborne heard on the BBC of the death, he wrote a note in his diary:

He was a great patriot, though perhaps more courageously outspoken regarding the Nazi persecution of the church and other offences against the laws of God and man than would please the hypersensitive neutrals of the Vatican. They probably do not realize how much he has done to counteract the unfavourable effects abroad of their neutrality.

To rub it in a little, he organized a great requiem mass for Cardinal Hinsley in St Peter's, no expense spared, at the cost of the British taxpayer, the Sistine choir at 7,500 lire, ten cardinals, eleven or more monsignori including Tardini and Montini and Kaas, Perosi's music written for the death of Pope Leo XIII, 14,000 lire altogether, none of which Osborne regretted.

But in long reflexion, he was satisfied with that Christmas broadcast. He never tried again, at least in the same way, to press the Pope to

---

[27] FO 371/34363; cf, Martin Gilbert, *Auschwitz and the Allies* (London, 1981), p. 105.
[28] Tittmann to Cordell Hull, 8 February 1943; NAW 866A/001/142.

public condemnation of German atrocities. And in 1943 the argument, and Osborne's work, turned the other way: how to keep the Pope silent, and how to prevent him from protesting, in the face of area bombing of great cities by American and British bombers.

10

The bombing of Rome

i. The sacredness of Rome

On the day that Italy entered the war Cardinal Maglione asked Osborne to ask the British not to bomb Rome. Italian newspapers picked up an extract from the *Daily Telegraph* threatening the bombing of Rome and other Italian cities. Maglione showed Osborne the extract from the newspaper. Osborne said that it was written by an imbecile and should be disregarded.

On the night of 13–14 June 1940 Allied aircraft flew over Rome and dropped pamphlets on Vatican City. This at least infringed neutrality. Maglione protested to London. London said that British aircraft had flown nowhere near Rome. But they retorted that if they decided to throw pamphlets at Rome, they could hardly avoid some of those pamphlets drifting down over Vatican City.[1]

This was the start of a very long correspondence which took much space in the archives of both sides and slowly became more anxious and more bitter.

London could see every reason for not bombing the Vatican. It could see no reason at all why it should undertake not to bomb Rome, especially if Italian aircraft bombed London. London said so to Rome, not uncertainly.

This argument went on for months and months. The British in London never came anywhere near understanding the Pope's point of view. They could not see that to the Pope Rome was quite as much *his* city as it was the capital of Italy; more his city. It was his capital of a thousand years.

The Vatican records show no recognition of an underlying motive in the British mind. Whether or not they bombed Rome, that was a question of policy and the future needs of war. Meanwhile they found it very useful to keep the Italian government on tenterhooks that at any moment bombs could rain down on Rome. They were confident that their threatening messages to Osborne would pass through the Vatican and so reach the Italian government. This confidence was not misplaced.

[1] ADSS, 4, 63–5, 70; cf. FO 371/24959/303.

The British found the attitude of the Vatican hard even to understand. That Vatican City should be unharmed, that they understood perfectly. But the Pope was a neutral. Why should he interfere more about Rome than about any other belligerent capital? Was he not taking the side of Italy? And the lack of neutrality depended, perhaps, on the circumstance that he not merely lived 'inside Italy', but was himself an Italian, and must want to help Italy?

The Vatican attitude rested upon a variety of sentiments and judgments.

The Pope is the Bishop of Rome. A bishop may care for the welfare of his people like any other bishop. But this feeling is little prominent in the Vatican records. For no other bishop possesses a diplomatic service enabling him to make such protests. As a bishop he hardly had status to intervene.

Secondly, the Pope had the feeling of Rome as a sacred city. To bomb Rome would be like bombing the Church of the Nativity at Bethlehem. It was a city sanctified by time and pilgrimages. It was a western Jerusalem. And it had works of art in profusion.

Thirdly, and this was important in the psychology, the defence of Rome from bombing was the last vestige of the old Papal States before 1870. Rome was taken away by the Italians. But still, somehow, it was Papal Rome. The Pope was still the legitimate lord, in a deep, hardly spoken consciousness, not only of the Vatican State but of all the city. That gave him the right and the duty to speak on behalf of all the city. Even Monsignor Tardini still had a memory of Pope Leo the Great going out to stop Attila the Hun from coming down to destroy the city, and of other Popes who went out to plead against barbarian invaders. He wondered sardonically whether this comparison between Pope Pius XII and Pope Leo the Great might do the British good since it implied that they were modern Huns.[2]

Fourthly, the defence of Rome from bombing had a necessary element in policy which could not be told to the British or the Americans. Vatican City was continually at risk of suppression. Many Fascists believed it to be a nest of spies. They also thought the more independent of the Pope's utterances to be a weakness in the war effort of the Axis.

Therefore, policy demanded that the Vatican be seen to be useful to Italy. Nothing could be more useful to Italy than the preventing of bombs on the capital. Of course this could not be said to the British. But with the Italian government Cardinal Maglione was perfectly frank. He kept them continuously informed of every move which he made to

2 ADSS, 7, 177.

interest the British and Americans in not bombing Rome. Since he made many such moves, he or his emissaries were able to say much. On 12 January 1943 Monsignor Montini found himself with Count Ciano at a luncheon given by Prince Colonna. Ciano said that he was very pleased with the Vatican for all its efforts to prevent the bombing of Rome.[3]

For the Vatican more was at stake than Roman lives or works of art; namely, its own continued existence as neutral territory.

ii. British bombing policy

From their refuge in Bordeaux the French, who were a beaten foe, cheerfully gave the assurance which the Pope wanted (17 June 1940). When it came to the British Cabinet, Cadogan minuted 'Cabinet agreed that we should say that we have no intention of attacking the Vatican City – and say nothing about Rome.' The actual Cabinet minute ran: 'that we should on no account molest the Vatican City, but that our action as regards the rest of Rome would depend upon how far the Italian government observed the rules of war'.[4]

Events soon put this moderation to the test. The Poles, desperate for help, wanted Rome bombed. As the raids on London grew in intensity, the Pope became ever more anxious. He raised it with Osborne at an audience of 2 October 1940. The Vatican minute reported no reply by Osborne or London. Osborne's letter to Lord Halifax was still able to be humorous: 'it was hardly necessary to bomb Rome. The dropping of leaflets and the resulting activity of Italian anti-aircraft fire seemed almost as damaging to the city as to the nerves of its inhabitants . . .' He felt nothing like so humorous as he sounded. He said to Tardini 'When I read such strong anti-English descriptions and expressions in Italian newspapers, a sort of rage comes over me and drives me to want English bombs to destroy Milan, Turin . . . and Rome.'[5]

That month tension grew because the Italians invaded Greece and men feared that they would bomb Athens. Osborne told Cardinal Maglione of his fear that if the Italians bombed Athens the British could hardly fail to bomb Rome by way of reprisal (26 October 1940). Maglione put the arguments for not bombing Rome and Osborne promised to put them to his government. Rome heard the story that a Caproni aircraft was shot down over London. Osborne asked London whether it was true, so that he could warn the Pope. London consulted the Royal Air Force who replied that Italian aircraft had crossed the east

[3] ADSS, 7, 186.
[4] FO 371/24959/304, 308; cf. Halifax to Godfrey, 15 June 1940, ibid., 307.
[5] ADSS, 4, 179; Osborne to Halifax, 3 October 1940, FO 380/106.

coast but none were known to have been over London. The Air Ministry instantly found a new use for Osborne. 'Anything Mr Osborne can do to keep the Italians guessing as to our intentions will be useful . . .'[6] Osborne was already in action in that sense:

I propose to tell the Cardinal Secretary of State this morning that I note from the Italian Press that it is proudly announcing that Italian aviation is now co-operating in the so-called 'retaliatory' bombing of England which is, in effect, attack by means of indiscriminate bombing on the civil population and morale; and that while I have no information or instructions from you on the subject, I shall be grateful if he will inform the Pope that, in my opinion, this must affect the results of His Holiness' plea to His Majesty's Government on behalf of the City of Rome.

I can only suppose that the much advertised Italian action is due either to the necessity for showing the German public some military activity on the part of the Italians or to the desire to prepare the Italian public for German assistance in Africa.

Three days later the Pope renewed his pleas. Osborne was truculent. 'I explained I appreciated the Pope's desire to spare the citizens of Rome, but I did not see that they had any better rights than the citizens of London and other British towns to be spared the horrors of direct attack.' He said that as the war was unpopular in Italy consistent bombing of Italian cities might trouble the Italian government. He hoped that they would soon be able to establish an air base in Greece and bomb Italy more easily.

This unusual fury in Osborne pleased the Foreign Office greatly. 'This seems quite the right spirit,' wrote Warner, 'and calculated to cause alarm and despondency when passed on to the Italians.' On 3 November Sir Alexander Cadogan wired to him encouraging him to keep up the game. 'Italian aircraft have so far been identified for certain over Dover and up the Medway . . . I approve your proposed language, and it will be useful if you can find further opportunities of dropping hints in Vatican circles which will result in playing on Italian fears regarding bombing of Rome. For your own information, we are anxious to keep them guessing as to our intentions in order to deter them from bombing Athens.'

The Greeks were very anxious that the Royal Air Force should not bomb Rome because they were afraid that Athens would suffer. They begged for the bombing of South Italy.

This also touched Osborne because Cardinal Maglione's home was in Naples. When Naples was bombed, Maglione happened to be there and 'sadly but resignedly' showed Osborne a map of Naples with his

[6] FO 371/24967/117–31; ADSS, 4, 204–5, 222; FO 380/106.

home outside the city. He was evidently anxious about his family. Every utterance of Osborne on this subject was indignant and uncompromising. He was believed in London to be, and felt himself to be, one of the principal agents in putting the fear of God and of British bombers into the Italians. His language was at times threatening about the dire future which awaited Italian cities. When Tardini pressed him (4 November 1940) he said 'But London, like Rome, has many artistic monuments which have been bombed!' – among them, St Paul's. Tardini said that history would not regard the bombers of St Paul's as friends of civilization, and the English would do ill if they followed the example.

However fiercely Osborne spoke, he went so far as to ask London whether in bombing Naples the bombers could spare Cardinal Maglione's house at Casoria. In London, Nichols asked the Royal Air Force[7] which sent a half-humorous answer: 'we would never make any attempt to cramp the style of our pilots'. But the squadron leader admitted that Cardinal Maglione's house was a long way from any likely target.

In the House of Commons, Sir Stanley Reed (7 November 1940) asked the Minister whether in view of the Italian claims that their men had bombed London, it was intended to continue to treat Rome as an open city. The point was thought sufficiently important to be laid before Churchill himself, who approved a menacing answer:

Mr R. A. Butler: His Majesty's Government have taken note of the Italian statement that Italian men and aircraft have participated in the bombing of London, and they must accordingly reserve full liberty of action in regard to Rome.

This answer worried the Greek allies almost more than the Italian foes.

On 5 November 1940 Sinclair at the Air Ministry assured Lord Halifax that they were ready to bomb Rome so soon as it was decided. He agreed that they must adhere to the pledge to the Vatican and be particularly careful not to bomb Vatican City. The targets would be the gasworks, the main railway station, and Mussolini's office in the Palazzo Venezia. Since the nearest of these, the Palazzo Venezia, was a mile from the Vatican he thought that if the night was moonlit the Vatican would be in no danger. Halifax had asked that the bombers (if they went) should avoid public monuments and buildings of great historical, antiquarian and artistic interest. The point, said Sinclair, 'is one which I certainly accept in principle, but which will, in practice, be extremely difficult to observe . . . It would be unfair to impose upon the pilots who, in attacking Rome, will certainly be undertaking an

[7] FO 371/24967/156.

arduous and difficult ask, more than the minimum of restrictions.' But Sinclair did not think it a sensible policy to bomb Rome. They could do more good to the Greeks by using their bombers on the Albanian front to attack the ports and lines of communication. The RAF did not like the job. The raid would come from Malta. The runway at Malta was not complete. Wellington bombers with full loads could not take off safely. And small bombs would not have much effect in Rome. The Foreign Office said that even a load of little bombs on Rome would have an effect on Italian psychology.

No bombs dropped on Rome as yet. The Greeks were pleased. The Pope was pleased. In Rome the reputation of the Pope rose. The Romans realized that he was far better security for their safety than any number of works of art.

On the night of 14–15 November the atmosphere changed when German bombers destroyed Coventry.

Osborne asked the Pope to condemn the bombing of civilians from the air. He talked of Birmingham and Coventry, of the number of deaths, of German boasting. In his speech of 24 November the Pope mentioned in a passing phrase, and in a prayer, his distress at cities destroyed and civilians killed. Tardini said to Osborne that the Pope was 'very distressed at these attacks' but would not comment. Cardinal Maglione said that the British were to be praised for sticking to military targets; 'but he would not be surprised if public opinion forced us to imitate the German example'.[8]

The Pope approached the Portuguese government for help, and the Portuguese ambassador (19 November 1940) called at the Foreign Office to express the pain which they and the whole Catholic world would feel if Rome were bombed. Sir Orme Sargent was mildly indignant. 'It might perhaps be suggested to the Pope that his attempts to organize pressure upon us not to bomb Rome because "it is the seat of the Papacy" would receive greater sympathy in this country if he simultaneously publicly condemned the bombing of St Paul's, Westminster Abbey, Canterbury Cathedral, Coventry Cathedral, Lambeth Palace. As far as I know he has not expressed any regret or surprise that these "seats of the Anglican Church" have been ruthlessly attacked by the German Air Force supported by the Italian Air Force.' He put it to Halifax who *more suo* shared a little, and to Vansittart who *more suo* shared a lot of this irritation. Vansittart minuted:

I would urge that he (Osborne) should put it merely as a retort, and not offer any opening by which the Pope might say 'Very well, I will condemn the bombing of English churches, and now you will spare Rome.' That would be the rottenest interchange imaginable.

[8] FO 380/61.

It is in fact too late for the Pope to use this gambit. Not that I think it would have been of any utility or advantage to sufferers in this country even if he had made it earlier.

At this point an entertaining suggestion reached the Royal Air Force from the other side of the Atlantic. A Mr Albert P. Segers wrote from a box number in Alabama to the British Ambassador in Washington Lord Lothian.

Through diplomatic sources secure the marking of Vatican City so that boundaries may be seen by day or night, in order that Mussolini may be bombed. This will shorten the war by giving some of its horrors to those who instigated it.[9]

The officers of the RAF received this suggestion with glee. Everyone saw it to be absurd, but it was entertaining and it would be good to put it up to the Vatican as though it were serious. They sent the wicked little idea up to Winston Churchill, whose sense of humour was perfectly attuned to such a mock-serious proposal.

You should make it clear [went off the order from Alexander Cadogan (28 November 1940)] that . . . H.M.G . . . reserve full liberty of action in regard to Rome. You should accordingly deprecate these attempts by the Vatican to organise pressure upon us, not merely because H.M. Government do not intend to be moved by them, but also because intervention by the Vatican in regard to Rome as distinct from the Vatican City, is bound to produce the unfortunate impression, that His Holiness is intervening to protect the Italian State and the Fascist government from the consequences of their own action in regard to the bombing of London.

Incidentally you should express disappointment that His Holiness should not have publicly condemned the bombing of the shrines of the Anglican Church, such as St Paul's Cathedral, Westminster Abbey, Canterbury Cathedral and Coventry Cathedral – not to mention Lambeth Palace – by the Germans supported in many cases by the Italian Air Force, as to which His Holiness does not appear to have expressed any regret. You should however make it perfectly clear that this does not imply that if the Pope were now to condemn the bombing of our churches we would reconsider our attitude of retaining full liberty of action as regards Rome . . .

You may . . . repeat that should we decide to bomb Rome every effort will be made to avoid Vatican City. You should point out that these efforts would be much facilitated if the Vatican precincts were suitably marked by night and day and suggest that immediate steps should be taken to make the confines of the Vatican City clearly distinguishable from the air. I am aware that the Italian government will certainly not permit such marking, but by making this urgent suggestion we shall place ourselves in a better position vis-à-vis the Vatican and the Catholic world if, as we hope will not be the case, the Vatican is hit by a

[9] FO 371/24967/165–6, 181.

stray bomb. Furthermore the question of marking the Vatican precincts may be expected to cause friction between the Holy See and the Italian government at a moment when you anticipate an endeavour by the Axis to associate the Vatican with their cause.[10]

Almost at the same time Lord Halifax saw the Apostolic Delegate Godfrey and criticized the Pope for his silence about the bombing of St Paul's Cathedral.

The Foreign Office were pleased with themselves. They had reminded the Pope that his attitude to the German and Italian bombing of civilians had been 'flabby' and simultaneously used him to make the Italians fear their future intentions.[11]

Osborne handed Cardinal Maglione this uncompromising memorandum on 5 December 1940.[12] It regretted Vatican pressure on London, accusing it of giving the impression that the Pope wanted to protect the Fascist State; lamented his silence at the bombing of four great cathedrals (no mention of Lambeth Palace, except by an *etc. etc.*). It stated that even if the Pope did condemn such bombing the British government retained its liberty to act. And it said how much easier it would be to respect Vatican neutrality if its frontiers were illuminated at night.

Of the resulting two interviews between Osborne and Maglione we have the notes of both men. Maglione was 'pained by the tone of my communication'. He said that the Pope had done nothing for the Fascist State. He only represented Catholic desires throughout the world that the sacred city be spared. He had blamed *all* bombardments of unarmed civilians, in his discourse of 24 November. Osborne said that the blame came in a little phrase and a prayer. Maglione replied that great things do not need a lot of words.

Two days later they met again to talk of lights at night. Maglione said that he was not willing to light up Rome to help British bombers. If he illuminated, the government and the Roman people would be furious, and rightly. He said that the Vatican City was 'unmistakably' indicated by the dome of St Peter's. He told Osborne how the Italian ambassador had said to him that no Italian aircraft had flown over London. Osborne said that this was not true.

'Trouble is,' reported Osborne to London (6 December), 'that Vatican thinks in centuries and they regard Fascism as a transitory interlude. I think the Pope will be upset, but I think it will be good for him.'[13]

[10] FO 371/24967/172; ADSS, 4, 281.
[11] Pierson Dixon, ap. FO 371/24967/167.   [12] ADSS, 4, 283.
[13] FO 380/106, Osborne to Halifax, 7 December 1940; FO 371/24967/176 and 179. ADSS, 4, 290–1, notes by Tardini.

Trenchant little Tardini was much more outspoken. To accuse the Pope of favouring Fascism was *falsissimo*. To ask for illumination of Vatican City was puerile. At this word Osborne was suddenly angry. 'Impracticable yes; puerile no!' Tardini said that the Vatican's electricity came from Italy. Osborne said that this had not occurred to him. Tardini said, 'If you want to do something to help Mussolini and harm yourselves, come and bomb Rome.' It is the diocese of the Pope; it contains many institutions which are ecclesiastical but not Italian; and many buildings belonging to the Pope. Osborne said only, 'But suppose a bishop gets a bandit into his diocese . . .?'

The documents show, as might be predicted, that Osborne's private attitude did not quite agree with that of his superiors. He also was pained by the uncompromising tone of the orders which he received, and in obeying them excused himself to Maglione for having to do what he was told. He accepted that his job was to keep the Italian government on tenterhooks. But he reminded London, in little phrases, inserted quietly into his telegrams, of another point of view. The bombing of Rome would swing world opinion to the side of Mussolini. The Fascists would be delighted and helped. Since we obviously could not bomb Rome, in our own interests (and the city contained no military objectives of importance), might it be better to take credit for it? – that is to say so and then say that the reason was nothing to do with Mussolini but only with the Pope. It would clinch our claim to be standing for Christian civilization. It could enlist the sympathy of all the Catholic world. It would weaken Mussolini among many Italians. We could keep Italian fears up by bombing nearby airfields or railways. The point of view failed to take account of the military pressures. But Osborne can be seen by his little phrases and occasional hints to be attracted by this more humane, if weaker, policy.[14]

From time to time, after that, Osborne suggested that the Pope might condemn the bombing of cities and civilian populations. But on occasion he would say 'This is a purely personal suggestion.' And it did not fit the policy of his government which knew already that it wanted to bomb cities, even if for expedient reasons it did not yet wish to bomb Rome.

During that winter of 1940–1 Osborne met a curious form of the argument. He found some Romans ready to believe that the British would deliberately bomb St Peter's and the Vatican. He therefore wondered whether Germans and Italians might do it, using British

[14] Cf. especially Osborne to London, 11 November and 21 November 1940, FO 371/ 24967/146, 188; ADSS, 4, 290.

bombs which failed to explode at Naples. He even suggested an assurance in the House of Commons, perhaps to a question put by a Catholic member, that we should never bomb the Vatican and that the Pope had been so informed.[15] This was indeed the policy of the British government, but it was also the policy not to say so aloud lest it benefit the Italians.

In the spring of 1941 came the Yugoslav crisis, and the German invasion of Greece, and British troops fought Germans in retreat on the road to Athens. Again the threat to bomb Athens caused fear that Rome would be bombed in reprisal. The British, trying desperately to protect Athens, told Osborne to tell the Pope that if Athens were bombed they would bomb Rome. The object was open; it was their way of warning the Italian government. The object was achieved. Osborne told Cardinal Maglione. Maglione told the Italians. Monsignor Tardini was again bitter. The English wanted to find any excuse for bombing Rome. The Germans would like to have the British bombing Rome, for it could do them nothing but good. Rome would be spared

if the Germans have a special regard for the famous city of Athens,
if the Germans want the good of Italy,
if the Germans want Rome to remain unharmed,
if the Germans were well disposed to the Holy See,
if the Germans were interested in not driving the British to acts of barbarity.
But who could answer *yes* to all these *ifs*?[16]

Early in April 1941 maps of Rome began to appear on the operations table at Bomber Command. The officers at headquarters argued. 'Oh well', said one, 'we don't propose to bomb St Peter's or the Vatican galleries, we shall go for the railway station or put in a precision attack on Mussolini's headquarters.' C. E. Carrington, the historian, was attached as an Army liaison officer to Bomber Command. He saw that the airmen had no idea of the difficulty of what they proposed; and his imagination boggled at the killing in Rome perhaps of some Irish-American priest, or the smashing of a famous baroque church. Yet when, as so often, the weather in northern Europe was shocking, Italy tempted the strategists; and with the German invasion of Greece there was public demand for reprisals against Italy.

Carrington rang up the most influential Roman Catholic he knew, Stanley Morison the typographer, a director of *The Times* and a close friend of Beaverbrook. They met for lunch that day in London (7 April). Morison went to see Heenan, then right-hand man to the cardinal.

[15] FO 371/24967/147.   [16] ADSS, 4, 425.

Two or three days later the maps of Rome disappeared from the operations table.[17]

To some observers the restraint of the British looked strange. D'Ormesson, now in hiding in Vichy France, even in 1942 saw that though the British reserved the right to bomb Rome they had not yet bombed Rome; and soliloquized charmingly, 'The British are too good gentlemen to behave like that.'[18]

So late as 4 March 1941 Osborne protested to the Pope that he ought to protest to the Italian government at a 'barbarity' over bombing from the air. In northern Greece an earthquake drove many of the people of Larissa to leave their houses and take refuge in tents because more than a third of their homes were destroyed. In the days following the earthquake Italian bombers attacked the camps, and Osborne commented with disgust to Cardinal Maglione, 'Even the Germans have never pushed total and totalitarian war so far.' Maglione accepted the mission, and talked to the Italian ambassador against this bombing.

Such protests were not all one-sided. A British submarine torpedoed an Italian hospital ship off the coast of Albania (14 March 1941). The ship was carrying Mussolini's daughter (Count Ciano's wife) Edda in her capacity as a dame of the Red Cross. The Italian embassy asked the Pope for a word of regret. Monsignor Montini said that the matter was difficult. If the Pope said something on the hospital ship, on how many other things on both sides would he need to speak in future? He had refrained from saying anything public on the Larissa bombing despite many requests. Montini suggested to the Secretary of State that perhaps he could send a note of congratulation to Edda on her rescue. To this the Pope agreed personally; and also agreed that the Secretary of State should take the matter up with Osborne in just the same way that Maglione took up the Larissa bombs with the Italian ambassador.

Osborne said to Maglione that he was sure the torpedoing of the hospital ship was in error and agreed to pass the message from the Vatican to his government. The Italian embassy was pleased with the Vatican.[19]

After the American entry into the war the weight of bombing changed sides. The German Air Force was busy in Russia. The British and Americans had no way to attack Germany except with bombs from the air, and bombing must mean area bombing, and therefore bombing of civilians, because the bomb-aimers could hit nothing smaller than an area. The Germans started area bombing but the British and Americans

---

[17] Unpublished memorandum by Carrington; Carrington to the author, 9 January 1981; Nicholas Barker, *Stanley Morison* (London, 1972), pp. 381–2; Morison to Carrington, 23 April 1941.

[18] *Ambassade tragique*, p. 187.   [19] ADSS, 4, 411–19.

now carried it much further. It was a sign of this change of weight when the German ambassador at the Vatican, Diego von Bergen, made a move (September 1942). Apparently he neither asked nor even told Berlin. He used a curious person for his manoeuvre, none other than that suspect carrier of messages Monsignor Pucci. But through Pucci he got a message to the Pope, that the Pope would do a very lovely thing if he could talk to the American envoy Myron Taylor, when he came to visit the Vatican in September 1942, against the bombing of civilians.

The Pope thought this good. Monsignor Tardini pointed out the danger. The British were already convinced that any such move was sure to be made because the Germans pressed the Pope. The Americans had not yet believed this but might be on the point of suspecting the same. Nevertheless, whether or not von Bergen suggested it and Monsignor Pucci brought it, the plea was right. The Pope did what he was asked, even though he saw that the Germans began it, and even though he could not help seeing that the persecution of the Church in Germany was growing.

Tardini took what little advantage he could out of the move by telling the Italian ambassador that the Pope had done what the German ambassador suggested.

Myron Taylor's reply was not quite uncompromising. He made the characteristic British retort, which was to ask whether the Pope had condemned the bombing of so many cities, St Paul's Cathedral etc., by the Germans. He denied any intention by the Allies to bomb indiscriminately. But he undertook to do what he could to discourage indiscriminate bombing, both in London and in Washington, and to persuade the Allies to warn the German public to stay away from areas containing military objectives.[20]

As the weight of bombing power grew, and the winter nights came longer, and the weather in northern Europe worse, the tacticians of the RAF started again to look for targets in Italian cities. In October 1942 (27–9) the RAF bombed Genoa, Turin and Milan. Early in November began rumours that Rome would soon be bombed. On the day of the first raid on the North Italian cities, Cardinal Maglione sent a message to the nuncio in Washingon Cicognani that if Rome were bombed the Pope would protest. The Americans were afraid that the British would bomb Rome and then could not help hitting something sacred to Catholic Americans. Myron Taylor suggested that the Americans could clear themselves of the danger of loss of reputation, and gain prestige in Italy and Spain and Portugal, if they told the Pope that

[20] ADSS, 5, 722–3, 730–1.

they distanced themselves from the British policy on bombing Rome and intended to be independent of their acts. But the Secretary of State Cordell Hull was uneasy at any such distancing from his Allies and preferred to try to win an agreement.

On 5 October 1942 Myron Taylor was in London, and with the American ambassador (Winant) went to dinner with Winston Churchill. Two of Churchill's daughters, as well as Mrs Churchill, were present. Taylor asked Churchill not to bomb Rome. Churchill said that he could give no such undertaking. Taylor then asked Churchill whether he could not say publicly that if Rome were bombed the targets would be limited to military objectives. Churchill thought such an undertaking impossible to give. 'Night bombing does not lend itself to accurate bombing of military objectives only . . . It would not be honest to state that night bombing would be confined to military objectives only.'[21] He said that he could not order the end of night bombing.

Mussolini was very irritable: 'The bombing of Genoa and Turin is all the Vatican's fault.' He misjudged Myron Taylor.

'In the Vatican,' said Mussolini, 'they are completely defeatist. Myron Taylor came here, and breathed that atmosphere of defeatism in the Vatican, and was convinced that it was shared by Italy. He went to London and suggested that they step up terror attacks, to get an Italian collapse.' He said: 'It would be very easy to send a few hundred men to attack the Vatican.'

Next day Farinacci printed in *Regime Fascista* the canard about the bombing of Turin and Genoa being caused by Myron Taylor's visit to Vatican. Cardinal Maglione protested. Mussolini told Count Ciano to tell Farinacci to correct. Farinacci said that he had the story from Mussolini.[22] Farinacci also said that Mussolini asked him to write the article.

On 15 November 1942 the Fascist minister Buffarini talked of putting interned Americans and British, including women, children, priests, monks and friars, into the places of danger from bombs so that they would be first to die. He said that he had Mussolini's approval for this mode of defence. He said that Rome had become 'the great centre of espionage' and he would put a ring of armed men round the Vatican. He was boiling with rage at the British bombing of hospitals in Genoa and seemed to want to take revenge out of the Vatican.[23]

But the Italian government offices still thought the Vatican a place more protected against bombs than the remainder of Rome. For into

[21] FRUS, 1942, 3, 794. Winant's report, Taylor Papers, Hyde Park, Box 10.
[22] R. Guariglia, *Ricordi, 1922–1946* (Naples, 1950), pp. 531–2.
[23] ADSS, 7, 93–4.

the Vatican they moved loads of famous pictures, for example from the Borghese gallery; and 63 paintings from the walls of the Chamber of Deputies. Some of the deposited pictures the Vatican sent to North Italy when closer danger threatened the city of Rome.[24]

That winter the efforts of the Vatican to prevent the bombing of Rome grew strenuous, at times even frantic. In the bombing of Genoa more than twenty churches were put out of use. The Americans bombed Reggio (Calabria) and killed the archbishop. What would happen if Rome were bombed, with historic churches in every square? The Pope enlisted Francis Spellman the Archbishop of New York, Cardinal Maglione enlisted the American bishops. The best policy to stop the British seemed to be to get the Americans to stop the British, for the Americans needed to take account of many Catholic and even Italian citizens. Cardinal Maglione enlisted the Apostolic Delegate in London, and then Cardinal Hinsley, to approach Anthony Eden direct. The Vatican also enlisted the dictator of Portugal Salazar to intercede with the British.

President Roosevelt kept making peaceable noises. The Americans liked to put the blame on the British. Their commanders had no desire to close any options. But it was convenient, in their relations with Catholic bishops and their people, to say that they could not stop the British from bombing Rome if the British so decided. Except for Myron Taylor, who thought that the bombing of Rome would be barbarity and a calamity for those who bombed, they would say a word to moderate the British but they would do nothing to prevent bombing if the British determined to bomb. Rome might be the seat of the Pope. It was full of history and monuments. But it was the capital of the other side in a war. Was the enemy government to be secure from threat? Were troops and supplies constantly passing through the railway yards to be exempt? The Americans made friendly noises as though they would do what they could. They had no desire to do anything important.

The British were uncompromising. They would bomb Rome whenever the needs of the war demanded. Eden said so in the House of Commons, more than once.

On 5 December 1942 the Pope published the message to the archbishops of Turin and Genoa, on the bombing of those cities. The Italians were very pleased with Cardinal Boetto of Genoa and his 'ringing patriotic message about the inhuman acts committed by the enemies of our Italy . . . in view of these innocent victims the Lord will lift a hand of mercy and give our beloved country a complete victory'.

---

[24] Cf. AE, Santā Sede, 1945, Busta 74, AE to Embassy, 24 December 1944; and report of 8 November 1944.

The Italians noted a wave of indignation, about the bombing of Genoa, sweeping through the Vatican.[25]

Osborne never forgave the Italian papers their glee over the bombing of London in 1940 and perhaps the bombing of Buckingham Palace was still in his mind. Tardini knew that this resentment still lived. On 8 December 1942 Tardini reminded him of the British statement that the Italian bombing of Britain was 'ineffective'. Osborne said emphatically 'It's the intention that matters!'

Tardini said: 'Excellency, we are talking here about bombs, not about intentions. If the British would drop intentions on the city . . .'. Osborne smiled; and would not budge. Tardini said, the bombing of central London is barbarism. And the bombing of Italian cities is barbarism. Osborne said that the British aimed only at military objectives. Of course there were bound to be mistakes. Tardini said, 'For me the objective is what gets hit, everything else is subjective. Anyway there are too many mistakes.' Osborne said that the dead in London far exceed the number of dead in Italian cities. Tardini said that London is a city of many millions, and that the bombing of Italian cities had only just begun.

Nearly a week later the two men met by chance outside the convent of Santa Marta. They fell to the same subject instantly. Osborne sounded dry, even angry. 'The British government will keep its right to bomb Rome if the way the war goes makes it useful.' Tardini said that nowadays rights count for nothing and he hoped that this right too would be kept among the rights that are unsatisfied.[26]

iii. Rome an open city?

The international laws of war recognized that a city could be declared 'open'. A belligerent could say that it would not defend the city, nor use it for military purposes. Then the enemy would accept that it had no reason to bombard, and the life of innocent civilians, or the treasures of history, or even a centre of ordinary civilized life, would not be endangered.

The precedents for this 'law' were few and uncertain. And its philosophy was contrary to that of the makers of German and American and British policy. Their bombers could not bomb by day because

---

[25] AE, Santa Sede, 1942, Busta 58; cf. Father McCormick's entry in his diary that day, in James Hennesey, 'An American Jesuit in War-Time Rome: the diary of Vincent A. McCormick, S.J., 1942–45', in *Mid-America*, 56 (1974), p. 35; Osborne's little indiscretion to the Uruguayan ambassador about the probable non-bombing of Rome but bombing of neighbouring towns (which the Uruguayan told his escort and so it came to the Italian police), AE, Santa Sede 1942, Busta 61, report of Ministry of Interior, 7 December 1942.   [26] *ADSS* 7, 138–9.

too many of them were shot down. Therefore they must bomb by night. There they could not hit military objectives. They could only hit areas inside which military targets were known to be. Therefore they needed to extend the idea of a military objective; until some of them were near the barbarous and false doctrine that if you kill the children of the soldiers at the front it will lower the morale of those soldiers and shorten the war.

Could Rome be an open city? There was precedent. In 1940 the French government left Paris for Bordeaux and said that Paris was an open city. A government could remove itself, its generals, its ministry of war; transfer its headquarters to a temporary capital and so preserve from destruction its permanent and historic capital.

In theory, then, Mussolini could move himself, his generals, his war apparatus, from Rome to Milan, or Turin, or an encampment of the wilderness like Hitler's Wolf's Lair. And then the British eyes upon the Palazzo Venezia at the centre of historic Rome could turn away to other targets.

If this was true in theory, it was almost unthinkable in practice.

Moving the headquarters of a belligerent nation is not the work of a few days. The French move to Bordeaux in 1940 was chaotic. When the Italian government moved from Florence to Rome in 1870–1, the result for a few months came near chaos. Even in peace, to rehouse a government took months.

Moreover, if Rome were sacred to the Pope, it had a touch of sacredness to Italians. It stood for a historic imperial mission. Its name echoed the memory of Italian greatness. It was a symbol of the unification of modern Italy. If united Italy fought a war, Rome as capital was part of Italian morale.

The war which the Italians then fought lay in North Africa. Italian bullets and tanks were made in North Italy. Petrol came from the north. In North Africa German allies fought at their side. General Rommel's supplies came through North Italy. Nearly all this material had to pass through Rome. The railways and roads of Italy were so designed that Rome could not be avoided. Even if Mussolini moved himself and all his staff to a wolf's lair, what of the railway station and sidings and goods yards of Rome? To make Rome a truly open city would strangle the throat of the armies in North Africa.

Because Rommel fought in Africa, German uniforms were seen all over Rome. The Germans had a headquarters at Frascati. They occupied a hotel in the Piazza del Popolo. They filled the Ministry of Marine. All round the Piazza della Oca they were billeted. In theory Mussolini could order the Germans to move out of Rome. The Italians might reasonably wonder whether they would go even if they were asked politely. The German army would hardly consent to throttle their lines of supply.

These were the reasons which made it almost impossible to turn Rome into an open city. And there was another reason, at first hidden, and slow to be perceived by either side. To make an open city requires the consent of two parties. At first dimly, and later clearly, the British perceived that they did not want Rome to be an open city. The doctrine of the 'soft' under-belly of Europe demanded that Rome be not an open city. If one day they invaded Germany from the south, they could not do without the roads and railways which ran through Rome. However the Italians talked of getting headquarters out of Rome, the British could not afford to accept that Rome be open.

Nevertheless Osborne saw that to suggest an open city to the Italians could disturb Italian planning and divide Italian morale. His original suggestion to Cardinal Maglione (December 1942) was doubtless intended to be a plea, like the plea to light the Vatican at night, in which you would almost need to wink as you said what you had to say.

Maglione took the plea very seriously. He thought it not impossible to persuade the Italian government to remove itself and its military headquarters from Rome and so get the city declared open. Nothing speaks more for the belief inside the Vatican that they could influence the Italian government. Maglione told the Italian ambassador Guariglia that the Italian government must remove *military objectives* from the city. Guariglia reported to his masters that the Vatican asked for the removal of the *principal military objectives*. Maglione told Guariglia that this was not what he said. Guariglia said that he saw no point in confronting Mussolini with an impossible demand.

Two days later Count Ciano talked with the King of Italy about moving headquarters out of Rome. The King wanted it to happen, and suggested a move to Fiuggi[27] the spa in the mountains beyond Palestrina. Guariglia told Maglione that they were already planning to remove headquarters. He told Maglione that he was free to tell Osborne and Tittmann. Whether the Italians really planned to move headquarters or not, they found it useful that the British should know as soon as possible, for the information, whether true or false, could postpone the bombing of Rome. On 13 December 1942 Guariglia told Maglione officially that the move was decided.[28] Maglione asked, what about the Germans in Rome? He told Guariglia that Osborne insisted, the Germans also must go. Guariglia said he would ask his government.

Maglione told all this to Osborne (14 December 1942). Osborne, as

[27] ADSS, 7, 133, 129; Ciano, *Diario (1939–43)*, 5th edn (2 vols., Milan, 1948), vol. 2, p. 227.
[28] ADSS, 7, 136; and ap. FRUS, 1942, Europe, III, 795–800.

may be imagined, was sceptical. 'But here are barracks, troops . . .' 'In a city of a million and a half people,' said Maglione, 'you need some troops to keep order.' Osborne said, 'Are there not enough police?' Maglione: 'I believe not.'

On 20 December Guariglia officially informed Maglione that the military and naval commands were at that moment moving out of Rome. He said that to stop the movement of troops through Rome was impossible. He said that Rome needed troops not only for public order but also as defence against invasion from the sea. On the following day he told Maglione that Mussolini was moving with his high command. He said that to move government out of Rome was impossible. The organization of the State prevented it, and it would hurt national dignity. Maglione heard a rumour that the Germans were resisting the move, and making remarks like 'We'll never get out of Rome just to please the Vatican.'

London was informed, and bristled with suspicion. This was an Italian idea. The Pope acted as an agent of the Italians. Cardinal Maglione had to keep protesting what was the truth, that the idea came from the Vatican. The Italian codebreakers followed with interest and apprehension the exchanges between Osborne and London, and recorded the particular intransigence of Anthony Eden, who 'wanted not to lose a good chance of humiliating Italy'.

All the same, they were in a difficulty at the Vatican. They thought of asking the Italians whether the move was complete, and realized that the question could not be asked, because it would be a request for information about the movement of troops. On 28 February 1943 Maglione regarded as safe a request for information couched in very general terms, but still insisting, not on *principal military objectives* but on *all military objectives of whatever kind*.[29] Can he really have thought that the request was feasible? He was an intelligent man, he must have seen that what he asked was impossible. Was he asking it in order that he might be seen by Osborne to be asking it, and thereby showing the British that Rome was at least half an open city?

Guariglia made a note on 9 March 1943. The move out of Rome had hardly happened. The doors of the commanding officers were closed. Flags disappeared from the bonnets of the cars of commanding officers. The officers wore mufti instead of uniform. But not much had moved out of Rome.[30] No Germans went anywhere. They stayed in their offices and billets.

As the plight of Italy worsened and North Africa fell to the Allies and the menace came nearer and sane Italian commanders knew that Italy

[29] ADSS, 7, 137, 151–2, 175, 230, 252; Guariglia, *Ricordi*, p. 516.
[30] Guariglia, *Ricordi*, p. 520.

was no longer capable of fighting a war, the pressure from the Vatican
began again. Five months after the undertaking by the Italian government to get out of Rome, Monsignor Tardini recorded a lament –
headquarters still in Rome, Mussolini still in Rome, members of the
high command walking round Rome in mufti – such a breach of faith
seemed to Tardini to provoke bombs, and compromised the Holy See
which promised that something had happened and now was proved
false. The Italian ambassador to the Holy See changed again, to no less
a man than Count Ciano.

On 23 May 1943 Maglione saw Ciano and asked for further
assurances that Rome was an open city. The Italian government took
its time and then assured that the high command was out of Rome.
Maglione said that he could not be satisfied; and suddenly in very
private conversation Ciano said that Mussolini had no intention of
getting out of Rome. He had played with the idea until one of the
Fascist Grand Council wrote him a violent letter that Rome ought to
share with other Italian cities the honour of being bombed. Mussolini
also realized,[31] it was later plain, that talk of making Rome an open city
played into the hands of the Vatican, by underlining its status as an
international possession and overlooking its status as the capital of a
nation at war. Farinacci, as was his way, later expressed Fascist
criticism of the Pope, under the heading *The Primate said nothing*:

It is true that the acclamations of the Roman crowd were imposing when
Pius XII insisted that his diocese be not bombed. But it is also true that Italians
of other dioceses are also men and Christians. They are mortified at being
abandoned to the terrorist bombing of the Anglo-Americans. There is no
Italian city without churches and Christian monuments. We would love to
hear, not only the Pope, not only the bishop of Rome, but the Primate of Italy.

(*Regime Fascista*, 14 March 1944)

On 29 May 1943 the Italian government gave another assurance that it
had removed principal military objectives from the city, except for the
garrison necessary for defence; and said that its motives were twofold,
first to spread the military targets in face of the threats from the air, and
second to meet the humane wishes of the Holy See. We have no record
of what the Vatican thought of this assurance. It probably took the first
motive more seriously than the second.

The Pope himself was in a state of faith about the bombing of Rome. He
felt that he had a mission from God to save the holy city. He was sure
that he would be able to prevent Rome being bombed. Sometimes he
would talk of it as a certainty, that he could succeed.[32] None of his three

---

[31] ADSS, 7, 345–6; 400–1; 715.   [32] Guariglia, *Ricordi*, p. 522.

colleagues in the Secretariat of State had the same feeling of assurance.

As danger approached the tone of the pleas became a little more desperate. To bomb Rome would be a crime before the face of history. If you bomb Rome the people will react violently and the Vatican may no longer be able to ensure the safety of the diplomats lodging in the Convent of Santa Marta. Though the Vatican now knew that Mussolini had no intention of leaving Rome, they also knew that a spreading out into the country of military objects was in progress as a protection against air raids, and duly informed the Allies. They said that the Allies had agreed that they would not bomb the Vatican and the only sure way of not bombing the Vatican was not to bomb Rome. The replies to these pleas were very disappointing. To the plea that if the Allies bombed Rome the Italian people might rise and kill the diplomats at Santa Marta, Tittmann as one of those diplomats replied that if the Allies thought that they could shorten the war they would not worry about the lives of a few diplomats. But neither Osborne nor Tittmann believed in this future riot, unless the Italian government organized murder. They thought that Cardinal Maglione was trying a specious plea to see whether it helped. Directly and formidably attacked by Osborne on the point, Maglione said that he was misunderstood.[33]

Tardini was infinitely depressed. These Protestant countries, they are deeply anti-Roman. The Italian government does everything to provoke bombing, insults the British, keeps military targets all over Rome, plays dirty tricks with the Vatican. The Papacy thinks the bombing of Rome would be a horror, the Fascists think it would be an honour. The Vatican could easily be seen as naive or even a liar because it gave assurances which were later proved false. The Allies claim that *everything* is a military objective, and they can bomb houses because the workers live there, and forget that the workers' wives and babies also live. 'The more military objectives go out of Rome the more the Allies will find in the city – they will never be satisfied.'[34] Tardini penned most of this gloom less than a week before the British and American armies invaded Sicily.

As the invasion of Sicily came nearer, British propaganda dropped leaflets on Italy. The archives of the Italian Ministry of Popular Culture contain a supply of these, collected by the police. Some of them are intelligent. There is an absurd picture of Hitler resolute to fight to the death of the last Italian. There is a map of future bombings – Turin, Milan, Genoa, *Rome*, Naples, Cagliari, Palermo, Catania – 'the Allied planes will obscure the sun from Italian soil'. One is headed 'Must Italy

[33] ADSS, 7, 456, 459–60; FRUS, 1943, II, 919, 921, 925.
[34] ADSS, 7, 462–3.

be Coventryized?' There is a warning that families should be got to safety; 'remind yourselves that your alliance with Germany is the only cause of Allied bombs on Italian cities'. 'Demand peace.' 'Demonstrate for peace.' 'We have bombed your ports and industries which work entirely for Germany. We don't hate the Italian people. We only hate the Fascist hierarchy who identified your country with the Nazis.' 'We shall bomb military objectives near Rome. We have no intention to destroy historic monuments, the glory not of Italy only but of the world.' 'Possibly to render its lies more credible, the Fascist government will itself bomb Rome, even Vatican City.'[35]

The contents of some of these leaflets gave an argument to Maglione. They distinguished between the Italian people and their government. Therefore they implied that if the Italian government was changed, the Italian people would be treated better. That meant the doctrine of unconditional surrender, announced by Churchill and Roosevelt at Casablanca, would not apply to an Italy which dropped Mussolini? Cardinal Maglione asked Osborne and Tittmann whether this meant a softening of the demand for unconditional surrender. London and Washington replied that it did not. Osborne suspected that Maglione was put up to this by the Pope. But it was a hint that Italians might consider dropping Mussolini and making a separate peace.

At the end of June 1943 Osborne came out of an audience with the Pope and told Tittmann that the Pope was 'worried sick' about the bombing of Rome.[36]

In July 1943 the British and Americans invaded Sicily. As part of the plan Rome was bombed by 500 American aircraft during the day of 19 July. They aimed at the central railway station and its yards. They also killed some 1,500 people and wounded more. They struck the old and famous church of San Lorenzo. At the moment of the raid there happened to be several full trams outside the church.

Late that afternoon the Pope left the Vatican accompanied by Montini. He was very sad. It was the first time he came out of the Vatican since his rabbling of summer 1940. He walked among the ruined houses of the working class, and came to San Lorenzo, where he knelt among the ruins and said the *De profundis*, 'Out of the deep have I called unto Thee, O Lord'; and the crowd hung about him and he did not get back to the Vatican for 2½ hours. Next day letters of bitterness went out to the nuncios, and a personal letter to President Roosevelt, telling him of the visit to San Lorenzo; not so much a protest

---

[35] AC, Min. Pop. Cult., Busta 29, fasc. 426.
[36] Tittmann Papers, Brussels, XII, 1943, 14ff.

as a dirge.[37] To make his protest without turning it into a formal protest against Britain and America which might be serviceable to German propaganda, he wrote (21 July) a letter to the Cardinal Vicar of Rome, of which the first draft was prepared by Tardini several days before in expectation or fear of just such a need.

He sang a hymn of praise to Rome – the holy city, radiant with Christ's name, rich in marvels of religion and of art, guardian of precious relics and documents; the underground haven of the perse-cuted in the earliest years of Christian faith; the headquarters of the Church; the home of international colleges of learning; with superb churches and libraries and museums; a lighthouse of civilization – and with Vatican City at its centre. He thought that he was neutral among the nations; that both sides recognized what he could do to save them from suffering. And now all those hopes were proved to be a delusion. We deplore what has happened . . . San Lorenzo, centre of pil-grimage, the tomb of Pope Pius IX. We have sought to do all we can for the injured in our diocese. And he called them all to prayers that arms might be laid down.

The Italian officials were very pleased with the Pope. The Chief of Police sent Mussolini a careful description of all that the Pope did at the ruins of San Lorenzo.[38]

The American officers thought the results of the raid excellent. Osborne had no sympathy at all for the Pope's protest. Yet he besought London not to do it again. Mussolini fell from power. 'I trust that there will not be another bombardment of Rome, i.e. of objectives within the city area, at any rate until the situation has clarified and the new government has had time to establish authority. I would also hope that other bombardments of Italy might temporarily be confined to military objectives of immediate vital importance. It will I am sure pay us to help to fortify the position of the new government by not saddling it with being made partially responsible for further loss of civilian life by air action. And this will of course in no way impair our liberty of action in the future.'[39]

The Catholic world was disturbed. Telegrams of sympathy poured in from bishops, some from Allied countries. Latin American ambas-sadors at the Vatican were cool to their British and American neighbours. President Roosevelt felt it necessary to broadcast (23 July 1943) that Rome was being bombed to save the lives of Allied soldiers fighting in Sicily and to assert (by now dubiously) that the attitude of the Axis prevented Rome from being declared an open city. Montini expressed a sense of hurt that Osborne and Tittmann did not at once

[37] ADSS, 7, 502–11, Eng. trans. FRUS, 1943, II, 931–3, 938.
[38] AC, PS, 1943, Busta 71, report of 19 July 1943.   [39] FO 954/31A/39.

express their regrets at the loss of life and the damage to a church. According to the observers, the Pope's sadness was part compassion and part sense of failure. So long Rome had been preserved from bombs, solitary among the European capitals at war, partly by the existence of the Vatican and perhaps partly by his efforts. He had longed to be able to feel at the end of the war that the city was spared out of respect for a common Father.

Behind the scenes Churchill was pressed by his commanders. They expected soon to acquire Rome. Then they would need to use its railways and roads and airfields. They would find it intolerable if they could not use these facilities because they had earlier agreed to Rome as an open city. Churchill hated the idea. What would the Russians think if the Allies were so kind to the Italians as to accept Rome as an open city?[40]

Rome was bombed for the second time on 13 August 1943. The raid attacked the railways and the airfields. It destroyed the church of S. Maria dell'Orto and damaged the church of St Helen on the Via Casilina where the second wave of bombers killed the parish priest as he tended the wounded. Instantly the Pope was out with the sufferers, and at St John Lateran found his white cassock stained with blood as he blessed an injured person.

Osborne thought these August bombings were mistaken policy. The new Italian government wanted peace badly and could not make it because of the presence of large German armies in Italy. Bombs on railway lines which supplied German forces were still useful; and bombs on railway yards might sometimes hit a church like San Lorenzo. Bombs on areas of Rome or Milan achieved nothing. They alienated the Italians and the Pope, and were immoral as area bombings without a sane motive. Osborne's *Diary* recorded his scruples:

13 August 1943: To my deep distress the BBC reports very heavy RAF raids on Milan (the nearest yet) and Turin last night . . . It is all too beastly . . . this detestable bombing.

The Italian government declared next day that Rome was an open city. It consulted the Vatican on the best wording of this declaration. But perforce it went on using the railways to carry troops. The Germans said (23 August) that they must run troop trains through Rome. The Italians gave an assurance to the German government (1 September) of free transit of German troops via Rome to the front, though without a stop in Rome. They sent the British a map of Rome as an open city, and told them that anti-aircraft guns would not fire, and

---

[40] Churchill to Roosevelt, 4 August 1943, FRUS, 1943, II, 939.

fighter-planes would not take off. They could get no answer out of Britain or America. For the British decided, though this was not known in Rome, that they would never recognize the city to be open. The notes of Tardini sank again towards despair.

11

The Italian Armistice

i. The first peace-feelers

An American Secret Service report went out of Italy to Washington on 16 July 1942.[1] It said that the Italians now hated Germany. Their monarchy was tottering. The Pope 'is strongly anti-Axis, and particularly anti-German. He is of the saintly type, and is essentially patriotic, but is opposed to war. He has proved himself a weak and cautious man, and an "appeaser"; his attitude has been somewhat akin to that of our isolationists. He looks upon the Fascists as "troublesome naughty children" in whose power he happens to be. In spite of all that has been said, source does not believe the Pope to be a power in Italy today, because there exists no deep [religious] feeling among the people.'

Such reports had the reliability of a single witness. A spy would gather news from a casual meeting, like a conversation in a bar. Other evidence does not suggest the morale of Italy to have been so low during the summer of 1942. In those months the Italians could still believe in Italian victory. With Rommel they advanced into Egypt, captured Tobruk, threatened to take Cairo. In Russia German forces still advanced with astounding speed. They neared the oil of the Caucasus. The British were devastated by the loss of Malaysia and Singapore and by the height of the U-boat successes. Casualties were not too terrible, most young Italian men served in Italy, war was still an adventure. Italian rationing was faulty, the black market was too prominent, but most Italian families still had members somewhere on a farm.

By the winter of 1942-3 these hopes had gone. Stalingrad held. Italy was driven out of Libya. Food was still more difficult, the discomforts of war more dreary. The Italians had never liked fighting in Hitler's war. Mussolini was not unpopular but was unimportant. The fate of Italy was being settled by Stalin and Roosevelt and Hitler and Churchill, and the Italians knew it. The nation never quite took the Fascist party to its heart and now began to find it repellent; the exhortations

[1] NAW, OSS, 18151.

246

and threats and struttings, the drive to manufacture bellicosity in a people that preferred peace, were seen by the people of Italy as emptiness. The hierarchs of the party intoned a Fascist war, the people wanted food.

On 20 December 1942 Marshal Badoglio, who had all the prestige of being a hero of the First World War, had a visit from an old anti-Fascist Tommasi della Torretta. Tommasi told him a strange story. The Pope, he said, had asked the Archbishop of Palermo, Cardinal Lavitrano, to meet the King to discuss the chance of a change of government. Lavitrano visited the King, but the King, recognizing how grave was the situation, thought that no decision could be taken. Tommasi also said that to another visitor from Milan, Gallarati-Scotti, the King had talked of a change of government with Marshal Badoglio as its new head, and that after seeing the new government into power he would abdicate and leave the crown to his son the Crown Prince Umberto. Tommasi also told Badoglio that Cardinal Maglione ought to be given the names of his collaborators in the government; and that the Pope would do all he could to win from the British and Americans a peace without an excess of dishonour.

Badoglio applied next day to the Vatican, sending a secret letter by the hand of his nephew. Was any of this true so far as concerned the Vatican? Did the Pope ask the Archbishop of Palermo to see the King and talk of a change of government? Was there anything in the talk of the King's acting to overthrow Mussolini and then abdicate? And was it true that the Pope was willing to arrange honourable terms of peace with the British and the Americans? Badoglio asked Cardinal Maglione only for a yes or a no. He said that (if it was yes) he could not yet give Cardinal Maglione any names for his future government.

On 21 December Cardinal Maglione received Badoglio's nephew. He was very uncompromising. He said that this whole story was fantasy; that he had never seen Signor Tommasi in his life. He did, however, confess that a month before, in November, Badoglio had sent a messenger to condole with him on the death of his (Maglione's) nephew. The messenger had talked of a possible call of Badoglio to power and said that he could not refuse the King's summons; and that in such circumstances he would naturally (Maglione was very struck by the word *naturally*) want to know that the Vatican would place no obstacles in his way. He said that he made no comment on this November message. He told Badoglio's nephew to tell his uncle that he was being fooled and that he ought to beware of his friends as well as his enemies.

Cardinal Maglione was evidently and not surprisingly perturbed by this conversation, and reported on it next morning to the Pope.[2] If conspirators against Mussolini already had spread rumours that the Vatican was a party to their plan, the danger to the Pope was very great.

The neutrality of the Vatican, achieved at such cost, was paying a dividend at last. The opponents of the Fascists trusted the senior Vatican officials with secrets which might mean the loss of their lives if they were open. The Americans and the British knew that in Tittmann and Osborne they had agents whose judgments they could trust and therefore that through the Vatican they possessed a measure of control to test what was happening – whether a man who said he was a conspirator was authentic, whether a soldier who said he could do this or that with the army or the King was capable of doing what he suggested. The two envoys in the Vatican assumed a new role as means of a secret communication; which yet must be conducted with the utmost prudence, for if it went wrong, Vatican City would be occupied by the enemy.

On 19 February 1943 another Italian commander appeared in the Vatican – a colonel who was secretary to Marshal Ettore Bastico the governor of Libya. He told the *maestro di camera* that he would like an appointment with the Pope. He also said that Italy was no longer capable of fighting this war, and that if it was to avoid total ruin it must get out of the clutches of Germany. He also said that the Italians needed to persuade the British to stop dropping bombs and instead to drop pamphlets with offers of peace.

Three days later Pius XII received Marshal Bastico – but the solitary audience lasted a very short time. Coming out of the audience he told the *maestro di camera*, 'I tried to interest the Pope in the present plight of Italy. But the Pope kept himself high above all that, flying right above the practical question, and left me without a hint what was his real opinion. . .'[3] The Vatican continued to protect itself by refusing to bless a conspiracy of which it was not yet sure.

In February 1943 Mussolini made drastic changes in his Cabinet. Among them he removed his son-in-law Count Ciano from the Foreign Ministry and sent him, at his own request, to be ambassador to the Holy See. This striking appointment caused furious speculation among everyone at the Vatican. Some even thought it a calculated insult to the Holy See, to send a man so identified with Mussolini and Fascism. The Vatican liked Guariglia and was sorry to lose him and only said that changing ambassadors too often was not good. Someone

---

[2] ADSS, 7, 155–7. For the earlier peace-feelers, see W. S. Lisenmeyer, 'Italian Peace Feelers before the Fall of Mussolini', in *Journal of Contemporary History* (1981), pp. 649ff.   [3] ADSS, 7, 240–1.

in the circle of the university called it 'a slap in the face to the Pope'. The American Jesuit McCormick recorded in his diary that the diplomatic corps accredited to the Holy See had sunk so low now that a decent ambassador would be quite justified in resigning.

But this was not the opinion of the more informed. Osborne had good reason, from his earlier and golfing knowledge of the man, to think that Ciano was much less in favour of this war than was Mussolini. He began to speculate: 'It seems plausible to suppose' that Ciano had come to work towards an Italian withdrawal from the war; perhaps towards a 'peace of compromise'; and for both these plans, 'I think', he would find a welcome in Cabinet circles. He reported to London that there was a committee in the Vatican studying the possible basis of 'une paix blanche', that is a peace where both sides receive honourable treatment and not oppression. This Vatican committee had even prepared a summary of the English book by E. H. Carr (who was then writing leaders for *The Times*), *Conditions of Peace*.

Osborne admitted to London that his ideas about Ciano were speculation.[4] But he probably knew more than he dared to put into a dispatch which he knew to be tapped. And it is very likely that he drafted the dispatch in this form to encourage Ciano to engage in negotiation.

Osborne asked London what to do if Ciano approached him inside the Vatican. He suggested that he be empowered to talk, provided that Tittmann were present and that Cardinal Maglione be informed. 'I should endeavour to ascertain whether he was to be considered as speaking for the Axis, for the Fascist government, or for himself. In the first two cases I should say it was sheer waste of time; we had taken our stand on unconditional surrender and no negotiated armistice and that left room for no other. If however he wanted to speak to me personally (I knew him before I came to the post here) I have no objection but he must understand that I could only reply personally and that nothing I might say must be taken as in any way committing my government. Do you approve? I do not see that it could do any harm to hear what he has to say.'

The doctrine of unconditional surrender, rashly enunciated at Casablanca by Roosevelt and Churchill, began at once to frustrate every sensible Allied activity to get Italy out of the war. But the Foreign Office was already more foolish about unconditional surrender than was necessary; or else, suspecting that the dispatches were tapped, wished the Italians to believe in their rigidity.

Anthony Eden replied to Osborne's reasonable request with a veto. Osborne must reject all approaches from Count Ciano, even on a

[4] Osborne to Norton, 11 February 1943, FO 371/37545.

personal basis. 'Even assuming that Ciano might be useful to us, as to which I am by no means convinced, it would be mistaken tactics for us to respond to advances from his side. You should therefore studiously cold-shoulder him.'[5] Eden took the trouble to get agreement for this veto out of the Americans. In the Foreign Office Orme Sargent and Pierson Dixon were not so sure.

A few days later they were more sure that Ciano went to be envoy at the Vatican for the sake of making peace. The American codebreakers intercepted a message from the Japanese envoy at the Holy See reporting what Ciano had said to him. Ciano said 'The Vatican is more important than ever to Italy now, and the day will come when it will play a superlative role.'[6]

By March 1943 a conspiracy existed within the Italian army. Its moving spirit was General Castellano, chief-of-staff to the commander-in-chief General Ambrosio. He drafted a plan for a coup d'état, which included the capture of Mussolini and the leading Fascists. Castellano gave the plan to General Ambrosio who said that it was 'premature'. He gave it to Ciano, who read it and locked it in his safe and did nothing. General Ambrosio would not act without an order from the King. Castellano won over the Under-Secretary at the Foreign Office, Bastianini, and got a promise at least of inaction out of the chief of police. He got into touch with a surviving elder statesman of the pre-Fascist era, Bonomi; and Bonomi started to try to influence the King.

There is evidence that both Count Ciano and Count Grandi that spring wanted to see Osborne. We have no evidence yet from the British side that they met, and after Eden's rigid instructions it sounds improbable. According to the Italian evidence Osborne expressed a desire that the Italians who overthrew Mussolini should not also overthrow the King.[7]

It is very hard to believe that such a meeting could have happened during those weeks. The point was whether the British would think the King so tarnished by Fascism that a palace revolution, in which a Fascist king toppled a Fascist dictator, was useless. The Italian conspirators knew that they had the best chance, probably their only chance, if they acted under the King's authority. They therefore must know whether the King would be acceptable to the Allied governments. The Vatican, with a congenital fear of disorder in Italy, and especially a fear that Communists might seize power during the

[5] Eden to Norton for Osborne, 24 February 1943, FO 371/37545.
[6] NAW, Magic Intercept, 3 March 1943.
[7] I. Bonomi, *Diario di un anno 2 giugno 1943–10 giugno, 1944* (Milan, 1947), pp. xxviii–xxix. Bonomi in his evidence called Osborne a person of absolute sincerity (*serietà*) and discretion.

anarchy of any change, wanted an orderly and constitutional change of government and saw that this could only be achieved with the help of the King.

On present evidence it is improbable that Osborne met Count Ciano. But it is very probable that the message came to him, to ask whether to get rid of the King was a *sine qua non* for talking to the British. Osborne must have taken the question to London when he went home in April 1943. And it is very possible that when he came back in June he passed the message which the conspirators wanted to hear. For the message was indispensable to their success. They could only get rid of Mussolini with the aid of the King and knew it. It is possible that Osborne needed to bring that message in June, so that they could act in July.

The conspirators must have consulted the British, because they certainly consulted the Americans. A report on this subject of a change of government was duly sent from Cardinal Maglione to Cicognani in Washington, in cypher, on 16 January 1943. But we do not know what it contained. For evidently it was so compromising that it was among the papers hastily destroyed that September.

On 10 February there was talk or argument whether in a new government the monarchy should be kept and if so, with the King himself, or with the Crown Prince as king, or with a regency for the King's grandson. The documentation is slender because the Vatican's agents were not waiting for the Germans to come before they destroyed, and in some cases they destroyed as they went along. But through Cicognani the Americans asked the Vatican for advice on monarchy or no monarchy in the post-Fascist government, and (surprisingly) got an answer out of Cardinal Maglione after a long delay and by special courier (who left 22 May 1943) – to the effect that the Italian people was much attached to its royal family and that the monarchical regime suited the inclinations of the people. Not surprisingly Maglione asked Cicognani in Washington to destroy the message. The delicate message, in fact, had passed through four drafts. One of the drafts even dared to mention three possible and acceptable men as prime ministers after the fall of Mussolini.[8] Tardini said this was dangerous and he was right. The names were removed.

Not for the first time, Osborne trod dangerous ground. He was again, as in 1940, a natural link between some conspirators and the British government. But as in 1940, if it were discovered, he compromised not only himself but all of Vatican City.

As early as March 1943, therefore, the British government began quietly to work with the Americans in drafting the terms of an

---

[8] They were Orlando, Caviglia and Federzoni, ADSS, 7, 365; cf. 222, 361–2.

armistice if the Italians should ask for peace. It took them more than four months to agree on anything.

On 10 May 1943 Monsignor Tardini made notes on the situation for the benefit of the Pope and Cardinal Maglione. Italy was suffering – bombs, hunger, loss of communications. It had no weapons nor air force and could not defend itself. Mussolini's only concern was to stay in power.

In such a state of affairs what were the prospects of an intervention by the Vatican? It was a neutral. But if it intervened it could hardly do other than look like a proposal for a separate peace for Italy – which would anger the Germans, and might weaken Italian resistance, and so would open itself to attack from the Italian government.

But the Papacy was very historic to Italy and could not shrug its shoulders while this went on. At the moment the Italian people held the institution and especially the present Pope in high regard. After-wards it would be good to be seen to have done everything possible for the welfare of Italy. ('We should never forget that the anticlericals and many of the antifascists accuse the Papacy of having backed Fascism.') The future would be good if the Papacy were shown to have saved Italy.

Naturally an intervention must not compromise the Pope's neutrality.

Conditions: such an intervention must be secret and not public – at least at first. It must be pastoral and fatherly – that is, be evidently the outcome of the Holy Father's care for his children. Anything suggesting a plan for a separate peace must be scrupulously avoided.

It could take the form of a letter to Mussolini, or a talk with Mussolini.

The King could be told. But it would not be right to send the letter, or a similar letter, to the King, because everyone at the moment was expecting the King to act against Mussolini, and the Pope must in no way whatever appear to be a backer of such a plan.

The Pope thought the plan good and sent Mussolini in a letter (12 May 1943) a 'verbal communication'. It said how deeply his fatherly heart was moved by the prospect of more ruin in Italy; and how he 'wants once more to tell Signor Mussolini that, as always, he is ready to do all he can to help the suffering people'. This was read to Count Ciano who took notes so that he could read it to Mussolini. Ciano said that Mussolini was in no mood to listen. He was still thinking of winning the war, over three or four years. Ciano said that the King would not move, and without him the Crown Prince could not move. Ciano said that negotiations must be started; but Mussolini would not negotiate at all and the Allies would not negotiate with Mussolini. 'It is tragic', Ciano kept saying. 'God and the Pope help our poor country!'

Ciano read his notes to Mussolini (13 May) and brought back to Maglione a very courteous response, lamenting the sufferings of Italy, and saying that Italy had no alternative but to fight on. And Ciano said that though the message was worded courteously, Mussolini disliked it.[9]

By mid-May the Italian opposition began to gather into the form of an embryo political party. The nuncio Borgongini Duca told Cardinal Maglione of its existence on 17 May and said that one of its leaders was the old Popular party secretary de Gasperi, who was now an employee of the Vatican Library.

He said that he had heard all this from the Under-Secretary for Foreign Affairs Bastianini. Borgongini Duca tried to protect the Papacy by pooh-poohing this whole story and saying that the charge of reviving a Catholic party was an old canard and that no one wanted a change of government in Italy at this moment.

Bastianini warned him that the Vatican was under suspicion of encouraging an anti-Fascist Catholic political party. Borgongini Duca knew that Bastianini came straight to this conversation from the Palazzo Venezia and could easily be repeating what Mussolini said.[10]

Among the more responsible Italian statesmen everything was less clear than it looked to the Allies. In Washington and in London the thing was obvious – Italy must drop Mussolini. And many of the Italian leaders began to agree. If Italy, as now looked certain, was losing the war, to drop Mussolini was the only way to persuade London and Washington not to treat Italy as an enemy.

But some Italians, who had no use for Mussolini, were not sure. If Italy was losing the war, it must make peace. But it could only make peace if Hitler could be persuaded to let it make peace. Only one Italian had any chance of getting Hitler to allow a separate Italian peace and that was Mussolini. If they dropped Mussolini in a coup d'état, it was more than probable that Hitler would occupy Italy and start a terrible war on Italian soil. There were strong anti-Fascists who yet could see that Mussolini was still necessary to Italy if they were to avoid war up and down the length of the peninsula. When Borgongini Duca said that no one wanted a change of government at the moment, he was wrong. But he knew of good men who thought that a change of government must bring more German panzer divisions into Italy. So late as 17 July Bastianini sent a note to Cardinal Maglione to say that it was in the interest of Britain and America not to demand the fall of Mussolini because only he could achieve the one thing that could help them – withdrawal of the German army.

[9] ADSS, 7, 318–20, 332, 334.   [10] ADSS, 7, 347–9.

This debate was settled when Mussolini sealed his fate. He made it very clear that he had no intention of suggesting to Hitler a separate peace for Italy. On 15 May 1943 the King approached him tentatively about the possibility of a separate peace. Mussolini said that they would need three months to prepare for a peace move.[11] His judgment of timing was correct. It seemed too long to those who saw that Italy could no longer fight a war.

At the end of May 1943 Tardini again wrote notes about the possibility of a démarche by the Pope to help get Italy out of the war.

What could happen? Only two things. Either the King would get rid of Mussolini, summon a new and vigorous military government which would make peace and so end the air bombardment of Italian cities; but the country would be occupied by the British and Americans and subjected to German reprisals; or the King would stick to Mussolini ('a prop-king' noted Tardini) and then the war would go on, the British and Americans would destroy the cities of Italy, the economy would be ruined, and a prostrate and massacred Italy would be occupied by the British and the Americans. Which future was worse? Evidently the second. For in the second case Italy had no defence against the air. In the first case it would have the help of British and American air forces. Therefore the Vatican ought to do what could be done to get the first future, the overthrow of Mussolini by the King.

But, asked Tardini, what if this became known? It would expose the Papacy to the vengeance of Fascists and Nazis. They would look for a scapegoat. But, wrote Tardini, with due care this ought not to get known. And even if the worst happened and it were betrayed, at least it would have the deep respect of the United States and might help to get a truce in air bombardment. 'It wouldn't be the first time the Papacy suffered only for doing good; and that would give it a new glory.'[12]

On the last day of May Tardini asked himself, who will tell Mussolini to go? Shall the Vatican ask the King to say, *Go*? If so, the first thing the King will do is to tell Mussolini and expose the Vatican to his vengeance. Therefore it is better to tell Mussolini direct. If so what are we to say to him? Could Count Ciano make him swallow the bitter pill without turning his enmity against the Pope? And suppose (Tardini went on with his meditations after a night's sleep) we tell Mussolini to go and he says *mind your own business* do we tell the Americans what he said? If we do, we risk more Allied bombs on Italian cities.

So Tardini concluded that in this business of belling the cat it was better for the Holy See not to try.

---

[11] For Bastianini's note, see Mario Toscano, 'Italian Soundings to abandon the conflict prior to Mussolini's fall', in his *Designs in Diplomacy*, Eng. trans. (London, 1970), p. 385.   [12] ADSS, 7, 381–3.

Peace talk was in the air of Rome. It kept rising. Count Dalla Torre kept Cardinal Maglione informed of the secret meetings in the circle round the King; and of how their minds moved away from the army commander General Ambrosio, because they doubted his political capacity, and turned towards Marshal Badoglio. Count Dalla Torre soon became one of Osborne's private informers on what was happening outside the Vatican.

By 1 June 1943 the Pope was convinced that something must be said to Mussolini. The next day he tried a public appeal for peace to all the powers. No one took the least notice.

Whisperers asked each other whether the Pope could not help them to peace. On 7 June the Japanese at the Vatican reported to Tokyo about these whispers and pooh-poohed the possibility that the Pope could do anything. 'The Vatican is observing a strict neutrality and it is practically impossible for either side to influence it. Incidentally, the Holy See does not wield as much influence as you think.'[13]

Inside the Vatican they argued, and drafted, and redrafted, a possible message from the Pope to Mussolini. Their problem was the King. They could not do without him. And they could not trust the King not to tell Mussolini. Mussolini, if he suspected, would do everything possible to put the blame on the Pope; and the Germans would help him with force; and if they could picture the Pope as the ally of the British and Americans they would try to throw all the blame for Italian defeat on the Pope. Tardini was afraid that to gain time the King would ask the Pope to find out Allied conditions for peace with Italy. The Pope could hardly refuse. Yet all it would get for an answer would be unconditional surrender. And how could the Pope make himself responsible for so brutal a reply?

The Portuguese ambassador in London approached Anthony Eden. Would it not be possible for the British to give a gloss to the phrase unconditional surrender? Eden said that it was not possible. The British had no intention of breaking up Italy. But they would tell the Italians nothing but unconditional surrender.[14]

Borgongini Duca saw the King of Italy on 17 June; ostensibly about medals to commemorate the anniversary of the Pope's consecration as a bishop. The King asked why the Italian press did not print the Pope's last message on peace. Borgongini Duca saw his chance; he said that America was not ill-disposed to Italy and if Italy got out of the war America would support her – and then the nuncio pronounced the weighty and dangerous words, *The Holy See knows it from official sources*.

Instantly the King saw the point. He bitterly attacked the British, the

[13] NAW, Magic Intercepts, 7 June 1943.
[14] Eden to R. Campbell at Lisbon, 18 June 1943, FO 954/31A.

unimaginable corruption of London, the façade of British society. He said he did not trust the American message. And then Borgongini Duca told him that the Pope had told the Americans how attached were the Italians to the House of Savoy. The King said 'I am not loved as the Pope is.' Then they discussed where the Allied landings would come.

Meanwhile in London, British Intelligence was preparing for the coup against Mussolini which they now thought certain. They weighed up the Italian generals – Roatta? – the record was against him – Ambrosio? – was he decisive? – Badoglio? – the record with Fascism was against him.

The knowledge of an Italian conspiracy made the British urgent to get Osborne home if they could achieve it in such a way that the Italians would allow him back to Rome. As early as the latter end of 1942 they decided that they needed him in London.

Osborne had an excuse. During the summer of 1942 he won from Mussolini the right to cross Italy to go to Switzerland for a week or two. His health suffered from the long confinement, and this he could reasonably plead. Italian counter-intelligence argued against the granting of this leave. They said that Switzerland was crammed with British agents. Who could know what he might do once in Switzerland? Why should he not recover his health at an Italian spa? The Italian Supreme Command had dangerous ideas about Osborne. They said that he behaved correctly 'on the surface'. But he had frequent contacts with agents outside the Vatican. He kept a radio transmitter. He financed propaganda inside Italy.[15]

Foreign Affairs said that under the Lateran Treaty leave could not be refused. And what harm could Osborne do in Switzerland? So the argument went up to Mussolini, who personally decided that the Lateran Treaty be observed.

Osborne then refused to use this leave, and never went to Switzerland. He realized that he would only get such leave once, and that he might need it at a more momentous time. Possibly he asked for the Swiss leave with the intention of later refusing it, so as to establish a precedent for later leave in England.

Accordingly in April 1943 he was in a strong position to ask for leave to go for his health to England. A telegram arrived from Orme Sargent on 6 March. The British wanted him. They did not say why. But they wanted his information on the Italian conspiracy; to discuss with him how to get the Italians out of the war; to find out what part if any the Vatican could play; and above all, since they were going to need a

---

[15] Report of Supreme Command, 10 May 1942.

means of communication with the Italian conspirators, to send him back with a more reliable and secret means than those cyphers which they now knew to be not only tappable but tapped.

The leave took him nearly a month to achieve. The problem was not to get leave to go out, but to make sure that he had leave to come back. By the end of March Monsignor Montini, who was responsible ex officio for securing this leave, had contacts inside Italian Foreign Affairs who wanted peace badly and wanted Osborne in London to this end.

Osborne left Rome by air on 8 April 1943 ('I wish I were going to have a holiday instead of some weeks of intense activity', *Diary*, 5 April). He flew to London through Seville and Lisbon. During his three months in London, he recovered, was knighted by the King and became Sir d'Arcy Osborne, and had many private talks at the Foreign Office. We possess as yet little information on these talks. Among other matters he had a long talk with Sir Orme Sargent about the choice of a successor to Cardinal Hinsley at Westminster, and Sargent told him to tell the Pope that they did not want 'an efficient administrator of a religious minority and nothing more'.[16] He settled at long last, to his own satisfaction, the wearisome quarrel over the Malta archbishopric.[17] Either he was given new cyphers or they arranged that he should

[16] Avon Papers, FO 954/31A.

[17] The problem of the Malta archbishopric lay in the succession to Archbishop Caruana, who lived but was senile. A Concordat of 1890 provided that though the Vatican chose the archbishop, it would only do so after consultation and in effect agreement with the British government. The Vatican and the British could not agree. Only one obvious candidate existed: Bishop Gonzi of Gozo. He was the only outstanding clergyman in Malta. The Vatican wanted him to be given the right of succession to Caruana. Gonzi wanted to succeed and made this plain. Caruana's illness was made a misery by worry about what would happen, and he also wanted Gonzi. Osborne thought it absurd to veto Gonzi. But in 1930 Gonzi signed a pastoral letter which forbade Roman Catholics, under pain of excommunication, to vote for Lord Strickland, the effective party leader on the island. Lord Strickland henceforth resented Gonzi as a political clergyman and an opponent; and Strickland was powerful in Maltese policy. Therefore the British government ransacked the world for a priest who could speak Maltese and would carry enough guns to equal Gonzi; and found none. The British postponed and postponed; only possible for them because Caruana still lived.

Osborne was helped in bringing sense to the Colonial Office by two pieces of good fortune: (1) Strickland died; his daughter still ran two newspapers in Malta, his nephew ran the party, but they had not quite the same fierce threat. (2) The former commander in France, Lord Gort, was made governor of Malta; and if Gort's main achievement was the defence of the island against overwhelming odds, his minor achievement was to agree with Osborne about the archbishopric. The Colonial Office was persuaded to withdraw opposition to Gonzi. The matter went up to Churchill. On 21 July 1943 the Foreign Office told Osborne to tell the Vatican that they could have Gonzi. On 31 July, in the midst of all the rumours about a German coup to seize Rome, Osborne went to see Cardinal Maglione and told him the news about the archbishopric of Malta and was pleased. The appointment of Gonzi as coadjutor with right of succession was announced in the *Osservatore Romano* of 24 October 1943.

receive new cyphers, indispensable to the secret Italian negotiations. He settled with the Foreign Office what would happen to British prisoners-of-war in Italy if a coup took place. He was told of the coming invasion of Sicily. He is also known to have discussed with the Foreign Office how to make the Vatican, and the institution of the Papacy, less Italian and more international.

By the same route in reverse, through a boiling Seville, he reached Rome on 18 June. Next day he saw Monsignor Tardini. He was very discouraging. He still had to talk of Italian surrender at discretion. He talked with a more dangerous frankness than ever before. On behalf of the Italians the Vatican asked whether if Italy made peace the British would give prior assurance about supplying fuel and food and *defence against the Germans*. Whether it liked it or not, whether it said so or not, the Vatican was once again in a conspiracy. The situation was parallel to that of the winter of 1939–40. Generals who disapproved of their dictator wanted the British to promise help before the event and used the Vatican as the secret channel of messages. The difference was, that in 1939–40 the German dictator was evidently winning, and in 1943 the Italian dictator had evidently lost.

Osborne disliked the doctrine of unconditional surrender. Publicly it was his duty to insist. He upset Monsignor Montini; upset Cardinal Maglione; depressed Monsignor Tardini infinitely. 'Italy,' Tardini wrote at the end of his personal report on the meeting, 'is in a tragic plight, between hammer and anvil.' On 28 June Osborne provided a formal document in English, still uncompromising on unconditional surrender, but adding a vital qualification: 'this does not portend any ill-treatment of the Italian people after surrender or any ill-will towards a future non-Fascist government and State'.[18] That amounted to a concession within the terms of surrender. Unconditional surrender was not quite unconditional.

Out of Madrid Sir Samuel Hoare had evidence from the Spanish general of the Trinitarian Order that the Vatican was at almost open war with Mussolini. Out of Portugal and Spain came the story that the Crown Princess of Piedmont was working to overthrow Mussolini. She tried to make soundings in Lisbon about Allied intentions. The men at the Foreign Office pooh-poohed these tales. They did not believe the Vatican to be at open war with Mussolini; and they were right. They had heard so often about the Princess of Piedmont and believed that she could do nothing; and they were right.[19]

Something must happen, but people did not know what. In Rome they felt uncomfortable and apprehensive. In the Vatican they felt

[18] ADSS, 7, 439 and 458.
[19] Hoare to Eden, 19 June 1943; notes by Laskey and Pierson Dixon, FO 371/37556.

uncomfortable and apprehensive. The American codebreakers who (to very little profit) tapped the messages of the Japanese envoy in the Vatican, recorded an intercept of 2 July: 'The atmosphere here is eerie. You know how it is in that heavy oppressive twilight time which precedes a thunderstorm. Everyone is silent and scared.'[20]

Inside the Vatican the atmosphere was subtly changing. Osborne and Tittmann (23 June) waited their turn in the anteroom of Cardinal Maglione. Count Ciano came out. He went up to them both and shook hands in a friendly fashion.[21] He no longer needed to obey Italian policy by cutting them dead. Osborne no longer needed to follow the Eden doctrine of the cold shoulder.

ii. *The fall of Mussolini*

On 10 July the British and Americans invaded Sicily. President Roosevelt sent a message to the Pope which was a propaganda and not a private message, of American intentions and idealism.[22] Mussolini was made so furious by this message that he accused the Pope of 'connivance' with the Americans, though he did not say so publicly. Mussolini's anger subsided within a few days. Rumours reached the Vatican from German sources that some inside the Vatican (though not the Pope himself) wanted the break-up of modern Italy and the return of a divided Italy, including the Bourbons. For a few days the Vatican was afraid of a total breach with the Italian government.

A week after that Mussolini was ousted, by constitutional methods. And in his ousting the Vatican had no hand. The King summoned Marshal Badoglio. We do not know how, but Osborne's *Diary* shows that he knew something two or three days before the event. The city was festive. Youths in the streets cried *Death to Mussolini* or *Down with Fascism*, blackshirts were attacked, Fascist symbols were pulled down, a few shots could be heard, the crowds in the streets celebrated a coming peace which did not come.

The diaries of Dr Goebbels show that on 26 July Hitler talked violently of seizing the Pope and occupying the Vatican at the same time as he arrested the King of Italy, Marshal Badoglio, the Cabinet and the Crown Prince.

The minute of Hitler's headquarters touched Osborne. It runs thus:

Hewel: Shouldn't we say that the Vatican and its exits will be occupied?
Hitler: That doesn't make any difference. Do you think the Vatican embarrasses me? We'll take that over right away. For one thing, the entire diplomatic

---

[20] NAW, Magic Intercept, 2 July 1943.
[21] Tittmann Papers, Brussels, XII (1943), 14ff.
[22] Cf. CAB 122/866 and ADSS, 7, 479.

corps are in there. It's all the same to me. That rabble are in there. We'll get that
bunch of swine out of there . . . Later we can make apologies . . .

Hewel: We will find documents in there.

Hitler: Yes, we'll get documents. The treason will come to light.[23]

The fierce mood of Berlin filtered through to Rome and so to the
Vatican. Cardinal Maglione urgently summoned the cardinals resident
in Rome to a meeting on 4 August. He said that the Italian government
feared a German coup, and with it a German invasion of the Vatican.
He reported that if this happened, the Italians predicted that the
Germans would seize the Pope and take him to Munich. This was
probably the moment when delicate Italian archives were carefully
hidden; and when some Vatican officials were told to have their bags
packed in case the Pope needed to leave Rome at a moment's notice.[24]

The Italian generals – Badoglio, the commander-in-chief Ambrosio,
his chief of staff Castellano, their new Foreign Secretary Guariglia (the
former ambassador to the Holy See, no doubt chosen as Foreign
Secretary because he had Vatican experience, just as Charles-Roux had
been summoned to the French Foreign Office in 1940) – knew only one
safe means of negotiating with London over an armistice: Guariglia–
Maglione–Osborne–Eden. Everything had to be done by night because
the Germans were everywhere and must not see the Foreign Secretary
of Italy calling at the Vatican. On 30 July Guariglia went to see Cardinal
Maglione who arranged that he saw Osborne. It did not help. Guariglia
reported that Osborne had no cypher which he could use apart from
the one which the Italians had broken and which had been given to the
Germans. Tittmann had no cypher at all.

It is certain that while Osborne was in London arrangements were
made that he should have a better cypher in Rome. Therefore either
Osborne would not disclose the fact to Guariglia because he knew that
he would soon need it for vital communication about the Armistice and
feared that if Guariglia knew the Germans would soon know; or he had
not dared to carry it with him when he flew in from Seville, in case he
were searched at the frontier (when Miss Tindall went on leave to
Switzerland, she had been searched humiliatingly at the frontier on
return), and the Foreign Office had arranged for other parties to carry
the cypher and it had not yet been delivered. The first time we find
Osborne using the new cypher is 17 August, a little more than a
fortnight later. If he used the cypher and the Germans discovered, he
jeopardized the existence of the Vatican. He only began to use it when

[23] *Hitler Directs his War*, ed. Felix Gilbert (Oxford, 1950), p. 53.
[24] Egidio Vagnozzi in *New York Times*, 21 March 1964; Robert A. Graham in *Civ. Catt.*
(1972), 1, 321, 327.

he could do no other, and when he was persuaded that the Vatican was already at risk from the Germans.

Possibly but not probably Osborne also had a radio transmitter inside the Vatican. The evidence is, first, that Italian Supreme Command (summer 1942) believed that he had a set; and they possessed the instruments for listening to whatever went out over the air from the Vatican; and secondly, the German ambassador Weizsäcker much later justified his own use of a secret radio transmitter by the plea that he only followed the example of Osborne; and he had at his disposal the reports of the Gestapo from their own listening devices. Despite this evidence it is hard to believe. Osborne refused the offer of a secret transmitter in June 1940. The use of a set without the knowledge of Monsignor Montini would have been contrary to everything else that we know about Osborne's sense of honour; and in view of the conditions set for messages by the diplomats, Montini could not have sanctioned the use of such a set. The British government shows no signs of knowing anything unusual other than by Osborne's new cyphers. And Sam Derry, who later in the war hid inside Osborne's flat, saw no sign of a transmitter. Therefore it is the more probable that Italian Supreme Command picked up the rumour off the streets of Rome, where gossip fancied that Osborne could send messages direct by radio to London, and then Italian Supreme Command told the Germans, and Weizsäcker picked it up, so to speak, second hand, and not from the listening gear of German Intelligence.

From the windows of Santa Marta the situation looked tense. Osborne had news (we do not know how, probably through Stückgold) that two German divisions lay at Viterbo ready to march on Rome and a third was being pulled back from Apulia. He asked himself what was likely to happen? The Italians would surrender, the German army would occupy Rome. Would they occupy the Vatican also? Probably. What would they do for an Italian government? Set up a government under Farinacci? Suppose German soldiers marched into the Vatican, was it his duty to defend his flat with his revolver and Jeremy the Cairn terrier? Was there any chance of the British and Americans landing from the sea and taking Rome before the Germans? He thought not, the logistics were impossible. The Allies would have to come to Rome, mostly, by land. Then what a plight for Italy! A war being fought up the peninsula, 'destruction following each mile of the war'.

His personal predicament was burdensome. He was the best and easiest means of communication between the Italian government and London. Therefore he must help. But he knew that every move of the Italian government at the Vatican was likely to be discovered by the Gestapo. And since he was confident that at the Armistice the German army would occupy not only Rome but the Vatican, he would fatally compromise the Pope if he used his communication with London freely. At all costs he must stay out of the business of the Armistice if he could; and yet he could not totally.

The British could not understand why the Italians did not at once surrender. It seemed to them absurd. Therefore the Italians must be bullied, terrified, bombed into submission. The only armistice would consist in the Italians laying down their arms. The British were first grieved and then angry at the delay. Some of them were so foolish as to wish to use Osborne openly to these ends.

The Italians knew that they *must* delay. They knew that they could not resist the Germans. Therefore they must not make an armistice until they had withdrawn their divisions from France and the Balkans, and until General Montgomery was far enough into Italy at least to protect Rome. They must lie to the Germans. They must tell the Germans that they meant to continue the war at Germany's side. They were confident that the Germans would not believe them. The Italians were right; the Germans did not. On 29 July German codebreakers listened to a telephone conversation between Churchill and Roosevelt about the Italian Armistice. From that moment they knew that secret negotiations were in train, and disbelieved every Italian denial. The Italians saw it as a vital interest of Italy that large British and American forces should land not only at the toe but far higher up the peninsula, certainly not further south than Rome. Some of the British (not all) had the fond illusion that if the Italians laid down their arms Allied armies would walk up Italy. The Italians knew better. Osborne shared their opinion. He was already inserting bits into his diary on the axiom that German eyes would read it when they occupied the Vatican.

The Vatican wanted an armistice because it wanted peace. It could see what the Italians saw. Guariglia and Cardinal Maglione met nearly every night. They must get *instant* British and American protection for Rome. Yet to ask for it compromised their neutrality fatally if the thing went wrong. If the result of an armistice was a line of British, Americans and Italians fighting Germans north of Rome, then the Vatican would be helped. If the result of an armistice was British and Americans fighting Germans south of Naples and German troops inside the Vatican and Italians not fighting at all, then it was the last thing the Vatican wanted. In August the tension increased almost unbearably.

The Italian government, in its ignorance, exaggerated the possibilities open to General Eisenhower and General Montgomery. The Italians saw how their own troops were ill-equipped with petrol and ammunition; how many of their best units were in the Balkans; how some of the units had been strongly Fascist and were not reliable for fighting Germans; how the morale of some of their units was so low that the men were hardly willing to fight anyone. Therefore they needed American and British help in strength. They could not realize that the strength necessary and the transport necessary were not available to Eisenhower. They could not realize that in Washington the American officers had no particular enthusiasm for an onslaught on the Germans in Italy. Unlike the British they had no belief in the soft under-belly of Europe. They had knocked out the Italian army and they saw a point in invading Sicily but little point in invading Italy. They were already withdrawing troops and transports to prepare for the invasion of France.

iii. The making of the Armistice

Since Osborne could not or would not yet use his new cypher, the Italians must send envoys to try to meet the British in Madrid or Lisbon; for by air or train they had fairly regular communication with Spain and Portugal.

On 3–4 August Guariglia tried feelers in three directions: Marquis D'Ajeta to Lisbon, Berio to Tangier because he was a friend of the British consul there, Alberto Pirelli to Switzerland to ask the Swiss to pass messages. Berio was useless because the level was too low; Pirelli was useless because the Swiss refused to risk their neutrality and would have nothing to do with the plan. D'Ajeta was authenticated by a letter of introduction from Osborne to Sir Ronald Campbell, who happened to be Osborne's cousin, and was the ambassador in Lisbon. He safely carried out of Rome a large valise of documents which would be fatal if found by German troops occupying Rome – it was put about that it contained Count Ciano's jewelry. He explained to the British that the Italians could not do other than *pretend* to go on fighting with the Germans and that when Guariglia met Ribbentrop at Tarvisio three days later he would assure the Germans that Italy was still their ally, but that this would be a lie. He gave the best guarantee of good faith by providing reliable information about the movement of German troops in Italy.[25]

The British look very stupid; saddled with the doctrine of unconditional surrender; refusing to talk to an evidently authentic envoy; treating an olive-branch with contempt; betraying vital secrets – for in August various guessing rumours reported that an emissary from

---

[25] R. Campbell, Lisbon, to Eden, 4 August 1943, FO 371/37333. It should be said that Berio was treated very seriously by the British when he first arrived at Tangier. He was superseded when the Castellano mission arrived at Lisbon.

Marshal Badoglio met Allied representatives in a neutral capital of the Iberian peninsula. The BBC accused Badoglio and Guariglia of 'cunning diplomacy'. The Italians desperately tried to keep a life-or-death secret from the Germans and the British shouted it all over Europe. The North African radio kept broadcasting threats – if you do not surrender at once we shall bomb you to bits.

On the evidence now available the British behaved stupidly. But we have not the evidence of Intelligence. Another theory of their curious actions is possible. Let us postulate such a theory:

The British accepted that it was not sensible, nor even desirable for the Italians to surrender until the Allies were ready to invade Italy from Sicily. They accepted the assurance of D'Ajeta that Badoglio did not mean to war at the side of Germany but must pretend that he would fight on and keep up the pretence till the time was ripe. Therefore because they could not be ready to invade Italy before September, there was no hurry for the Armistice. There was time for the Italian generals to send one of themselves as a principal. Meanwhile they must help the Italians by giving Germany the impression that they, the British, still fought Italy to the limit. The bombing of Rome in August, which Osborne thought mad, hurt German communications and was necessary to the plan. The denunciation of Badoglio by the BBC must help Badoglio in lying to the Germans. The betrayal of the Italian secret from Lisbon fits. Lisbon was full of the Gestapo. Hints might have reached British Intelligence that the Germans had discovered the presence of D'Ajeta; and if so it was of the first importance to jettison D'Ajeta publicly and treat Italian peace feelers with the maximum public scorn and reiterate unconditional surrender.

We have not the materials to put forward or to refute such a theory. But it has this on its side. If it or something like it is not true, the British behaved very stupidly. Although the British sometimes behaved stupidly in war, there were also times when it suited them to appear very stupid indeed.

Such a theory helps to explain the leisureliness of the negotiations. The bargainers proceeded at a snail's pace. They could be dilatory because they knew that nothing could be done until September.

The theory helps to explain a curious telegram. The Germans, afraid of what was coming, demanded to be given the prisoners-of-war under Italian guard in Italy. They said that they had captured most of them. The Italians perforce agreed. The idea infuriated the British. Churchill sent a brutal telegram to the King of Italy. *Expect no mercy if you deliver to Germans British prisoners now in your hands.* The Italians regarded this as a blundering bomb thrown into their tensions.[26] They

---

[26] R. Guariglia, *Ricordi, 1922–1946* (Naples, 1950), pp. 635–6.

had no intention whatever of handing over British prisoners except at the point of a gun. They thought that Churchill must know this. Yet the telegram had merit, even for the Italians. It reassured the Germans that the British regarded the Axis as in being.

Osborne tried to persuade London that the British press should be less offensive about the King and Marshal Badoglio. But at that moment it was in Italy's interest, as well as Britain's, that the Italian and British governments should be seen to be as far apart as possible.

On 12 August General Castellano set out for Lisbon. He dared carry no official documents. The Italian generals told him that he must not fall into German hands or the Germans would shoot the entire Italian government. He was to travel as Signor Raimondi. Unlike General Ambrosio, whom even in his pyjamas everyone knew to be a soldier, Castellano had no presence. He could pass for the junior clerk of a small business. But they asked Osborne for another letter to authenticate him.

The more letters Osborne provided the more danger to the Vatican. He expected all this effort to fail. He expected the Germans soon inside the Vatican. But he could not refuse to authenticate a man going off to see his own cousin, when what was at stake was getting a whole nation out of a war.[27]

Osborne asked for, and got, a signed statement from Marshal Badoglio authorizing Castellano to speak to the British on his behalf. (What Osborne afterwards did with such a perilous document is far from clear – probably he burnt it less than a fortnight later.) Then Osborne gave Castellano a signed introduction to Sir Samuel Hoare the ambassador in Madrid. He made this letter as bare and brief as possible. Castellano called it 'a laconic ticket'. Simultaneously, unknown to Castellano, Osborne sent to London a telegram in his new cypher. He confirmed that this was real; and that he had in his possession Marshal Badoglio's signed statement.[28]

The reader will perceive, hidden behind this information, an enormous concession on the part of the Pope. Since Italy came into the war Osborne was under a solemn obligation to communicate to London only what concerned his mission as an envoy to the Holy See. Now, from 17 August frequently, Osborne's cypher was used in the business of the Italian armistice. He cannot have done that without telling, in honour bound, Monsignor Montini and getting an assent out of the Curia.

This is certain. For Guariglia learnt, at one of his secret meetings with

---

[27] Ibid., p. 646; FO to Berne, 16 August 1943, CAB 954/31A; Castellano, *Come firmai l'armistizio di Cassibile* (Milan, 1945), p. 87.

[28] Harold Macmillan, *The Blast of War, 1939–45* (London, 1967), p. 379; cf. Macmillan, *War Diaries: Politics and War in the Mediterranean 1943–1945* (London, 1984), p. 185.

Cardinal Maglione under cover of night, that Osborne had these cyphers and could use them for purposes of the Armistice. But part of the reason for the Vatican's permission was not the Armistice. Osborne's cyphers were a direct way to talk to London, and they were still deeply worried about the bombing of Rome.[29]

Yet the risk was extraordinary. Osborne believed that the Germans would occupy the Vatican. A few days later we meet Monsignor Tardini with 'mild jitters' because he expected the same. Vatican self-interest was to stay out of all this and hold a rigid neutrality. But peace for Italy was at stake. And constitutionally the only thing that was happening, in the Curia's eyes, was a constitutional prime minister of Italy sending a duly accredited representative to talk about peace to two Powers with which it was at war. Osborne's cypher only made the talk about peace easier and faster. The Vatican was helping towards peace in the world, which the Pope saw as his divine vocation. It made no difference to the Pope's decision that Hitler would regard everyone who had anything to do with this whole affair as traitors.

Thus the Legation at the Vatican set up the negotiations for the Armistice.

On 23 August, Osborne told London that a Vatican 'source of reputation' told him that the Germans would advance on Rome, that the Italian defence would hardly last more than a day or two, that the King and Badoglio would flee to Sardinia, and that the Germans would set up a Quisling Fascist government in Rome. They would then demand from the Pope that he hand over 'certain persons in Vatican City'; that the Pope would refuse the demand; and that the Germans might then come in and fetch them (i.e. Osborne and the diplomats). He suggested to London that these reports might be put about by Germany as 'blackmail'. Four days later he contradicted all this – 'I learn from my direct and secret source that reports given in my telegram 287 are almost wholly fantasy.' But they were not fantasy. In almost all respects they were correct; except that they had the wrong destination for the flight of the King of Italy, and except that the demand for the diplomats was only a vague notion in Berlin and not a decision.[30]

Osborne was working very hard – 'a hellish day of unwonted and unwanted activity' (*Diary*, 17 August); 'often rather tricky matters on hand' (18 August); 'Dalla Torre came in and told me about – well, several things' (25 August); 'I wish I could put down all the facts and rumours of these days, but I can't. It is a pity for the sake of the diary!'

---

[29] Guariglia, *Ricordi*, p. 648; Tittmann Papers, Brussels, xii, 90ff., 109; cf. Tittmann to Cordell Hull, NAW 121/866A/341.
[30] Osborne to London, 23 and 27 August 1943, CAB 122/855.

(26 August). He later made a post-war note on the margin of the *Diary*. 'The bits cut out of this were a precaution against the Germans coming into Vatican City and finding it. I didn't want to risk incriminating anybody' (ap. 1 September 1943).

The British were very interested in General Castellano. In Lisbon he gave them the sensation that the Italians hated and feared the Germans 'intensely'. On 16 August a *most secret* telegram went from London to Berne for Osborne, so that he could find out more about Castellano and his plan for peace.[31]

On 22 August Castellano left Lisbon for Rome, carrying with him a radio transmitter and a cypher, with which he could at certain precise times communicate with Allied headquarters in Algiers. They instructed him in how to work the radio and the cypher. They decided to use an SOE officer named Mallaby, who had been dropped into Italy and captured, to work Castellano's radio. It is evident that the radio was of a special type, no doubt for the sake of security; since otherwise it is odd that Castellano could not use an Italian radio, and odd that he needed a Briton to transmit. It was agreed that if Castellano failed to communicate with Algiers by 29 August, he should go to the Vatican and give Osborne a message with the words: 'The Italian government protests against the delay in the release of complete names of Italian prisoners taken in Sicily.' This message did not mean what it said. It was agreed in Lisbon that if Osborne sent this message the Italian government accepted the (very severe) terms of surrender. Simultaneously Osborne was warned by London to hold himself ready to pass on urgent information.

A ludicrous accident hampered this plan. The trouble was, these new cyphers were not working smoothly. At the crux Osborne could not decypher a whole telegram from London, nor could he decypher part of a second telegram. He decyphered a garbled message about prisoners. As he had little idea what was happening, he sent the following telegram (25 August):[32] 'I am assured from a sure source that there is no need for any anxiety about our prisoners as far as Italians are concerned.' The 'sure source' is likely to have been Guariglia to Maglione.

This message gave London furiously to think. Was this the code message, four days early, which said that the Italians accepted the terms of surrender? It was suspiciously similar, and surprisingly unlike. 'Highly ambiguous' the Foreign Office called it. They sent off

---

[31] FO 954/31A/40; for the negotiations, K. W. D. Strong, *Intelligence at the Top* (London, 1968), pp. 100ff.; R. Murphy, *Diplomat among Warriors* (London, 1964); and the files CAB 122/855–9.

[32] FO 371/37333/291; for the plan, CAB 122/855, 21 August 1943, Lisbon to Foreign Office.

(27 August) another *most secret* telegram to Osborne asking what he meant, and repeating the instruction about the unmentionable but forthcoming Armistice.

Osborne (28 August) assured them that he had received no message about prisoners from the Italian government. (Foreign Office note: 'This is a relief . . . it is now clear that it [Osborne's message] has nothing to do with General Castellano and his message.')

Osborne had his secret source of information about the Germans. The anti-Nazi German doctor Stückgold hid inside the Vatican during the summer of 1943. Vatican employees were willing to hide him in a corner provided that they were well remunerated. An appeal came to Osborne to lend 100,000 lire. He provided Stückgold with the loan, for repayment after liberation. For nearly a year Stückgold passed Osborne information gleaned from German sources in the city. Some of the information was helpful and some not, but mostly it was rumour. Osborne was glad of the help but thought the affair shameful for the employees of the Vatican.

Probably Stückgold now passed him the information that the Germans would occupy the Vatican on 25 August and would demand from the Vatican the handing over of 'certain persons unnamed'. Osborne went down to the Tittmann apartment which was the only one to have an old-fashioned grate. They lit a fire (evening of 24 August) and enlisted the two Tittmann boys to feed it with documents.

Osborne carefully wrote up his Diary, on the axiom that the Germans would read it when they occupied the Vatican. He hoped that in reading it they would find material to acquit the Vatican of any part in these shadowy acts. He wrote that there was nothing in his files of any interest. He cut out large chunks and thereby made it willy-nilly suspect to any German intelligence officer who found it. He put into it a certain amount of affection for one of the young sons of Tittmann, perhaps to provide an innocent motive for the excisions (it was an affection which he felt, after more than three years of celibate solitude, but it was not corrupting, for both the Tittmann boys looked back for the rest of their lives upon Osborne's friendship as a matter for gratitude).

Meanwhile a still stranger contact was made in Lisbon. Carton de Wiart was one of the famous soldiers of Europe. After marrying a German princess he came out of the First World War with one eye and one arm and the Victoria Cross. With his black patch and his empty sleeve he was one of the dramatic personalities of the war. In April 1941 he was sent to Yugoslavia and was shot down on the way and captured by the Italians. They found him no easy prisoner. They now fetched him out of the camp, gave him civilian clothes and brought him to Rome with the idea of sending him to England about the Armistice.

While in Rome Carton de Wiart avoided the Vatican. His reasons were two. He did not wish to compromise the neutrality of the Vatican. Like everyone else in the know, he was aware of the danger of a German occupation of the Vatican, and he was not an easy figure to disguise. His second reason startles. 'I was avoiding the Vatican . . . because the British Minister . . . had shown himself unfriendly to me, and I had no wish to see him.'[33]

This is a puzzle, and not only because no one else is found to make this criticism of the friendly Osborne. How, and under what circumstances could Osborne have offended Carton de Wiart? There was no place or time when they could have met?

On 26 August Carton de Wiart, escorted by an Italian general Zanussi, appeared in Lisbon. The British were not pleased. Algiers thought Zanussi might be a spy to discover the negotiations. The British thought it absurd to put Carton de Wiart, who would have been remarkable to look at it even if he had not had a black eye-patch and an empty sleeve, into a place full of German agents. They flew him home with qualms, under a French name. They were at last persuaded that Zanussi was on the right side.

On the Allied side the negotiators were further hampered when first the Russians and then General Smuts and then the Dominion governments asked to send representatives to the signing of the Armistice. Not the French, because the French were being excluded from the information on grounds of security, to their later fury. Harold Macmillan thought that the idea of a vast gathering of representatives was absurd and embarrassing. 'We have at the same time to embark upon one of the most perilous adventures in military history, conquer a country with inferior forces, opposed by formidable and ever increasing German armaments, and at the same time impose upon the country we are invading unconditional surrender . . . I would be sorry to see the guests arrive at a "ceremony" when there is still a strong chance that neither the bride nor the bridegroom will be present.'[34]

Everyone was afraid that Castellano had been captured by the Germans. London asked Osborne to trace him. Osborne reported (30 August) that he had arrived in Rome.

[33] Carton de Wiart, *Happy Odyssey* (London, 1950), p. 228.
[34] Macmillan from Algiers to London, telegram no. 1614, 1 September 1943, CAB 122/ 856. General Alexander (31 August) calculated the unpromising nature of the venture thus: German divisions in Italy, 19 well-equipped: Italian divisions in Italy, 16 ill-equipped; Anglo-American divisions 3–5 at first, could build up to 8 over two weeks. Therefore Italian help was indispensable – and would it be given?

Castellano landed in Sicily on 31 August. The Sicilian journey happened thus. Confronted with the Allied terms of surrender Marshal Badoglio said that they were impossible because instantly the Germans would occupy Rome. He would only sign if the Allied armies undertook to land at least fifteen divisions near Rome. He told Castellano to fly to Sicily to say so.

At Cassibile airfield near Syracuse: long difficult angry debate;[35] 2 September, Castellano went to North Africa to meet General Eisenhower, long difficult angry debate; 2 September, German intelligence reported their suspicion that the Vatican was the centre of anti-German espionage; 3 September, Castellano back in Cassibile. General Alexander threatened him that unless he signed the Allies would bomb Rome again. The difficulty was not obstructiveness. To sign the Armistice as it stood was to invite the Germans to take over North Italy and Rome and Central Italy. The Italians saw no point in signing an armistice which failed to take them out of the war and put them under Nazi rule. They would only sign if the British and Americans would land enough troops to protect Rome. Eisenhower and Alexander knew that they could not possibly land enough troops to protect Rome. Yet they must have the Armistice, because they were about to invade Southern Italy and did not want to be fired on, however half-heartedly, by Fascist-minded Italian troops. Alexander must have Castellano's signature. They made promises, vague enough, of landings near Rome. They agreed to send an American airborne division to land near Rome. At Algiers Castellano was bullied by Macmillan and Eisenhower. They sent a radio message to Rome that confirmation must be given and deposited with Osborne at the Vatican and he must acknowledge its receipt. Osborne inserted in his Diary for that day a note for future German readers: 'During the afternoon and after tea we did [= decyphered] a telegram of a very Phillips Oppenheim nature, which was clearly not intended for us, as I am replying' (Phillips Oppenheim was a writer of thrillers well-known during the thirties). On 3 September the message came that Castellano was authorized to sign and that a declaration by Osborne would be fixed that day. In this way Osborne became the guarantor of the good faith of the Italian Armistice.[36]

---

[35] At Cassibile on 31 August Castellano asked, among much else, what the Allies were going to do about protecting the Vatican from the Germans. The Allies knew, but did not want the Italians to know, that they had no possible way of protecting the Vatican from the Germans. Bedell-Smith replied to the question that the protection of the Vatican would be part of the protection of Rome. Algiers to War Office, 1 September 1943, in CAB 122/856.

[36] Macmillan, *Blast of War*, p. 379; cf. CAB 122/856, Osborne to Foreign Office, 3 September 1943, telegram no. 334; 'I have just received a message of which the following is a literal translation from the Italian. It is signed Badoglio. "I declare that General Castellano is authorized by (group undecyphered) to sign acceptance of Armistice terms proposed by the Supreme Commander of the Allied Forces".'

On 3 September General Montgomery's army began to land on the toe of Italy.

The last argument about the Armistice was when. The Allies were determined to have 8 September. Badoglio saw that he had slightly more military chance if it was delayed for even four days or a week after that. Finally the Allies had to force the Italians into an armistice of 8 September. On the day before, Osborne who knew what was coming, inserted in his *Diary*, for the benefit of the German eyes which might now come any hour, his first hearing from the Portuguese ambassador and Father Mistiaen that the Armistice would be *signed* tomorrow (he knew that it had been signed already).

At this point the Chiefs of Staff in Algiers made a proposal which alarmed the British Minister there, Harold Macmillan. They suggested that the Armistice might not be believed, might be suspected of being Allied propaganda, and would need authenticating. They asked that Osborne should go to Cardinal Maglione, show the Cardinal Marshal Badoglio's authority for the Armistice, and ask that Vatican radio broadcast that the Secretary of State had seen the document and knew it to be genuine. In this way the armistice broadcast would be certified to be true by the Pope.

Macmillan reported the proposal to the King and the Chiefs of Staff in London, but dissented:

I personally consider this an unwise proposal because it would
   (a) involve the Vatican to a dangerous extent;
   (b) quite likely provoke and partially justify German invasion of the Vatican;
   (c) be almost sure to meet with a refusal and
   (d) compromise His Majesty's Minister at the Vatican.[37]

Events were to prove that this judgment of Macmillan was wisdom. If the course suggested by the Chiefs of Staff had been taken, Osborne would have become useless to the British government after 10 September 1943 when the Germans occupied Rome. And he was still to be of much use. The last stages of Osborne's service within enemy country owed something to Harold Macmillan.

So on 8 September the Allies announced the Armistice, whether the Italians liked the timing or not. The drop of the airborne division on Rome was cancelled. The elder Tittmann boy kept a diary and best records the excitement inside the Vatican:

8 September. Exciting day. D'Arcy was able to get the film *Desert Victory* down here so we are showing it today to Santa Marta. [Osborne saw most of it in London a few months before and Brendan Bracken sent it to the Vatican by Vatican courier.] It is really a wonderful film . . . Somebody turned on the

---

[37] FO 954/31A/42; cf. FO 371/37333, Algiers to Foreign Office, 7 September 1943.

radio and we heard that an armistice had been declared . . . We went out to St Peter's Square to see how the people react but most of them had not heard it . . . Then we went up the gardens and everybody was yelling and kissing each other and shaking hands.

In his *Diary* Osborne recorded his astonishment at this turn of events and also tried to help the Pope from the coming Germans. 'The Pope, poor man, with the best will in the world, has had nothing to do with restoring peace to Italy. If it is peace.' He destroyed nearly all his entry for 9 September. On 12 September he summarized what he now heard about the Armistice from the BBC, as though he knew no more than the BBC told him. On 13 September another entry for German eyes: 'I had burnt a lot more papers of no particular importance and I think I shall probably burn the remainder of our telegram files. Not that there is anything in them but they are such a mess that they offend me. And in their absence I shall be able to avoid writing an Annual Report!' . . . 'our innocent files' – to a suspicious eye he might protest too much. It is certain that this was for German eyes because he later told London that he destroyed *all archives not innocuous*.[38]

Cardinal Maglione, who was trying to protect the Pope and not the diplomats, asked the diplomats to burn their files. The diplomats held a meeting (14 September) and agreed. At the meeting they found that Osborne and Tittmann had already burnt nearly all theirs in the boys' holocaust of 24 August.[39]

Italian troops fought courageously against the Germans in the southern suburbs of Rome. In the northern suburbs a truce was soon arranged. Some of the officers had Fascist sympathies and no motive for fighting to let British and American soldiers conquer Italy. The private soldier was fed up with war, and saw a chance of going home. And since Badoglio and the King were advised that they were unsafe, they left Rome for Southern Italy, leaving no head of resistance in the city of Rome.

Would the Germans cross the border into Vatican City? The Pope's troops occupied its frontier as a symbol of defence. But they were under orders not to shoot, a direct order from the Pope. The commander of the Swiss demanded to see the order in writing. On 9 September, with fighting on the edges of the city, Cardinal Maglione summoned the new German ambassador Ernst von Weizsäcker and begged him to get Berlin to respect Vatican neutrality. Weizsäcker telegraphed Berlin that afternoon. And at that moment it was German policy to respect Vatican neutrality. On 10 September German detachments halted at the frontier of the Vatican.

[38] FO 371/44237/3.   [39] Tittmann Papers, Brussels, XIII.

Monsignor Tardini much admired the Pope that day. He was serene and smiling.

Each day, 8 and 9 and 10 and 11 September, Osborne sent off to London what news he could of the battle in the streets of Rome.[40] 9 September he half-suggested that the RAF should bomb the advancing Germans. This was not very sensible.

On his side Anthony Eden was now willing to use Osborne openly. On 10 September a desperate-sounding telegram went off from Eden, that Osborne should pass Marshal Badoglio a personal message from Eden, begging him to inspire the Italians to resistance with a clarion call. We have no evidence that Osborne got this message to Badoglio before Badoglio fled from Rome.[41] 'In general', reported Osborne to Eden, 'the situation is full of unpleasant possibilities.'

In August Osborne had heard a rumour that if fighting broke out in the streets of Rome the Pope would leave the city. He thought the rumour improbable ('and, if true, discreditable'). In the three or four days of fighting the Pope gave the envoys reason to think that he would only move if seized. The Brazilian ambassador had the idea that the envoys should inform the Pope that if he were kidnapped they would demand the right to go with him – naturally they would not ask Weizsäcker. On 15 September the Brazilian held a meeting of the immured diplomats at his lodgings; and two days later sent the Pope this sign of dedication. The Pope said he was touched. But he cannot have found it a comforting message.[42]

At some time, which we cannot yet date precisely, but very early in these secret negotiations, the German conspirators revived. Josef Müller and General Beck met, and again discussed the chance of treating with London through the Vatican and Osborne.[43] Both were aware that their chances were less than in 1939–40. They agreed that the attempt should be made.

Müller came again to Rome. He met Monsignor Kaas. He was again in touch with Father Leiber.

The Gestapo, however, had begun to suspect German Intelligence. Not evidence, but rumour, reached them that someone inside German Intelligence had put out a peace-feeler through the Vatican. For the moment they stored the information. Meanwhile they arrested Josef

---

[40] D. Tardini, *Pio XII* (Rome, 1959), p. 6. For Osborne's reports, CAB 122/856.
[41] Eden to Osborne, 10 September 1943; telegram no. 229, Osborne to Foreign Office, 11 September 1943; CAB 122/856.
[42] Maglione to Accioly, 29 September 1943, copy in FO 371/37539.
[43] K. Sendtner, 'Die deutsche Militäropposition im ersten Kriegsjahr', in *Die Vollmacht des Gewissens* (Munich, 1956), pp. 470–2.

Müller on a charge of treason. He stayed in gaol the rest of the war and was lucky to survive.

The British papers (so far) show nothing of this. The German sources show that the Pope, by one of his staff, talked to Osborne, putting the question whether, if Hitler were overthrown by Germans, there would be a chance of agreement – that is, did the formula *unconditional surrender* rule out such a chance? According to Müller the Pope said that after a German coup he would be willing to act as mediator between the parties. This is probable enough. The Pope repeated again and again his willingness to act as mediator between the warring parties whoever they were. Someone suggested – perhaps Monsignor Kaas – that the Pope should send to Berlin after the coup a special envoy and not Monsignor Orsenigo, and this would show the world that a new start had come to Germany. All this talk between Müller and Beck, and between Müller and Kaas and Leiber, sounds woolly. It does not sound as though it got precise enough to make it worth Osborne transmitting.

But just at this moment Beck found a young Catholic officer fanatically determined to overthrow Hitler at whatever cost to himself. In August 1943 Stauffenberg came out of hospital after treatment for terrible wounds sustained in North Africa, with one eye and an artificial hand. He refused further treatment which the surgeons said to be necessary. He said that he had a high mission, that there was something which he must do for Germany. The vacillating conspirators found that they had acquired a man resolute to kill. General Beck could see a chance that the German government might change overnight.

12

The German Occupation

i. *Surveillance*

Hitler had only one of Mussolini's reasons for respecting the neutrality of Vatican City. The Nazi Foreign Office, intent on happiness at home and German influence in other countries, and more squeamish than William Nogaret or Napoleon Bonaparte or Vittorio Emanuele II, shrank from the consequences of a seizure of the Vatican. But anything could change the mood.

One of Hitler's favourite occupations was to imprison the famous – King Leopold, Admiral Horthy, Marshal Pétain, Blum, Daladier, Schuschnigg etc. Several German reminiscences of the time mention the possibility of removing the Pope to Germany.

The rumour that the Germans meant to kidnap the Pope kept appearing. This was partly because the idea was obvious – if the Germans had to evacuate Rome why should they leave behind them in the Vatican a moral force who might help the new occupiers of Rome? But one reason the story kept going about was British propaganda. The British Political Warfare Executive found it excellent propaganda to put it about that Hitler was just about to kidnap the Pope. A bogus 'German' wireless broadcast the message (9 October) that all preparations were made for the removal of the Pope to the Reich. Two days later the bogus radio said that the castle of Lichtenstein in Württemberg was now ready to receive the Pope and the cardinals. These broadcasts appear to have taken in some of German Intelligence.[1]

There is evidence that Martin Bormann thought it better to remove the Pope. Weizsäcker kept hearing rumours about it. The Pope's only protection was the belief of several German leaders, including perhaps Himmler, that an unseized Pope could be useful in a negotiated peace. The protection was flimsy. The Vatican was on probation for good behaviour.

Osborne's role changed again. Under Italian rule he had to persuade the Italians that the Vatican was useful to the Italian war. Under German rule he could do nothing to persuade the Germans that the Vatican was useful to the German war – other than by making it

[1] FO 898/72; Robert A. Graham in *Civ. Catt.*, 129, (1978), 1 125; and (1972), 1, 459.

difficult, still, for the British to bomb a key of communications for the German army fighting in Southern Italy.

The danger was not past when the German troops halted at the frontier of Vatican City. And some Germans suspected the Vatican of a hand in the 'treachery' of the Italian Armistice. If Carton de Wiart was the only Briton so far known to criticize Osborne, Hitler was the only person so far to call him a swine. It was therefore important that the Germans should not be able to prove that the Vatican had a part in the Armistice. Ribbentrop ordered that the Italian archives be seized and sent to Germany. The Germans found a lot of the chests empty. They learnt that Guariglia had sent some out of the country, and that others were systematically destroyed. The Italians did not tell the Germans that they had hidden a lot in the cellars of the Palazzo Lancellotti. Still, forty chests of documents were sent off on a train to Germany and no one could be quite sure what they might find. They found nothing worth while, either to prove treachery, or to be useful in German propaganda.[2]

The Vatican now began to be helped by the German ambassador. He was determined to do all he could to prevent the Vatican's being occupied. A Rome newspaper, *Popolo di Roma*, made sensational 'disclosures' about the Vatican's hand in the Armistice. It said that the Pope had a long personal conversation on the telephone with President Roosevelt. Then Weizsäcker must accept the assurance of Monsignor Montini that this was false and pass the assurance to Berlin.[3] No one did more than Weizsäcker to keep the Vatican unoccupied, and therefore Osborne relatively free, during the next nine months. From being a mere German post of observation, the German embassy to the Holy See became one of the weighty executive centres in Rome.

Weizsäcker himself had to behave correctly. The Gestapo did not trust him. That August Martin Bormann put into his embassy an agent, Dr Ludwig Wemmer, partly with the duty of seeing that the ambassador did not negotiate with the British and the Americans. Weizsäcker noted with amusement that it took the Pope only two minutes to enchant Dr Wemmer.[4]

At this point the German security service, Reichssicherheitshauptamt, woke up to the fact that they also ought to put one of their men into the Vatican embassy. Weizsäcker must have had the impression that every corner of his embassy would be occupied by secret agents.

---

[2] Best in Mario Toscano, *Nuova Antologia* (March 1961), pp. 299ff.; and *Pagine di Storia diplomatica contemporanea* (Milan, 1963), pp. 249–81.
[3] Leonidas Hill, *Die Weizsäcker-Papiere 1933–1950* (Frankfurt, 1974), p. 349; cf. ADSS, 7, 614. [4] Hill., p. 353.

The first object of Reichssicherheit was to check on the enemy news that went out of the Vatican from Osborne and Tittmann. Their agents in Rome found access to the Vatican difficult and they thought they would do better if one of their men was in the embassy. They proposed to Weizsäcker one Georg Elling. He had been a free-lance writer doing research on the life of St Francis of Assisi, and spoke perfect Italian and French and English.

Weizsäcker protested. He said that his embassy was overstaffed already. 'There is no case for any more people.' We already get a mass of news out of the Vatican, our informers overwhelm us with information, the trouble is deciding which is the small amount of truth that all this information contains. 'You need to be known in the Vatican, if you are to do any good, and some of my present staff are known.' He invented a saying: 'In the Vatican anyone who knows anything says nothing, anyone who tells you anything knows nothing.'[5] When Georg Elling nevertheless came to Rome, Weizsäcker at once sent him home for Christmas. When he came back in January Weizsäcker could resist Reichsicherheit no longer, though he said that Elling 'will meet passive resistance in the Vatican'. To give him a title he made him 'research auxiliary' or 'collaborator in scientific studies'. He said that Georg Elling was not at all enthusiastic to be given this work. He said that this was a balancing act between the rival secret services.

However by January 1944 two separate agents, of different German secret services, were on Weizsäcker's staff in the embassy; this was apart from the reports that went to Berlin from the Gestapo chief in the city of Rome, Herbert Kappler.[6]

Georg Elling, reluctant though he might seem to Weizsäcker, received the job of reporting on Osborne and the other diplomats. To this end he was allowed the use of the private radio of the Gestapo chief. He was also given the job of organizing a network of spies inside Rome, in expectation of the time when the Allied armies took the city.[7] Thus Martin Bormann's man Wemmer kept an eye, naturally a discreet eye, on Weizsäcker, and the security man Elling kept an eye on Osborne and the diplomats.

ii. Allied bombing

On 5 November 1943, about 8.10 p.m. on a clear moonlit evening, bombs fell inside Vatican City. One dropped 100 metres from St Peter's and blew out windows; one fell near the Governatorato, destroying

[5] Ibid., p. 374.   [6] See the file in AA, Inland, II.G.330658.
[7] Robert A. Graham, 'Spie naziste attorno al Vaticano durante la seconda guerra mondiale', in Civ. Catt. (1970), 1, 26.

glass, including the glass of Tardini's flat (he was heard to exclaim 'Open City!'); one hit the laboratory of the mosaics; and one hit the Vatican aqueduct. No one was hurt.

German propaganda made great play about the incident. Osborne did not believe that the plane could be British. He asked London. RAF headquarters reported that they had nine planes in the neighbourhood of Rome but none of them dropped bombs on the city. They admitted that one of the planes was a Boston with engine trouble which unloaded its bombs through the cloud without quite knowing where it was. This was a clearance because the sky over Rome was fine. The British pointed out that German aircraft were known to be over Naples. Three questions were asked in the House of Commons (10 November 1943). The *Giornale d'Italia* printed a story that Stalin sent congratulations on the raid to Winston Churchill. The Foreign Office decided that they need not bother to deny the canard.[8]

Tardini could not help noticing that the date, 5 November, was an anti-Catholic date in Britain. General Eisenhower officially denied that the aircraft could be American. Weizsäcker officially denied that the aircraft could be German. Count Dalla Torre told Cardinal Maglione that Farinacci organized the raid from an airfield near Viterbo. Rumour in the city of Rome pointed at Farinacci, who did not deny the story. It was very unlikely.

On 23 January 1944 the Allies landed at Anzio and the distant rumble of guns rattled the windows of Rome. The city came into the front line. Aircraft raided into Latium. The first trouble came from the bombing of the papal palace to the south of Rome at Castel Gandolfo. Into this estate were crammed thousands of refugees from the war, who had nowhere to go or who believed that they would be safe on papal territory.

But the anxious confidence of the Pope and his staff was shattered by the affair of Monte Cassino.

The Allied armies were held up for months at the Cassino line north of Naples. They suffered heavy casualties and were very weary at the fruitless efforts to advance. High above the town of Cassino stood the monastery of St Benedict, the most historic religious house in all western Europe.

Miserable and wet at the foot of the mountain, the Allied soldiers found it impossible not to believe that German troops held the monastery, for it dominated the valley and the ridge. The German commanders gave Rome an assurance, for transmission to the British

---

[8] Papers in FO 371/37548; cf. ADSS, 7, 688 and 705; Moelhausen, *La carta pendente*, pp. 151–4; R. Trevelyan, *Rome '44: the battle for the Eternal City* (London, 1981), p. 183.

and Americans, that no German troops were in the monastery. The ordinary soldier and some of his commanders believed no word that the Germans said. They had been beaten back from Monastery Hill and were angry.

Italian directors of museums pointed out to the advancing armies the historical importance of the abbey of Monte Cassino. The Air Command in the Mediterranean instructed its units that they take every precaution not to bomb the abbey.

During October 1943 the abbey hill became part of the line of German defence known as the Gustav Line. On 16 October German officers persuaded the abbot that despite the promise of both sides to conserve cultural and religious treasures, it would be wise to send away his treasures. From 17 October German lorries made several journeys, removing the treasures of art and the manuscripts to Rome. Most of the monks went, all the nuns and the school children. That left the abbot, ten monks, and about 150 people, nearly all refugees.

On 7 December the German army commander asked how he could use the abbey in defence. 'To respect its extraterritoriality is not possible: its position makes it the centre of any defence.' Kesselring, who had promised the Vatican that German troops would not enter the monastery, replied that this was to stand – but only to apply to the monastery buildings. Accordingly the Germans destroyed all the outbuildings of the monastery, fortified an observation post just under the monastery wall, and stored ammunition in a cave which ran into the monastery under the mountain.

By the end of December occasional shells were beginning to drop on the monastery. The Vatican protested to Osborne and Tittmann. By the usual roundabout route this came through to the commanders in Southern Italy. They investigated. They reported that it was perfectly possible in error, but if it had happened it was not intentional. The Allied command ordered its officers to make every effort to avoid hitting the monastery, even though it would be excellent as an observation post for the enemy.

The Germans, realizing what was coming, tried to persuade the abbot to leave. He refused. They evacuated all the refugees except a few too ill to be moved. In February, as the fight over the surrounding countryside grew hotter, workers from their farms with their wives and families sought refuge in the abbey.

In February fresh troops arrived in the Allied line, the New Zealand division under General Freyberg, with the 4th Indian division under him as well as the New Zealanders. As soon as he looked at the abbey sitting on the mountain which he had to capture he said it ought to be blown down if the Germans used it. The commander of the Indian division, Tuker, was depressed by the miserable morale of the men whom he was relieving. He had no desire for a direct attack; if he must attack, he said that heavy bombing was necessary. On 12 February at 7 p.m. Freyberg asked the headquarters of the Fifth Army that the monastery be bombed the next day. The responsible general, the American Mark Clark, was away in Anzio. Various American officers said that destroying the monastery was not warranted. Someone said that inside the monastery were 2,000 refugees. The chief of staff sent the argument up to the supreme commander, Sir Harold Alexander. At 9.30 p.m. the message came that Alexander ordered the monastery to be bombed if Freyberg believed it a military necessity. He said that he trusted Freyberg's judgment.

Mark Clark had now been consulted and was against. Bombs would risk civilian lives, and the monastery would be a better fortress ruined than whole. It was a work of art; a sacred shrine; and probably it had many children inside.

Next morning (13 February) Alexander talked with Clark on the telephone. He admitted all Clark's arguments. But he said, if Freyberg wanted the monastery bombed, the monastery must be bombed.

There were no Germans inside the monastery. But vague evidence kept coming in that there were. Someone 'saw' the glint from field glasses inside. A civilian who came into the lines said that he was lately in the monastery and saw 30 machine-guns and about 80 soldiers. Someone thought he was wounded by a sniper who fired from inside the abbey; two senior American airmen, low over the abbey, 'saw' a military aerial poking up and soldiers moving in and out of the building. On 14 February the French general Juin visited Mark Clark to get the decision reversed. It was too late.

On the same day the German ambassador Weizsäcker assured the Vatican that no artillery, mortars, machine-guns, nor even troops were posted in the monastery or *in its immediate surroundings*.[9]

Late on 14 February Allied aircraft dropped leaflets on the monastery hill. They warned that bombs would follow, that all Italians must evacuate at once, that this was urgent. One of the refugees saw one of the leaflets on the hill, and not without danger, fetched it and took it to the abbot. The abbot arranged with the Germans that everyone should leave by a mule path at dawn on 16 February.

But nineteen hours before the evacuation, the raid came. The watching British, and even the bombing airmen were sure that they were justified, when both claimed to have seen German soldiers running from the monastery buildings. After two days nothing was

[9] FRUS, 1944, IV, 1282, 1299; ADSS, 10, 142.

left but rubble, and a hundred or more dead bodies of refugees who had sheltered in the monastery.

For a few days the lot of Osborne and Tittmann was unhappy. Cardinal Maglione used language unlike himself. He said that this was a colossal blunder and *'a piece of gross stupidity'*. Tardini said that it showed the Allies to have *a mania for destruction*. The Allied envoys argued that German troops must have been posted inside the monastery but they were not persuasive. After about two months they were formally assured by their governments that the abbey was proved to be part of the German defensive system.[10] The Americans announced to their people that it was a German fortress. A Benedictine abbot in Ottawa said that the bombing was justifiable as a regrettable necessity.

The abbot came out of his ruins enraged against the Allies. The place was sacred. The Allies knew that it contained not only himself and his monks but hundreds of refugees. He was 78 years old and he walked down the mountain over a mule path to a waiting German car. The car took him (17 February) to the local German general, Senger. German press photographers poured in. Film cameras recorded the interview (18 February) between the abbot and General Senger. For home consumption in Germany they excised parts of the interview. But it contained everything that the Germans wanted. The general was thanked for all he had done to keep the abbey out of use by his troops. The abbot certified that until the moment of destruction no single German soldier or weapon was inside the building. The abbot was very angry that the Allies dropped leaflets warning of bombs and urging evacuation, and then gave no time for the evacuation. Before the cameras he even accused the Allies of intending to drop the leaflets so late that evacuation would be impossible. When the raid started he and his monks laid out white cloths everywhere possible in the abbey, 'in order to say to them, do nothing to us, we are without arms, we are not a military objective, here is a holy place'. And despite the white cloths the bombers killed hundreds of innocent people. The abbot finally tore into the barbarian Allies by his thanks to the German army. 'I . . . thank you and the German Armed Forces for all the consideration given to the original abode of the Benedictine Order both before and after the bombardment.'[11]

General Senger put the abbot into a car and sent him off to Rome. He reached only the suburbs of Rome in that car, for the SS stopped it and took charge of the abbot. They took him circuitously round the city.

[10] Martin Blumenson, *Salerno to Cassino* (Washington, 1966), pp. 414–15.
[11] Hill, *Weizsäcker-Papiere*, p. 369; ADSS, 10, 148–9; Senger in Blumenson, *Salerno to Cassino*, p. 415.

The abbot expected to be taken to Benedictine headquarters at Sant' Anselmo. Instead he found himself at the Italian radio station. There he was interviewed and his answers to questions said everything that the Germans could wish. He spoke in inflammatory language.

The Germans were not finished with this wonderful opportunity for propaganda; a barbaric act by their enemies, a godly man who was very old and did not care what he said. They now took him to Weizsäcker's embassy. Out to the world went a press photograph of the abbot standing with Weizsäcker. The ambassador had prepared a written statement which he asked the abbot to sign. The abbot did not want to sign without reading it carefully. Weizsäcker pressed him and got his way. Then appeared more Germans, 'representatives of the press', actually men from Dr Goebbels and the Ministry of Propaganda in Berlin. They started more questions. The abbot at last lost all patience. He was tired and angry and would say not a word more. Then a German car at last drove him to Sant' Anselmo. Privately Weizsäcker was sorry for Abbot Diamare; a very old man, forced to talk when he was shaking, exhausted and filthy.[12]

The bombing of Monte Cassino remained in the books as one of the vandal acts of an air force. No one has believed that the monastery contained a German soldier.

But Osborne's plight, as the representative in Rome of a barbarian race, did not last long.

It was Tardini who asked the key question. We must know whether the British are right in saying that this was a German fortress, or the Germans are right in saying that it contained no military objective. We cannot trust either side. But there is a man we can trust – Abbot Diamare. We ought not to be seen to interview him. But we should bring him, surreptitiously, into the Vatican and ask him what happened.[13] We shall have to give him the assurance that whatever he tells us is secure and that we shall not publish any of his evidence. For that would be to help the Allies about the disposition of German troops.

On 20 February Abbot Diamare and the monk who was his secretary came into the Vatican. They were received by the Pope at 9 a.m. and at 10 went to Tardini. And there Tardini recorded some fascinating evidence.

The monastery, said Abbot Diamare, was half-destroyed before the air-raids. It was in the line of fire. Each side lobbed shells at each other over the hill. The gunners had not meant to hit the monastery but sometimes their aim was poor. This had been happening since mid-January. No one was killed. But the place was half-ruined.

[12] FO 371/50084/7.   [13] ADSS, 10, 141ff.

Inside the abbey were no German soldiers, no observation post, no cannon, no machine-guns. Tardini asked Abbot Diamare again and again. He was sure. At first some German soldiers came in as sight-seers or to make their confessions. But as the battle came close, not a single soldier was inside the precincts. The Germans had agreed with the abbot that the precincts, and circle of 300 metres round, should be free of troops or weapons. The abbot said that this precinct had the agreement of the Vatican, but no record of such an agreement has been found in the Vatican archives. To measure 300 metres was not simple because the radius went over precipices. Measuring the metres hardly mattered because the Germans failed to respect the agreement. Soldiers and weapons crept nearer and nearer to the monastery, until finally they were under its outside wall. Two tanks (or perhaps self-propelling guns) drove round and round the wall firing off, especially at night. Just under the abbey was an observation post which at night fired lights to guide the guns and light up the British position. Lastly, a cave stretched into the mountain right under the monastery. This cave was full of munitions.

Abbot Diamare had protested to the Germans that all this was dangerous for the abbey. They gave him a vague promise but moved nothing.

Osborne could know nothing of this conversation. The British government never learnt the truth. It continued to justify itself by trusting the word of some of its commanders that the abbey was a strongpoint. But Osborne's life was again more comfortable because the Vatican knew that though the British were barbarians they were not the only barbarians.

Cardinal Maglione had attacked Osborne and Tittmann fiercely and staked the attack on the evidence that no Germans were in the 'immediate neighbourhood' of the abbey. Now he knew this to be false.

He had another reason for being kinder to Osborne and Tittmann, though this second reason was likewise not plain to them. It was the German treatment of Abbot Diamare.

The use or misuse of a holy old man for the purpose of propaganda helped Osborne and Tittmann. The Vatican resented. They had dis-covered the truth, that no one could fire at the Germans on the mountain without firing at the abbey; and they found the Germans making war capital out of someone whom they saw as one of their own people. They lifted the pressure on the British and American envoys.

But even towards the end of May Osborne still believed that the Germans deliberately sought to make the Allies think the abbey to be a strongpoint. Only a month after the bombing Osborne was convinced, and told London, that it was a mistake; that the propaganda loss outweighed the military gain. In the Foreign Office they did not disagree. Here is a note of 22 March made at a Foreign Office desk on a letter about it from the Apostolic Delegate in London:

There is no doubt that the Military made a blunder in bombing the Abbey to bits, that the evidence of its use by the Germans is of the slenderest description, and that its destruction has provided German propaganda with a bull-point . . . Our best policy is really to preserve silence on Monte Cassino.[14]

So for the fourth time in its long history was destroyed Monte Cassino. The architecture was not what mattered principally, though it mattered, because most of it was of the late sixteenth century. It was the symbol, the razing of a sacred sanctuary, and (as many even then believed) to no purpose. Nearly everyone was to blame. The Germans fortified the mountain in such a way that no one could fire on them without firing on the abbey. General Freyberg was never aesthetic in his sensibility and cared only about the morale of his fighting men. General Alexander could have refused a British commander but could not dare to refuse a New Zealand commander and so have to bear the blame if or when the attack failed. And the ultimate culprit was one of the greatest of saints, Benedict himself, who chose a natural fortress as his home and shrine; or perhaps, long before him, the priests of Apollo, who found a spring of water upon the mountain and consecrated the place to the sun-god, and built for their temple pillars which St Benedict used in his courtyard and which were now, at long last, blasted into dust.

Nevertheless, the ruin of Monte Cassino shocked the Vatican, and not only because of the loss of a great and sacred and historic building. They had argued for the safety of Rome from bombs because it was a city great and historic and sacred and full of works of art. The end of the old Monte Cassino proved that this argument counted for nothing if it stood in the way of victory; that if these two armies fought through the streets of Rome the only rule would be to kill the enemy even if he hid inside the dome of St Peter's. From 17 February 1944 began three and a half months of the acutest anxiety. What would happen to Rome if it became part of no man's land like Monte Cassino?

And now the bombing of Rome started again and became frequent: the destruction of Ostia station, where the raid blew up a train full of munitions and damaged two churches; bombs on the Janiculum (1 March) damaging the palace of the Inquisition; heavy loss of life on

---

[14] Osborne to Foreign Office, 16 March 1944, FO 371/43870; and 24 May 1944; cf. Craven and Cate, *The Army Air Forces in World War II*, vol. 3, p. 847 note.

3 March when a bomb fell on a crowded shelter. Osborne got into trouble again. The Pope issued leaflets and advertisements that he would address the people in St Peter's Square on the anniversary of his coronation (12 March). He easily got the German authorities in Rome to agree. Then he asked the British and Americans to promise not to raid Rome that day while the crowd was in St Peter's Square. Osborne, who for obvious reasons was refusing to recognize Rome to be an open city, not merely transmitted his government's refusal but dared a rebuke: 'Rome is now close to the battle area and the expediency of arranging for a large assembly to be held in Rome, even on Vatican territory, could not but seem open to question.' This was a cool time between the British Minister and the Curia. Later the Pope himself gave audience to Osborne and cast blame for his attitude and that of his government. His speech to the crowd was only a part-success. Some of them had hoped that he would announce an arrangement for an open city, and were bitterly disappointed at his generalities. As the day was very cloudy no aircraft came anywhere near Rome.

Two days later, on 14 March, came another raid, in which many civilians were killed; on 19 March a hospital was destroyed; the raids were followed by papal protests each time. Tardini talked of the methodical coldness of the Anglo-Saxons. The RAF denied that they were anywhere near Rome on 19 March. At the end of the month the Vatican was shocked to find a German munition train stopped on the line by the Vatican railway station. What would have happened if it had been bombed? The Germans pleaded weakly that these were only old Italian munitions. They promised never to do it again.[15] A rumour spread that the Germans used the Coliseum to store munitions, and the Vatican had to take the trouble to prove it false. And all the time Latin American bishops, Spanish, Portuguese, neutrals everywhere, did what they could to influence the uninfluenceable British and Americans not to bomb Rome and not to fight through the streets of Rome. The Vatican found the Irish government to be of special help. To the south the palace at Castel Gandolfo suffered several bombs. It lay between two main roads, both used by the retreating German army. One bomb destroyed the summer villa of the College of Propaganda, killing several hundred refugees. Another bomb killed seventeen nuns in a convent on the edge of the estate. On 29 April 1944 Osborne formally apologized to Cardinal Maglione for the losses at Castel Gandolfo.

This apology was accompanied by a sting. The Vatican kept appeal-

---

[15] ADSS, 11, 219, 245, 263–4, 276, 282.

ing to the Lateran Treaty. Osborne said that the British government was not bound by the Lateran Treaty. And that even neutral territory lost its immunity when used or occupied by enemy forces.

The second mother-house of western monks suffered in May. The Vatican asked Britain to take care that the house at Subiaco, first retreat of St Benedict, should be spared. In January 1944 the Foreign Office told Osborne that they had so instructed the Allied commanders in Italy. The Germans put into the famous monastery a hospital and painted a red cross on the roof. Early in April the hospital was moved out, though the red cross remained on the roof. After 28 April no German soldier came anywhere near the monastery and there were no troops in the neighbourhood. On 24 May Allied aircraft bombed and severely damaged the lower monastery, and traces of the damage may be seen to this day. The abbot used strong language. So did the Curia to Osborne.

Osborne's situation in the Vatican was changing. On the one hand he grew more formidable as the physical force of his conquering country drew nearer to Rome. For a few months he was like the ambassador inside the Papacy of some medieval northern invader whose men could not be trusted not to sack the city. On the other hand his predicament was uncomfortable. He had made close friendships with Montini and Tardini. It was not pleasant to be told that his country was barbarian and Philistine in its destruction of civilian life and irreplaceable historical monuments.

In March Osborne protested to the Foreign Office. He said that the cumulative effect of the bombing was slowly but surely turning Italian opinion from the Allied side, 'especially as all reports indicated that the destruction of civilian life and property was altogether disproportionate to the military results attained'. He told London that one of the men in the Vatican (it was almost certainly Tardini) poured contempt on President Roosevelt's talk of 'a moral crusade to rescue Rome' when this was 'stultified' by civilian casualties and damage. The Foreign Office took no notice. The armies must beat the Germans. They would not promise to refrain from attacking anything which (they imagined) stood in the way. Within this general principle, they kept telling Osborne to tell the Pope, the commanders had instruction to avoid all damage to historical monuments or to innocent civilians.

Osborne was grieved at his own predicament, or the ruthlessness of his government. He told the Pope (22 April 1944) that he disapproved of his government. Even to London he compared its behaviour adversely with that of the Americans. He told the Pope that he could not but sympathize with some of the papal grievances against the British government.[16]

The nearer the fight came to Rome, the more difficult to find food for the Romans. The Vatican helped. They bought lorries and sent them into the countryside to fetch food. Soon the country nearby was exhausted. Then the lorries must travel further. Out on the roads they were easily mistaken for German transport and were bombed or machine-gunned, with the loss of several lives. Usually the convoys stopped as Allied aircraft approached, hoping to be safer if seen to be stationary, though their drivers took to the fields and ditches. The Vatican kept protesting to Osborne. The lorries were given special Vatican markings but the markings could hardly be seen from the air and were unfamiliar to the airmen. Montini and Galeazzi took Osborne and Tittmann on the roof of St Peter's to show how easily they could be identified from the air, markings of a lurid yellow and white. On 3 May a Vatican note accused the British and Americans of 'deliberate aggression or at least . . . extreme negligence'. It was a very stiff note indeed. It pointed out that if the city was saved from starvation and therefore revolution it would not be because of the Allies. Meanwhile retreating Germans also took food from the countryside and the shortage grew desperate. Osborne advised London not to bomb convoys but the RAF still could not tell a convoy of food for starving Romans from a convoy of munitions for German soldiers. Winston Churchill himself grew angry at the stupidity of bombing Vatican convoys: Prime Minister to Foreign Secretary and Chiefs of Staff (8 May 1944): 'It looks as if some stupid and spiteful person of the fourth grade has got hold of this matter. I regard this matter as most urgent. Action should be taken on it at once.' He added in his own hand, 'Why should we *now* plan for a starving Rome?'[17]

On 30 May Osborne reported to London that Vatican organizations were supplying about 100,000 of the poor of Rome with a meal at one lira a head. They also supplied the hospitals with food. The children and the middle class were the worst sufferers.

Meanwhile the Vatican tried to persuade Osborne and Weizsäcker and Tittmann to get a scheme for relief ships by sea. The ships should sail from the ports of Northern Italy and fly a papal flag. The Germans kept the negotiations going. The Allies hardly liked to refuse but would not agree, and at last on 4 June refused the plan. At that moment the stocks of flour were down to a few days. The Allied armies occupied Rome not a moment too soon.

[16] FO 371/50084/8 and 18.
[17] FO 371/43873/31. Churchill discussed it with Eden on 10 May, ibid., 105.

Weizsäcker believed that Pius XII was not wrong in thinking that he (the Pope) contributed to the saving of Rome from destruction. The British would never agree that it be an open city. But both sides began to treat it more like an open city during that winter; the British and Americans were more careful than in Germany to try to confine their bombing to military objectives. The German commander Kesselring did all he could to reduce the number of German troops or munitions of war passing or stopping in Rome. Weizsäcker privately diagnosed that this was because the city acquired a *nimbus* with both sides. He kept being surprised, in view of the persecution of the Church in Germany, how messages from Berlin talked about Rome as the cradle of culture and Christianity. He wondered whether that one-time artist and amateur architect Adolf Hitler had a romantic feeling about the buildings of Rome. He noticed how Kesselring's attitude to the Church and clergy, which started friendly, grew ever more hostile as the war moved up Italy. But Weizsäcker thought that much could be conceded to the Pope. 'During the last few months he has created an awe, which neither side felt before, about the venerable qualities of the city.'[18]

iii. The Jews of Rome

On the morning of 16 October 1943 a special squad of the SS tried to round up the Jews of Rome. They ransacked the old ghetto and sent a number not quite certain, probably 1,007, by train to Auschwitz, of which fifteen survived to the end of the war.

The Pope's silence at this atrocity was used twenty years later by Rolf Hochhuth for a violent attack on the Pope. We need not enter this problem, which has been often argued by historians.[19]

On the day after the train set off for Auschwitz Osborne had an audience with the Pope. In his mind rose again the question whether the Pope would have to leave Rome. Might there come a moment when conditions in the city were so vile, or so immoral, or so impossible, that it would be better for the Pope to follow the example of some of his predecessors and go away till better days? Osborne asked the Pope directly whether, and under what conditions, he would leave the city. The Pope said emphatically that he would never leave Rome, for his 'protection' or otherwise, unless he were removed by force. He said that he had no complaints against General Stahel, the German army commander in the city, nor against the German police,

---

[18] Weizsäcker, 11 June 1944, that is, five days after he knew at last that the city was now safe from destruction, in Hill, *Weizsäcker-Papiere*, p. 378.
[19] Cf., for example, Owen Chadwick, 'Weizsäcker, the Vatican and the Jews of Rome', in *Journal of Ecclesiastical History*, 28, 2 (April 1977), 179ff.

who had hitherto respected the neutrality of the Vatican. It was true that General Stahel, and even a few of the police officers, had done what little they could for the Jews.

Osborne said to the Pope (Osborne told London) 'it was the opinion of a number of people that he underestimated his own moral authority and the reluctant respect in which he was held by the Nazis because of the Catholic population of Germany; I added I was inclined to share the opinion and I urged him to bear it in mind in case in the course of coming events an occasion might arise for taking a strong line'.[20]

One other letter from Osborne to the Foreign Office throws a small shaft of light. It was written on the last day of that month.

As soon as he heard of the arrests of the Jews in Rome the Cardinal Secretary of State sent for the German ambassador and formulated some sort (?, unde-cyphered word) of protest.[21] The Ambassador took immediate action with the result that large numbers were released . . . Vatican intervention thus seems to have been effective in saving a large number of these unfortunate people.

Osborne was under an illusion that the number released (it was about a hundred) was thanks to action by Weizsäcker.

I enquired whether I might report this and was told that I might do but strictly for your information and on no account for publicity since any publication of information would probably lead to renewed persecution.[22]

iv. The Ardeatine caves

On the afternoon of 23 March 1944 Communist partisans exploded a bomb in the Via Rasella in Rome, just as a company of German soldiers marched by. Thirty-three Germans were killed. Some of them were ex-members of the Italian army from the Italian Tyrol. Berlin ordered the death of ten Italians for each German soldier killed, and that this must happen within 24 hours. The German notice in Rome said 'criminals, Jews, Badoglians'. This went down in history as the massacre of the Ardeatine caves, from the caves south of Rome where the Gestapo shot 335 Italians and dynamited the entrace to the caves.

The Pope cannot have known that the massacre was planned, for several high German officers in Rome did not know. But everyone with experience of the European occupation could prophesy that something like it would happen, from the moment the German soldiers died on the street. An Italian predicted the ratio of ten Italians to one German in a message to the Secretariat of State on the day before the massacre.

---

[20] Osborne to Berne for London, 18 October 1943, FO 371/37571/R10995.
[21] Minutes of this interview in ADSS, 9, 505.   [22] FO 371/37255/19.

Evidence, not quite certain, shows Weizsäcker telephoning Kesselring repeatedly in the effort to stop or limit what was bound to happen; and this is probable enough. Evidence exists, also a little uncertain, that the Pope asked his usual intermediary with the German commanders, Father Pancrazio Pfeiffer, the Salvatorian from Bavaria, to intervene with the German command. If he applied, there is no evidence to whom he applied, except that it was not to the Gestapo chief Herbert Kappler. To whomsoever he applied, he was turned away.[23]

Osborne told London that the *Osservatore Romano* printed a warning to the people of Rome to abstain from acts of violence; and this warning was plainly directed towards the bomb in the Via Rasella. A desk in the Foreign Office (McDermott) noted only: 'The Germans massacred over 300 Italians in return, yet the *Osservatore* says nothing of it . . .'

The Italian embassy to the Holy See had a different view of this article in the *Osservatore*. Babuscio Rizzo said that it demanded respect for human life; that the Germans protested to Cardinal Maglione about the article; and that the Cardinal replied energetically.[24]

v. The interval between occupations

Rumour ran in Rome even in October 1943 that Hitler would abandon the city and fight in the hills to the north, and therefore the Germans would soon evacuate Rome. In January 1944, with the landing of Allied armies at Anzio near Rome, came stronger rumours, even that the Germans would evacuate the city by the end of that month.

The Pope worried. What would happen in a city between the end of German power and the coming of Allied power? A city without effective police to prevent crime? A city where Communist partisans staged a coup for power? He wanted a sort of undertaking that the Allies would occupy the moment the Germans left. He had no clear proposal. He made Osborne and Tittmann aware of the anxiety.

He had one request.

Osborne to Foreign Office, 26 January 1944: The Cardinal Secretary of State sent for me today to say that the Pope hoped that no Allied coloured troops would be among the small number that might be garrisoned at Rome after the occupation. He hastened to add that the Holy See did not draw the colour line but it was hoped that it would be found possible to meet the request.[25]

---

[23] See A. Ascarelli, *Le Fosse Ardeatine*, 2nd edn (Rome, 1974); Robert A. Graham, 'La rappresaglia nazista alle Fosse Ardeatine. P. Pfeiffer, messaggero della carità di Pio XII', in *Civ. Catt.*, 124 (1973), 4, 467ff.

[24] FO 371/43870, Osborne to Foreign Office, 25 March 1944; Babuscio Rizzo to Italian government, 30 March 1944, AE, Santa Sede, 1944, Busta 72.

[25] FO 371/43869/21.

In the event there was no interval. American troops entered the southern suburbs as German troops left the northern suburbs. For a few weeks all was not well with the policing of Rome. But the Vatican's worst fears were not realized.

vi. The escape line

The Italian surrender led to the strangest and most improper activity in which Osborne engaged.

The terms of the Armistice agreed that the Italians release their prisoners-of-war. Therefore thousands of ex-prisoners were loose in Italy. The Germans rounded up where they could. But thousands still hid in the mountains or the countryside. They looked to rejoin their advancing army. If that proved impossible, they would escape into a neutral country. Where was a neutral country? Spain, or Switzerland, or the Vatican. In June 1943 the BBC advised escapers in Italy to make for the Vatican. The advice was foolish. The BBC probably expected ten or twelve. No one expected thousands. If even two hundred escaped prisoners got into Vatican City, the Germans would occupy at once. Fortunately many prisoners were not aware that the Vatican was outside Italy.

This trouble threatened Osborne, and the Vatican's safety, for several months. Technically the Vatican was a neutral State, with duties under international law to intern escaped prisoners. But this was like the right to illuminate the Vatican by night, it was a right which could hardly be used.

We have seen Albert Penny riding his stolen or borrowed bicycle into the Vatican and causing the fall of the most pleasant of Vatican policemen. Before the Armistice three airmen walked into the Vatican by following a group of workmen at 5.30 a.m. Monsignor Montini got them a football, John May found them a radio, they lived on the top floor of a barracks, they were taken separately for walks in the Vatican gardens, the Pope gave them an audience and finally they were exchanged for three Italian prisoners.[26]

But now thousands of prisoners were free in the Apennines. They were in leaderless groups, having little idea where to go next. Italian peasants helped them but they were near starvation because they had no money and wore North African clothes in an Italian mountain autumn and coming winter. They had no medicines. If they tried to go south across the mountains to join General Montgomery, a few got over but many perished. If they tried a route southward by sea on the

[26] FO 380/87.

west coast, it was always fatal. If they tried by sea on the east coast, a few got through but only a few. Some got to Switzerland. Most thought it best to stay where they were till the southern armies arrived. And so they starved or froze or got ill or risked the lives of the Italians who fed them.[27]

No one in the Vatican could tolerate lots of prisoners escaping into Vatican City. For they would mean the end of Vatican City. Stringent instructions were given to the guards to prevent them coming in or to throw them out if they slipped in. Hugh Montgomery rescued two British soldiers who got into St Peter's disguised as Italian soldiers and were being fought down the steps by the gendarmes back into German territory. On his way to see Tardini Osborne happened to pass papal gendarmes when they were expelling a captain in the Royal Engineers and rescued him. But quite a number of prisoners were rejected or ejected without the knowledge of Osborne and some at least without the knowledge of Cardinal Maglione or Monsignor Montini. After the fight on the steps of St Peter's the Vatican authorities argued that as St Peter's was a public place it was not (for purposes of sanctuary) part of the Vatican State.[28] Osborne had no difficulty in demolishing this bizarre plea. So Cardinal Canali instituted a system of identity cards, without which no one could enter St Peter's.

Nearly a week after the German occupation of Rome, fourteen British prisoners, hungry and in rags on the streets of Rome, ran into an Italian carabiniere. They were very lucky. He was Anton Call. He explained to them how to get inside the Vatican, in parties of not more than two or three. When they were inside and stopped they should say that they were escaped prisoners and should ask for John May. But they all ended up under arrest at an Italian police barracks which the Germans later took over and only two were not recaptured. When they had asked for John May, the gendarmes handed them over to the carabinieri.

As appeals for food or money from hidden and starving men were brought into the Vatican by Italian messengers, Osborne realized that he could no longer behave with propriety. He could not leave British prisoners in the bush to starve. But if he helped them and this was discovered by the Germans, they would threaten the Pope and the Vatican would expel Osborne for trading disgracefully on his diplomatic status, and the British Legation in Rome would be at an end. If he failed to find them an alternative means of survival outside Vatican

---

[27] For a beautifully written account of the experiences of one prisoner, see Lord Clifford of Chudleigh's papers in the Imperial War Museum; see also the papers of Roger M. Freer and M. A. Glass and D. I. Jones.   [28] FO 371/44237/4.

City they would try to get into Vatican City and all of Vatican City would be at an end.

He does not seem to have framed the problem to himself, it is better to risk destruction of the British Legation in the Vatican than to risk the destruction of all the Vatican. He had a simpler duty, that of helping British servicemen.

He decided to help. He had to have money, and agents. Yet his every move was watched. He found his indispensable assistant in an unlikely place, the office of the Inquisition. Hugh O'Flaherty was an Irish monsignor who had resided in the Curia since 1922. He was learned, and tall, with blue eyes behind steel spectacles, a rugged knobbly face, a lilting Irish brogue, and a very Irish humour.

He was almost an ideal ally for more than one reason. His office, and two storeys above it his bedsitter, were in the Collegium Teutonicum, the German College. This building was not inside the Vatican State but, as extraterritorial, was not examined by Italian police. And it was very near the walls of the Vatican, just on the other side from the Convent of Santa Marta and the British Legation. He had easy access to the Vatican. He could move in Rome freely. And with care and a sufficient disguise he could smuggle men in to see Osborne or John May. He affected strongly Irish and anti-British sentiments.

He had a second advantage. He was an expert, the Vatican expert, on prisoners-of-war. In 1941 the Curia appointed him secretary to the nuncio to the Italian government, Borgongini Duca; and together they toured the prison camps of northern Italy. O'Flaherty started making lists of prisoners for Vatican radio to transmit to relatives, and organized the distribution of Red Cross parcels. He made himself responsible for the parcels, and for getting adequate clothing to prisoners who only had their North African uniforms. Over two and a half years of war he distributed more than 10,000 books. He compiled and gave out prayer-books for the camps.

He was a fine golfer and so knew Osborne before the war. Despite the Irish record, Osborne reported no sign in him of real anti-British feeling. He seemed to be specially offended when the Jews were rounded up in Rome and set to scrubbing roads near the Tiber. He achieved the removal of two nasty commandants of camps, one at Modena and the other at Piacenza hospital.[29] He championed refugees of every description, including Jews and anti-Fascists.

This work started to end in the last days of 1942. At Christmas that year the Italian censors discovered a letter from a British prisoner-of-war to his home, which said: 'The Monsignor had told them that the

[29] Ryan's report, WO 204/1012/2.

war was going well.' This was reported to High Command which refused to let O'Flaherty go again with Borgongini Duca.

Nevertheless, three months later we find him in trouble again, this time in the company of Monsignor Riberi, visiting the camp for Australian and South African prisoners at Tuturano near Brindisi. The local Fascist party said that the visit raised the morale of the prisoners and lowered that of their guards. It was especially criticized that the visitors distributed accordions, mandolins, and guitars.[30]

That August, High Command had a secret report on O'Flaherty. He was a notorious Anglophile. He was suspected of passing military information to the enemy. He certainly passed information to Osborne.[31]

Osborne was organizing a service to keep escaped prisoners alive. But so far as possible he must be able to defend himself against the charge that he was abusing diplomatic privilege. Once he is recorded as saying (not long after 20 October 1943) that it would be better if the prisoners surrendered to the Germans, winter was coming and they could not stay alive; and if they surrendered Her Majesty's government would avoid 'acute embarrassment'. When O'Flaherty and Tittmann protested at this utterance of the tongue-in-cheek, Osborne said 'Let us see what we can do about organizing things.'

This was an untypical utterance. He did what he could not to seem to organize.

O'Flaherty recorded him as saying: 'I must not be seen to compromise the tacit conditions under which I am here in the Vatican State. What I suggest you do is to have a quiet word with John May. *I don't want to know any details*, but I have a good idea he can help you.'[32] O'Flaherty reported John May as saying to him 'You needn't tell Sir d'Arcy too much.' But we find Osborne taking curious little precautions; refusal to date letters lest they be found by the Germans; pretending not to notice O'Flaherty when he found him in his own hallway planning an escape with John May; pretending not to know that for a few days John May helped to conceal an escaping Italian prince[33] – a hard pretence for Osborne, who was rather one for princes.

Inside Santa Marta they found Osborne detached about the work.

[30] AE, Santa Sede, 1943, Busta 69, report of 22 April 1943.

[31] AE, Santa Sede, 1943, Busta 68/1, report of 11 August 1943.

[32] J. P. Gallagher, *Scarlet Pimpernel of the Vatican* (London, 1967), pp. 35 and 48. For the escaped prisoners, S. I. Derry's book, *The Rome Escape Line* (London, 1961), is far the best study. The principal PRO document is Ryan's Report, WO 204/1012. Others have written, especially John Furman, *Be not Fearful* (London, 1959). J. P. Gallagher's book studies O'Flaherty. More on O'Flaherty is in Robert A. Graham, 'La "Primula Rossa" del Vaticano e l'Intelligence Service. Assistenza o Spionaggio', in *Civ. Catt.* (1974), 2, 230ff.

[33] Gallagher, *Scarlet Pimpernel*, p. 59.

His communications to London show that the heart was engaged – sick men, dying men, men without blankets, 'precious lives' to be saved.

In London the Foreign Office asked themselves whether they risked Osborne's Legation by handing him money to help escaped British prisoners. They decided that obviously they ran that risk. Did they now mind the danger to their post in Rome? And did they mind that Osborne could not guarantee that all his money reached the people whom it was intended to help and that some of it might end up among crooks? They decided that these risks had to be accepted. 'My own view,' commented Rumbold, 'is that it is worth taking a good many risks, including that of compromising his position in the Vatican, to send money to British prisoners, wherever they may be in Italy.'[34]

Osborne needed large sums of money. He had to have it on credit from the Vatican Bank. It complicated his life that he dare not go near the Vatican Bank personally. The Foreign Office needed therefore to give the Vatican Bank a guarantee that it would cover this credit on terms of repayment after the liberation of Rome. They secured him a loan of 3 million lire on terms that it would be for three months or within one month of the liberation of Rome.[35]

After a time he found that some of the escapers were not British but Russian. And on 10 December Cardinal Tisserant pointed out to him that there were 92 Greek soldiers known to be hiding in Rome. He took the Greeks and Russians also under his wing, like the Americans. The Foreign Office was prudent enough, first to decide that it was the War Office and not the Foreign Office which ought to pay for all this, and then that they should ask the Russian and Greek governments for a proportionate contribution.

The sums were considerable. Osborne borrowed 2 more million lire from the Vatican Bank in April. By 23 April he had spent a total of £27,500. In May he told London that his further needs were met by the French Canadian head of a religious order who offered to lend him up to 20 million lire on credit, against credit in London, from a fund held in suspense to build a new house for the order in Rome; the aim of the French Canadian was to preserve the value of the money against the depreciation of the lira.[36]

Tittmann obtained from the State Department ('for charitable

---

[34] FO 371/37566.

[35] 29 January 1944, cf. FO 371/44215. R. A. B. Mynors was the Treasury official concerned.

[36] Papers in FO 371/44215. Despite the credit from the French-Canadian, at the end of May 1944 Osborne asked that the equivalent of £2,000 in lire should be credited by London to the Banca Svizzera Italiana in Lugano, to an account number which was a Jesuit account. Money could be brought to the Vatican from Switzerland by Vatican courier.

purposes') the equivalent of 5,000 dollars, and later some more in Swiss francs, to be brought from Switzerland by Vatican courier. He also asked for money to help Jewish refugees inside Rome.[37]

Prince Doria Pamphilj, a courageous anti-Fascist married to an equally courageous Scottish wife, gave a gift from his hiding-place of 150,000 lire for prisoners and refugees and added more later.

In this way Osborne was enabled to spend freely. The Foreign Office could not imagine how he got the money out of the Vatican into the hands of the escapers.

Another part of the work he needed to know, however he preferred to say that he did not wish to know. He needed agents; that is, British officers not interned inside the Vatican but able to move in disguise through Rome. The organizers had no check, except through Osborne, on the people whom they chose to work for them. It would be easy for the Gestapo to plant an agent inside the organization. One genuine British SOE man, who made touch, the organizers treated with such suspicion that they could not use him. But if they brought in a British officer and gave him responsibility (they each came in disguised by O'Flaherty as a monsignor), Osborne interviewed him over a meal or a drink; asked a lot of questions about his home and background; sent a cyphered telegram to London; and got back the clearance from London after policemen had gone round to the family. Thus there were two things which he must do for the organization because no one else could do them. One was to supply the money. The other was to get a check from Britain on the reliability of the agents.

The change from Italian threat to German threat meant a certain easing of the restrictions. O'Flaherty could not have taken a British officer disguised as a monsignor to see Osborne because the Vatican police under Fascist domination would have known about monsignori and who they were; and if they did not know, would have asked his name, to report it to the quaestor of Rome. The new German occupiers were better armed, but more easily bewildered by monsignori. Gestapo agents were inside the Vatican, and had Italian agents. But they had not the old control among the Pontifical gendarmes. Meetings could happen in Osborne's Legation, which could not have happened at all before 25 July 1943.

We have a full account of Osborne interviewing the candidate for being put in charge of the escape line. Early in November 1943, though with precautions, they got Major Sam Derry out of the bush (he had

---

[37] The total American expenditure was 8,928 dollars; some of it disbursed through Derry, the rest through Father McGeogh. NAW 121/866A/372, Tittmann to Cordell Hull, 21 December 1943 and 10 March 1944; NAW, RG, 59, Tittmann to Wesley Jones, 2 August 1944.

jumped a train taking him off to Germany, and sent Osborne a message). He passed a German road-block under a pile of cabbages on a peasant's farm cart. Monsignor O'Flaherty met him on the steps of St Peter's. That night he was dressed as a monsignor, and so passed the Vatican frontier to dine with Osborne.

The dinner in Santa Marta was extraordinary; a man who had not eaten properly for eighteen months, came out of the wilderness and dined on a polished table with polished glass and silver-candlesticks, waited on by an English butler and an Italian footman. Derry's description was very perceptive about Osborne:

Unruffled poise . . . Seldom have I met any man in whom I had such immediate confidence. He welcomed us warmly, yet I found it impossible to behave with anything but strict formality. Apart from the restraining influence of my clothing [he was not used to being dressed as a monsignor] I was almost overwhelmed by an atmosphere of old-world English courtliness and grace, which I had thought belonged only to the country-house parties of long ago. Sir D'Arcy was spry, trim, a young sixty, but he had spent years enough in the diplomatic service to develop an astonishing aptitude for creating around himself an aura of all that was most civilized in English life. I felt as though I had returned home after long travels, to find that royalty had come to dinner, and I had to be on my best behaviour.

He would not have been so happy if he had known that the Italian footman who helped John May was in the pay of the Fascist police. They did not talk business over dinner.

After dinner, though with a certain 'studied reticence', Osborne offered him the command of the escape organization. While Derry returned to the bush to arrange for the men with whom he had been living, a coded message went to the Foreign Office; Foreign Office to War Office; War Office to New Scotland Yard; Scotland Yard to Newark police; and when the information came back Osborne asked him more questions about his home and family and regiment.

We notice the extent of the play with diplomatic privilege. They might pretend that Osborne had nothing to do with the organization. But he personally offered the headship of the organization, personally interviewed another officer (Lesslie) who was given the headship of a hide-out of escapers on the Janiculum (where he was helped by Anton Call the former Vatican gendarme and by an American Monsignor in the Vatican, McGeogh). The ultimate headquarters was not O'Flaherty's flat in the Collegium Teutonicum but in Santa Marta. Osborne told Derry that all he could do was to supply cash, and interned British officers as secretaries to do the clerical work.

Sam Derry now took charge. He handed out the cash, controlled the billeting officers, threatened the cases of indiscipline which risked the lives of the Italian hosts, arranged with the RAF at Bari for drops of supplies into the countryside. John May made at least one microfilm and baked it in a loaf of bread for transmission to Bari.[38] Osborne said he did not want to know details, but he was kept continuously informed and attended meetings of the inner ring. From the Vichy embassy, de Blesson helped with all his energy. The Irish minister's daughter Blon Kiernan helped, but as yet there is no evidence that her father knew. John May used big bribes on the black market, and once to get documents into the pile signed by the German ambassador.

With so many ex-prisoners held in flats in the city, and with privates with nothing to do and an ability to get drunk, and an Irish monsignor with no idea of secrecy, and an English butler who liked to show that he was in the know, and Gestapo informers inside the Vatican, the Germans could not but become aware of what was happening. It took them a surprisingly long time, a little more than a month.

On 5 January they caught an Italian girl who was used to carry money to escapers hidden in the country round Sulmona. They threatened her mother and baby and she talked. On 6 January they captured two key billeting officers, one of whom (a Yugoslav) they shot. On 8 January they raided three apartments in Rome and caught fourteen men and another of the billeting officers. Secundo Costantini was the Italian caretaker at the closed British Legation in the city, where the furniture was covered in dust-sheets but where escaped prisoners sometimes slept till a better place could be found. The Germans discovered that Costantini was part of the organization and forced him to play the part of a double agent. He had a long history of being an agent and perhaps needed no forcing.

On 11 January Hugh O'Flaherty went to a reception at the Hungarian Embassy and met Weizsäcker. Weizsäcker told O'Flaherty that they knew about the escape organization and 'if you leave the area of the Vatican you will be arrested on sight'.[39] The Vatican Secretariat of State gave O'Flaherty the same warning. The Rector of the Collegium Teutonicum told O'Flaherty that the Germans knew about the activities of himself and Derry, and said that Derry must leave the building.

Thirty years later, while he was still a prisoner of the Italians, the ex-chief of the Rome Gestapo Herbert Kappler said that Hugh O'Flaherty organized a spy ring from inside the Vatican. By that date, O'Flaherty was nine years dead, but Kappler knew him well during his last years. The statement is very improbable. No other evidence exists for the charge. But Kappler doubtless believed it. The ring was closing on O'Flaherty and he must retreat into the Vatican.

[38] Derry, *Escape Line*, p. 65.   [39] Ibid., p. 108.

With O'Flaherty forced into the Vatican and Derry forced out of the Collegium Teutonicum, Osborne lost his two main agents in Rome for organizing the escape line. He now took his most undiplomatic decision. Derry dressed up as a monsignor and went to see him. Osborne told him to take up residence inside Santa Marta; not as an interned officer, which would stop his work, but secretly. He and O'Flaherty now directed operations from inside the Vatican. Derry was very careful to remain hidden. If his presence became known, the Legation might be closed.

Osborne kept his distance. He had a British officer hiding illegally in his flat. His relations with Derry never crossed the frontier into informality. Once a week he would send his butler across the passage to invite Derry to take luncheon or dinner as his guest.

The worst time for the organization was between 15 March and early May 1944. They lost five of their Italian helpers in the shootings at the Ardeatine caves. Two of their prisoners (at least) were shot as they were being recaptured, and they lost at least 44 men recaptured. On 22 April Osborne learnt from the Swiss that Weizsäcker knew that he supplied the money. It was not a difficult deduction. Derry called this 'a very black time'. They were encouraged because John May found a clerk in the Questura who in return for suitable palm-greasing provided them with copies of police orders. The number of ex-prisoners continued to grow: mid-March 1944, 3,423; mid-April 3,739; 4 June, 3,925 (of whom British 1,695; South African, 896; Russian, 429; Greek 425; American 185).

The question remains why Weizsäcker did not force the Pope to close the Legation and expel Osborne.

Weizsäcker could not wish to uncover the organization in a way that would hurt the Vatican. Convinced that it was the interest of Germany to be seen to respect the Pope's neutrality, and believing that the Vatican might be useful in the quest for a peace of compromise, which was now Germany's only hope, he was resolute to prevent Hitler from occupying the Vatican. He knew that this was running risks. He could not want to tell Berlin too plainly that British agents operated out of the Vatican. Yet he could not control what the Gestapo were reporting to Berlin. And he had this justification. The expensive operation might be held to help the British war effort only at the margin.

Why did not Cardinal Maglione or Monsignor Montini say to Osborne this must stop? It is impossible that they did not know. O'Flaherty was a blurter, John May had too wide a mouth. Monsignor Montini must have known, at least in outline. The relations of honour between Osborne and Montini were such that we can assume a need in Osborne's conscience to tell Montini. Sam Derry believed that Osborne was so honest a man, and so close to Montini in friendship, that he must have told him.

We must suppose that the Vatican justified its inaction on grounds which were part-diplomatic and part-moral. To close the British Legation at this stage of the war, when the Allies were winning, would look to the future winners like a shout of propaganda on the side of Germany. And on moral grounds they could refrain.

For Osborne had a defence ready, and he stuck to that defence to the end. He was not helping anyone to win a war. He was helping refugees not to starve. And the Vatican was in the business of helping refugees not to starve. Even to London he tried to make the distinction. He knew that these copious baskets of lire that went out of the walls of the Vatican to unknown Italian hands might end up buying weapons for North Italian partisans to shoot Germans. But he consciously tried, so far as he could, to restrict the cash (as he once told London)[40] to refugees near Rome and not to 'large military bands'. He hoped London would agree. London had not the same reason for minding, and after an early hesitation asked no questions about how he used the money.

After the Allies occupied Rome, Osborne sent the Foreign Office[41] (14 September 1944) words of praise for his Italian helpers.

I take this opportunity to record my admiration for, and gratitude to the numberless Italians, mostly of the poorest peasant class in the country districts, who displayed boundless generosity and kindness to our men over a long and trying period; it must be remembered that, in so doing, not only did they refuse the financial rewards for the denunciation of British prisoners of war which the Germans offered and which would have been a fortune to them, but they also showed magnificent abnegation and courage in sharing their few clothes and scanty food and, above all, in risking their lives and the lives of their families and friends in disregarding the increasingly severe German injunctions against harbouring or helping British prisoners. A number of them indeed were shot by the Germans. We owe a debt to the Italian people in this respect that should not be forgotten and cannot be repaid.

Characteristically, he failed to mention that three groups of British soldiers absconded with their share of his funds.

[40] FO 371/37566, Osborne to London, 11 November 1943.
[41] FO 954/31A, HH 06876.

13
Aftermath

On 19 October 1943 Harold Macmillan, in Algiers, thought that the armies advanced fast, that they might reach Rome within a week or two, and that the British and Americans would be unprepared to deal with the Vatican politically. He telegraphed the Foreign Office suggesting that General Eisenhower be given instructions as soon as possible. The reply came back two days later not from the officers in the Foreign Office but from the Prime Minister himself. The message was Churchillian in its laconic quality. 'How could we treat it except with the utmost respect?'[1]

Seven and a half months later the attitude was the same.

The Allied armies entered Rome on 4–5 June 1944. They reported that they found the Vatican in perfect order and many Italian treasures safe because hidden in the Vatican. At the victory parade, General Mark Clark insisted that Osborne stand beside him on the saluting base at Porta Pia.[2] Osborne told London that the discipline of the American troops in Rome was not good, and that 'the over-eagerness of collaborationism of Roman women is somewhat of a public scandal'; and accompanied this with a formal complaint about morality from the Vatican. General Alexander used Osborne's help to persuade Mark Clark to reduce the number of American soldiers in Rome, a concentration which had danger.

When the Allied armies entered Rome, the Pope was the most important person in Italy. Vast crowds came repeatedly to St Peter's Square. Romans attributed to his presence their relative freedom from bombing and their exemption from a battle through the streets. The Italians saw that the Allies respected him and that he had a chance of securing favourable peace terms for Italy. Towards the outside world the Pope was for a few months the strongest political force in the peninsula. The King was tarnished with Fascism. For the first time since 1860 the Pope had no competitor for the prestige of a head of State.

During the next few months it seemed not unrealistic to talk of an extension of Vatican territory. The Allies had a not coherent feeling

[1] FO 371/37539.
[2] FO 371/43874, Osborne to London, 12 June 1944; 23 June 1944; 4 July 1944.

that they would like to make the Vatican a little more independent of the Italian State which surrounded it, and that if they made the Vatican a little larger, perhaps with an airport, or even with a port and a corridor to the sea, it might have this effect. There was also responsible talk that after all the Pope might be allowed a seat at the future peace conference. There was discussion whether the internal treaty, which was the Lateran Treaty, applicable only to Italy and the Vatican, should not be replaced by an international guarantee. In Catholic Milan could be heard less responsible talk of a return of all Rome to the Pope. The Pope started to help feed Rome with motor-boats flying the Vatican flag, and this reappearance of a 'papal fleet' bothered the Italian government, which said that it was not contemplated in the Lateran Treaty.

Allied soldiers applied for audiences, and the Pope loved to greet them as a few months before he had loved to give audience to men of the Afrika Korps. At first Osborne could hardly bear the sudden influx of cameras and flashlights and 'the Hollywood publicity bug. But you can't do that if you are Pope without hopelessly cheapening and vulgarizing your office. It makes me sick when I think of Pius XI' (*Diary*, 7 June 1944).

The leaders of the Allies came to Rome and were received. Myron Taylor came at once and was at once influential. Winston Churchill came in August 1944 and had an audience. Anthony Eden came in November but failed to make time for a visit to the Pope. The Curia observed that he made time for a visit to the pictures at the Palazzo Venezia. Osborne's defence of Eden's busy timetable failed to persuade the Vatican that Eden was not an anti-Catholic politician. Osborne to Eden 3 November 1944: 'I have not been entirely successful in convincing the Vatican that you are not, as they suspect, anti-Pope or anti-Catholic . . . His Holiness has a very feminine sensitiveness and all of the vanity of his race – or at any rate as much as is compatible with a really saintly character. But I am sure I can satisfy him next week that it was simply not physically possible for you to see him.'[3] Harold Macmillan came, as the chief political officer in Italy, and Osborne arranged for an audience. Macmillan found the Pope sad and depressed, with a bird-like mind which moved on from one point to another:

I think I murmured encouraging little sentences, as to a child . . . A sense of timelessness – time means nothing here, centuries come and go, but this is like living in a sort of fourth dimension. And at the centre of it all, past the papal guards, and the noble guards, and the monsignori, and the bishops, and the

[3] FO 954/31A.

cardinals, and all the show of ages – sits the little saintly man, rather worried, obviously quite selfless and holy – at once a pathetic and a tremendous figure.[4]

As early as October 1944 the abbot of Monte Cassino, who longed for his pastoral care, returned to the ruins of the abbey, installed himself in a church nearby, and put five monks into the caves. He was determined that the shrine of St Benedict be not left unguarded. He found that the ruins had already been picked over by looters and souvenir-hunters. The abbey lost more of its surviving treasures during the time of desolation. The British asked Monsignor Tardini about Monte Cassino (28 July 1944) and were pleased to find that he blamed both sides. But Osborne soon needed to protest against the guide book for sale to visitors at the abbey. The abbot refused to withdraw it from sale. He still thought the bombing of the abbey to be a barbarous act. The British helped the monks to start a restoration. On 15 March 1945 the foundation stone of a great new monastery was solemnly laid. The mood was to restore what was before, for the old seemed now consecrated by a martyrdom. So the restorers lost a chance to make the monastery more the size, and more the simplicity, needed by modern Benedictines. Restoration did not really begin till 1947, and the congregation could not return fully till 1952. It required much money. When Montini as Pope consecrated the abbey in 1964, his words showed that he had not forgiven.

In December 1945 Osborne protested to Tardini both against the abbey's booklet and against a Vatican memorandum which Tardini provided in defence of the booklet. Both Tittmann and Osborne resented the statement that the abbey was only made part of the German defences after the bombing. In conversation Tardini accepted that the German commander Kesselring told a lie when he told all Europe that the abbey was no part of German defences. But he refused to agree that therefore the destruction of the abbey could be justified militarily. In March 1946 the Foreign Office was still asking whether the booklet was still on sale.[5]

The Russian successes filled the Vatican with foreboding. Casimir Papée the Polish ambassador, for obvious reasons. Osborne found that the Vatican needed persuasion that the Russians were less bad than the Nazis. As early as February 1943 he embarked upon the task of giving Cardinal Maglione what he called 'anti-Bolshevist bogey dope' (*Diary*, 20 February 1943). The problem was that Russia could only be

---

[4] *The Blast of War, 1939–45* (London, 1967), pp. 555–6; *War Diaries: Politics and War in the Mediterranean 1943–1945* (London, 1984), pp. 585–7.

[5] FO 371/60797; especially Osborne to Foreign Office, 20 December 1945 and Foreign Office to Osborne, 6 March 1946; for Tardini blaming both sides on 28 July 1944, see FO 371/43946/101.

kept out of central Europe if a reasonably strong though democratic Germany were left after the war; and against this worked the doctrine of unconditional surrender, which the Vatican continued to dislike very much. But the Pope wanted Austria to be separated from the future Germany, as a protection both for Italy and for the Catholicism of Austria. During the winter of 1944-5 he consulted much with Monsignor Kaas, who was believed to favour a divided Germany and became for a time the close adviser of the Pope. The Pope befriended the move to restore a Habsburg to the throne of Vienna, in which the Americans were also much interested. But he had no interest in the far weaker move to think of a restored monarchy in France. He wanted an international organization to keep the peace, and thought it possible that such an organization could protect the Poles against the Russians. He thought the plan for a trial of war criminals 'reasonable'.[6] He pressed for a long American presence in Europe as the only protection against Russian advance. He wanted Roosevelt re-elected for his third term, and was downcast at his death.

Cardinal Maglione fell ill and died in August 1944. Osborne recorded that he had lost a personal friend. No new Secretary of State was appointed. Some thought that the Pope was now so dependent on the Americans that he wanted Archbishop Spellman of New York as his Secretary of State and only failed to have him on the fierce opposition of the Curia. Some thought that Cardinal Maglione acted too independently for him and that he preferred to have no successor. Some thought that he was not capable of making up his mind on so far-reaching an appointment. And some thought that he, who for so long was Secretary of State, preferred to take back into his own hands work which he understood, and trusted Tardini and Montini to give him the subordinate help which he needed.

Later he offered the cardinal's hat to both Tardini and Montini. They asked leave to decline. The Pope refused to order them to accept. They became cardinals only after his death; Tardini to write the best study of the character of the Pope, Montini to be a lovable and hesitant successor to Pope John XXIII.

At New Year 1945 the vacancies in the Curia were more numerous than ever before. There was no Secretary of State; no Camerlengo; no Chancellor; no Prefect of the Congregation of Religious. There were only 41 cardinals, of whom 24 were Italian and 17 non-Italian. The last cardinals to be created were made in 1937. Rumour said that the Pope must have decided to fill no office while the war lasted, because any appointment would look political. Part of the difficulty was expense. A new cardinal needed to spend about 3 million lire on clothes and other

[6] Audience to Myron Taylor, June 1944, Hyde Park Papers, Box 11.

appurtenances of his office. The see of Boston was vacant, Prague had been vacant for three years.

At the end of December 1945 the Pope created 32 new cardinals – one of them was Griffin the new Archbishop of Westminster. This was the largest creation of cardinals for four centuries. It filled all the vacancies in the cardinals' college. And it was historic. For the first time in history the Italian cardinals were a minority. Before he was Pope, Pacelli had long experience of the Catholic Church outside Italy. He was elected Pope with the strong assistance of non-Italian cardinals. His experience of Fascist Italy during the war made him wish to elevate the see of Rome above the Italian nationality. Some of the Italian clergy were like the King of Italy, with a record over Fascism which did not satisfy the Allies who were now all-important to the future of Italy. During the war he came under steady pressure, especially from Osborne but also from Accioly of Brazil, to 'internationalize' the Curia. This was among the subjects discussed by Osborne with the Foreign Office when he was 'on leave' during the early summer of 1943. About this the Foreign Office consulted an intelligent young Roman Catholic bishop, David Mathew. Mathew warned them that the business was not simple; that in the Curia quality counted more than quantity; that a single Cardinal Tisserant weighed more than ten English nonentities would weigh; and that to broaden the Curia was not to make it Anglo-Saxon but to make it Spanish-American or Mediterranean-Latin.[7]

The creation of a majority of non-Italian cardinals was a decision with long consequences for the future.

For a time Monsignor Pucci still operated his news service; and then vanished.

Allied power in Italy, and the Italian and papal necessity for Allied help, led to other pressures on the Curia. It was a law of history that whenever liberal governments pressed on the Papacy, the Jesuits were in trouble. A main part of this was historical memory or anachronism. But the charge was put about that the Jesuits were strong behind the government of General Franco in Spain, and that in Italy they were compromised by their association with Fascism. At the end of August 1944 a body of senior Jesuits, with Montini's knowledge, was said to have discussed the possibility of a papal dissolution of the Society of Jesus if it should prove to be in the interests of the Church. The Pope was reported to have said that he would do all in his power to defend and safeguard the unity of the Society;[8] all this, however, was blown up by that faker of news, Scattolini, out of very little.

---

[7] FO 371/37554/46, October 1943.
[8] NAW, OSS, 102367, report from Rome of 6 October 1944; cf. also Robert A. Graham in *Civ. Catt.* (1973) 3, 477.

On 29 July 1944, for the first time in history, the Pope received in audience a bishop of the Church of England: Edward Woods, the Bishop of Lichfield.

General de Gaulle came to the Vatican on 30 June 1944, with due solemnity, in a motorcade of six cars, as though he were already a head of State. In one of the cars rode de Blesson, who resigned his post the day before to adhere to the Gaullist cause. De Gaulle visited St Peter's where he was met by Monsignor Fontenelle. Leon Bérard held on for nearly two months longer. On 24 August 1944 he resigned as French ambassador on the ground that since Marshal Pétain could no longer exercise his functions as head of State, he (Bérard) regarded his charge as ended. He continued to live 'as a guest' inside the Vatican. De Gaulle asked (January 1945) that he be succeeded by the philosopher Jacques Maritain.

The Pope's quick recognition of de Gaulle (December 1944) provided the material for some of Farinacci's heaviest bombardment of the Pope's person. It was contrary to the usual Vatican practice with belligerents. Normally the Vatican refused to recognize any government, created by force during a war, until the signing of the peace treaty. The Vatican had to defend the Pope. This was historic France, not a new State or an occupied country. And the last act of the legitimate government – that of Pétain – was to ask the French to adhere to de Gaulle. Nevertheless Monsignor Tardini had to endure a heavy onslaught from Baron von Weizsäcker about the legal wrong of receiving de Gaulle.

Vatican Radio perforce remained neutral. But Father Mistiaen managed to celebrate VE Day by introducing the French bulletin with the opening bars of Beethoven's Fifth Symphony – the victory notes. In 1945 Father Mistiaen went back to Belgium and spent the rest of his life quietly, in teaching or in parish ministry or retreats, and died at Ghent in 1970 aged 76. Father Soccorsi remained the director of Radio Vaticana till 1953 and then went on teaching about religion and science at the Gregorian University till his death in 1961.

The Vatican rebuilt the gaps where their walls had become scalable. They persuaded the police to clear St Peter's Square of the hawkers and teenagers who moved in there when the people started to regard it as the safest place under Allied bombing.

During the last few months of the war the Vatican was able to act as an intermediary to help protect Italian works of art from Allied bombing. The German army moved 58 cases from the Villa Poggio at Caiano to the castle at Neumelane in Sand (Campo Tures). The German army told the German Foreign Office and then the message went through Orsenigo, the Vatican Secretariat, the Italian chargé

Babuscio Rizzo, the Italian Foreign Office, to the Allied commanders in Italy.[9]

From Cremona in the north Roberto Farinacci issued his worst attacks on the Pope. He encouraged a little group – it remained a very little group – of patriotic Italian priests who believed that the Pope had betrayed Italy. He mocked the Pope's concern that Rome be not bombed and reminded readers that Italy had other cities. He called the Vatican a partisan of the Allies; assailed the Pope for 'blessing terroristic bombers' – 'not a word from that high cathedra to deplore this criminal and barbarous banditry' (14 June 1944); not a word to defend Polish churches persecuted by Russians; 'our enemies are a triumvirate – Stalin, de Gaulle, Pius XII' (29 December 1944); no word to condemn the immorality of the agreement reached at Yalta; a blessing on partisan murderers in Italy – 'it is evident that into the house of the vicar of Christ Satan has entered'. 'For a few years', wrote Farinacci (17 January 1945), 'Pope Pius XII has fully espoused the Jewish cause to the point of offending the sensibilities of his flock . . . We never imagined that our Pastor, the Vicar of Christ, the Head of our Church, could one day be regarded as the most influential defender of the interests of the Jewish people. True enough, this war turns people upside down and creates absurdity.'

Or again, under the heading, *Now he is silent* (16 February 1945):

Who does not remember the protests, tirades, humbug of Vatican Radio on behalf of the Catholics of Poland? Three times a week they broadcast – patience, the Holy Father prays for you, and will do all that he can – you will live again. But now a Russian government is in Warsaw, and the Yalta agreement has liquidated the Polish government in London. We are sure that Vatican Radio will not say a word.

On 17 April 1945, only a few days before his judicial murder (at which he displayed courage of a high order) Farinacci declared the Pope to be only the political head of the Vatican State.

The group which he encouraged was headed by Tullio Calcagno, the former archpriest of Terni cathedral. Calcagno published a weekly, *Crociata Italica*, without many clear ideas, but in every number with pictures of Italian churches or cemeteries destroyed by bombers. In its more ardent moments it advocated a national Italian Catholic Church. Like Farinacci and Pavolini and Mussolini himself, Calcagno was shot by partisans.

By contrast to Farinacci, the Russian media of 1945–6 – *Pravda, Izvestia*, the radio – often attacked the Vatican for its Fascist attitudes.[10]

---

[9] AE, Italia, Busta 95/1, memorandum of 30 November 1944.
[10] Documented in FO 371/50060; cf. FO 371/44227/3–23; *Tablet*, 12 February 1944.

The cold war of Europe began to take shape. The Catholic Church in Albania was destroyed. The Uniat Church in Romania was forced to abandon Rome and put itself under the Orthodox see of Bucharest. These changes were done with brutality and sometimes murder. In Yugoslavia and Hungary the leading Catholic prelates were on trial or danger of trial for collaboration with the Nazis. The Vatican watched helplessly while the consequences of Hitler's invasion of Russia, and the resulting Russian domination of eastern Europe, worked their way in the affairs of the Catholic Church.

The Vatican did what little it could to stop anti-Fascist zealots digging up Fascist bodies from graveyards. Monsignor Borgongini Duca did whatever could be done to get altered the death penalties imposed upon collaborators. Osborne was grieved (18 September 1944) when the governor of the Regina Coeli prison was lynched by a mob because he knew him to be no war criminal but one who helped escapers whenever he could. The Pope himself begged Allied leaders for mercy 'towards those responsible for the Italian tragedy'. The Italian chargé Babuscio Rizzo had an interview with him before he gave an audience to Winston Churchill: 'I felt his affection vibrate towards Italy', 'He shares the suffering of Italy both as an Italian and as a priest.'[11]

The Allies were more respectful than the Germans, outwardly, towards the Pope. And internally their leaders felt more benevolent towards all that the Pope stood for. But for a time they treated the Pope's organization worse than the Germans had treated it. The Germans were not bound by the Lateran Treaty, which was an agreement only between the Pope and the kingdom of Italy. Yet they respected its provisions, both over the neutrality of Vatican City and the rights (more or less) of Osborne and the other diplomats. The Allies were not bound by the Lateran Treaty and saw no reason why they should observe its provisions unless it suited their interests. Communications between the Pope and the outside world were worse hampered in the first six months of Allied rule of Rome than under the German occupation. The reason was more clumsiness, stupidity and red tape than viciousness or anti-Catholicism.[12]

The situation was now reversed. The Vatican found itself housing and interning a few German soldiers who escaped from camps in Southern Italy. In June 1944 the Slovakian minister first, then in July Weizsäcker and the Japanese Harada moved perforce into Vatican

---

[11] AE, Santa Sede, Busta 71, Babuscio Rizzo to Italian government, 20 August 1944.
[12] Cf. Robert A. Graham in AHP (1980), p. 454.

City. Weizsäcker took up his lodging in the former flat of de Blesson in Santa Marta.[13]

London told Osborne to tell Cardinal Maglione again that the British were not bound by the Lateran Treaty. This disturbed the Vatican.

Prince Carlo Pacelli was the Pope's nephew. (As a compliment to the Pope, Mussolini made him a prince.) He now wrote a memorandum, which Osborne forwarded to London. This memorandum argued that though the Lateran Treaty was a 'bilateral instrument' (that is, an agreement only between Italy and the Pope and not a treaty with international agreement), it acquired a 'sort of additional and universal sanction' because its conclusions were applauded, and given a 'spontaneous adhesion' by the diplomats then (1929) accredited to the Holy See, who were 29 in number. This argument was legally thin. It did not convince Osborne, who could not mind if it was valid, and certainly did not convince London, who needed to be sure that it was invalid.[14]

On 6 June 1944 Allied Military Police arrested Dr Ludwig Wemmer and Albrecht von Kessel, Weizsäcker's counsellor and minister. This was back to the days of Mirosevic the Yugoslav with a vengeance, an occupying power seizing diplomats who by the Lateran Treaty had the immunity of diplomats. Cardinal Maglione protested strongly. The German government lodged a protest with Monsignor Orsenigo in Berlin. Further protests in June and July got a little result. They let Kessel join Weizsäcker inside the Vatican, but sent Wemmer and the attaché Georg Elling to Sicily where they remained under house arrest in a hotel at Taormina. The reason for this strange conduct was impossible to disclose to the Vatican, in the same way that Mussolini had not been able to tell the Vatican the reason for his misbehaviour over Mirosevic. The American Magic codebreakers intercepted a message from Harada to Tokyo (3 June 1944) which said that all the members of the German embassy had now left for Florence except those engaged in intelligence work.[15] Moreover they had good (and, as we know already, well-founded) reasons for suspecting that Dr Wemmer worked for the Gestapo, and they soon collected evidence that Georg Elling was a member of the Sicherheitsdienst. About Wemmer and Elling the British had every reason to maltreat the diplomatic immunities of the Vatican. But they could not explain why to the Vatican, because their methods of enquiry and their proofs were not suitable for the light of day. Dr Wemmer was soon telling the Vatican

[13] He first went for four days into the Palazzo Tribunale. Harada went into the former flat of the Bolivians in the Palazzo Tribunale.

[14] FO 371/44225/26–8.

[15] NAW, RG, 59, Myron Taylor, Box 28.

that the confinement of the Germans at Taormina constituted a permanent violation of international law.[16] The British took no notice.

The British were far more frightened of Weizsäcker and what he might do than were the Americans. For this fear they had reasons. The first was a priori: they suspected at sight a man who was Ribbentrop's Under-Secretary when Stalin made his pact with Hitler and Germany invaded Poland and later the Low Countries and France. His record, a priori, was not in their eyes that of an honourable German. They also knew him to be able. Then, they knew that their own man, Osborne, served his country very effectively while under the closest enemy surveillance. If he could do that for Britain, it was to be presumed that Weizsäcker in the Vatican could do it for Germany. And finally they very soon had evidence that Weizsäcker had done what Osborne refused to do. He had taken into the Vatican a secret radio transmitter. They did not protest to the Vatican. They preferred to listen to Weizsäcker's messages.

Osborne's situation was painful. The Italians and even the Germans had treated the Vatican fairly over diplomats. His own country should do no less. He did not like the attitude of his government over Weizsäcker. Meanwhile he had to represent the wishes of his government to Cardinal Maglione, whom he liked and who was dying, and to Monsignor Montini, whom he liked still more and who had behaved very honourably towards the Allies; and both Cardinal Maglione and Monsignor Montini were shocked by the attitude of the British. They did not know, but British Intelligence had recommended that Weizsäcker be not even allowed inside Vatican City but expelled from Italy. So also Harold Macmillan had recommended from Algiers.

Osborne's opinion was at the opposite extreme. He thought that the British had a moral duty, though confessedly not a legal duty, to observe the provisions of the Lateran Treaty. Therefore they should gain political advantage by observing it even more strictly than Mussolini and allowing Weizsäcker to remain inside the city of Rome and not need to move inside the Vatican. He said that Weizsäcker under surveillance in Rome could do no harm.[17] He also had a point about accommodation. Monsignor Montini told him that if Weizsäcker moved in, there was no room and he, Osborne, would have to move out. He realized, and argued to the British government, that his own physical proximity to Tardini and Montini was an important part of his effectiveness.

London thought that Osborne was being naive. Their portrait of Weizsäcker was different. They did not believe that any amount of

[16] Osborne to Foreign Office, 10 December 1944, FO 371/44226/133.
[17] Osborne to Foreign Office, 15 October 1943, FO 371/37539.

surveillance could stop him, loose in the city, from being effective as an enemy spy. They wondered whether he might also be a centre of disaffection for Italians still loyal to Mussolini; Cavendish-Bentinck, senior in British Intelligence, even asked whether Osborne's judgment had been weakened by being 'too long in the holy atmosphere of the Vatican'. They were agreed that Weizsäcker would be less of a menace if he were immured, like Osborne, inside the Vatican.

But they were sure that Osborne should for a time refuse to leave Vatican City. The more rooms in the Vatican were occupied by himself and Tittmann, the less room for the German and Japanese diplomats who might be dangerous. This policy was agreed with the Americans before the liberation of Rome. And if Weizsäcker and Harada were in the Vatican, it was better that Osborne should be near. From being under surveillance, he became part of a system of surveillance.

Osborne's perfect manners were at risk. London was saying to him, go on squatting in the Vatican (Cadogan used the actual verb *squat*), refuse to leave when you are asked to leave, so that there is no room in the Vatican for any more Germans. Osborne hated these instructions. He was in the position of a guest, whose host has treated him with generous hospitality, and who now is asked that for hospitable reasons he should move out of his room. He was sure that to bring Weizsäcker inside the Vatican was to increase German influence with the Pope. He made his discomfort plain to London. The Foreign Office was not pleased at his attitude. To themselves they accused him of not listening to their instructions. 'We deprecate the overkindly attitude of the military authorities and Sir D'Arcy Osborne.'[18] He was quite crisp with them. 'I am sick of being the football between the Army and the Church in this matter of the accommodation of Axis diplomats' (Osborne to Foreign Office, 18 June 1944). When they told him to refuse to leave, he told them that he could not refuse to leave. And the next day he asked them whether it was justice to arrest Axis diplomats because they could not get into the Vatican by a specified hour, when they could not get in because he was instructed to keep them out. 'If the Pope has not room,' said the Foreign Office unrelentingly (1 July 1944), 'he must give first choice to Allied diplomats . . . This may be very embarrassing for the Pope, but in wartime neutrals are being continually forced to adapt themselves to the exigencies of the military situation.'

The impasse between Osborne and his masters was solved by the Americans. On 5 July Stimson came from Washington and was taken by Myron Taylor to see the Pope. The Pope made a special request

[18] FO 371/44225/85.

about the diplomats' rooms. The Americans could not but agree. 'It rather sickens me', wrote Osborne, 'this pandering to His Holiness . . . Myron's love-feast with the Pope rather nauseates me.' The Americans ordered Tittmann (who agreed with Osborne) to suspend all cooperation with the British over Axis diplomats, and they ordered Tittmann at once to move out of the Vatican. They further angered London by ordering that American troops take no part in any arrest of Axis diplomats in Rome.

This was called 'a shocking breach of the Allied front'. Anthony Eden begged Churchill to discuss the matter with Stimson as he passed through London on his way home (Eden to Prime Minister, 14 July 1944).[19] Eden said that the Americans no doubt had their eye on the Catholic vote in the coming election for President. London attacked Cordell Hull in Washington. Cordell Hull said that he knew nothing about it but would enquire.

Finally the Foreign Office desks, angry not only with the Americans, but with Osborne, washed their hands and accepted defeat. 'Anyhow now Sir d'Arcy Osborne can clear out of the Vatican and go to a better hole if he can find one. I am sick of the whole business and of his eternal complaints and non-cooperation' (note of 17 July 1944).[20]

Three days later Stauffenberg's attempt to assassinate Hitler failed. Weizsäcker was suspect to the Nazi hunters and was lucky to be immured inside the Vatican. One of the conspirators under investigation was content to mention his name, knowing that he was safe. Weizsäcker's wife dared not return to Germany till the war ended.

American intelligence thought it worth recording that Osborne once met Weizsäcker in the Vatican gardens and shook hands.

Weizsäcker was finally confronted with the secret radio in June 1945 after the end of the German War. He 'appeared very much ashamed and confused'. He excused himself saying that the Nazis forced him to take the radio by threats of reprisal against his family. He said that he had sent no military or espionage information. He pleaded also that the Vatican had never forbidden radio transmitters expressly and that he had heard that the Allies had used one from the Vatican and so he 'expected reciprocity'. All the cryptographic material in the German lodging at Santa Marta was handed over to American intelligence.

While the trials of war criminals began at Nuremberg, the Vatican continued to shelter Weizsäcker. In the Vatican Library he worked quietly on a new constitution for Germany, and studied the question of Church and State, and painted water-colours in the Vatican gardens. He interested the Pope in the suffering of Germany and sought to

---

[19] PREM 3/243/1.   [20] FO 371/44226/28.

persuade the Pope that Germany was no longer a military problem of the future but simply an object now of charity. In April 1946 Tittmann begged the Vatican to persuade Weizsäcker to go to Nuremberg to give evidence on behalf of Grand Admiral Raeder. He went under a promise of safe conduct and returned. He thought the Allies were vindictive against Germany. In his turn he wanted the Pope to speak. He wanted the Vatican to say something like this: 'He who cannot forget and liquidate the past is no Christian and is at the same time a bad politician.' But, he said, 'the Vatican knows the limits of its influence'. It 'knows what it could not risk on behalf of the vanquished'.[21]

In June he was assured of freedom if he settled in the American zone of Germany. In August the French gave him leave to settle in the French zone. On 26 August he and his wife at last left the Vatican. They had been immured only two and a quarter years, less than half the time of Osborne. He left in a Vatican car, followed by his luggage on a Vatican lorry, and under a strong Allied escort.[22] He started to farm a little estate near Lake Constance.

But then the Americans decided to try him as a war criminal at Nuremberg. The prosecution demanded the death penalty. The Vatican begged for leniency. More than one lawyer doubted the justice of the trial. He was sentenced to seven years; sentence reduced; he finally served eighteen months (not including the two and a quarter years of investigation and trial). While in prison he wrote a pallid and uninformative autobiography. In reviewing the English translation of this book Lewis Namier launched a scornful attack upon Weizsäcker, elevating the issue above the person into a moral indictment of a whole civil administration, the 'honourable' men who served Hitler and refused to resign in the face of vilest immorality on the plea that only worse would follow. But the Vatican evidence argues that Weizsäcker was indeed an honourable German who tried to do his best in impossible circumstances. The autobiography had a unique feature. He defended Monsignor Orsenigo. Weizsäcker thought that the Berlin nuncio's policy of not breaking with Hitler's Reich was the best policy.

Sam Derry was taken into British Intelligence and served with distinction during the Cold War.

Monsignor O'Flaherty did a lot for returning prisoners-of-war. He received a CBE from the British government, and was not quite approved of in the post-war Vatican. He kept visiting the ex-chief of the Rome Gestapo, Herbert Kappler, in his life imprisonment and in 1959 converted him to the Catholic faith. A romantic and unreliable

---

[21] *Memoirs*, Eng. trans. (London, 1951), p. 300.
[22] Cf. the file in FO 371/60811.

and impressionistic picture of this delicious priest was portrayed by Gregory Peck in an American film entitled *The Scarlet and the Black*. O'Flaherty became a legend during his life. He had a first stroke in June 1960, a second in May 1963, and died 30 October 1963.

Osborne received thanks by name in the House of Commons (7 June 1944). Not by the right name, because Anthony Eden called him Sir Francis. Eden told the House of Commons the truth; that he served for a prolonged period of exceptional difficulty under conditions which must be unique in diplomatic experience.

Osborne realized that his life inside the Vatican was breaking up and had a curious sensation of regretting the disturbance. But a month later he longed to be away from the Vatican. He played golf again but kept missing the ball. A doctor prescribed pills to recover weight and he was in danger of diabetes and was put on a very strict diet. He was stale, and felt the Vatican a place of tiresome petty problems. His work was no longer so important or exciting, and he was depressed. He grieved that his footman Livio was discovered to have accepted pay from the enemy and had to be sacked ('It is not nice to learn that you have been nourishing (and nourishing damn well too) a viper in your bosom.') Livio nevertheless asked him for a character reference. Osborne was also depressed by the coming home to roost of the anarchy in the accounts, or non-accounts, of payments for escaped prisoners. The financiers in the Foreign Office asked fiendish questions for a man not good at sums, like the demand to know the lire equivalents of the various sterling payments, and how much went to each nationality among the escapers.[23]

We have a portrait of him at this time from the hand of a master. On 29 July, nearly two months after the fall of Rome to the Allies, Harold Macmillan took luncheon with Osborne in the flat in Santa Marta. Macmillan recorded his impression, which summarized the experience inside Vatican City:

He was charming, and so were his tiny suite of rooms. Not a bad prison, in which this attractive and rather whimsical man has been for four years incarcerated. His only sorrow is that close association with the Vatican and its atmosphere of petty intrigue has been a disillusionment![24]

This criticism of pettiness rarely appeared in Osborne's dispatches during the war. He had told Anthony Eden (12 November 1943) of 'certain elements or tendencies in the backstairs life of Vatican City which are anything but edifying'.[25] He attributed them not to the

[23] Osborne's *Diary*, 19 August 1944; cf. FO 371/44215, Foreign Office to Vatican Chancery, 26 September 1944.
[24] Macmillan, *War Diaries*, p. 494. [25] FO 371/37554/56.

Church but to one side of the Italian character. That he should specially talk of them in July 1944 was no doubt to do with that mood of staleness which he felt oppressive.

He finally moved out of the Vatican, the last Allied diplomat to go, in the first days of November 1944; to a flat in San Saba, and a chancellery at Via del Parlamento 14. He wrote a collins to Monsignor Montini for his hospitality over four and a half years. 'We must have been awful bores at times.'

Just before he retired from the diplomatic service, he made the first of two defences of the wartime record of his host at the Holy See.

Through 1945 and 1946 Russian newspapers and radio assailed the record of the Pope. They said that he was a prop of Fascism. On 26 February 1947 Sir Oliver Harvey, who succeeded Sir Orme Sargent at the Foreign Office and was concerned as a British diplomat with the Russians, wrote a private letter to Osborne which, though moderately, took up the accusation. Harvey wrote that the Pope had 'a facing-both-ways attitude'; that he had no 'positive line' towards 'the Nazis and Fascists, their heirs and assigns and those who collaborated with them'.

On 4 March 1947 Osborne wrote to Oliver Harvey a little apologia for the Pope.

Papal charity aspires to being absolute and universal. I have often discussed this at the Vatican and pointed out the dangers of such an aspiration. It goes back, I suppose, to the medieval right of sanctuary. During the German occupation of Rome the Vatican and the extra-territorial Vatican premises in Rome were full of fugitives and refugees from Nazi and Fascist persecution, including de Gasperi, Nenni, and a number of leading anti-Fascist politicians. It may be, and I think it likely, that some Fascist refugees were also helped and hidden when their time came to hide and be helped, but these would be exceptions; nothing like the wholesale protection of the victims of Fascism. And the Pope is on record that the authors of war crimes should pay for their evil-doing . . .

He confessed that the Pope's neutrality was 'meticulous and seemingly pusillanimous'. He confessed that there was no line 'indicating reprobation by name, or cursing by bell book and candle'.

But he is genuinely convinced – and nothing will shake his opinion – that he specifically condemned all Nazi war crimes in his public speeches during the war. . .

Not only is the atmosphere of the Vatican supranational and universal, at any rate to an extent sufficient to affect political judgement and decision, but it is also fourth-dimensional and, so to speak, outside of time. That is to say, that the Pope and his advisers do not consider and resolve a problem solely in the light of its temporary and obviously apparent elements. Their approach and survey are by habit and tradition unlimited in space and in time so that, for example, they can regard the Savoy dynasty as an interlude, and the Fascist era as an incident, in the history of Rome and of Italy. They reckon in centuries and plan for eternity and this inevitably renders their policy inscrutable, confusing, and on occasion reprehensible to practical and time-conditioned minds.[26]

Osborne complained to the last that, despite these new non-Italian cardinals, the Curia still needed to be made less Italian. One of his late reports reminded London that the only non-Italian in a responsible post at the Curia was still Cardinal Tisserant. Pius XII continued to refuse to appoint a Secretary of State as successor to Cardinal Maglione. He told Osborne that he liked the system. Osborne thought that though the Pope liked it, it was less satisfactory for himself[27] and for the other diplomats, and that it was awkward for the substitutes Tardini and Montini. He finally retired from his post and from the diplomatic service in June 1947. The retirement was unwelcome to the Pope, to Tardini, and to Montini.

He loved Italy and the Italians too warmly to leave the country. He settled in a flat at Via Giulia 66, looking over the Tiber towards St Peter's. He organized and financed a boys' club run by the Salesian fathers, which fed 1,000 boys a day and educated 300. There he was visited by Princess Elizabeth, the future Queen of England.

In 1963 Rolf Hochhuth published his onslaught upon Pope Pius XII, then dead five years. Hochhuth attacked the Pope for unpardonable silence during the war years, especially over the Jews.

Osborne, then aged 77, was moved to come out of his privacy with a letter to *The Times* (20 May 1963). It was his last judgment on the Pope. It was generous and sincere but not quite ecstatic:

So far from being a cool (which, I suppose, implies cold-blooded and inhumane) diplomatist, Pius XII was the most warmly humane, kind, generous, sympathetic (and incidentally saintly) character that it has been my privilege to meet in the course of a long life. I know that his sensitive nature was acutely and incessantly alive to the tragic volume of human suffering caused by the war and, without the slightest doubt, he would have been ready and glad to give his life to redeem humanity from its consequences. And this quite irrespective of nationality or faith. But what could he effectively do?

Osborne agreed that the Pope was concerned to keep 'meticulous' neutrality in the hope of being able to mediate; that he liked the German people, or at least the German Catholics; and that he believed that he condemned Nazi atrocities in his Christmas messages and speeches.

[26] FO 371/67917C.
[27] FO 371/67920B, Osborne to Foreign Office, 12 February 1946.

There was admittedly no clearcut and unequivocal condemnation. For, unfortunately, the language . . . was too often so prolix and obscure that it was difficult to extract his meaning from its extraneous verbal envelope . . . I feel assured that Pope Pius XII has been grossly misjudged in Herr Hochhuth's drama.

He ended by saying that he was not a Roman Catholic.

Montini, now a cardinal and about to be Pope, hoped that Osborne would become a Roman Catholic. He watched and waited, that it might happen before the end. Even as Pope he told a friend that if Osborne summoned him he would go at once whatever his engagements.

But Osborne's mind, though sympathetic to religion, and capable of understanding the essence of Catholicism, was still a long way from Christian orthodoxy. The old age had sadness, because his memory contrasted a world of his childhood with the pollution and smoke and crowds of modernity. His last poem was a yearning for a land which he remembered, of lonely woods and golden corn, without motor-cars or aeroplanes or traffic blocks. But he consciously preferred to live in a city which at that time had the worst traffic blocks in the world. His once-arrested maid, Giuseppina, served him to the end.

He became the last Duke of Leeds in 1963 and lamented that he had not seen such money earlier in his life. He died on 20 March 1964 and was buried in the Protestant cemetery at Rome. Queen Elizabeth II, and Queen Elizabeth the Queen Mother, were each represented at his funeral.

Select bibliography

Actes et Documents du Saint Siège pendant la seconde guerre mondiale, ed. P. Blet, Robert A. Graham, Angelo Martini and Burkhart Schneider. 11 volumes in 12. Vatican City, 1965–81

Adolf, Walter. *Geheime Aufzeichnungen aus dem nationalsozialistischen Kirchenkampf, 1935–43.* Mainz 1979

Akten zur deutschen auswärtigen Politik, 1918–45. Series D 1937–45. Baden-Baden 1950–8

Albrecht, D. (ed.) *Der Notenwechsel zwischen dem H. Stuhl und der deutschen Regierung, Bd. III: Die Akten und Demarchen des Nuntius Orsenigo 1933–45.* Mainz 1980

Ascarelli, A. *Le Fosse Ardeatine.* 2nd edn, Rome 1974

Amè, C. *Guerra Segreta in Italia 1940–43.* Rome 1954

Badoglio, P. *Italy in the Second World War: memories and documents.* Eng. trans. London 1948

Barker, Nicholas. *Stanley Morison.* London 1972

Bastianini, G. *Uomini, case, fatti.* Milan 1959

Blumenson, M. *Salerno to Cassino.* Washington 1966

Boelcke, W. A. (ed.) *The Secret Conferences of Dr Goebbels, October 1939–March 1943.* Eng. trans. London 1970

Bonomi, I. *Diario di un anno 2 giugno 1943 – 10 giugno, 1944.* Milan 1947

Breitman, R. 'The Allied War Effort and the Jews, 1942–3', in *Journal of Contemporary History*, 20, 1, 1985, 135ff.

Caravaglios, M. G. 'La Santa Sede e l'Inghilterra in Etiopia durante il Secondo Conflitto Mondiale', in *Africa*, March 1980, 217–54

Cavalli, F. 'La Sante Sede contro la deportazioni degli ebrei dalla Slovacchia durante la seconda guerra mondiale'. *Civiltà Cattolica*, 1961, 3, 6ff.

Carton de Wiart, A. *Happy Odyssey.* London 1950

Chadwick, O. 'Weizsäcker, the Vatican, and the Jews of Rome' in *Journal of Ecclesiastical History*, 28, 2, April 1977, 179ff.

Charles-Roux, F. *Huit Ans au Vatican 1932–1940.* Paris 1947

Cianfarra, C. M. *The War and the Vatican.* London 1945

Ciano, G. *Diario (1939–43)*, 5th edn., 2 vols. Milan 1948

Clauss, M. 'Der Besuch Ribbentrops im Vatican', in *Zeitschrift für Kirchengeschichte*, 1976, 54ff.

Conway, J. S. 'The meeting between Pope Pius XII and Ribbentrop' in *Historical Papers of the Canadian Historical Association*, 1968, 103ff.
    'Myron C. Taylor's Mission to the Vatican 1940–1950', in *Church History*, 1975, 44, i, 85ff.

Craven, W. F. and Cate, J. L. *The Army Air Forces in World War II*, 7 vols., Chicago 1948–58

Dalla Torre, G. *Memorie*, 2nd edn., Verona 1967

Deakin, F. W. D. *The brutal friendship: Mussolini, Hitler, and the fall of Italian Fascism*, rev. edn., 2 vols. London 1966

De Felice, R. *Mussolini il Duce: II, Lo Stato totalitario 1936–40*. Turin 1981

Delzell, C. (ed.) *The Papacy and Totalitarianism between the two world wars*. New York 1974

Delzell, C. 'Pius XII, Italy, and the outbreak of the War', in *Journal of Contemporary History*, 2 (1967), 137–61

De Risio, C. *Generali, Servizi Segreti e Fascismo*. Milan 1978

Derry, S. I. *The Rome Escape Line*. London 1961

Deutsch, H. C. *The conspiracy against Hitler in the twilight war*. Minneapolis 1968

Dilks, D. (ed.) *The Diaries of Sir Alexander Cadogan, 1938–1945*. London 1971

Di Nolfo, E. *Vaticano e Stati Uniti 1939–52*. Milan 1978

Discorsi e radiomessagi di Sua Santità Pio XII, 20 vols. Vatican City 1955–9

I Documenti diplomatici italiani. Series 9, 1939–43. Rome 1954–

Documents on British Foreign Policy Third Series, 1938–9, 1949ff.

Documents on German Foreign Policy 1918–45 Series C, London 1957ff.

Dordoni, A. '*Crociata italiana*', fascismo e religione nella republica di Salo. Milan 1976

D'Ormesson, W. *De St Pétersbourg à Rome*. Paris 1969

Duclos, P. *Le Vatican et le Seconde Guerre Mondiale*. Paris 1955

Eden, Anthony *Facing the Dictators*. London 1962

Ellwood, D. W. *L'Alleato nemico e la politica dell'occupazione anglo-americana in Italia 1943–46*. Milan 1977

Falconi, Carlo *The Silence of the Pope*, Eng. trans. London 1970

Fappani, A. and Molinari, F. *Chiesa e repubblica di Salò*. Turin 1981

Fappani, A. and Molinari, F. *G.B. Montini giovane, 1897–1944*. Turin 1979

Fargion, L. P. *L'occupazione tedesca e gli ebrei di Roma*. Rome 1979

Fogarty, Gerald. *The Vatican and the American Hierarchy from 1870 to 1965*. Stuttgart 1982

Friedländer, S. *Pius XII and the Third Reich: a documentation*, Eng. trans. London 1966

Counterfeit Nazi. London 1969

Furman, John. *Be not fearful*. London 1959

Gallagher, J. P. *Scarlet Pimpernel of the Vatican*. London 1967

Garland, A. N. and Smyth, H. M. *Sicily and the Surrender of Italy* (US Army in World War II). *Washington 1965*

Gilbert, Felix (ed.) *Hitler directs his War*. Oxford 1950

Gilbert, Martin *Auschwitz and the Allies*. London 1981

Giovanetti, A. *Il Vaticano e la Guerra 1939–40*. Vatican 1960

Roma città aperta. Milan 1962

Gonella, G. *The Papacy and World Peace*, Eng. trans. (abridged) London 1945

Graham, Robert A. *The Pope and Poland in World War Two*. London 1968

'Spie naziste attorno al Vaticano durante la seconda guerra mondiale' in *Civiltà Cattolica*, 1970, 1, 21ff.

'La strana condotta di E. von Weizsäcker ambasciatore del Reich in Vaticano' in *Civiltà Cattolica*, 1970, 2, 455ff.

'Contatti di pace fra americani e giapponesi in Vaticano nel 1945' in *Civiltà Cattolica*, 1971, 2, 31ff.

'La rappresaglia nazista alle Fosse Ardeatine. P. Pfeiffer, messaggero della carità di Pio XII' in *Civiltà Cattolica*, 1973, 4, 467ff.

'Voleva Hitler allontanare da Roma Pio XII?' in *Civiltà Cattolica*, 1972, 1, 319ff., 454ff.

'Il vaticanista falsario. L'incredibile successo di Virgilio Scattolini' in *Civiltà Cattolica*, 1973, 3, 467ff.

'La Missione di W. d'Ormesson in Vaticano nel 1940' in *Civiltà Cattolica*, 1973, 4, 145ff.

'La "Primula Rossa" del Vaticano e l'Intelligence Service. Assistenza o Spionaggio', in *Civiltà Cattolica*, 1974, 2, 230ff.

'Goebbels e il Vaticano nel 1943', in *Civiltà Cattolica*, 1974, 4, 130ff.

'La Radio Vaticana tra Londra e Berlino' in *Civiltà Cattolica*, 1976, 1, 132ff.

'Il Vaticano nella guerra psicologia inglese 1939–45, in *Civiltà Cattolica*, 1978, 1, 125ff.

'L'occhio del SIM sulla Città del Vaticano', in *Civiltà Cattolica*, 1978, 4, 44ff.

'L'enciclica Summi Pontificatus e i belligeranti nel 1939', in *Civiltà Cattolica*, 1984, 4

Grimaldi, U. A. and Bozzetti, G. *Farinacci il piu fascista*. Milan 1972

Guariglia, R. *Ricordi, 1922–1946*. Naples 1950

Guerri, G. B. *Galeazzo Ciano*. Milan 1979

Hachey, T. E. (ed.) *Anglo-Vatican Relations 1914–1939; Confidential Annual Reports of the British Ministers to the Holy See*. Boston, Mass. 1972

Hassell, C. A. U. von *The von Hassell diaries, 1938–1944*. Eng. trans. London 1948

Heenan, J. C. *Cardinal Hinsley*. London 1944

Hennesey, James 'An American Jesuit in War-Time Rome: the Diary of Vincent A. McCormick, S. J., 1942–45': in *Mid-America*, 56, (1974), 50

Hill, Leonidas *Die Weizsäcker-Papiere 1933-1950*. Frankfurt 1974

'The Vatican Embassy of Ernst von Weizsäcker 1943', in *Journal of Modern History*, 1967, 39, 2, 138ff.

Hinsley, F. H. *British Intelligence in the Second World War*. 4 vols. London 1979

Hoffman, P. *Widerstand, Staatsstreich, Attentat* 3rd edn. Munich 1979

The Jews of Czechoslovakia. Historical Studies and Surveys. 2 vols. New York 1968–71

Katz, R. *Black Sabbath*. London 1969

Death in Rome. London 1967

Kostich, L. M. *The Holocaust in the Independent State of Croatia*. Chicago 1981

Laqueur, Walter *The Terrible Secret*. London 1980

Leiber, R. 'Pio XII e gli ebrei di Roma', in *Civiltà Cattolica*, 1961, 1, 449ff.

Liesenmeyer, W. S. 'Italian Peace Feelers before the fall of Mussolini' in *Journal of Contemporary History*, 1981, 649ff.

Lipscher, L. *Die Juden im Slowakischen Staat 1939–1945*. Munich 1980

Ludlow, P. 'Papst Pius XII, die britische Regierung und die deutsche Opposition im Winter 1939–40' in *Vierteljahreshefte für Zeitgeschichte*. Munich, 22, 1974, 229ff.

Macmillan, Harold *The Blast of War, 1939–45*. London 1967
  War Diaries: Politics and War in the Mediterranean 1943–1945. London 1984

Magister, S. *La politica vaticana e l'Italia, 1943–1978*. Rome 1978

Manvell, R. and Fraenkel, H. *The Canaris Conspiracy*, London 1969

Marrus, M. R. and Paxton, R. O. *Vichy France and the Jews*. New York 1981

Mayda, Giuseppe, *Ebrei sotto Salò*. Milan 1978

Molinari, F. and Neri, V. *Olio santo e olivo di ricino: rapporto su Chiesa e Fascismo*. Turin 1976

Moloney, T. *Westminster, Whitehall and the Vatican: the Role of Cardinal Hinsley, 1935–43*. London 1985

Morley, J. F. *Vatican Diplomacy and the Jews during the Holocaust*. New York 1980

Murphy, R. *Diplomat among Warriors*. London 1964

Nicolini, Giulio *Il Cardinale Domenico Tardini*. Padua 1980

Noel, G. E. *The Montini Story: a portrait of Paul VI*. London 1963

L'Opera per la pace della Santa Sede Milan, 1940

Padellaro, N. *Portrait of Pius XII* Eng. trans. London 1956

Papée, Kazimierz. *Pius XII e Polska*. Rome 1954

Papers relating to the foreign relations of the United States. Washington 1939ff., 1954ff.

Papeleux, Léon *Les silences de Pie XII*. Brussels 1980

Paul VI et la modernité dans l'Eglise (Actes du colloque 1983) Ecole française de Rome 1984

Pieri, P. and Rochat, G. *Pietro Badoglio*. Turin 1974

Poliakov, L. *Harvest of Hate*. London 1960

The Pope Speaks. London 1940

Randall, A. W. G. *Vatican Assignment*. London 1956
  The Pope, the Jews and the Nazis. London 1963

Rhodes, A. *The Vatican in the Age of the Dictators*. London 1973

Rossi, E. A. 'La politica del Vaticano durante la Seconda guerra mondiale', in *Storia Contemporanea*, 1975, 881–928

Rotkirchen, L. 'Vatican Policy and the "Jewish Problem" in "Independent" Slovakia (1939–45)', in *Yad Vashem Studies on the European Jewish Catastrophe and Resistance* 6 (1967)

Schneider, Burkhart 'Dr Friedensappel Papst Pius XII vom 24 August 1939' in *Archivum Historiae Pontificae* 6 (1968) 415ff

Scoppola, P. *La Chiesa e il Fascismo*. Bari 1971

Scrivener, Jane (pseud) *Inside Rome with the Germans*. New York 1945 (Author's diary – 8.9.43 – 5.6.44)

Sendtner, K. 'Die deutsche Militäropposition im ersten Kriegsjahr' in *Die Vollmacht des Gewissens*. Munich 1956

Senise, C. *Quando ero capo della Polizia 1940–1943*. Rome 1946

Sheils, W. J. (ed.) *Persecution and Toleration*. Oxford 1984

Speaight, Robert. *Voice of the Vatican*. London 1942

Strong, K. W. D. *Intelligence at the Top*. London 1968

Tarchiani, A. *Dieci anni tra Roma e Washington*. Milan 1955

Tardini, D. *Pio XII*. Rome 1959

Toscano, Mario *Designs in Diplomacy*. Eng. trans. London 1970
  Dal 25 luglio all' 8 Settembre – nuove rivelazioni sugli armistizi fra l'Italia e le Nazioni Unite. Florence 1966
  Pagine di Storia diplomatica contemporanea. 2 vols. Milan 1963

Trevelyan, R. *Rome '44: the battle for the Eternal City*. London 1981

Villani, G. *Il vescovo Elia della Costa*. Florence 1974

Walker, R. F. *Pius of Peace: A Study of the pacific work of His Holiness Pope Pius XII in the World War 1939–45*. London 1946

Wartime Correspondence between President Roosevelt and Pope Pius XII. New York 1947

Wasserstein, S. *Britain and the Jews of Europe, 1939–1945*. Oxford 1979

Zangrandi, R. *1943: 25 luglio–8 settembre*. Milan 1964
  L'Italia Tradita: 8 Settembre 1943. Milan 1971

Zizola, Giancarlo *Quale Papa?* Rome 1977

Index